Woman, Women, and the Priesthood in the Trinitarian Theology of Elisabeth Behr-Sigel

Woman, Women, and the Priesthood in the Trinitarian Theology of Elisabeth Behr-Sigel

Sarah Hinlicky Wilson

BLOOMSBURY

LONDON • NEW DELHI • NEW YORK • SYDNEY

Bloomsbury T&T Clark

An imprint of Bloomsbury Publishing Plc

50 Bedford Square   1385 Broadway
London   New York
WC1B 3DP   NY 10018
UK   USA

www.bloomsbury.com

First published 2013

Bloomsbury is a registered trade mark of Bloomsbury Publishing Plc

British Library Cataloguing-in-Publication Data
A catalogue record for this book is available from the British Library.

ISBN: HB: 978-0-567-06110-2
ePDF: 978-0-567-48078-1
epub: 978-0-567-21777-0

Library of Congress Cataloging-in-Publication Data
Wilson, Sarah Hinlicky
Woman, Women, and the Priesthood in the Trinitarian Theology of
Elisabeth Behr-Sigel / Sarah Hinlicky Wilson p.cm
Includes bibliographic references and index.
ISBN 978-0-567-06110-2 (hardcover)

Typeset by Newgen Imaging Systems Pvt Ltd, Chennai, India
Printed and bound in Great Britain

Contents

Acknowledgments   vi

Preface   vii

1   The Grandmother of Western Orthodoxy   1

2   Paul Evdokimov on "Woman"   11

3   Agapia to Sheffield   29

4   The Path to Rhodes   53

5   After Rhodes   79

6   The Female Diaconate   105

7   Feminist, Protestant, Orthodox?   113

8   Tradition, Priesthood, Gender and Personhood   143

Published Works of Elisabeth Behr-Sigel   167

Works Cited and Consulted   183

Index   197

Acknowledgments

It would not have been possible for this American Lutheran to write about a French Orthodox theologian without a great deal of help across national and ecumenical boundaries. I am indebted to Cyrille Sollogoub, who located and sent to me a great number of Behr-Sigel's articles that are unavailable in the United States. Olga Lossky helped him as well and also permitted me to read the manuscript of her biography of Behr-Sigel before it was published. This study could not have been written without either of them. Leonie B. Liveris in Australia provided me with a number of hard-to-find pieces by Behr-Sigel and copies of original letters by her. Brandon Gallaher exchanged a number of emails with me about the various "schools" of Orthodox theology.

Stateside, Teva Regule and Maria Gwyn McDowell of the *St. Nina Quarterly* gave me transcripts of the interviews with Behr-Sigel during her trip to the United States in 2003 and helped me locate a number of documents. Valerie Karras sent me a copy of a letter from Anthony Bloom to Behr-Sigel. Paul Valliere also answered questions about the "schools" of Orthodox theology and sent me a manuscript of one of his unpublished papers.

At Princeton Theological Seminary, Kate Skrebutenas tracked down all sorts of things for me; she is a reference librarian extraordinaire. Darrell Guder offered to be a reader when I knew not where to turn. Michael Plekon introduced me to Behr-Sigel's writings in the first place, encouraged me to work on this topic, and connected me to a number of the people mentioned above. His many years of friendship have been a great blessing to me. Ellen Charry directed my dissertation as the culmination of many years' study with her. I have been deeply formed by her conviction that a theologian must also live and act like a Christian.

All dissertations need revision before they are publishable. My gratitude to the Institute for Ecumenical Research in Strasbourg, France, is immense for both allowing and encouraging me to devote the necessary time to the rewriting process. My colleagues at the Institute were also able to clarify some points regarding the church in France and Behr-Sigel's own life in Strasbourg.

Andrew L. Wilson made it possible for me to write this work in a relatively short period of time by taking care of our son Ezekiel, cleaning up the kitchen, and keeping me going when I started to droop. I certainly couldn't have done it without him.

Last of all I would like to acknowledge and thank the star of this show, Elisabeth Behr-Sigel. I found her book at just the right time and she put me on to a course of thought that has proved to be tremendously fruitful in my life, not only academically but also personally and spiritually. It was an honor to meet her several years before she died, and I hope this study of her writings will honor her further and do justice to her contribution to the church catholic.

Preface

As a rule, the name of Elisabeth Behr-Sigel is associated with this long-lived theologian's defense of the ordination of women in the Orthodox church. This is true, though somewhat misleading, for Behr-Sigel devoted much of her considerable corpus to other topics, such as Orthodox spirituality, Russian saints, and ecumenism. This work will do little to amend the common perception about her interests.

But this book does seek to make a correction to the general use of Behr-Sigel on the topic of women's ordination. Both admirers and detractors tend to cite her earliest work and to assume a continuity between her first forays into the question of women in the church and her mature position on women's ordination. Specifically, Behr-Sigel is often thought to defend the necessity of uplifting and incorporating "feminine charisms" into the life of the Orthodox church. Such an inclusion would be a corrective to masculine excess and vice in both church and society. Women are of a unique essence and therefore it is vital that their contributions be appreciated to reflect the full catholicity of the church.

Behr-Sigel certainly did wish for a broader inclusion of women in the life of the church and at all levels of the church. But less than ten years after her first reflections on women, she came to reject the concept of "feminine charisms" altogether. The notion of an ontological difference between men and women—perhaps indicating their alignment with the Son and the Spirit respectively, as her friend and fellow theologian Paul Evdokimov had proposed—no longer seemed to her a valid explication of the relationship between trinitarian being and human being. The real force of her thought tended toward the meaning of *personhood*, not womanhood. Being a woman colors how one is person, but neither encloses nor determines nor exhausts it. This distinction is tremendously important to understanding her overall theological vision as well as her specific arguments about the Christian priesthood.

It is also commonly thought, especially among those who do not favor the ordination of women, that the push for ordination is nothing more than the impingement of the secular world on the church. Feminism drives the quest, not the gospel or the Tradition of the one, holy, catholic, and apostolic church. This book makes the case that Behr-Sigel's consideration of the ordination of women and eventual support for it are generated from within, a result of her immersion in the Scriptures, the church fathers, and the theology of the Orthodox church, occasioned but not determined by changes in the status of women in worldly society. Such an approach to theology and society, I will further claim, should be understood as a properly Orthodox one.

This is because Behr-Sigel was the heir to a stream of Orthodoxy that, quite the contrary to being invaded by the secular world, deliberately went out in search of it. Orthodox thinkers like Alexander Bukharev and Vladimir Soloviev in the nineteenth century were convinced that the faithful Christian witness is to engage the world constantly, in its developments and regressions, in its philosophy and politics and art. Soloviev was an ecumenical pioneer decades before the incipient ecumenical movement at Edinburgh in 1910; he studied continental philosophy in order both to learn things from it and teach things to it. Bukharev left the monastery, finding his Christian vocation to be properly in the world, addressing questions that trouble the hearts of everyday people. It would be quite wrong to construe their efforts as the encroachment of a secular juggernaut on a whole and wholesome church. Instead, the very real flaws of the church, and the very real movements of the world, caused these figures to take the gospel out with them, rather than retreating behind church walls. Thus when, a 100 years later, Behr-Sigel turned her attention to the status of women in church and society, she was following in their footsteps out into the world, holding the burning torch of the gospel to light the way.

Finally, this book makes the case that the discussion surrounding the ordination of women in the Orthodox church is, in a certain sense, not chiefly about women or ordination at all. Although there was certainly some ecumenical pressure on the Orthodox to consider it, there was no strong internal pressure—no equivalent of the "Philadelphia Eleven" in the Episcopal Church (USA) staging noncanonical ordinations to force the issue. In Behr-Sigel's time, and still in the present, the ordination question has been entirely theoretical.

It is more accurate to see the discussion about the ordination of women, as it has actually evolved in the Orthodox church, as a subset of the reevaluation and reclamation of trinitarianism in the nineteenth and twentieth centuries across the whole church. Theologians of the East and West alike have sought to understand human personhood and society on the basis of the triune nature of God, a community of distinct persons living in a fellowship of perfect love. As we will see in the following chapters, Paul Evdokimov—the first Orthodox theologian to reflect extensively on the spiritual meaning of femininity—can and must ground his reflections in the Trinity, not only figuratively but even ontologically. Thomas Hopko, an American Orthodox making similar arguments, follows suit. Behr-Sigel accepts the necessity of a trinitarian grounding for understanding human personhood, but she differs significantly from Evdokimov and Hopko's reading of the trinitarian evidence. This is the real meat of the disagreement on the theological level, and so we now turn to the unfolding of the dispute in the chapters that follow.

1

The Grandmother of Western Orthodoxy

Elisabeth Behr-Sigel, the "grandmother of western Orthodoxy," was born to a Bohemian Jewish mother and an Alsatian Lutheran father on July 21, 1907, in the town of Schiltigheim, near Strasbourg.[1] Neither parent cared much for religious observance during Elisabeth's childhood.

Her father, Charles Sigel, saw to it that Elisabeth was baptized by a Lutheran pastor friend of his when she was a year old. When she was 6, he enrolled her as a day student at a Protestant boarding school with excellent teachers of religion. That was the full extent of his religious direction of his daughter's life. His own father, Eugene Sigel, had planned on becoming a pastor, but in the milieu of German liberal Protestantism in the nineteenth century and especially under the influence of David Friedrich Strauss, he lost his faith altogether and opted for a military career instead. Charles inherited the cultural Christianity, but it meant little to him personally.

Elisabeth's mother, Emma Altschul Sigel, was fluent in German and Czech but never felt at ease in the local francophone synagogue, so she did not attend services, nor did she ever seem to regret it. Her own religious practice was limited to praying the traditional prayers once a year on Yom Kippur, but she did so in such privacy that Elisabeth didn't even realize that her mother was a Jew till much later in her childhood. Emma did, however, teach her daughter to pray every night, a habit that Elisabeth kept her whole life long. The young Elisabeth, nicknamed Liselotte, spent her summers

---

[1] The material here is drawn almost entirely from Olga Lossky's biography, *Vers le Jour sans Déclin: Une Vie d'Elisabeth Behr-Sigel (1907–2005)* (Paris: Cerf, 2007). Citations are taken from the English translation, *Toward the Endless Day: The Life of Elisabeth Behr-Sigel (1907–2005)* (ed. Michael Plekon; trans. Jerry Ryan; South Bend, IN: University of Notre Dame Press, 2010). Olga Lossky describes the process of writing the biography and her interviews with Behr-Sigel in "Les Déjeuners du Samedi," *Contacts* 59, no. 4 (2007), pp. 498–502. See also Olga Lossky, "Une Chrétienne Engagée au Coeur de son Epoque," *Lumière du Thabor* 28 (2006), pp. 1–5, and "Elisabeth Behr-Sigel: Her Vision and Contribution," in *Many Women Were Also There . . .: The Participation of Orthodox Women in the Ecumenical Movement*, pp. 181–83 (ed. Eleni Kasselouri-Hatzivassiliadi, Fulata Mbano Moyo, and Aikaterini Pekridou; Geneva/Volos: WCC Publications/Volos Academy for Theological Studies, 2010); and Lyn Breck, "Nearly a Century of Life," in Elisabeth Behr-Sigel, *Discerning the Signs of the Times: The Vision of Elisabeth Behr-Sigel*, pp. 125–36 (ed. Michael Plekon and Sarah E. Hinlicky; Crestwood, NY: St. Vladimir's Seminary Press, 2001).

in Bohemia with her Jewish cousins and grandparents, the only baptized Christian among them, their "little goy."[2] Several decades later, all but one of her Jewish relatives from Bohemia lost their lives in the Nazi death camps.

As an Alsatian, Elisabeth's earliest experience was of living on the borders of different worlds. Her family was mixed not only in religion but in language and culture, constantly crossing borders of both political and social kinds. The "first shadow" on her happy childhood was the First World War,[3] and the fervid nationalism that went with it instilled in the young girl a hatred of all kinds of barriers between human beings. Openness to the truly other was a constant theme in her life.

And yet the barriers could not be avoided or discounted. When Elisabeth enrolled in a French lycée, she enthusiastically adopted French language and culture, which created a barrier between herself and her German-speaking mother. Another and more significant barrier followed when Elisabeth, as a teenager, became active in the Christian students' association, the Fédération Universelle de l'Association Chrétienne des Etudiants (FUACE), and through its ministrations came to a personal acceptance of Christ as the lord of her life. As Elisabeth recalled it,

> It is in this circle that I had the spiritual experiences that determined the direction my life would take: up to this time I considered the Gospel as, essentially, a code, or rather a moral atmosphere. For the first time, I felt personally loved by God, called by Christ, as was the rich young man, to follow Him without worrying about the rest.[4]

But the love of Christ was something her mother did not and could not understand, and from then on there was a lack of intimacy between them, profound enough to leave Elisabeth with great sorrow and a sense of personal failure when Emma died young in 1927.

Through FUACE and its local branch called the Fédé, Elisabeth made the acquaintance of significant Protestant movers and shakers in the budding ecumenical movement, among them Suzanne de Dietrich, Marc Boegner, and Pierre Maury. She read Paul Claudel and Charles Péguy with enthusiasm. From her Protestant compatriots she gained a rigorous knowledge of Scripture and genuine liberty of conscience, as well as a desire for living faith and ecumenical dialogue. At the same time she was wracked with metaphysical questions of all kinds and turned to the study of philosophy at the University of Strasbourg. Her closest classmate and friend was Emmanuel Levinas, with whom she kept up a correspondence until his death in 1995. Their professors were interested in Thomas Aquinas, Emile Durkheim, Henri Bergson, and Edmund Husserl. Elisabeth was not satisfied with philosophical answers, however: she wanted theological ones. Providentially, the Protestant faculty of theology in Strasbourg opened its doors to women, and after finishing her philosophy degree Elisabeth enrolled, eventually to graduate with top honors in her class.

---

[2] Breck, "Nearly a Century of Life," p. 126.
[3] O. Lossky, *Toward the Endless Day*, p. 8.
[4] Ibid., p. 11.

Among her peers at the theological faculty were three students from traditionally Orthodox countries, a Romanian and two Russians. One of the latter, Paul Fidler, became a particular friend of Elisabeth's. He introduced her to Russian religious thought, especially Alexis Khomiakov's writings on the church. By her own testimony, it was the ecclesiology of the Orthodox church that drew Elisabeth to the East. She had always thought of the church as an institution; for the first time, in Khomiakov, she heard of it as "a communion lived in faith and love." The individualism that distressed her in Protestantism was transcended: according to Khomiakov, "No one is saved alone. The person who is saved is saved in the Church, in union with all its other members. If a person believes, it is within a community of faith; if a person loves, it is within a community of love; if a person prays, it is within a community of prayer."[5] The new ecclesiological outlook dovetailed with her growing ecumenical passion. In Orthodoxy she saw the undivided church of the fathers, at the same time that the Orthodox church was joining in the fledgling hopes of reunion signaled by the first Faith and Order Conference in 1927.

Russian culture and spirituality attracted her, too, and the attraction only grew as she came to know more and more Russian émigrés fleeing the Revolution and its aftermath. She joined Action Chrétienne des Etudiants Russes (l'ACER) and in the spring of 1928 during a Fédé event in Paris she attended the paschal vigil at the new Institut de Théologie Orthodoxe Saint-Serge, founded in 1925. It astounded her: it was heaven on earth. Elisabeth knew then that she had to find out more about Orthodoxy, but there was no parish as of yet in Strasbourg, so she arranged to spend the next year of her studies at the Protestant faculty in Paris.

During her time there she met Lev Gillet, "A Monk of the Eastern Church," as he liked to sign his books. He and Elisabeth corresponded through all of their long lives until his death in 1980, nurturing a friendship of great intimacy and occasional conflict on that account. At the time, Gillet was a recent convert himself, from the Roman Catholic church, distressed by the papal encyclical *Mortalium Animos* that rejected ecumenism in favor of universal conversion to Rome. He, too, shared the passion for all things Russian. And he was open to the contemporary and changing world, a matter of vital importance to Elisabeth. He led the Orthodox liturgy in an "evangelical" manner, speaking the prayers loudly enough for the assembly to hear, and attracted the great lights of Orthodoxy in France to his parish: Paul Evdokimov, Vladimir Lossky, Ilya Fondaminsky, Nikolai Berdiaev, George Fedotov, Leon Zander, and Sergius Bulgakov. A number of women were active in the parish too, several of French rather than Russian extraction, who helped Elisabeth to feel more at home.

The Paris year came to an end and Elisabeth returned to Strasbourg. Despite her limited worship options, she decided to be chrismated—but not baptized or "rebaptized"—into the Orthodox church. Gillet came to celebrate the liturgy in December 1929. Not wanting to cause offense by using the only church available to them—a Protestant one—he did it instead in the apartment of a Russian Orthodox student. The student was André Behr, whom, in time, the young convert married.

---

[5] Ibid., p. 16.

In the Orthodox church, Elisabeth hoped to find "a tradition incarnated in life." Her biographer Olga Lossky suggests that this desire is the indirect impact of her Jewish family background.[6] Elisabeth also admired in Orthodoxy a "rich, fruitful tension between tradition and freedom," an admiration that she admitted later to be perhaps idealistic.[7] Indeed, the very ecclesiology of communion that initially attracted her received its first major blow during an unpleasant jurisdictional crisis: the Orthodox congregations in France disputed whether they should be under the umbrella of Moscow or of the ecumenical patriarchate. Some went one way, some the other.

Elisabeth was no longer living in Paris during the jurisdictional disputes. She was instead in Berlin, studying with Fedotov and writing her master's degree thesis on the Russian ideal of holiness through an assessment of the saints canonized by the Russian Orthodox church. As Lossky observes, it is a striking choice of topic: Elisabeth deliberately immersed herself in an area of theological study completely foreign to her Lutheran past—hagiography—in order to assimilate herself fully to her new church home.[8] Her proposal to categorize Russian saints as either "sufferers, fools for Christ, or *startsy*" remains the classic typology.[9] This study also did much to influence her own way of witnessing to the Christian faith throughout the rest of her life; as Michel Evdokimov put it, Behr Sigel "had the impatience of prophetic voices, and in this sense she is situated in the line of Russian holiness."[10] Her sojourn in Germany also alerted her for the first time to issues of social justice. In her own way she foresaw the inevitable Second World War, given the dreadful conditions in Germany after the First.

While Elisabeth studied in Berlin, her by-then fiancé André was doing his military service, and since she was anxious about the possibility of continuing her studies and working once she became a wife, they delayed their marriage for awhile. Before André finished his service, Elisabeth returned to Strasbourg, and there an unexpected proposition was put to her. She was asked to fill in as an "auxiliary pastor" for a Reformed parish encompassing the two tiny villages of Villé and Climont in the Vosges Mountains to the west of Strasbourg—making visits, teaching catechism, and conducting worship, though not presiding at the sacraments since she would not be ordained.[11] She had all the same qualifications as male graduates of the Protestant faculty, and many parishes had been long without pastors since the First World War, so there was no objection on the Reformed side. Lev Gillet and Sergius Bulgakov were both in favor, so she accepted and carried out her ministry for eight months. Another friend, Paul Evdokimov, was rather more uncomfortable with the situation and pushed

---

[6]　Ibid., p. 27.

[7]　Ibid.

[8]　Ibid., p. 36.

[9]　*Startsy* can be translated as something like "wise old hermits." See also Michel Evdokimov, "Les Racines Russes de la Pensée Théologique d'Elisabeth Behr-Sigel," *Contacts* 59, no. 4 (2007), pp. 403–12 (406).

[10]　Ibid., p. 407.

[11]　See the important study by Elisabeth Parmentier, "Elisabeth Behr-Sigel's Theological Formation and Ministry in Strasbourg," in *"A Communion Lived in Faith and Love": Reflections on Elisabeth Behr-Sigel's Ecclesiology* (ed. Eleni Kasselouri-Hatzivassiliadi and Sarah Hinlicky Wilson; Doxa and Praxis; Geneva: WCC Publications, 2013) for a detailed account of the clerical offices open to women in the French Protestant churches during the twentieth century.

Elisabeth to get explicit permission to continue from Bishop Vladimir, the Orthodox auxiliary bishop of Metropolitan Evlogy. Elisabeth at this point felt compelled to tell the leaders of the Reformed church about her conversion—a fact that apparently was not quite out in the open when she first accepted the position, though the Reformed leadership seemed to have already guessed as much when they offered her the job and brooked no objection.

Nevertheless, the ambiguity of the situation got the better of Elisabeth, and she at last concluded that she had to make a clean break with Protestantism. It was not a happy decision; the rift in Christendom felt like a personal wound. It violated her newfound Orthodox ecclesiology, which did not perceive the church in terms of jurisdictional divisions at all but only as "plenitude of life in Christ." In her remaining Sundays she devoted her sermons to discussing the mystery of the church, not proselytizing but "awaken[ing] a sense of the Church in my parishioners."[12] At another level, though, the problem was solved by Elisabeth's impending marriage: at that time, even the Protestants didn't think it was fitting for a married woman to exercise a public ministry.

At the end of 1932, Elisabeth graduated from Strasbourg's Protestant faculty and finished her ministry at Villé-Climont, and that was the end of her service in any Protestant church. Lev Gillet encouraged her, though, to continue to see herself as a bridge between East and West, religiously as well as culturally, just as he himself, Evdokimov, and Vladimir Lossky understood their own work. This vocation was the one Behr-Sigel ultimately adopted for herself, even as its outward expression varied greatly over the years. The vocation manifests itself in her earliest publications: an essay on paschal worship in the Orthodox church for *La Quinzaine Protestante*, another on the life and thought of young Protestants for the Roman Catholic journal *La Vie Intellectuelle*. At the same time, her master's work on Russian holiness was serially published in *Irénikon*, an ecumenical journal based at the Roman Catholic monastery of Chevetogne in Belgium. As Olga Lossky observes, "Her reception into the Orthodox Church did not imply any abandonment of her Lutheran origins but rather accentuated her quest for unity in Christ. Elisabeth showed herself most attentive to the theological development of other Christian denominations."[13] She was also still interested in philosophy, becoming friends with Henri-Irénée Marrou, a close collaborator of Emmanuel Mounier's, the founder of the French Personalist movement.[14] Behr-Sigel became a faithful subscriber to their Personalist journal *Esprit* and even faced a Nazi inquiry in the 1940s because she was *Esprit*'s regional representative.

During the 1930s, Behr-Sigel's friendships and family expanded. Her first child was born in 1934 after a difficult labor; and when the doctor suggested Behr-Sigel offer up her sufferings to God, she snapped back, "No way!"—furious at any suggestion that her pains of parturition were punishment for being Eve's descendent.[15] She visited Paris regularly and became friends with Maria Skobtsova, the nun who would deeply

---

12 O. Lossky, *Toward the Endless Day*, p. 49.
13 Ibid., p. 57.
14 Mounier's French personalism is not to be confused with the American personalist movement founded in Boston by Borden Bowne. See Emmanuel Mounier, *A Personalist Manifesto* (London: Longmans, Green, and Co., 1938).
15 O. Lossky, *Toward the Endless Day*, p. 58.

form Behr-Sigel's ideas about the diaconate, and Sergius Bulgakov, with whom she exchanged frequent letters. She wrote, in fact, the first study in French on this Russian theologian's notorious sophiology: a theology of which she herself was critical—as Bulgakov knew—but did not consider deserving of the condemnation it received from Moscow.

During these years, Behr-Sigel worked as a teacher here and there, finding whatever positions she could, but never settling into anything satisfying. She described her labors as a teacher of technical German as "eighteen hours of boredom a week."[16] And then the war came, sending her and everyone else into five years of constant crisis. The shining light of the time for Elisabeth was a clandestine support group of Protestants, Roman Catholics, and Orthodox, sharing not only prayer but a common desire to act on their Christian convictions against the barbarism of the Nazis. This group was, of all the communities she was a part of in her life, the church that Khomiakov had described and Elisabeth had longed for. It was also representative of the fact that Behr-Sigel always got more joy and strength from her friends than her family, whether as a child or as an adult. On top of the partial estrangement from her mother, Behr-Sigel suffered an unhappy relationship with her husband André following his return from a year of service at the beginning of the war. He came back shattered, in poor physical health, and with an alcohol problem that he would never shed despite frequent hospitalizations and detox treatments. The years after the war were particularly dismal for their family.

In 1947 Behr-Sigel began her lifelong involvement with another ecumenical group, the Fellowship of St. Alban and St. Sergius, for Anglicans and Orthodox. At the time there was a profound feeling of kinship between these two church bodies, and a number of significant Orthodox thinkers got involved, including Vladimir Lossky and Sergius Bulgakov. (Ironically, it was the Anglican communion's decision to start ordaining women that was the profoundest blow to this feeling of kinship—ironic because that is precisely what Behr-Sigel spent the last 30 years of her life arguing *for* within the Orthodox church.) Behr-Sigel published an article on the Jesus prayer in its English language periodical *Eastern Churches Quarterly* that year, also attending a conference of the Fellowship in Abingdon, England. The next year she met Timothy Ware, soon to convert to Orthodoxy himself, and Anthony Bloom, eventual metropolitan of Britain and Behr-Sigel's greatest public supporter in her work on the ordination of women in the Orthodox church. Ware, too, collaborated with Behr-Sigel on the subject 50 years later. Behr-Sigel spent every summer that she could in England after that, participating in Fellowship activities. It was a nice contrast to the rather dull parish life available to her in Nancy, where she and André had settled: the priest had no theological education and recited the liturgy in Old Church Slavonic. Behr-Sigel never made any headway in becoming part of parish life there.

Prospects were a bit brighter for Behr-Sigel in the 1950s. In 1952 she started work on her doctorate, and from 1954 to 1956 she received a scholarship that allowed her to study full time without working. Even so, she did not graduate with her degree until 1976. Her subject was the little known and widely reviled Alexander Bukharev. He was a nineteenth-century Russian theologian whose clarion call was the "ecclesialization"

---

[16] Ibid., p. 119.

of life, the engagement of the church with the modern world. Olga Lossky observes, "As a former Lutheran, Elisabeth was deeply moved by this marginal person, who both accepted unjustified calumnies—a trait characteristic of Russian spirituality—and intended to live an evangelical Orthodoxy freed from the institutional straitjacket that distorted its message."[17] His emphasis on kenosis and self-renunciation was especially meaningful during the hard years of family crisis and deadening employment. Sadly, even late twentieth-century France was not ready for Bukharev; Elisabeth's completed dissertation, released by Beauchesne, was quickly withdrawn from publication without further consultation with the author.[18]

Another hopeful prospect was the "rebirth" of the journal *Contacts* in 1958. Behr-Sigel became one of its editors, along with Olivier Clément, another convert (from atheism, rather than from another Christian church). John Meyendorff was on the board. The journal was to provide a common forum for French Orthodox belonging to parishes of different jurisdictions and ethnicities, leading the way toward healing the breach. Behr-Sigel's editorship was another instance of mediation between East and West. Olga Lossky identifies three types of articles that Behr-Sigel contributed over the years. The first type was simply theology, by topic or by theologian, in systematic presentation and often pressing for answers to contemporary questions. A second type addressed particular burning issues: ecumenical rapprochement or the ordination of women. The third type was generally the shortest, reports on conferences or events she attended.[19]

In the 1960s Behr-Sigel looked outward more and more: she spent time in Paris, wrote more for *Contacts*, and traveled around the world: Greece, Israel, the Soviet Union. Her husband lived occasionally with a family friend who looked after him in his illness and alcoholism; it became impossible for him to hold a job anymore, and his chief interest was philately. Despite the understandable strain this caused, it also allowed for more kindness and mutual understanding to grow between them again. André died in 1968. By then all their children had grown up and moved out of the house, and Behr-Sigel had no tie to Nancy anymore. She was free to put herself in the thick of things, so that is exactly what she did: she moved to a suburb of Paris, Epinay-sur-Seine, and settled down to the most productive period of her life. She was in her early 60s at the time.

As soon as she moved to Paris, Behr-Sigel joined the francophone Holy Trinity parish, under the ecumenical patriarch, that met in the crypt of St. Alexander Nevsky cathedral. The priest, Boris Bobrinskoy, promptly put her to work as lay president and, "faithful to her Protestant upbringing," as Olga Lossky puts it,[20] she wasted no time in improving its organization and money management. She also started a newsletter for the parish, *Bulletin de la Crypte*, to which she contributed many articles over the years. She published a number of times in other Orthodox news publications, too, such as *Le Messager Orthodoxe* and *Service Orthodoxe de Presse*. All along she continued her work

---

[17] Ibid., p. 117.
[18] Ibid., p. 119.
[19] Ibid., pp. 136–37.
[20] Ibid., p. 183.

editing *Contacts* and writing for it. She participated in the activities of the Orthodox Fraternity as well as the Comité de Coordination de la Jeunesse Orthodoxe.

New teaching opportunities arose from her writing. First *Contacts* and then Saint-Serge hired her to offer correspondence courses, from which developed her book *Le Lieu du Coeur*, a study of Orthodox spirituality. It was in this capacity alone that she taught for Saint-Serge; despite her doctorate, it was clear that the Orthodox seminary had no intention of hiring a woman to its faculty. However, a Roman Catholic center for ecumenical studies, l'Institut Supérieur d'Etudes Oecuméniques (ISEO), was very interested in Behr-Sigel's work. She taught a number of courses for them through 1982, starting with her basic Russian spirituality studies, eventually including courses on Orthodox anthropology, the place of women in the Orthodox church, and the lay priesthood. In 1983 and 1984 she had a similar experience teaching at the Tantur Ecumenical Institute in Israel.

Behr-Sigel tirelessly advocated for deeper involvement by Orthodox church and people alike in the besetting problems of contemporary society. One way she modeled her convictions was by becoming the vice-president of Action de Chrétiens pour l'Abolition de la Torture (ACAT), an ecumenical anti-torture organization. In a draft of an article for its newsletter *Courrier de l'ACAT*, Behr-Sigel expressed her basic convictions:

> From their Catholic and Protestant brothers and sisters, the Orthodox receive the impetus of a more active spirituality that is present in the world without being of the world. The Orthodox know how to sing the joy of Christ's Resurrection perhaps better than others do. But they have to learn—and adherence to the ACAT could facilitate this—to pose acts that bear witness to their faith *here and now*.[21]

"Here and now" was Behr-Sigel's favorite phrase; it appears again and again in her writings over the years. She remained vice-president of ACAT until 1993 and stayed on its theological commission until her death. She was also a member of another ecumenical relief organization, Comité Inter-Mouvements Auprès Des Evacués (CIMADE), which began with Protestant efforts to care for those displaced during the Second World War; to this day it addresses the needs of displaced populations.

Behr-Sigel perceived no discontinuity between social engagement and contemplation, so while she was the vice-president of ACAT she was also instrumental in the founding of an Eastern-rite Carmelite monastery, Saint-Elie (St. Elijah). Eventually in 1991 a group of supporters formed the Fraternité Saint-Elie, which strove for the unity of all Christians through prayer, charity, evangelical truth, and a journal called *Mikhtav*. The following year Jews were also welcomed into the Fraternité.[22] In 2003, the Fraternité honored Elisabeth with a festschrift, *"Toi, Suis-Moi," Mélanges Offerts en Hommage à Elisabeth Behr-Sigel*. This same year she took her last tour

---

[21] Ibid., p. 250.
[22] Eliane Poirot, O. C. D. I., "Elisabeth Behr-Sigel et le Carmel Saint-Elie," *Contacts* 59, no. 4 (2007), pp. 459–66.

abroad, lecturing at Holy Cross and St. Vladimir's Orthodox seminaries in the United States. She died on November 26, 2005.

This is an impressive résumé for anyone's life.[23] But although Behr-Sigel was recognized and honored for many of these things, especially her book on Russian spirituality,[24] it was her studies of the place of women in the Orthodox church that gained her the greatest fame. Perhaps this is not surprising; the second half of the twentieth century was particularly occupied with the impact of feminism and the growing practice of ordaining women to clerical offices. Behr-Sigel took these changes as "signs of the times," demanding careful and thoughtful theological study from the Orthodox church. But she did not begin her work as a partisan of the ordination of women. She began with distinct theological objections to it. As her studies led her deeper into the Scriptures, the church fathers, and Orthodox theology, she changed her mind and began to articulate a different theological conviction, one that recognizes the call for *persons* to become priests, whether those persons are male or female.

In the chapters to follow, we will trace the evolution of Elisabeth Behr-Sigel's thought on women and the priesthood, accounting for both her starting and ending points, and exploring the changes that took her from the former to the latter.[25] To do so, we must begin with a chapter reviewing the work of Paul Evdokimov, Behr-Sigel's dear friend and among the first theologians to write on "woman" as a theological topos in an entirely positive light. Chapter 2 therefore deals with Evdokimov. Chapter 3 turns to Behr-Sigel's first forays into the question herself, starting with an invitation to deliver the keynote address at the first-ever international gathering of Orthodox women at the Agapia monastery in Romania and following her work through the last of the WCC-sponsored conferences on "The Community of Men and Women in the Church" in Sheffield, England. Chapter 4 demonstrates how Behr-Sigel began to shake off Evdokimov's ideas and move to her own mature position in favor of the ordination of women. During the same period, the Orthodox church finally recognized the need to address the question and in 1988 met on the island of Rhodes to discuss it. Though Behr-Sigel attended the consultation, she was not given the opportunity to speak. In the end it was a theology shaped very much by Evdokimov's work, and not at all by hers, that carried the day. Chapter 5 covers the rest of Behr-Sigel's working life, including her responses to other Orthodox theologians' work and their challenges to her own.

---

[23] A nice, brief summary of her life's work can be found in Paul Ladouceur, "Aperçu de l'Oeuvre Littéraire d'Elisabeth Behr-Sigel," *Lumière du Thabor* 28 (2006), pp. 5–8. See also his "Pensée et Oeuvre d'Elisabeth Behr-Sigel," *Contacts* 59, no. 4 (2007), pp. 430–54.

[24] Her book, *Prière et Sainteté dans l'Eglise Russe* (Paris: Cerf, 1950), is cited in Steven Runciman, *The Great Church in Captivity: A Study of the Patriarchate of Constantinople from the Eve of the Turkish Conquest to the Greek War of Independence* (London: Cambridge University Press, 1968); James Billington, *The Icon and the Axe: An Interpretive History of Russian Culture* (New York: Knopf, 1966); and Sergei Hackel, "Russian," in *The Study of Spirituality*, pp. 259–76 (ed. Cheslyn Jones, Geoffrey Wainwright, and Edward Yarnold; New York: Oxford University Press, 1986).

[25] The bibliography of Behr-Sigel's writings at the end of this book is the most comprehensive to date. I am heavily indebted to the first compiled bibliography that appears in the festschrift, *"Toi, Suis-Moi," Mélanges Offerts en Hommage à Elisabeth Behr-Sigel* (Iasi, Romania: Editura Trinitas, 2nd edn, 2003). The bibliography in Olga Lossky's biography is also based on the one in *"Toi, Suis-Moi,"* which makes some needed corrections though also retains a number of errors that I have tried to correct here.

Chapter 6 is an excursus on the female diaconate, which won not only Behr-Sigel's endorsement but also the Rhodes Consultation's. The diaconate's relevance to a study otherwise on the priesthood lies in its being the only live opportunity for ordination, or at least some kind of consecration to clerical office, for women in the Orthodox church. Chapter 7 then deals with three interpretative questions that arise from Behr-Sigel's life and work: namely, how influenced she was by feminism, by Protestantism, and by the two competing schools of Orthodox theology among the Russian émigrés in France. Finally, Chapter 8 attempts to draw together the various strands of her arguments and to offer a slightly more systematic construction anchored in her thought.

2

Paul Evdokimov on "Woman"

Elisabeth Behr-Sigel began to think theologically about women in the priesthood because of her friendship with an unordained man.[1]

---

[1] There is only one book-length study on Evdokimov, Peter C. Phan's *Culture and Eschatology: The Iconographical Vision of Paul Evdokimov* (New York: Peter Lang, 1985), which also contains the most complete bibliography of Evdokimov's writings. Olivier Clément discusses Evdokimov and Vladimir Lossky together in *Orient-Occident—Deux Passeurs: Vladimir Lossky, Paul Evdokimov* (Perspective Orthodoxe, 6; Geneva: Labor et Fides, 1985). Articles on various aspects of Evdokimov's thought include the following. Olivier Clément, "The Eucharist in the Thought of Paul Evdokimov," *Eastern Churches Review* 7, no. 2 (1975), pp. 113–24; "La Vie et l'Oeuvre de Paul Evdokimov," *Contacts* 23 (1971), pp. 88–106; and "Paul Evdokimov 1901–1970," in *Ecumenical Pilgrims: Profiles of Pioneers in Christian Reconciliation*, pp. 86–92 (ed. Ion Bria and Dagmar Heller; Geneva: WCC Publications, 1995). Rowan Williams, "Christian Art and Cultural Pluralism: Reflections on 'L'Art de l'Icone,' by Paul Evdokimov," *Eastern Churches Review* 8, no. 1 (1976), pp. 38–44; and "Bread in the Wilderness: The Monastic Ideal in Thomas Merton and Paul Evdokimov," in *One Yet Two: Monastic Tradition East and West*, pp. 452–73 (ed. M. Basil Pennington; Kalamazoo: Cistercian Publications, 1976). Peter C. Phan, "Mariage, Monachisme et Eschatologie: Contribution de Paul Evdokimov à la Spiritualité Chrétienne," *Ephemerides Liturgicae* 93 (1979), pp. 352–80; "The Eschatological Dimension of Unity: Paul Evdokimov's Contribution to Ecumenism," *Salesianum* 42 (1980), pp. 475–99; and "Evdokimov and the Monk Within," *Sobornost* 3, no. 1 (1981), pp. 53–61 [N.B.: Peter C. Phan and Cho D. Phan are the same person]. Michael Plekon, "An 'Offering of Prayer': The Witness of Paul Evdokimov (1901–1970)," *Sobornost* 17, no. 2 (1995), pp. 28–37; "The God Whose Power is Weakness, Whose Love is Foolish: Divine Philanthropy in the Theology of Paul Evdokimov," *Sourozh* 60 (1995), pp. 15–26; "Paul Evdokimov: A Theologian Within and Beyond the Church and the World," *Modern Theology* 12, no. 1 (1996), pp. 85–107; "Interiorized Monasticism: A Reconsideration of Paul Evdokimov on the Spiritual Life," *American Benedictine Review* 48, no. 3 (1997), pp. 227–40; "Tradition's Freedom and Beauty: The Enduring Vision of Paul Evdokimov and Elisabeth Behr-Sigel," *Lutheran Forum* 37, no. 2 (2003), pp. 28–32; "Becoming What We Pray: Three Images, Three Lives," *Ecumenical Review* 57, no. 4 (2003), pp. 395–405; and "Sacrement Frère/Soeur chez Paul Evdokimov et Mère Marie Skobtsov," *Contacts* 56 (2004), pp. 5–28, translated as "The 'Sacrament of the Brother/Sister': The Lives and Thought of Mother Maria Skobtsova and Paul Evdokimov," *St. Vladimir's Theological Quarterly* 49, no. 3 (2005), pp. 313–34. Olivier Rousseau, "Le Professeur Paul Evdokimov (1901–1970)," *Irénikon* 43, no. 4 (1970), pp. 588–91. Jean-François Roussel, "Evidence et Indicibilité dans l'Apologétique de Paul Evdokimov," *Contacts* 47 (1995), pp. 287–307. Lars Thunberg, "Paul Evdokimov, Théologien Oecuménique," *Contacts* 47 (1995), pp. 270–86. William J. F. Keenan, "Rediscovering the Theological in Sociology: Foundation and Possibilities," *Theory, Culture and Society* 20, no. 1 (2003), pp. 19–42. Articles that directly concern Evdokimov's work on women and gender include the following. Roman Ginn, "Paul Evdokimov on the Question on Women's Ordination," *The Priest* 41 (1985), pp. 40–45. Peter C. Phan, "Gender Roles in the History of Salvation: Man and Woman in the Thought of Paul Evdokimov," *Heythrop Journal*

Paul Evdokimov and Behr-Sigel met through a mutual friend. As she testified later, he embodied for her "l'Orthodoxie vivante."[2] An expatriate Russian, he and his family had been driven out of their homeland by the Revolution.[3] Although his studies had begun at the Kiev Academy, they were completed in France, first with a degree in philosophy from the Sorbonne, then from the newly founded Saint-Serge in Paris as a member of the first graduating class and a student of Berdiaev and Bulgakov. He earned a doctorate in philosophy at Aix-en-Provence in 1942 and ten years later began to teach at Saint-Serge.

Evdokimov was not a priest. He was more like a deacon, though without the title. During the Second World War and for a number of years thereafter he worked in hostels caring for the poor and displaced. Service and theological study went hand in hand for Evdokimov, even as a layman—perhaps especially as a layman. His passion was to develop fully the priesthood of all believers, the royal priesthood of 1 Peter 3. Despite its better renown in Protestant circles, the lay priesthood—as both Evdokimov and Behr-Sigel were convinced—ought also to be exalted in Orthodoxy, because Orthodox ecclesiology is not fundamentally vertical, with ascending ladders of offices instituted to maintain hierarchical discipline, but horizontal in the sense of *sobornost*, the Russian word for "communion" or "conciliarity," a dynamic and mutually interdependent relationship of love intended to mirror that of the three persons of God. Building on this insight, Evdokimov spoke often of "interiorized monasticism," a notion he drew from the nineteenth-century Russian theologian Alexander Bukharev. Evdokimov agreed with his predecessor that the modern world requires a Christian presence not so much in cloisters as in cities; correspondingly, chastity is as much a virtue of marriage as of monasticism.[4] The tasks of Christian service and theological reflection belong to lay "priests" just as much as they do to their clerical counterparts. Because of this conviction, Behr-Sigel approvingly called Evdokimov the "herald and prophet" of "the royal priesthood of all the baptized."[5] Sharing his commitment to Christian service in the world, Behr-Sigel explored its roots further through her doctoral studies of Alexander Bukharev, encouraged by Evdokimov.

Evdokimov's theology was further characterized by two impulses: first, a return to the patristic sources, and second, a dialogue between those patristic sources and

31 (1990), pp. 53–66. Michael Plekon, "Le Visage du Père dans la Mère de Dieu: Marie dans les Ecrits Théologiques de Paul Evdokimov," *Contacts* 47 (1995), pp. 250–69. Christopher P. Klofft, "Gender and the Process of Moral Development in the Thought of Paul Evdokimov," *Theological Studies* 66 (2005), pp. 69–95. Joachim Illies, "Eva und das Heil der Welt: In der Sicht des russisch-orthodoxen Christen Paul Evdokimov," in *Die Sache mit dem Apfel: Eine moderne Wissenschaft vom Sündenfall*, pp. 116–26 (ed. Joachim Illies; Freiburg: Herderbücherei, 1972), which is simply a summary of Evdokimov on Eve and the division of man and woman in the garden without critical analysis, so I will not deal with it further here.

[2] Behr-Sigel, "Témoignage sur Paul Evdokimov," *Contacts* 23 (1971), pp. 237–40.

[3] The biographical information provided here can be found in the introduction of Clément's *Orient-Occident—Deux Passeurs* and in the introduction to Evdokimov, *Ages of the Spiritual Life* (trans. Sister Gertrude; rev. trans. Michael Plekon and Alexis Vinogradov; Crestwood, NY: St. Vladimir's Seminary Press, 1998).

[4] See Plekon, "Interiorized Monasticism."

[5] Behr-Sigel, "The Ordination of Women: Also a Question for the Orthodox Churches," in Elisabeth Behr-Sigel and Kallistos Ware, *The Ordination of Women in the Orthodox Church* (Geneva: WCC Publications, 2000), p. 17.

the contemporary world. This marks Evdokimov as an heir of the stream of Russian Orthodoxy flowing from Bukharev through Soloviev and later Bulgakov. A return to the sources, though essential, by itself remains inadequate, degenerating all too easily into cranky repristination. Evdokimov attempted a fresh claim on the common faith of the modern and ancient Christian alike, based on his conviction that patristic insights could speak potently to modern dilemmas, just as modern dilemmas could draw out aspects of the Christian faith that simply did not appear in the early church.[6] Bukharev had once sought to reconcile the heart and mind of the nineteenth-century Russian intelligentsia with the theology of the church fathers, and Evdokimov sought to do the same in French Orthodoxy. This, if anything, is the golden thread that runs through all of Behr-Sigel's work, too.[7]

Evdokimov and Behr-Sigel's common formation was at the feet of Sergius Bulgakov, who believed that, "however basic [the patristic sources] may be for the Eastern Orthodox tradition, [they] are nonetheless not inexhaustible; indeed, they are already exhausted. Theological reflection must enter into dialogue with modern philosophy in order to withstand its challenges."[8] And in one key area Bukharev, Soloviev, Evdokimov, and Behr-Sigel all took up the challenge: in the pressing questions of the status of women.

"Woman" in Evdokimov's Orthodox predecessors

Capping his exuberant vision of lay Christianity, and of dialogue between patristic faith and modern times, was Evdokimov's interest in "woman" as a theological topos. There was a hint of this interest already in Bukharev, who shockingly (for his time) left the monastery and eventually married, later writing on the common chastity of monasticism and marriage.[9] Bukharev did, however, tend toward what we might call abstraction, interested more in "woman" than in "women." Behr-Sigel describes Bukharev's view as "integrating sexuality and marriage into a vision of womanhood which, in the work of salvation, is a complementary spiritual principle to that of manhood."[10] This sounds innocent enough. In its own way, it is even strikingly progressive, insisting on the irreplaceable role of the feminine in the realm of divine action. But what do "spiritual principles" have to do with actual women? And in what precisely does their "complementarity" to the masculine lie?

---

6   See Behr-Sigel, review of *Orient-Occident—Deux Passeurs: Vladimir Lossky et Paul Evdokimov*, by O. Clément, *Contacts* 37 (1985), pp. 317–20 (320).

7   Behr-Sigel, "Témoignage sur Paul Evdokimov," pp. 239–40.

8   Michael Aksionov Meerson, *The Trinity of Love in Modern Russian Theology: The Love Paradigm and the Retrieval of Western Medieval Love Mysticism in Modern Russian Trinitarian Thought from Solovyov to Bulgakov* (Quincy, IL: Franciscan Press, 1998), p. xix.

9   Behr-Sigel notes Bukharev's seminal work on women and also on modernity; the two go together. "[H]e was the first modern Orthodox theologian to dare to address the problems of human sexuality with boldness, depth and delicacy." Behr-Sigel, "Women in the Orthodox Church: Heavenly Vision and Historical Realities," in Elisabeth Behr-Sigel, *The Ministry of Women in the Church* (trans. Steven Bigham; Redondo Beach, CA: Oakwood Publications, 1991), pp. 123–24.

10   Ibid., p. 124.

Bukharev had sown the seed of reflection on the feminine in Orthodox theology. Vladimir Soloviev, the religious philosopher, and Sergius Bulgakov, the theologian, were the first to reap it. Both produced "sophiologies," studies on the wisdom of God, depicting Sophia with a distinct feminine character.

In one of her earliest articles, Behr-Sigel analyzed these two sophiologies in order to introduce Bulgakov's writings to a French Orthodox audience.[11] In Bulgakov's teaching, Sophia, or wisdom, is a distinct reality. Bulgakov characterizes "her" as "ontologically distinct, and 'in a way personal,' capable of loving God with a certain 'passive love,'" as Behr-Sigel reports. She notes parenthetically, though, that "passive love" is generally equated with "feminine love," which opens the door to romanticizing Sophia as an "Eternal Feminine," though Bulgakov himself never did so.[12] Although this essay predates Behr-Sigel's extensive reflection on women in the church by nearly 40 years, we can already hear a note of skepticism about theological ruminations on the feminine.

Behr-Sigel's real criticism, though, is reserved for Vladimir Soloviev, Bulgakov's predecessor, whose articles of the early 1890s were collected in the volume *The Sense of Love*. Soloviev posits that the sexual relationship between man and woman mirrors the relationship between the Absolute (i.e. God) and "Its Other." It is worth quoting Behr-Sigel's summary of Soloviev here at length, as it sets the stage for Evdokimov's own variations on the same theme. The Absolute's Other,

> which is only in itself pure potentiality, receives from the Absolute from all eternity the plenitude of the divine life and realizes itself for Him as the "Eternal Feminine." In the same way, the woman who "represents" the essence of all nature, the definitive expression of the material world in its interior passivity, receives from the man by whom she is loved the possibility of realizing the divine image, the sophianic germ hidden in her and which the amorous exaltation permits the man to discover. But, from her side, the woman helps man to leave his egoistic ipseity that separates him from the Universe and permits him, thanks to the amorous ecstasy, to participate anew in the organic unity of the Cosmos. The genuine meaning of marriage is the total union of man and woman, a union never realized in its "totality" by empirical marriages but that appears as the far-off end toward which they strive. The realization of the ideal marriage would have to result, according to Soloviev, in the emergence of a new being, "integral," reuniting in itself the characteristics of the two sexes, and who would be the "new Adam," the definitive incarnation of the divine image of man such as exists in the celestial Sophia. Soloviev defends himself from having introduced in God traits of carnal eroticism and of teaching

---

[11] Behr-Sigel, "La Sophiologie du Père Serge Boulgakoff," *Revue d'Histoire et de Philosophie Religieuses* 2 (1939), pp. 130–58; reprinted in *Le Messager Orthodoxe* 57 (1972), pp. 21–48. Quotations are from the latter version and are my translation. It so happens that Bulgakov was also Behr-Sigel's confessor and correspondent until his death. Bulgakov was unknown to French readers not only because he wrote in Russian but also because his sophiology had been condemned by the Moscow patriarchate. In fact, it was the equally eminent Orthodox theologian Vladimir Lossky who alerted Moscow to Bulgakov's works, an act that has been called "patricide." See Clément, *Orient-Occident—Deux Passeurs*, p. 12.

[12] Behr-Sigel, "La Sophiologie du Père Serge Boulgakoff," p. 45.

the adoration of the "Feminine in oneself." It is nevertheless undeniable that an air of eroticism, an eroticism certainly spiritualized and sublimated, traverses all his work.[13]

Behr-Sigel concludes by complimenting Bulgakov on avoiding Soloviev's approach to marriage. Instead, Bulgakov considers marriage to be the exit of man and woman alike from egoism to a community of love, in this way imitating the Trinity.

"Woman" in Evdokimov's theological anthropology

Even though his predecessors paved the way for theological reflection on women, Evdokimov's own work was unique and unprecedented. This is perhaps because he wrote in a time and place—the mid-twentieth century and western Europe, Paris in particular—where burning questions concerning women were occupying the secular mind.

For instance, Evdokimov read and commented at some length on Simone de Beauvoir's *The Second Sex.* On one level his criticism is directed toward the existentialist philosophy that underlies it.[14] He could accept the existentialist formula that "man is what man does" only insofar as "man" exists within the divine life, "when an objective, normative value structure is accepted freely—the submission to which is sovereignly free because freedom itself is found among such values."[15] He could appreciate de Beauvoir's complaint that women have become merely the product of a civilization created and controlled by men, leading an artificial and secondary life, but he finds no solution within her godless framework. In Evdokimov's view, the only way out of this problem is to posit a "transcendental origin" of woman.[16] It is not enough to define men and women through their physical being, as Evdokimov interprets de Beauvoir's view: "Through his body, man has a grip on the world; in her subjugation to her body, woman endures the world." But "de Beauvoir refuses to see in woman the mystery praised by the poets . . . [Instead there is] a metaphysical void."[17]

We will return shortly to Evdokimov's own solution to the metaphysical void. The salient point here is that Evdokimov was, until Behr-Sigel herself, the only theologian in French Orthodoxy to consider the secular women's movement with great sympathy, seeing in it even an "ethical imperative" and, in another of Behr-Sigel's favorite phrases, one of the "signs of the times" that Christ exhorted his disciples to mind.[18]

In this way Evdokimov proved himself again a disciple of Bukharev. The latter, as Behr-Sigel reports, encouraged a male student to see the same image of Christ in

---

[13] Ibid., pp. 39–40.

[14] Klofft notes this also in "Gender and the Process of Moral Development," p. 72.

[15] Paul Evdokimov, *Woman and the Salvation of the World* (trans. Anthony P. Gythiel; Crestwood, NY: St. Vladimir's Seminary Press, 1994), pp. 13–14.

[16] Ibid., p. 21.

[17] Ibid., p. 22.

[18] Behr-Sigel, "Introduction," in *The Ministry of Women in the Church*, pp. 2–3. Despite the seminal work of Bukharev, Soloviev, and Bulgakov, it cannot be said that they were involved in the feminist movement of the West, which postdated their lifetimes.

women as in men, by virtue of their common humanity, for "this was the only attitude that could meet the challenge of an embryonic feminism taking form in the Russian intelligentsia. He felt that the Church should not condemn this feminism but rather baptize, purify, and enlighten it."[19] Evdokimov followed suit. He respected women as human beings.[20] He noted, and was grieved by, the inverse proportionality between marian piety and respect for Mary's ordinary sisters.[21] He discerned in Ephesians a call to *mutual* submission, not only the submission of wife to husband, and argued that the analogy must refer to a *good* marriage, not just to any marriage at all.[22] As a twice-married (widowed the first time) lay theologian, he held sexual love in high esteem. He consequently had little use for "clumsy" definitions of women with sole reference to their biological function and concomitant understandings of erotic love as merely a means to the ultimate end of reproduction.[23] As he so pithily put it, "Scholasticism promotes procreation, but castrates love."[24] The explicit or implicit meaning of such definitions is that women are fundamentally inferior to men, which Evdokimov would not tolerate.[25] He identified the source of this Christian tendency in the "inhuman asceticism" of Platonic mind-body dualism and so, following Bukharev's lead, he strove to rehabilitate sexuality as a legitimate, integral part of personhood.

However—and this is a big however—Evdokimov's principled interest in real, everyday women did not save him from the abstraction common in thinkers before him. If anything, he indulged in the most high-flown abstractions yet. In his defense, this is perhaps to be expected from a pioneer breaking new ground and one who happened to be doing so prior to mature developments in feminist thought. But either way, Evdokimov proved to be more Soloviev's heir than Bulgakov's.[26]

---

[19]   Behr-Sigel, "Mary, the Mother of God," in *The Ministry of Women in the Church*, p. 212.

[20]   Behr-Sigel, review of *Orient-Occident—Deux Passeurs*, p. 319.

[21]   Behr-Sigel, "The Otherness of Men and Women in the Context of a Christian Civilization," in *The Ministry of Women in the Church*, p. 36. See also in *The Ministry of Women in the Church* the articles "Women in the Orthodox Church: Heavenly Vision and Historical Realities," p. 116, and "Mary, the Mother of God," p. 208. In Evdokimov, see *Woman and the Salvation of the World*, pp. 23–24.

[22]   Evdokimov, *Woman and the Salvation of the World*, p. 18.

[23]   Behr-Sigel, though, comments that Bukharev essentially thought the same thing about sexuality, though none of her studies spend much time on this aspect of his work. See "Un Prophète Orthodoxe: Alexandre Boukharev," *Contacts* 25, no. 2 (1973), pp. 93–111 (97–98).

[24]   Evdokimov, *Woman and the Salvation of the World*, p. 27.

[25]   Behr-Sigel, "Women in the Orthodox Church: Heavenly Vision and Historical Realities," in *The Ministry of Women in the Church*, pp. 124–25.

[26]   Evdokimov wrote two books principally devoted to a theology of women and femininity; they are substantially similar on all points, in places even down to identical phrasing. Here I will follow mainly the argument of the later of the two, noting corresponding points in the first and the occasional additional thought. *Le Mariage, Sacrement de l'Amour* (Lyon: Livre Français, 1944) has seen multiple reprintings in French since its initial publication. It was published in English as *The Sacrament of Love: The Nuptial Mystery in the Light of the Orthodox Tradition* (trans. Anthony P. Gythiel and Victoria Steadman; Crestwood, NY: St. Vladimir's Seminary Press, 1985). *La Femme et le Salut du Monde: Etude d'Anthropologie Chrétienne sur les Charismes de la Femme* (Paris-Tournai: Casterman, 1958) has also been reprinted in French several times. It was published in English as *Woman and the Salvation of the World* in 1994. There are two relevant essays in the posthumous collection *La Nouveauté de l'Esprit: Etudes de Spiritualité* (Spiritualité Orientale, 20; Bégrolles: Abbaye de Bellefontaine, 1977): "Les Charismes de la Femme," pp. 237–52, first published in 1959, and "La Saint Esprit et la Mère de Dieu," pp. 253–78, first published in 1971. Both are translated into English and appear in the collection *In the World, Of the Church: A Paul Evdokimov Reader* (ed.

Evdokimov's book *Woman and the Salvation of the World* is a work on soteriology, developing, naturally, an Eastern theology of deification.[27] He takes a long time to say anything about women at all, but that is because he prepares the way by developing a theological anthropology. Only toward the end does he begin to offer reasons for two distinct kinds of human beings, male and female, each moving toward deification and each contributing something unique to the work of salvation. The whole argument turns on archetypes (there are many references to Jung): people must become the image of their designated archetypes in the process of deification.[28]

Following Soloviev's lead, Evdokimov describes a femininity that connects Sophia to the Mother of God. He writes, "It is the vocation of Sophia to bring forth divine thoughts, and to give them a human form; this is the humanization of Yahweh. Through the feminine principle of Sophia, the awe-inspiring countenance of Yahweh transforms itself into a human face."[29] Mary, analogously, is maternity and chastity alike, the manifestation of divine love that is too dreadful to be grasped in God's own face.[30] The paternity is beyond human recognition, so the Theotokos makes it available in her humanity; there is a commonality of parental love in God the Father and Mary the Mother of God that even Christ, it would seem, does not express, being the Son.[31] The humanized face of God is, in addition, the church, the bride, ultimately a feminine kind of being.

These archetypes are not mere symbols. In Evdokimov's thought, the archetype reveals a deeper truth: that gender is, in fact, a transcendental category of being;

Michael Plekon and Alexis Vinogradov; Crestwood, NY: St. Vladimir's Seminary Press, 2001): "The Charisms of Woman," pp. 231–42, and "Panagion and Panagia: The Holy Spirit and the Mother of God," pp. 155–73, respectively. Behr-Sigel makes explicit reference only to the material in these two books and two articles, so I will restrict myself to dealing with them, though there are a few other articles by Evdokimov on the subject of women.

27 With unfortunate, and generally inaccurate, sideswipes at Western theology. In one place (p. 154) he even makes the astonishing claim that no woman could or would ever have developed the doctrine of predestination! Cf. Jennifer L. Bayne and Sarah E. Hinlicky, "Free to Be Creatures Again," *Christianity Today* (October 23, 2000), pp. 38–44. Behr-Sigel apparently follows Evdokimov in criticizing predestination as a "dark doctrine" in her own book, *The Place of the Heart: An Introduction to Orthodox Spirituality* (trans. Steven Bigham; Torrance, CA: Oakwood Publications, 1992), p. 4. This book is a translation of *Le Lieu du Coeur: Initiation à la Spiritualité Orthodoxe* (Paris: Cerf, 1989).

28 Despite Evdokimov's concern over "Platonic mind-body dualism," he is unable to escape it and Platonism more generally in his theories of archetypes. He may also have been following again the lead of Soloviev, who developed the notion that ideas are "metaphysical entities rather than products of abstract thinking . . . Person (subject) and idea (object) imply each other, because a person without an idea would be empty and meaningless, whereas an idea without a person would remain passive and impotent." Meerson, *The Trinity of Love in Modern Russian Theology*, p. 27. If this is the case, a woman can only be a woman insofar as she images the metaphysical entity of womanhood. For a different approach to archetypal imagery, with considerably more elbow room and human freedom, see Anthony Ugolnik, "Nymphios and Sophia: Gender as a Spiritual Dialectic in the Thought of the East-Slavs," *Logos: A Journal of Eastern Christian Studies* 35, nos 1–4 (1994), pp. 11–40. Although Ugolnik draws on Evdokimov, the difference between them is substantial.

29 Evdokimov, *Woman and the Salvation of the World*, p. 203.

30 Ibid., p. 219. Also in "Panagion and Panagia," p. 161: "This humanizing of God in the Incarnation is articulated mariologically, that is, through the person of the Mother of God." Here also he aligns the Theotokos with Sophia.

31 Evdokimov, "Panagion and Panagia," p. 172.

archetypes are the condition for the possibility of sexual differentiation in material creatures.[32] The differences between the sexes are no mere matter of the roles they play or of their physical biology—de Beauvoir's mistake. They are ontological differences in the very structure of reality that give rise to biological differences in males and females. For Evdokimov these differences are no ground for discrimination or oppression, however; they are the source of complementarity, mutual need, and mutual fulfillment.

Evdokimov declares that sexual differentiation came *after* the first creation of "humanity." This primal separation of men and women from one another drives the intense desire between them. Curiously, Evdokimov does not cite either the Cappadocians or Maximus the Confessor, the latter of whom especially insisted on this point.[33] Nor does he use the bipartite-creation principle to relativize the depth of ontological difference between male and female once they have been separated, as other Orthodox writers often do.[34] Rather, he writes:

> The creation of Adam (in Hebrew, 'adam is to be understood in a collective sense, "mankind") is the creation of the original human cell, of man as man-woman, of the male and female elements in their original, not-yet-differentiated fusion . . . the biblical story clearly shows that these two aspects of man are inseparable to such a degree that a male or female human being taken separately and viewed *in se* is not a perfect human being.[35]

The first creation emphasizes their unity and belonging to each other; the second, the great difference between them.

But because the difference is archetypal, ontological, and not merely physical, the movement is not from body to quality, but from quality to body, thus:

> A woman is not maternal because her body is able to give birth: it is from her maternal spirit that the corresponding physiological and anatomical capabilities are derived. Likewise, man is more virile and physically stronger because in his spirit there is something that corresponds to the "violence" of which the Gospel speaks. The true hierarchy of principles must be reestablished; we must understand that the physiological and the psychic depend upon the spirit *normatively*, serving it and expressing it.[36]

---

[32] Ginn writes in his appreciative article, "Evdokimov distinguishes very carefully between masculine and feminine charisms. He had great interest in the work of Jung, with whom he occasionally corresponded, and his distinctions are based on the latter's doctrine of archetypes. These belong to man's structure and are located in the collective unconscious. They are not merely psychological but metaphysical realities that look to the 'arche', the ultimate principle." "Paul Evdokimov on the Question of Women's Ordination," p. 40.

[33] Another parallel to Maximus the Confessor appears in "Panagion and Panagia," p. 166, where he says that Mary's virginity is not about a physical state per se but a time before the fall when giving birth was not a function of sexual activity.

[34] See, for instance, the work of Verna Harrison.

[35] Evdokimov, *Woman and the Salvation of the World*, p. 139.

[36] Ibid., p. 16.

If, then, the differences between men and women have a transcendental source, and if men and women are at their most fulfilled—and most deified—when they most fully emulate their distinct archetypes, it follows logically that we can and must delineate just what those differences are. Human happiness and possibly even salvation depend on it.

Here is where Evdokimov is at his most speculative—and troubling, in the end, to Behr-Sigel. His thesis statement, as it were, is this: "The conflict between man and woman, between creation and giving birth, between the person—who is unique—and the species—procreation—remains irreducible."[37] Remember that this is not an observation on the cultural impact of biological differences; women give birth not because of their wombs, but they have wombs for giving birth because of their fundamental birthgiving spirituality. It is best here to let Evdokimov speak for himself.

> While man extends himself in the world by means of tools, woman does so by her gift of self. In her very being she is linked to the rhythms of nature, attuned to the order that rules the universe. It is through this gift that every woman is potentially a mother, and carries the world's treasure in the depths of her soul . . . While man's aim is to act, woman's is to be, which is the pre-eminent religious category. Woman could accumulate intellectual values, but such values provide no joy. The excessively intellectualized woman, man's equal and constructress of the world, will find herself despoiled of her essence, for what woman is meant to contribute to culture is femininity as an irreplaceable mode of being and way of living. Man creates science, art, philosophy, and even theology as systems, but all these lead to a frightening objectification of the truth. Woman, fortunately, is present; she is predestined to become the bearer of the values obscured by this objectification, the place where they become flesh and live . . . This is woman's vocation: to protect the world of humans as mother, and to save it as a virgin, by giving to this world a soul, her soul . . . Woman has her vocation not in terms of society but in terms of humanity; her field of action is not civilization, but human "culture."[38]

So Evdokimov, for all his sympathy to the women's movement, lamented anything that led women into men's roles, fearing a loss of their proper spiritual gifts or even an all-out annihilation of the feminine.[39] He says, for instance, "A woman who takes the place of a man does not add anything special to the role; on the contrary, she loses the sense of her own femininity, of her own vocation."[40]

But this is a largely negative approach, focusing on the differences. What interested Evdokimov far more was the distinctive charisms proper to women, charisms that the church had shamefully neglected or even devalued. For instance, in a break from the usual exegesis, he reads the 1 Corinthians 11 passage on the woman's veil as a symbol of

[37] Ibid., p. 175.
[38] Ibid., pp. 184–85.
[39] Ibid., p. 267.
[40] Ibid., p. 163.

the mystery of her charisms to be uplifted, not one of submission or shame.[41] Woman's principal gift is "weaving her entire being through her special relationship to God, others, and self."[42] Furthermore,

> [h]er charism of interiorized and universal "maternity" carries every woman toward the hungry and the needy and admirably defines the feminine essence: virgin or spouse, every woman is a mother for all eternity (*in aeternum*). The structure of her soul predisposes her "to protect" all that crosses her path, to discover in the strongest and most virile being a weak, defenseless child.[43]

Maternity, clearly, is of the essence in woman. There is no corresponding charism of paternity in men, though. In fact, Evdokimov asserts that men have no natural gift for paternity whatsoever: "Though he may be conqueror, adventurer, builder, a man is not paternal in his essence."[44] Religious fatherhood, as of God, has no correspondence in human experience. This explains to Evdokimov why even in biblical texts the fatherhood of God must occasionally be described in maternal terms.[45] And this is another reason why mariology must play an essential role in soteriology: "While it is Christ who saves the world, it is the Theotokos who protects it, and introduces into its 'dehumanization' a tender attention to grace."[46] If anything, to be religious is to be feminine. In the spiritual realm, woman is the stronger sex—thus, from the serpent's point of view, the woman was the one who had to be assaulted first. Evdokimov will not have Eve depicted as a weakling responsible for sin.[47]

"Woman" in Evdokimov's trinitarian theology

One is tempted to congratulate Evdokimov on his creativity and then demand how he can get away with it. Maybe his notions about feminine charisms and ontological distinctions logically follow the transcendental reality of sexual differentiation. But what are his grounds for saying such a differentiation exists at all? Evdokimov, good Orthodox theologian that he is, knows that there is only one possible foundation for his house. It has to be built on the solid rock of the Holy Trinity. And Evdokimov claims that it is.[48]

---

[41] Evdokimov, *The Sacrament of Love*, p. 32.

[42] Ibid., p. 31.

[43] Ibid., p. 33.

[44] One of the most mysterious ironies here is that Evdokimov was the househusband in his family, at home with the children, while Mme. Evdokimov worked as a teacher of Italian! See Behr-Sigel's reminiscences in "Témoignage sur Paul Evdokimov," p. 238.

[45] Evdokimov, *Woman and the Salvation of the World*, p. 152. Cf. Gal. 4.19.

[46] Ibid., p. 153.

[47] Ibid., p. 157.

[48] There are remarkable parallels to the Orthodox use of the Trinity in elaborating male-female relationships to be found among Protestant evangelicals, as documented by Kevin Giles in *The Trinity and Subordinationism: The Doctrine of God and the Contemporary Gender Debate* (Downers Grove, IL: InterVarsity Press, 2002). Though the details of the story differ—evangelicals argue for the eternal subordination of the Son to the Father as the template for the eternal subordination of

Orthodox trinitarianism insists, far more strongly than in the West, that the Father is the source or fountain of divinity. The Son and the Spirit are not inferior or "subordinated" to the Father in the sense of being less divine or mere creatures. Nor is there any reason to think that obedience itself implies a secondary status within God's being. Yet it is still necessary to insist on order within God. The Son and the Spirit express the Father; Irenaeus of Lyons speaks of them as the two hands of the Father. According to Evdokimov, the Son and the Spirit make knowledge of the Father possible: "The Father is enveloped in the silence of *apophasis*, of what cannot be said. It is the hidden face of the Father that the Son and the Spirit reveal to the world."[49] In point of fact, Evdokimov made a doctrinal misstep at this point. Properly speaking, from an apophatic point of view, all three persons of the Trinity are equally unknowable to humans. The Father is not less knowable *in se* than the Son or Spirit.[50] To add a further complication, Evdokimov himself elsewhere posits that the Theotokos *also* images the hidden face of the Father to the world, but how she compares to the Son and the Spirit in doing so is never made clear.

Nevertheless, Evdokimov assumes that the Son and the Spirit uniquely image the unknowable Father. Further, as Orthodox anthropology teaches, humanity is itself analogous to the Trinity. The Genesis 1 creation story says that male and female together are the image of God. The existence of a male implies a female, while a female implies a male. So it is also in the Trinity, Evdokimov says, wherein the existence of a Father implies a Son and a Son implies a Father. Even within the Son there is mutual implication of the divine nature by the human nature and vice versa.[51]

If both men and women are in the image of God, and God (the Father) is known in the revelation of the Son and the Spirit, then, Evdokimov infers, one will find those distinctively male and female qualities in God—but not in the Godhead generally. They will be distinguished in the different persons of God. The one Father is expressed by the two, Son and Spirit. The one humanity is expressed by the two, male and female. The correspondence, then, between God and God's created image, is this: "[T]here is an ontic affinity between the masculine and the Word, as there is an ontic affinity between the feminine and the Holy Spirit. Within the Trinity, the uni-duality of the Son and the Spirit expresses the Father."[52] Evdokimov is unconcerned, it would seem, with the fact

---

women to men—there is in common a defense of what turns out to be a trinitarian heresy, and the arguments employed are all less than 50 years old despite their claims for being as old as the church itself.

[49]　Evdokimov, "Panagion and Panagia," p. 172.

[50]　See, for instance, John Meyendorff, *A Study of Gregory Palamas* (trans. George Lawrence; London: The Faith Press, 1964), p. 219.

[51]　Evdokimov, *Woman and the Salvation of the World*, p. 16.

[52]　Ibid., p. 27. This move is not unknown in the West. A fairly conservative Catholic approach is found in Joan Schaupp, *Woman: Image of the Holy Spirit* (Bethesda, MD: International Scholars Publications, 1996). A feminist Episcopal approach is found in Alla Bozarth-Campbell, *Womanpriest: A Personal Odyssey* (New York: Paulist Press, 1978), pp. 214–15. Vladimir Lossky, back East, makes a comparison between Eve and the Holy Spirit, but in a way quite different from Evdokimov's: he notes the patristic comparison of the Spirit's procession from the Father with the "procession" of Eve from Adam in a "unity of nature and plurality of persons." *Orthodox Theology: An Introduction* (trans. Ian and Ihita Kesarcodi-Watson; Crestwood, NY: St. Vladimir's Seminary Press, 1978), p. 70. Kenneth Paul Wesche strongly objects to the identification of women with the Holy Spirit, arguing that both men and women's humanity is grounded in the Logos. He does so, however, to award

that the Trinity is *one* self-identical God, and the incarnate Son is *one* self-identical person, in a way that actual human males and females are clearly not. But he has now connected the being of God to the archetypes: this trinitarian anthropology "leads from the divine universal Archetype to the archetypes of the masculine and the feminine."[53]

Why is the Son masculine and the Spirit feminine? The former is apparently so obvious to Evdokimov that he doesn't discuss it, but it is easy enough to infer. The Son, who took the human flesh of a man and is called the Son of God from eternity, is the Logos, reason, which seems to Evdokimov to fit better with the masculine character. The Spirit, in the eternal triune relationship, "is hypostatic motherhood, since He reveals the Son to the Father and the Father to the Son," a notion Evdokimov borrowed from Bulgakov.[54] The motherhood of the Spirit is connected also to Sophia and to Mary the Virgin Mother.[55] "Feminine spirituality is sophianic, intimately linked to the Holy Spirit," he writes.[56] "It is the Spirit who 'forms' Christ, brings Him forth in the soul of each believer; and He prepares the eschatological birth of the age of the Kingdom. The charismatic vocation of woman is most explicit here; it is spiritual motherhood that brings forth Christ in every human being through the power of the Holy Spirit."[57]

Evdokimov assures the reader (though only in a footnote) that "such expressions do not touch upon the essence of God in the least, nor do they introduce any feminine element in God. They refer to the feminine dimension of certain manifestations (energies) of God in the world."[58] He defends this on the grounds of the sharp Orthodox distinction between the essence of God and the energies of God.[59] Here again, Evdokimov's speculations got the better of his orthodoxy. Gregory of Palamas had developed the energy-essence distinction in Orthodox trinitarianism to safeguard the hesychasts' mystical experience of union with God. Clearly, they could not have united with God in His essence, since that is reserved for the three persons of the Trinity alone; nor could it be a union of the hypostatic type, which exists only between the divine and human natures of Christ. A third type of union was therefore posited, between human nature and the "energies" of God. While humans cannot unite with the eternal, hidden, and unknowable essence of God, they can indeed unite with the energies of the essence of God. The point on which to critique Evdokimov is this: "No energy is to be associated with one divine person to the exclusion of the other two, but the energies are shared in common by all three persons of the Trinity. This is, of course, a reaffirmation of the basic Cappadocian principle that, in their operations *ad extra*, the three persons of the Godhead always act together."[60]

---

primacy to males over females. See his "Man and Woman in the Orthodox Tradition: The Mystery of Gender," *St. Vladimir's Theological Quarterly* 37, nos 2–3 (1993), pp. 213–51 (223).

53 Evdokimov, *Woman and the Salvation of the World*, p. 27.

54 Ibid., p. 220. He specifically mentions Bulgakov's book, in Russian, *Chapters on the Trinity*.

55 Ibid., p. 219.

56 Ibid., p. 153.

57 Ibid., p. 222.

58 Ibid., p. 220, fn. 24.

59 Ibid.

60 Kallistos Ware, "God Hidden and Revealed: The Apophatic Way and the Essence-Energies Distinction," *Eastern Churches Review* 7, no. 2 (1975), pp. 125–36 (130). John Meyendorff makes

We will see in the following chapter how Thomas Hopko shares Evdokimov's trinitarian alignments with men and women. Though Hopko will not invoke the energy-essence distinction, he will argue that the Holy Spirit "associates" Himself with particularly "feminine" actions, such as the conception of Jesus in Mary's womb and the "birth" of Christ in the hearts of believers. But this too would appear to drive against the Cappadocian principle of trinitarian unity in all actions, to say nothing of the difficulty in ascertaining what exactly count as "feminine" actions—though it would certainly seem that causing Mary's pregnancy should be considered more "paternal" than "maternal!"

To reiterate, Evdokimov finds that men reflect the masculinity of the Son and women reflect the femininity of the Spirit. Men have christic charisms and women have pneumatic charisms. On these grounds he concludes—rather as an afterthought, since the question was not being asked when he wrote this book—that a woman could never be a priest, not without betraying her own being,[61] despite the fact that, as he himself said, "the essential charism of the priesthood is 'maternal tenderness.'"[62] Priesthood is christic, modeled on Christ the unique high priest, and women are not christic. To women belongs, of course, the royal priesthood of the baptized, and in that office women are to express their pneumatic charisms. (Presumably lay men are included in the lay priesthood too, though it is not clear how they exercise their christic charisms outside of the clerical office.) Granted the foundation, this insight pulls everything together beautifully.

> The question of the priesthood of woman finds its solution at the very precise level of charisms. The Virgin in no way resembles a bishop. If, iconographically, she is often represented wearing an omophorion [episcopal garment], that is only a sign of her maternal protection, without any trace of priestly powers. The priesthood of orders lies in the masculine function of witnessing. Bishops attest to the validity of the sacraments, and have the power to celebrate them. They possess the charism of watching over the purity of the tradition, and exercise pastoral authority. But the ministry of woman does not lie in "functions"; it resides in her nature. The ministry of orders does not belong to her charisms; that would be a betrayal of her being. Man is, by means of his priestly functions, in his essence linked to Christ the Priest. "Man the Overseer" sacramentally penetrates the elements of this world, in order to consecrate them and transform them into the Kingdom. "Man the Witness" acts through his virile energy; by means of his priestly powers he pierces the flesh of this world. He is the "violent one" of which the Gospel speaks, who seizes the treasury of the Kingdom—and this treasury is hagiophany, holiness of being, and it is woman who symbolizes it. Linked in her very essence to the Holy Spirit, the life-giving Paraclete, woman is Eve—("Life") who safeguards, vivifies, and protects every part of the masculine creation . . . Masculine nature is expressed

the same point in the chapter, "An Existential Theology: Essence and Energy," in *A Study of Gregory Palamas*. See also the chapter on "The Triune God" in his *Byzantine Theology: Historical Trends and Doctrinal Themes* (New York: Fordham University Press, 1979).

61   Evdokimov, *Woman and the Salvation of the World*, p. 216.
62   Evdokimov, "Panagion and Panagia," p. 163.

on the level of deeds that project him beyond himself. Tools lengthen the arm of Man the Worker (Homo faber), and the entire world becomes his extended body. All the activities of the builder, the inventor, and the reformer construct the world and order it . . . While "ecstatic" man resides essentially in the extension of himself into the world, "enstatic" woman exists within herself; she is turned inward, into her own being.[63]

Whatever Evdokimov's intentions, the charisms here seem to be more anatomical than spiritual, leading to a metaphor that resembles nothing so much as rape.[64]

The action/being divide illustrated by the respective characters of men and women is fundamental for Evdokimov and extends to religious practice. "But while asceticism as effort and struggle is essentially 'violence,' and in this form essentially masculine, inward purity and the immediate intuition of the beautiful are proper to the feminine. Man must acquire these through hard work, in the sweat of his brow; woman can express them directly through the plain grace of her nature."[65] The feminine is expressed in festivals of "being," like the Nativity and Pentecost; the masculine is expressed in festivals of "energy," like the Resurrection and the Transfiguration.[66] Women correspond to the eucharist, a state of being; men correspond to baptism, a violent act.[67] The preference for being over action in women actually earns them Evdokimov's praise, for they are more like God, for Whom existence and essence are identical. Female humility is a mirror of divine humility.[68]

Interestingly, despite Evdokimov's association of men with the Son, he does not assign the incarnate Christ the part of archetype for human males. Among other things, it would be unbalanced to set even the holy Theotokos next to the incarnate Son of God, even if the former does represent the Spirit—after all, she is not actually the Spirit and in this way fully divine. Furthermore, Christ is the new Adam in the sense of the one humanity protologically before sexual differentiation and again eschatologically after their reunion.[69] The masculine and the feminine among humans are "the two dimensions of the one *plêrôma* of Christ."[70] John the Baptist, it turns out, is the masculine archetype. He epitomizes the "violence" of masculine ministry, preparing the way of the Lord with the "virility" of witness to the point of martyrdom.[71] Mary, by contrast, the archetype for women, is "entirely a birth-giving being."[72]

---

[63] Evdokimov, *Woman and the Salvation of the World*, pp. 214–15.

[64] Another such extraordinary sentence: "With the Theotokos, Virginity has returned to earth; ontologically, Virginity is ready to contain in its depths the One who cannot be contained." Ibid., p. 222.

[65] Ibid., p. 218.

[66] Ibid., p. 222.

[67] Ibid., p. 260.

[68] Ibid., p. 225.

[69] Ibid., pp. 24, 227. Though if Christ is the truly human before and after sexual differentiation, and men and women are both accurate "dimensions" of Christ's "plêrôma," it remains unclear why in Evdokimov's view it is ontologically impossible for a woman to represent Christ as a priest just as well as a man.

[70] Ibid., p. 25.

[71] Ibid., p. 243.

[72] Ibid., p. 249.

Thus, "[t]he Virgin and St. John are God's thoughts on the masculine and the feminine; the two are their normative, hypostasized truths. By looking at them, everyone judges himself or herself."[73] And again: "In their unity, the masculine and the feminine exclude any common denominator . . . neither do the masculine and the feminine permit any reduction of the one into the other, although both are counterparts created by God Himself."[74] Despite the chasm of difference between them, only in cooperation will either man or woman understand the depths of his or her own being. Evdokimov envisions this as the goal of the eschaton— whether it will mean peaceful union of men and women, or actual transcendence of their respective maleness and femaleness is not entirely clear—but what is certain is that "[t]he Kingdom will come when the two are completely one" in a way only forecast now by marriage. In the meanwhile, "[t]he domain of signs remains, however, and man cannot change anything in it."[75]

With the trinitarian and anthropological bases firmly in place, Evdokimov can now turn to criticize the modern world for its extreme masculinity that has no place for femininity. He devotes so much time and interest to feminine charisms because he thinks they are the only way to save modernity from catapulting itself toward destruction—hence the double meaning in the title of his book, *Woman and the Salvation of the World*.[76] The problem exists with equal intensity in the church, where women are not treated as equal companions by Christian men. Evdokimov goes so far as to say, "A woman is not admitted to the parish, she is used by it."[77] He objects to the ongoing observation of "ancient curses" and taboos applied to women of the new covenant, especially the notion of ritual impurity during menstrual bleeding and after childbirth.[78]

In the end, Evdokimov's intention is to award a divine origin to human sexuality, not just as divinely created, but as divinely participating in and reflecting God's own being. He writes, "In the East, it is most emphatically the *divine element* in human nature, the image of God *(imago Dei)* which is the foundation of every anthropology."[79] Sexuality is too powerful and too deeply connected to personhood to be a fact of mere creation. At the same time, though, Evdokimov posits both a protological and eschatological absence of differentiation into male and female. It is only for the interim of earthly life that the differences exist distinctly in individual persons.

Behr-Sigel's appropriation of Evdokimov on "woman"

Evdokimov promotes a high and holy calling for women. And yet one gets the distinct impression that women exist chiefly as auxiliaries to poorly behaved, immature, and

73 Ibid., p. 231.
74 Ibid., p. 250.
75 Ibid., p. 252.
76 Ibid., p. 251.
77 Ibid., p. 255.
78 Ibid.
79 Ibid., p. 33.

foolishly aggressive men, who are finally drawn back to peace by the constancy of contemplative, calm, centering, sensible women. His overall picture is not only limiting to women; it is demeaning to men. He writes in a typical passage to this effect:

> More interiorized, more closely related to the root of existence, woman is completely at ease within the limits of her being. She works to develop her own gifts, and make of her own person a clear, limpid symphony. She fills the world with her inward presence. Woman is in complicity with time; for her, time has no "duration," for she carries within herself a greater part of eternity; she is in gestation. Man overreaches his being; his charism of expansion makes him look outward, beyond himself.[80]

A little later he continues:

> Man is called to "subdue the earth" (Gen. 1:28), to "cultivate the garden" (Gen. 2:15), to show the creative, inventive power of his mind. He welcomes the woman to his side, a helper who inspires and completes him. Destined to procreate, protect, and be the source of life and the wellspring of holiness, the woman sees at her side the man from whom she is bride, wife, and mother. As "the glory of man," according to St. Paul (1 Cor. 11:7), she is, in her luminous purity, like a mirror that reflects the man's countenance, reveals it to himself, and thereby corrects it. Through an intuition of what is concrete and living—the opposite of all abstraction—woman has the gift of entering directly into the life of another. She has the spontaneous, immediate ability to grasp the intangible in the human person. Through this ability, she helps man to understand himself and actualize the meaning of his own being. She completes him by deciphering his destiny. It is through woman that man more easily becomes what he is. The prophetic function of woman that is directed toward his being changes him, and the offering of self that is typical of woman unleashes the irruption of the Other.[81]

Furthermore, women exist to counteract warmongering men. "Woman sees an absolute, priceless value in the human form, and through this she humanizes and personalizes the world. Instinctively, she will always uphold the primacy of being over theory, of the operative over the speculative, of the intuitive over the discursive."[82] He continues, "Woman, the 'enstatic' one, interiorizes . . . she reveals the root of her being, her Sophia, the original, immaculate righteousness. The 'ecstatic' one, man, moves out of himself, extends and enlarges himself through his energies, inseminates, actualizes, and builds. In the dominant aspects of their respective beings, the masculine is 'Christ-bearing' (Christophoros), the feminine 'Spirit-bearing' (Pneumatophoros)."[83]

---

80 Ibid., p. 258.
81 Ibid., pp. 258–59.
82 Ibid., p. 260.
83 Ibid., p. 261. Klofft too suggests that excessive adulation of women is a weak point in Evdokimov's thought, along with his "thoroughly mythical" view of history, especially positing a prehistoric

Stepping back now from the more speculative parts of his work—the trinitarian analogies and rather glossy depictions of "woman"—it is clear why Behr-Sigel admired Evdokimov and gained so much from him. He stridently rejected a merely sociological construction of women that could only say what roles history had shoved women into but not who women truly are. Likewise, in Evdokimov's view, women were not to be thought of as merely biology, accessories to procreation but little else.[84] He could even acknowledge that there was something finally artificial about men inquiring into the "women question," as if women were so far removed from men that they could be studied as an external topic.[85] And he did make a breakthrough in his writings by treating "sexuality as a naturally spiritual subject."[86]

The point is, even if Evdokimov wandered too far afield in his speculations on women and sexuality, he nevertheless finally made it possible for Orthodox theologians to talk about these matters. And above all he insisted that men and women needed each other, not just reproductively but also spiritually, sharing both a common humanity and a common call to holiness. In this light we can understand what precisely Evdokimov believed he was fighting against.

> We must make a choice. Either man and woman, in their very difference, possess equally—but according to his or her own nature—light and shadow, the positive and the negative, a right side and a wrong side, and they reveal themselves as a felicitous and indispensable *complementarity* (the power of logical analysis paired with the direct, intuitive power of understanding and so forth); or we have the irreducible opposition between Yang and Ying, passive and active; between earth, night air and chaos, on the one hand, and day and order on the other. Such a simplistic method of easy contrasts leads unfailingly to the no-win conflict of contradictions (the solar being eternally opposite to the earthly being), to the total dependency of the one upon the other (woman as the lunar being), or else to the autonomy and complete independence of spheres.[87]

Given the options, Evdokimov's choice is laudable. But it is also telling that the only options he perceived were ones that posited profound differences in the respective spiritual existences of men and women.

This strong defense of the fundamental differences between men and women was essential for Behr-Sigel in her early thinking on the subject. It was actually what

---

matriarchy, and his use of gnostic sources on occasion; see "Gender and the Process of Moral Development," pp. 92–93. Ginn, by contrast, an uncritical fan, begins his essay with the remark, "It would be hard to accuse the Russian Orthodox theologian Paul Evdokimov of male chauvinism," as if this absolves Evdokimov of all error. "Paul Evdokimov on the Question of Women's Ordination," p. 40.

84 Evdokimov, *Woman and the Salvation of the World*, p. 253. Evdokimov disapproved of Thomas Aquinas's take on the matter—that except where making babies is concerned, men are in all respects better than women.

85 Ibid., p. 249.

86 Behr-Sigel, "Orthodoxy and Women in France," with Nicole Maillard, in *Women, Religion and Sexuality: Studies on the Impact of Religious Teachings on Women* (ed. Jeanne Becher; Geneva: WCC Publications, 1990), p. 188.

87 Evdokimov, *Woman and the Salvation of the World*, p. 21.

gave her *permission* to speak. If men and women are in fact so different and possess incommensurate spiritual charisms, then women must have something to say about themselves that men *cannot* know. Therefore the church must, at peril of ignoring nothing less than the wisdom of the Holy Spirit—to whom women are ontically aligned—listen to what women have to say. Evdokimov puts it bluntly: "Christianity is behind the times. The Church has the message of liberation, but it is others who 'liberate.'"[88] Evdokimov provides a reason for a women's movement in the church; a reason for Behr-Sigel herself to get involved in ecumenical efforts to listen to Christian women's voices; a reason even to start asking questions about the priesthood. Evdokimov permits a challenge to the status quo of women's social submission to men. He demands to know whether "the types of women created by history are true? Do they correspond to women's metaphysical truth? *Are they normative?*"[89] Behr-Sigel, along with Evdokimov, will answer no. But she will be considerably less convinced by the normative metaphysical structures Evdokimov erects to defend his answer, and she will become increasingly skeptical of his romanticization of women.[90]

The irony of all of this is nicely captured in an observation of Evdokimov's. He laments the general hostility of celibate monks and clergy to the married life, and so he asks: "Can one write, except in the case of special revelation, something correct about one's opposite where neither agenda nor resentment, neither illusion nor theory intervenes? It is not appropriate for the married to discourse on the monastic life, nor does it suit the unmarried to construct a phenomenology of Eros."[91] In reaction to his mystification of woman, one might be tempted to apply the same rule to him—that men ought not write about women. But Behr-Sigel herself would not do so. She would instead reject the supposed chasm between men and women that, Evdokimov always insisted, divides them from one another.

It is rather unfortunate to leave our discussion of Evdokimov here, for his writings on women represent only a small portion of his life's work and do not represent him at his best. In fact, toward the end of his life, he desired to go back and completely rewrite his books on women but died before he had the opportunity.[92] It should be clear by now that whatever errors Evdokimov may have made in his discussions about women, he was certainly not a misogynist. It was the misogyny he saw in the Orthodox church that horrified and disgusted him. His own writings on women were ultimately intended to combat this misogyny, not to reinforce it.

Be that as it may, Evdokimov's published works discussed here are the ones that Behr-Sigel knew and to which responded, so we must now shift our attention to her.

<hr>

[88]   Ibid., p. 19.
[89]   Ibid. His italics.
[90]   A danger of which Evdokimov himself seems to have been aware; see *The Sacrament of Love*, p. 33.
[91]   Ibid., p. 19.
[92]   Tomoko Evdokimoff [*sic*], letter to Michael Plekon, 1996.

3

Agapia to Sheffield

Until 1976, Behr-Sigel put nothing in print about women in the church. She devoted her first 43 years of scholarship to Russian spirituality and literature; the history of prayer, hesychasm in particular; Alexander Bukharev and other Orthodox figures such as Tikhon of Zadonsk, Mother Maria Skobtsova, Nil Sorsky, and Juliana Lazarevskaya; and occasional ecumenical questions. What set Behr-Sigel, nearly 70 years old, onto the subject for which she would become best known was the World Council of Churches' undertaking of a worldwide cross-confessional study of gender issues. The precise beginning point for Behr-Sigel was an international gathering for Orthodox women at the Agapia monastery in Romania. That in turn led her to participate in a series of three WCC-sponsored conferences on women, culminating in Sheffield, England, in 1981.

A common theme runs through all of Behr-Sigel's writings during this period. She accepts Evdokimov's vision of positive charisms unique to women but rejects female-specific vices or limitations as mere stereotypes. The evident inconsistency grows into an intellectual obstacle. In the late 1970s and early 1980s she takes the first steps toward dismantling the gender typology, but it will not be until after Sheffield, as she plunges into deeper study, that Behr-Sigel will make her break from Evdokimov altogether—a move that in turn opens the door for the ordination of women.

The first step: Agapia

The Agapia gathering took place from September 11 to 17, 1976.[1] The WCC sponsored and organized the conference, Protestant women paid for it, and it was a historical

---

[1] Certain presentations (including all of Behr-Sigel's keynote address), photographs of the participants, and reports of their activities were published in *Orthodox Women: Their Role and Participation in the Orthodox Church. Report on the Consultation of Orthodox Women, September 11–17, 1976, Agapia, Roumania* (ed. Constance J. Tarasar and Irina Kirillova; Geneva: WCC Publications, 1977). John H. Erickson reports with evident relief the absence of both "strident language" and any desire for "certain abstract 'rights'" in the conference's official recommendations; see his review of *Orthodox Women* in *St. Vladimir's Theological Quarterly* 21, no. 3 (1977), p. 170. Sergei Hackel similarly reports

"first"—a gathering specifically for Orthodox women (with a few men as observers and speakers), lay and religious, married and celibate, theologically educated as well as trained in other professions, to discuss their experiences of the Orthodox church and the theology that undergirds women's participation in it.[2]

Behr-Sigel was invited not only to attend but also to give the keynote address, undoubtedly on the strength of her qualifications as a Professor of Philosophy at the Graduate Institute of Ecumenical Studies (ISEO) in Paris with a newly minted Docteur ès Lettres (Histoire Religieuse), as well as coeditor of the journal *Contacts* and lay president of the French Orthodox parish of the Holy Trinity in Paris. Behr-Sigel was reluctant at first to take on a new project of such monumental proportions; in fact, the prospect filled her with terror.[3] She wanted, "like the aged Sarah at the announcement of Isaac's birth," just to laugh,[4] but in the end she accepted. In the years to follow, she took it upon herself to remind the Orthodox community again and again of what began at Agapia.

The conference revolved around the basic question of what part Orthodox women could play in church and society, especially now in the rapid changes of modernity—a question already dear to Behr-Sigel's heart. Her keynote address, at the birth of public Orthodox interest in women, has four distinctly interesting facets.[5]

First, she is entirely guided by Evdokimov's thought, without a whisper of challenge. He is the first person she mentions in connection with the question, though Bukharev and Soloviev merit a brief notice as well. Her theological reflections on "woman" are drawn substantially from Evdokimov's *Woman and the Salvation of the World*. She endorses his lament against the dehumanizing of women, just as she concurs with his descriptions of the true nature of femininity—it is "the spiritual organ of human nature and might be defined as the capacity to receive divine grace"[6]—even to the point of the transcendental origin of gender: "The biological becomes a sign of the spiritual which goes beyond it. Humanity in its fullness, of which the Church is the model, can only be realized by the conjunction of the masculine and feminine principles."[7] She praises Evdokimov's efforts to describe the "mystery of woman" and agrees with his interpretation of 1 Corinthians 11 that "woman keeps preserved deep within herself the mystery of her being and her gifts."[8] Behr-Sigel does raise the question of whether the difference between the sexes entails different missions or a common mission carried

that, contrary to misleading journalists, the ordination of women is simply a closed issue for the Orthodox. "The Agapia Consultation," *Sobornost Series* 7, no. 6 (1978), p. 431. Tarasar, one of the editors of the book, expresses disappointment in her own report that the presentations delivered by the men at the conference either glorified motherhood or condemned female priesthood—neither issue being terribly pressing to the women present or part of the conference agenda. "Orthodox Women's Consultation," *St. Vladimir's Theological Quarterly* 20, no. 4 (1976), pp. 242–44.

2 Leonie B. Liveris, *Ancient Taboos and Gender Prejudice: Challenges for Orthodox Women and the Church* (Burlington, VT: Ashgate, 2005), p. 65.
3 Lyn Breck, "Elisabeth Behr-Sigel—Entretien," *MaryMartha* 5, no. 2 (1997), pp. 13–14 (13).
4 Behr-Sigel, "Introduction," in *The Ministry of Women in the Church*, p. 5.
5 Behr-Sigel, "Keynote," in *Orthodox Women*.
6 Ibid., p. 25.
7 Ibid., p. 24.
8 Ibid.

out in two different ways, but in either case a distinct spiritual difference is simply assumed. She perceives no conflict between this assumption and her own discovery that the Scriptures contain no "theoretical exposition on the nature of women and their specific charisms."[9]

The second facet of her keynote essay is a willingness to listen to feminist critiques of the church. Although she will never be entirely comfortable with the feminists' solutions to the problems they identify, Behr-Sigel regularly finds their insights helpful. She begins her keynote by reporting her amusement that the Orthodox church was going to organize a conference to listen to women at all, and her less-than-amusement at the usual Orthodox assertion of women's perfect happiness in their church, an assertion generally made by Orthodox *men*.[10] She notes historical tendencies toward patriarchy and hierarchy, the limitations placed on women by their natural and social roles, and even the pernicious tendency to exalt women so as to keep them in their place, though as yet she does not notice that Evdokimov did the same. She sees a need to address not only the changes wrought by the industrialization of Western society but also the objectification of women's bodies that has gone hand in hand with it.[11]

At the same time—the third facet—Behr-Sigel proudly proclaims that social improvements for women are ultimately the work of the gospel, of the leaven that has taken a long time to raise the heavy lump of ancient pagan societies. It may have taken two millennia for Gal. 3.28 to do its work, but it is still undoubtedly Gal. 3.28 transforming society in the present under the "ambiguous and sometimes irritating sign" of secular feminism.[12] Through the lens of the gospel, Behr-Sigel perceives a calling toward "an imaginative new style of relationships and new structures in which liberated men and women can join together to work at their common task in a spirit of fraternal or conjugal love, respecting one another's dignity and distinctiveness."[13] This is the "new community" that will haunt her imagination for the next several years. The new community cannot be a simple repetition of a past community from a more pristine era, though. Tradition can guide but it cannot be flatly recreated, any more than a new community can be imposed without a spirit of charity.[14]

Fourth and finally, Behr-Sigel makes her first mention of women in the priesthood. She is quick to say that not all arguments against it are equal, particularly not the *ad*

---

9 Ibid., p. 22. Behr-Sigel's employment of the notion of female charisms is observed in the article, "The Ecumenical Consultation at Agapia Convent—Romania," *Romanian Orthodox Church News Quarterly Bulletin* 6, no. 4 (1976), pp. 25–29. The (unnamed) author reports how Behr-Sigel "pointed out that women possess qualities and energies of their own, like: spiritual sensitivity, intuition, love, compassion," p. 27. The author notes the same theme in the paper by Prof. Dumitru Staniloae (not in the *Orthodox Women* collection). "The basic idea of this paper was that mankind is represented integrally by the two poles—man and woman—which complete each other without any clash, each having his or her vocation. If the priest has his prototype in Christ, the woman, as a mother, wife, or collaborator of the priest, has her prototype in our lady," p. 27.

10 Behr-Sigel, "Keynote," in *Orthodox Women*, p. 17. Though Zernov, an Orthodox woman, does the same.

11 Ibid., p. 19.

12 Behr-Sigel, "Women in the Orthodox Church: Heavenly Vision and Historical Realities," in *The Ministry of Women in the Church*, p. 107.

13 Behr-Sigel, "Keynote," in *Orthodox Women*, p. 21.

14 Ibid.

hominem ones that see women's aspiration to the priesthood as inherently a form of spiritual pride. In particular, the argument that Gal. 3.28 applies to baptism and not to priesthood is inadequate, in her judgment, since baptism is the source of the royal priesthood of all Christians, which is in turn the source of the clerical priesthood. If, she asks, we say that some members of Christ's body cannot under any circumstances exercise a particular spiritual gift, "are we not in fact subordinating grace to a biological determinism, to nature which it can and will transform as the fire blazes in the burning bush yet does not consume it?"[15]

The reason Behr-Sigel does not, finally, decide in favor of the ordination of women is because of the iconic significance of the priest. In this she follows Thomas Hopko's essay "On the Male Character of the Christian Priesthood."[16] She explains, "[T]he priest represents Christ; he is the sacramental presentation of Christ, the Word incarnate who assumed full humanity in the masculine mode of being."[17] She endorses Hopko's position with an Evdokimovian insight: "Between the masculine and the Word which creates and restores, as between the feminine and the Spirit which inspires and invisibly fulfills the Word, faith and love prefigure mysterious correspondences."[18] For now she is content with this answer, though she warns that the Orthodox church must ponder the question deeply, not just write it off as a Western problem irrelevant to the East.

The reflections of other participants at this early stage in the discussion mirror Behr-Sigel's. For instance, an observer named Ekaterina Braniste reports that everyone present affirmed the valuable role women can play in society because, "[b]y her very nature, woman has a special vocation in the education of children and men, and in bringing consolation, affection, and a softening of the harshness of the human heart."[19] This is, of course, the same logic as Evdokimov's. Women have distinctive gifts because of what they essentially are. Therefore it is good to listen to them and allow them a place in the church. The participants also concluded, writes Braniste, that educating women theologically could only benefit their communities. Overall there was an understanding that women can contribute to harmony, justice, and the abolition of war.[20]

An address by Metropolitan Emilianos Timiadis, bishop of Calabria and representative of the ecumenical patriarchate to the WCC, also exemplifies the early and still rather confused nature of reflection on the subject. He, too, rolls out the same logic as Evdokimov, though he gives no indication as to whether he was familiar with Evdokimov's writings. Timiadis unmistakably favors the participation of women in the life of church and society alike, emphasizes mutuality in male-female relations, says that

---

[15]   Ibid., pp. 27–28.

[16]   This essay was first published in *St. Vladimir's Theological Quarterly* in 1975 and later appeared in the first edition of the book that Hopko edited, *Women and the Priesthood*, pp. 97–134. Behr-Sigel cites the essay in her "Keynote," in *Orthodox Women*, p. 28.

[17]   Behr-Sigel, "Keynote," in *Orthodox Women*, p. 28.

[18]   Ibid.

[19]   Ekaterina Braniste, "Reflection of a Participant," in *Orthodox Women*, p. 7. Braniste herself was a former professor of religion at the university of Bucharest. At the time of the conference she taught Romanian literature at the same place, being both a Licensiée en Théologie as well as a Licensiée ès Lettres.

[20]   Ibid.

children need mothers and fathers alike to flourish, worries at how discrimination has unjustly limited women's options, and insists that women are called to holiness every bit as much as men. On the other hand, he gives cryptic warnings about what happens when, "[i]nstead of finding the right place for everyone in the universe, people launch into dangerous innovations as a pretext for returning to woman what she has lost. In such cases, strange, inappropriate possibilities are offered, resulting in a betrayal of roles."[21] He goes on to assert that the "order" established by the creator gives a place to everyone and cannot be disrupted without grave consequences.

It is not hard to imagine that the "strange, inappropriate possibilities" mentioned here refer to women in the priesthood. And yet the idea of a "place" for women is not envisioned as a limiting factor but rather as a way of insisting that women do, in fact, belong in the life of the church. Timiadis means it as a score for inclusivity, not exclusivity. He states, "The place of woman—this is a key phrase. It implies that one recognizes her right to a unique place which is in accord with her own nature, her own particular vocation, as one half of the world is indispensable to the other if there is to be wholeness, even the hope of salvation."[22] It would be a mistake to see this order-of-creation theology as having an oppressive *intention*, whatever its practical outcome might be. In fact, just like Evdokimov, Timiadis frets over the excessive masculinization of modern society that has kept women out and longs for more "feminine" characteristics like compassion and nurture. Even men, he says, benefit from displaying "slightly feminine emotional characteristics," though which ones precisely he does not say.[23] He also rejects reducing women to their reproductive capacities, pointing out that women were students of Pantainus, Clement of Alexandria, and Origen, as well as coworkers with the Apostle Paul.[24]

Timiadis concludes with nine observations and proposals, mostly directed toward getting women more involved in church life, decision-making, and evangelism. He concretely proposes allowing women into the minor orders of acolyte and reader and reestablishing the female diaconate, which had fallen into disuse around the time of the final conquest of the Byzantine empire, though it was never canonically abolished. Furthermore, he hopes to see the revival of orders of widows and virgins, female teachers too, and perhaps even new orders invented to suit the needs of modernity.[25]

Noteworthy is Timiadis's final sentence. "The differentiation between man and woman is secondary; we have first to understand what it means to be a person, and when we have understood that, we can consider the relatively minor differences between them."[26] Here, for all the other accidental or not resemblances to Evdokimov, Timiadis says something substantially different. Perhaps it was this remark that opened the door for Behr-Sigel to walk out of Evdokimov's thought-world and into a place where the

---

[21] Emilianos Timiadis, "*Excerpts from* The Concern for Women in the Orthodox Tradition: New Challenges," in *Orthodox Women*, pp. 30–36 (30–31). Citations will be taken from this version. The complete text was published the year after the Agapia conference as "The Concern for Women in the Orthodox Tradition," *Diakonia* 12, no. 1 (1977), pp. 8–23.

[22] Timiadis, "*Excerpts from* The Concern for Women," in *Orthodox Women*, p. 32.

[23] Ibid.

[24] Ibid., pp. 33–34.

[25] Ibid., pp. 34–35.

[26] Ibid., p. 36.

differences between men and women, far from being transcendentally grounded in the trinitarian life, are relegated to "relatively minor" status, allowing a more fruitful reflection to take place on personhood itself.

Agapia at home

With enthusiasm and delight Behr-Sigel reported on the Agapia conference in her parish newsletter. She discussed the beautiful setting, profound spirituality, and impressive array of delegates from Orthodox churches around the world. She relayed the passion of the "women of Agapia" to engage the world "here and now" along with their difficult questions regarding their place in the church. She mentioned the matter of women's ordination in passing, noting the differing opinions on the matter and recommending that the issue be studied "under the guidance of the Spirit, and at the same time in a climate of charity and with theological rigor."[27]

Behr-Sigel reported on Agapia at greater length for *Service Orthodoxe de Presse* (*SOP*).[28] The women at the conference, Behr-Sigel writes, declared their desire to be equal partners in life and in church. Women want to offer "our 'talent,' our energies, our femininity itself, complementary to the masculine gifts of our partners." To do so, structural changes will be required of the church but not a break from the church's "authentic Tradition." Instead, the accumulated falsehoods and humiliating practices must be removed and a new way envisioned in the spirit of "creative fidelity."[29]

To do this, feminine values must challenge "masculine values distorted by sin" like domination and egotistical competition—again, the same notes sounded by Evdokimov and Timiadis. At this point Behr-Sigel invokes the Trinity in order to ground the charisms of sexuality and gender in something deeper than biology. The church, Behr-Sigel intuits, must rely on the revelation

> of God, One in Three distinct Persons, of the same nature and equal dignity, united, according to a sacred ordering but without subordination, in an eternal movement of love, of generosity, and of self-sacrifice; God, One in Three Persons, always acting jointly in the world, but each, the Creator, the Redeemer, the Consoler, according to his mission and his own modalities, according to his *difference*, in supreme communion and supreme liberty; Tri-Unity in the image of which humanity is created at the same time one and multiple, man and woman, to rule the earth.[30]

---

27. "Consultation des Femmes Orthodoxes à Agapia (Roumanie) 11–17 septembre 1976," *Bulletin de la Crypte* 47 (1976), pp. 11–13. My translation.

28. Behr-Sigel, "Femmes et Hommes dans l'Eglise," *Service Orthodoxe de Presse* 12 (1976), pp. 8–11, from which citations here will be taken; it was reprinted the following year in *Unité Chrétienne* 46 (1977), pp. 40–45, with the addition of subheadings and one footnote on scriptural interpretation, and again in *Supplément au Service Orthodoxe de Presse* 64 (1982), pp. 8–11. All quotations are my translation.

29. Behr-Sigel, "Femmes et Hommes dans l'Eglise," p. 8.

30. Ibid., p. 9.

Though the image is distorted by sin, it is restored by Christ. In the church, which is Christ's body, men and women are called to work together, according to their own different modalities but always with the other and for the other.[31] It is the trinitarian combination of unity and difference that makes reconciliation and partnership possible for men and women. Behr-Sigel draws a parallel between the persons of the Trinity and sexually differentiated human persons, a parallel that she would later come to reject. But the trinitarian move made here remains key to the whole discussion to unfold over the next two and a half decades.

Behr-Sigel speaks in this essay also of the church's obligation to "invent" new ways of living that better affirm the unity of male and female and especially the oft-violated dignity of the latter. A good starting point is the abolition of all purity taboos.[32] But that alone is not enough. Women need to participate, Behr-Sigel argues, at all levels of church leadership open to laypeople, thus in the liturgy, catechetical instruction, theological research, parish administration, conciliar assemblies, even prophetic witness in the world. To these tasks women will bring the "charism of their femininity": spiritual intuition, care for all living things, passionate energy in the service of various causes, compassion for the "shipwrecks of life." An active laity would combat the Orthodox tendency to clericalism, reminding the Orthodox that the difference between priest and lay is matter of vocation and service, not of ontology.[33]

At the end of the essay, Behr-Sigel deals briefly with the ordination of women to the priesthood and the diaconate. Though she calls for deeper and better thinking on the former, she again rejects sacerdotal ordination for women. While dismissing a number of arguments against it, such as the unchangeability of tradition, she still endorses the iconic character of the priest that requires him to share the "masculine modality" of Christ. She mentions the "mysterious analogies" between Christ and men, and the Holy Spirit and women, straight out of Evdokimov. But she argues that there is every reason to reinstate women as deaconesses, as the Greek and Coptic Orthodox churches had already done to some extent.[34]

Some time later Behr-Sigel collected her thoughts up to this point in a longer essay called "Women in the Orthodox Church: Heavenly Vision and Historical Realities," the fruit of her conversations about Agapia with other women.[35] She begins with the conviction that, all things considered, the Orthodox church is a rewarding place to be a Christian woman.

---

[31] Ibid.

[32] Ibid.

[33] Ibid., p. 10.

[34] Ibid., pp. 10–11.

[35] The initial French article was "La Femme dans l'Eglise Orthodoxe: Vision Céleste et Histoire," *Contacts* 29, no. 4 (1977), pp. 285–326. It was reprinted with a new introductory section in *Unité Chrétienne* 53–54 (1979), pp. 7–43, and again in the collection of Behr-Sigel's writings, *Le Ministère de la Femme dans l'Eglise* (Paris: Cerf, 1987). Quotations here are taken from the English translation, "Women in the Orthodox Church: Heavenly Vision and Historical Realities," in *The Ministry of Women in the Church*, pp. 103–47, which was also reprinted in *Woman in Prism and Focus: Her Profile in Major World Religions and in Christian Tradition*, pp. 81–112 (ed. Prasanna Vazheeparampil, CMC; Rome: Mar Thoma Yogam [The St. Thomas Christian Fellowship], 1996).

For instance, contrary to sweeping claims of patriarchal oppression, Behr-Sigel outlines all the ways in which women have in fact been a part of the very center of Christian life and faith. They have always been baptized, chrismated, called to the royal priesthood of the laity, and communed. Individual women have been confessors, martyrs, apostles, evangelists, prophets, and saints, married and celibate women alike.[36] The marian ideal has always been held up for women to imitate, an ideal that affirms their femininity, complete with the roles of virgin, wife, and mother. Orthodox cultures have praised strong evangelical women, especially in Russian culture and literature—Behr-Sigel sees examples in Tolstoy, Dostoevsky, and Pasternak.[37] She adds, perhaps under Evdokimov's influence, that this is in contrast to the Western church, which made efforts to "supply rational grounds" for the subordinate status of women, considering them good for nothing but procreation. She concedes, however, that even if the Eastern church didn't try to account for the assumption of women's inferiority, it didn't do much of anything to dispel it, either.[38]

The liturgy itself has a pervasive "feminine" air, chiefly through the omnipresent icons of the Theotokos. Behr-Sigel favorably cites Militza Zernov, who wrote, "In our churches, women feel not only tolerated but honored. They are at home in the house of the heavenly Father. They come with their children carrying their babies in their arms. Their children bring to church their noise, their toys and sometimes their disorder."[39] Behr-Sigel does not notice, at this point, that women here are spoken of as guests more than as members of the household, nor that the only role imagined for them is motherhood. Behr-Sigel cites with equal favor Evdokimov's observation that children get their first intimations of the kingdom of heaven from their mothers—before they are ready to get it at a later stage from their priests and bishops.[40] Altogether, she asserts, Orthodox women feel that the church is a lateral structure of communion, not a vertical one of hierarchy,[41] which is quite different from the rationalized hierarchies and subordination of women in the West and in Thomas Aquinas.[42]

However, none of this means that Behr-Sigel is altogether satisfied with the status quo. If the Orthodox church really believes what it confesses about human nature—that males and females both are in the image of God, that Christ assumed the full humanity of both—then why are women, even freshly baptized baby girls, kept out of the sanctuary, except to clean it? Why is there still ritual purification after childbirth for women of the new covenant? Why is there a lingering taboo discouraging women from

---

[36] Behr-Sigel, "Women in the Orthodox Church: Heavenly Vision and Historical Realities," in *The Ministry of Women in the Church*, pp. 116–17.

[37] Ibid., p. 119.

[38] Ibid., p. 125. For similar thoughts, see her essay, "The Place of Women in the Church," in *The Ministry of Women in the Church*, pp. 154–55.

[39] Behr-Sigel, "Women in the Orthodox Church: Heavenly Vision and Historical Realities," in *The Ministry of Women in the Church*, p. 122, citing Militza Zernov, "Women's Ministry in Church," *Eastern Churches Review* 7, no. 1 (1975), pp. 34–39 (38). For all its breezy dismissal of the issue of women's priesthood in the East, the bulk of Zernov's article discusses the female diaconate and insists that its consecration is a proper ordination to a (formerly) major order. Behr-Sigel's essay ends by making substantially the same point.

[40] Zernov also quotes Evdokimov on this point in her "Women's Ministry in Church," p. 38.

[41] Behr-Sigel, "Women in the Orthodox Church: Heavenly Vision and Historical Realities," in *The Ministry of Women in the Church*, p. 122.

[42] Ibid., pp. 119, 125. Behr-Sigel is following Evdokimov here.

communion during menstruation? There is even inconsistency in the discrimination: while women are not allowed into the minor orders of acolyte, reader, and subdeacon, they *are* permitted to instruct children in the faith—a task that requires quite a bit more skill and talent—yet this work is considered inferior.[43] When Behr-Sigel first came to Orthodoxy, it was in large part because she found herself in the company of progressive, creative thinkers like Lev Gillet and Sergius Bulgakov; as such, she was always "particularly shocked to discover that in its empirical reality, Orthodoxy is often weighed down with archaic prejudices and Old Testament taboos about women."[44] She asserts that the time has come for Orthodox women to be

> called out of their silence. I am not referring to the blessed and fruitful silence of prayer from which flow strong and inspired words, but rather to the sterile silence of resignation and indifference, a silence that does not exclude but rather produces futile chatter. It was probably that useless noise that St. Paul had in mind when he issued his famous injunction which people never fail to bring up. (1 Cor. 14.34)[45]

Behr-Sigel declares, further, that the Orthodox church dare not refuse to discuss the ordination of women question. At the same time, it is certainly legitimate to criticize the hasty and unconciliar way in which other churches went about it.[46] She distinguishes between tradition and Tradition, the former being historically conditioned non-essentials, the latter being the living logic of the gospel carried by the church through time.[47] After a cursory discussion of the priesthood and its meaning, Behr-Sigel concludes that both the royal and the clerical priesthood derive from the unique high priesthood of Christ, and it is "the delicate balance between them that explains the serenity of Orthodox women. Even though they are not called to the special liturgical priesthood, they do not feel frustrated; they rather feel called in a positive way to a personal prayerful communion which is intensified all the more in the divine mysteries."[48] If women cannot be priests, it is not because femininity lacks worth but because of the great worth in a liturgical symbolism that "obeys the rules of a grammar that is the work of the Church inspired by the Holy Spirit." The priest is an icon of Jesus Christ, not in a crude naturalistic sense, of course, yet the eternal Son "clothed himself with that humanity in its masculine modality and this was no simply accidental happening." Masculinity then is an "appropriate sign" of Christ the Bridegroom, a sign that a woman herself cannot be.[49]

Behr-Sigel then argues that the restoration of fallen humanity in Christ did not abolish the difference between men and women but rather the quarrel between them. The trinitarian analogy again casts light on the situation. The two kinds of humans mirror the two persons of the Trinity. "The Son and the Spirit are united for the joint

---

43 Ibid., p. 137.
44 Behr-Sigel, "Introduction," in *The Ministry of Women in the Church*, p. 8.
45 Behr-Sigel, "Women in the Orthodox Church: Heavenly Vision and Historical Realities," in *The Ministry of Women in the Church*, p. 105.
46 Ibid., p. 139.
47 Ibid. In my use of the word "tradition" from here on out, I will capitalize the word or not depending on the intended meaning, acknowledging that sometimes it is a difficult distinction to make.
48 Ibid., p. 142.
49 Ibid., p. 144.

accomplishment of the Father's will, each One according to his proper modality and mission. In the same way, men and women in the Church are called to work together for their salvation and the world's."[50] Behr-Sigel credits Evdokimov with discerning "a mysterious relationship, an analogy, on the one hand between the masculine principle and the Word who expresses, orders and structures, and on the other between the feminine principle and the Spirit who incarnates, inspires, and consoles," who is, in the phrase Evdokimov borrowed from Bulgakov, "hypostatic maternity." Like Evdokimov, Behr-Sigel is quick to say that such notions in no way introduce "sexual differentiation into the Trinity, and apophaticism, that is, silent respect in the face of the divine mystery, must constantly correct the analogy." But the clear attraction for Behr-Sigel is the "feminine aspect in the image of God."[51]

While Behr-Sigel agrees that the trinitarian arguments for excluding women from the priesthood are valid, she insists again that many other common arguments are not. The whole question, though, is an opportunity for women to deepen their own awareness of their roles in the life of the church and to discover "their most authentic vocation: a vocation of personal charisms, of inspiration and of prophecy rather than of the objective and cultic expression of the divine mystery."[52] Again the voice of Evdokimov rings through loud and clear: Behr-Sigel feels qualified to speak on behalf of all Orthodox women, equal sharers of serenity, who ought not waste their distinctive feminine gifts by chasing after masculine roles.[53]

A related issue is the secular women's movement. By its logic, industrialization and the emerging nuclear family no longer do justice to women's gifts, and this judgment Behr-Sigel accepts, not least of all because it assumes that there *are* gifts distinctive to women.[54] Some women have dealt with modern degradations by rejecting altogether "any idealization of womanhood" or feminine charisms, but Behr-Sigel judges that to be a temptation best avoided by faith in the triune God who is "supreme distinction in supreme communion"—a trinitarian corrective.[55] Otherwise, "women end up denying their own most profound being," and "[s]exual differentiation is reduced to a biological accident and femininity becomes the product of social pressures."[56] This is a mistake because human sexual polarity is a blessing, not the result of sin.[57] Behr-Sigel looks again to her predecessor to resolve the conflict.

> Carrying on Evdokimov's thinking, we may say that the distinctiveness of women belongs to two areas at the same time: the transmission and preservation of life and the relation with the other, with concrete others who are loved and accepted

---

[50] Ibid., p. 113.

[51] Ibid., p. 126.

[52] Ibid., pp. 143–44.

[53] In the reprint of the essay in *The Ministry of Women in the Church*, published first in French in 1987, Behr-Sigel appends her own footnote to this essay, directing the reader to the "Introduction" where she explains her change of mind on the issue.

[54] Behr-Sigel, "Women in the Orthodox Church: Heavenly Vision and Historical Realities," in *The Ministry of Women in the Church*, p. 109.

[55] Ibid., pp. 108–09.

[56] Ibid., p. 110.

[57] Ibid., p. 112.

in their otherness. To be a woman means to aspire to fulfill oneself by welcoming the other, by bringing into the world "an other" life that has been allowed to grow inside oneself and which must be lovingly cared for. This is at the opposite end from solipsism which is the masculine temptation par excellence.[58]

Behr-Sigel acknowledges that women's "openness" carries a bit of danger with it, too—Eve's openness to the serpent meant falling prey to temptation, and men detect a "primitive chaos" in the "cosmic and spiritual energies" of women that threaten masculine order and hierarchy.[59]

But then a slight rewriting of Evdokimov ensues.

> The masculine mind is at home in the world of ideas, though individual women also participate in this world; it runs the risk, however, of getting lost in the infinity of abstractions and in the desert of ideologies. The charism that is proper to women, *without excluding an aptitude for intellectual activity*, is to give life and care for it.[60]

Behr-Sigel will not accept Evdokimov's easy assertion that women gain no joy from intellectual labors, have no place in the construction of civilization, and are entirely birth-giving beings. But she *does* accept the judgment on the male mind as solipsistic and abstracting as well as the salutary corrective of feminine attention to life.

> *Here and now*, could not there be an authentic dialogue between men and women that would bring about the renewal of the aborted dialogue in the West between humanism and faith? In place of a Cartesian humanism of the male, "master and possessor of the earth," we must substitute a new humanism pervaded with respect for *the other*, with tenderness and compassion for mankind and the whole of God's creation. Would not a genuinely feminine presence in all domains of culture, including the concrete life of our ecclesial communities, contribute to such a humanism?[61]

It is an uneasy combination—rejecting negative stereotypes about women but maintaining positive generalizations about them, and doing just the opposite where men are concerned—and one that won't stay the course in Behr-Sigel's maturing thought. Already in this essay, she asks whether mariology and feminine charisms don't provide (however inadvertently) a pious excuse for keeping women out of men's world of church. She cautiously suggests that Evdokimov went a little too far at times. "Do we not have here" in Evdokimov, she asks, "a very distinguished way of expressing the ancestral and naïve conviction of the intellectual superiority of the masculine sex?" Behr-Sigel has not yet seen that Evdokimov himself was guilty of the abstractions he denounced.[62] He didn't want to collapse distinctions by making all men identical to

---

[58] Ibid., p. 128.
[59] Ibid., p. 127.
[60] Ibid., p. 129. My italics.
[61] Ibid., p. 106. Her italics.
[62] Ibid., p. 130.

all women, but he ended up collapsing distinctions anyway by making all women identical to each other (and all men identical to each other, too). Yet Behr-Sigel herself is only a shade beyond Evdokimov's abstractions when she suggests that women should employ their "proper gifts: intuition, sympathy, attention to the other, a natural propensity to love and protect life," while avoiding the "worst aspects of masculinity: self-centeredness, hardness, dominating spirit."[63]

Still, a tentative new course is suggested when Behr-Sigel quotes Olivier Clément's comment that "every human being, whether man or woman, is called to a certain virility in relation to his nature—we think of the 'strong women' of the Bible—but also to a certain femininity in relation to God."[64] Behr-Sigel then says, "We would add: and to his fellow creatures."[65] Here she perceives a way of distributing specific gender-based charisms to the opposite gender as well, which is a notable departure from Evdokimov, though she continues to assume the validity of basing charisms on gender at all.[66] And Behr-Sigel, like Evdokimov, still takes the logic all the way to the Godhead: we get an "intuition of a mysterious and ineffable correlation between the feminine as a way of being, as an ontological and constituent structure of humanity and something or rather someone in the superessential Deity. God is not only Being but also openness and interpersonal tension."[67] Femininity is thus grounded in the Trinity.

The essay concludes with another vision of the "new community." A church in which both the masculine and the feminine are equally welcomed—welcoming the latter would be the innovation—could transform all of society. Behr-Sigel imagines that "a new art of living could bloom, even if it were only on a few islands, like the first Christian communities or medieval monasteries. These communities would be places where being would have priority over having, where inner fulfillment would be more important than competing for power and where science and technology would serve life, not death."[68] Only a true collaboration between men and women, on the basis of the Truth revealed in Christ, could enable such a "utopia" to exist.[69]

Agapia and Behr-Sigel's reflections on it bore practical fruit in the French Orthodox community. Conjointly with three other women, in 1978, Behr-Sigel sponsored a workshop on the place of women in the Orthodox church. The workshop placed, in her words, an audacious bet: to permit each person complete freedom of speech. The result was at times tense, since the participants ranged in age from teenagers to the elderly, and included men and women, lay and religious, even one Roman Catholic and one Protestant. The principal point of convergence for all the participants, though,

---

[63] Ibid., p. 132.

[64] Ibid., p. 131.

[65] Ibid.

[66] Ibid.

[67] Ibid., p. 127.

[68] Ibid., p. 134.

[69] Ibid. In May of 1977, Behr-Sigel gave an introductory talk on trinitarian theology and spirituality at Kaire, an international conference for Orthodox and Roman Catholic nuns and Protestant deaconesses. The talk appears never to have been published, and she herself only mentioned the meeting briefly in her parish newsletter. The only point made in the short article was the request pressed on the Orthodox to translate "their theology into a praxis capable of responding to the concrete problems posed to our generation," p. 19. Behr-Sigel, "Rencontre Oecuménique Féminine [Kaire]," *Bulletin de la Crypte* 57 (1977), pp. 18–19. My translation.

was the common offense taken at the lingering impurity taboos that, though fallen into disuse in the West, had never been officially repudiated.[70]

The following year a document was published in *Service Orthodoxe de Presse*, "Questions about Men and Women in the People of God," intended as a survey of the range of thinking in Orthodoxy on the matter and also as a starting-point for further discussion. It was signed by 36 people, including men and women, clergy and laity.[71] No author is identified by name, but Behr-Sigel and Michel Stavrou were the principal drafters of the document, and she included it as an appendix to her book of essays, *The Ministry of Women in the Church*.[72]

The document calls upon Orthodoxy to take seriously the issues regarding women, instead of dismissing them as irrelevant to the Mary-loving Eastern church or as the inevitable problems of wayward filioque churches. Evdokimov is cited as the only Orthodox theologian to consider the women's movement sympathetically. Agapia is identified as a key event, followed by books, articles, local meetings, and dialogues. Hard questions are asked about Orthodoxy—whether it is "the last bastion of traditionalist conservatism"—but the document is quick to assert that its signers are not "a bunch of modernists who are unconcerned with the Church's Tradition which is Spirit and Life."[73] They recognize with joy the Orthodox affirmation of women in the veneration of the Theotokos, in its rich theology of marriage, and in its blessing of clerical marriage. At the same time they lament, as in the workshop Behr-Sigel sponsored, the lingering taboos. The scandal to the weak lies more in preserving these customs than in eliminating them. The Tradition has no investment in stereotypes. It certainly affirms biological motherhood, but it can also recognize the gifts of women (and men) in the education of all children and in spiritual motherhood. The document concludes with a suggestion to restore and reenvision the female diaconate.

Behr-Sigel in the ecumenical conversation

It was some time before the question about women attracted wider interest in Orthodoxy. Behr-Sigel herself identifies the Rhodes Consultation of 1988 as the real turning point. But the wider church was in the grip of disputes over this question, and by virtue of her ecumenical engagement on behalf of Orthodoxy Behr-Sigel found herself on the front line of the ecclesial battle. A brief review of the ecumenical history is thus in order.

In 1947, under the guidance of W. A. Visser't Hooft, a study was undertaken by the Faith and Order Commission, shortly before its incorporation into the nascent World

[70] Behr-Sigel, "Atelier sur la Place de la Femme dans l'Eglise Orthodoxe," *Contacts* 30 (1978), pp. 391–92.

[71] Included among them are two of Behr-Sigel's children and their spouses, Paul Evdokimov's son Michel and his wife Marie-Claire, and Olivier Clément with his wife Monique. Behr-Sigel, "Questions about Men and Women in the People of God," in *The Ministry of Women in the Church*, pp. 217–26, originally published in *Service Orthodoxe de Presse* 40 (1979).

[72] Michel Stavrou, "Elisabeth Behr-Sigel et la Question du Diaconat Féminin," *Contacts* 59, no. 4 (2007), pp. 483–90 (486).

[73] Behr-Sigel, "Questions about Men and Women," in *The Ministry of Women in the Church*, p. 220.

Council of Churches, on "The Life and Work of Women in the Church," by means of a questionnaire sent to women in 58 countries.[74] A summary of the responses was presented at the inaugural assembly of the WCC in 1948. Kathleen Bliss compiled the answers from the questionnaires in her book on *The Service and Status of Women in the Church*.[75] In 1958, Swedish bishops asked the WCC to collect reports on member churches' deliberations over the ordination of women. Five years later a study called *Concerning the Ordination of Women*[76] emerged jointly from the WCC's Department on Faith and Order and Department on Cooperation of Men and Women in Church, Family, and Society, as preparation for the fourth Faith and Order world conference in Montreal in 1963. In this study appear the first public ecumenical statements by Orthodox theologians Nicolae Chitescu and George Khodre about the ordination of women.[77] At the Fourth WCC Assembly in Uppsala, Sweden, in 1968, another formal request was made for a study on the ordination of women. In 1974, the WCC Sub-Unit on Women in Church and Society held a session on "Sexism in the 70s," which led to a recommendation to Faith and Order for still further study during its meeting later in the same year in Accra, Ghana.

The delegates of this last group prompted a resolution in Nairobi in 1975 to study in depth and detail the church's theology of gender, the participation of women in the church, and the relationships of Christian women and men to one another. Under the name "The Community of Men and Women in the Church," the study was authorized by the WCC Central Committee in 1976, immediately leading to the Agapia conference for Orthodox women and later to three broader ecumenical conferences in which Behr-Sigel participated. These three main events were held in Klingenthal (outside of Strasbourg) in 1978, on the subject of the ordination of women;[78] at Niederaltaich Abbey in Bavaria in 1979, on theological anthropology;[79] and finally in Sheffield, England, in 1981, on the collective theme of men and women in the church. The study as a whole "enjoyed the most extensive grassroots participation of any such project in the history of the World Council of Churches."[80]

Thus the ecumenical background. After her good experience at Agapia, Behr-Sigel entered the churchwide discussions hopefully, and at the beginning her hopes were

---

[74] The history recounted in this paragraph comes from Liveris, *Ancient Taboos*, pp. 20–22, 27, 54–55.

[75] Kathleen Bliss, *The Service and Status of Women in the Churches* (London: SCM Press, 1952).

[76] See *Concerning the Ordination of Women* (Department on Faith and Order and Department on Cooperation of Men and Women in Church, Family, and Society; Geneva: WCC Publications, 1964).

[77] Nicolae Chitescu, "The Ordination of Women: A Comment on the Attitude of the Church," in *Concerning the Ordination of Women*, pp. 57–60, and George Khodre, "The Ordination of Women," in *Concerning the Ordination of Women*, pp. 61–64.

[78] The results of the study are published as *The Ordination of Women in Ecumenical Perspective: Workbook for the Church's Future* (ed. Constance F. Parvey; Geneva: WCC Publications, 1980).

[79] The results of this study are published as *In God's Image: Reflections on Identity, Human Wholeness, and the Authority of Scripture* (ed. Janet Crawford and Michael Kinnamon; Geneva: WCC Publications, 1983).

[80] William H. Lazareth and Bärbel von Wartenberg, "Preface," in *The Community of Women and Men in the Church: A Report of the World Council of Churches' Conference, Sheffield, England, 1981* (ed. Constance F. Parvey; Philadelphia: Fortress, 1983), p. ix. The history recounted in this paragraph is drawn from Parvey's essay, "The Church—Women and Men in Community," in *The Community of Women and Men in the Church*, pp. 2–18.

rewarded. In a report on the conference at Klingenthal—which, since it was dealing with such a disputed issue, could easily have become tense and ugly—she was happy to say that the Orthodox learned from it, as did the Westerners, in a spirit of mutual understanding. After all, the Orthodox churches had joined the WCC when some Western churches were already ordaining women, so in certain respects nothing had changed from the initial situation.[81] At any rate, the conference's purpose was not to resolve but to think through the issue and all its implications. Behr-Sigel was pleased that there was a strong Orthodox plug for the female diaconate, despite minor disagreement over its mode of consecration: Evangelos Theodorou of Athens saw it as a proper ordination that could therefore be considered a "middle way" between ordaining women to the priesthood and neglecting their gifts altogether, while Bishop Anthony Plamadeala of Romania demurred at the use of the term "ordination," though still agreeing that women's gifts were tragically undervalued in the church. More broadly, the conference spoke of the impact of symbolism and scriptural language vis-à-vis women, as well as the relationship between the royal ministry of the baptized, the clerical ministry of the priests, and the unique ministry of Christ the high priest.[82]

At Niederaltaich, Behr-Sigel spoke: she presented a brief statement on Orthodox anthropology as a source for sorting out gender relations. She hoped that the Cappadocian fathers especially could offer a corrective to the Augustinian and Thomist heritage in the West.[83] In the Cappadocians, Behr-Sigel found a theological anthropology that is not static, not caught in an atemporal Platonism of chains of being and immersion in the One, but that is ultimately relational. It is the infinite difference between God and humans that allows a genuine self-transcending relationship to take place—humans transcending their finitude and God transcending His transcendence. Any relationship between the two must be entirely the work of divine grace.[84] The image of God is "not a *thing* or a part of man [*l'homme*]. It relates to the dynamic and global orientation of an existing being who is endlessly called upon to go beyond himself and to transcend his nature. As such, the image of God is both a gift and a task: the task of *becoming* 'the likeness of God.'"[85] The reference to transcendence of one's

---

[81] However, both the Bulgarian and Georgian Orthodox churches withdrew from the WCC in the late 1990s, in large part because of the ordination of women in other member churches.

[82] Behr-Sigel, "Consultation du C.O.E. à Strasbourg-Klingenthal sur l'Ordination des Femmes," *Contacts* 32 (1980), pp. 68–70. Behr-Sigel wrote another brief summary of the conference, "Consultation de Klingenthal," *Bulletin de la Crypte* 76 (1979), p. 23. It simply reports on the event with no editorial comment on her part.

[83] Behr-Sigel's report on the conference was "Oecuménisme au Féminin: A Propos des Colloques de Bad Segeberg (Juin 1980) et de Niederaltaïch (Septembre 1980)," *Contacts* 32, no. 4 (1980), pp. 337–41. Her presentation at the event was published as "La Femme Aussi Est à l'Image de Dieu," *Supplément au Service Orthodoxe de Presse* 64 (1982), pp. 15–23, later reprinted in *Contacts* 35, no. 1 (1983), pp. 62–70. It appeared first in English as "Woman Too in the Likeness of God" in *Mid-Stream* 21, no. 3 (1982), pp. 369–75; no translator is identified. The essay appears in both the French and English editions of *The Ministry of Women in the Church*. The English edition contains Steven Bigham's translation of the essay from the French book, so it reads slightly differently from the *Mid-Stream* version, although it is otherwise exactly the same essay. He also gives it a slightly different title, "Woman Is Also Made in the Image of God." Quotations here are taken from Bigham's translation.

[84] Behr-Sigel, "Woman Is Also Made in the Image of God," in *The Ministry of Women in the Church*, p. 82.

[85] Ibid., p. 84.

own nature reveals the anthropology of Vladimir Lossky in the background of her thought, but it will be quite some time before Behr-Sigel makes more explicit use of his ideas in her defense of the ordination of women. And again we see the importance of the fact that the Holy Trinity is a community of different persons and therefore the archetype of human community restored to its original unbrokenness.[86] All humans are one, in the image of the Son, who is the image of the Father.

The apparent fact of the oneness of humanity is challenged, though, by the more obvious fact of the twoness of humanity: there are men and there are women. Behr-Sigel observes that the church fathers do not handle this challenge in uniform fashion. This observation already indicates some maturation in her own thought; previously she had asserted that the fathers as one considered human sexual duality to be a blessing in no way connected to original sin.[87] Now she explains how Gregory of Nyssa, for instance, posited a double creation. According to him, God first created the human as such, the universal archetypal Adam made after the image of the eternal Son. Then, and only second, in anticipation of human sin, God created the one human in distinct male and female forms for the sake of procreation. It is good to be male and female, sort of—God intended it that way, but only as a remedy against the fall. Otherwise the distinctive qualities of male and female have no part in the divine image. As Behr-Sigel explains, "Although sexuality is used for a transcendent purpose, that is, the ultimate deification of humanity, it is not itself transfigured."[88] She detects in this view a certain angelism and ambivalence toward women, who are not really bad in themselves but inevitably become a source of temptation for men seeking holiness. She supposes that Gregory's ambivalent feelings stem from his own life situation—being married and later regretting that he could not make the great sacrifice of lifelong virginity. He was further prey to the pagan cultural belief that femininity was a "synonym for weakness" and the Christian cultural belief that a holy vocation was best fulfilled by rejecting sexuality in one's own life.

For her part, Behr-Sigel prefers Basil of Caesarea's perspective on human duality, one that is "more scriptural and pastoral and less influenced by philosophical speculation."[89] She cites approvingly Basil's corrective to a female acquaintance who read "man" in Genesis 1 to mean "husband," which would exclude herself. Basil insisted, rather, that both husbands and wives are in the image of God; their "two natures are equally honorable; equal are their virtues; equal are their rewards; and alike are their condemnations." In fact, Basil observed that women are generally the stronger sex when it comes to enduring fasting and performing good works in Christian love. Behr-Sigel notes that Basil used "masculine" traits to describe holy Christian women—strength in soul, strength in body, boldness—along with the more typical "feminine" ones of gentleness and patience. Behr-Sigel concludes that in patristic thought "we can see that the revolutionary idea of the equal dignity and responsibility of human persons, male

---

[86] Ibid., p. 85.

[87] Behr-Sigel, "Women in the Orthodox Church: Heavenly Vision and Historical Realities," in *The Ministry of Women in the Church*, p. 112.

[88] Behr-Sigel, "Woman Is Also Made in the Image of God," in *The Ministry of Women in the Church*, p. 87.

[89] Ibid., p. 88.

and female, was opening a path through the language of a culture that saw the male as the paradigm of humanity."[90]

Behr-Sigel acknowledges the "verbal excesses" of the fathers in their excoriations of women, yet it is their affirmations in the midst of these excesses that are so striking. Gregory of Nazianzus, the same theologian who argued that "what He has not assumed He has not healed," made the equally powerful statement, "The same Creator for man and woman, for both of them the same clay, the same image, the same law, the same death, and the same resurrection."[91] If that was their belief, Behr-Sigel wonders, why did they not draw the conclusion that men and women might also have the same calling, the same vocation, the same priesthood? Some of the reasons are culturally and historically relative, and thus invalid today; others are theologically and scripturally based. But Behr-Sigel now finds herself dissatisfied with the theological and scriptural reasons, too. The best answer she can find is the "intuition of a symbolism of the masculine and the feminine in their reciprocity, a symbolism whose meaning is revealed in the body as well as in a book."[92] Behr-Sigel concludes her essay with a charge to study this image more deeply in the stream of the living Tradition.

Despite the honor of being a speaker, Behr-Sigel was rather more disappointed by the Niederaltaich gathering, chiefly because it was so underrepresented by the Orthodox. She swiftly absolves organizer Constance Parvey of any blame, directing it instead to the dearth of qualified Orthodox male and female theologians interested in the subject at all. She comments:

> Too often, indeed, where it could develop freely, the Orthodox reflection on the double polarity, feminine and masculine, of the anthropos, has remained singularly timid and void of creativity. Disconcerted by the excess of an aggressive feminism—a Christian idea "gone wild" in the climate of Western nihilism—, haunted by the fear of raising the problem of the ordination of women to the ecclesial ministry, it has taken refuge most often in a fearful conservatism. Nevertheless, under the superstructures where the ancestral taboos persist, shines the evangelical vision of a community of men and women reconciled in Christ, in the radiance of the trinitarian mystery. Today it is time to dare to think further! Conducted in a spirit of both intellectual honesty and creative fidelity to the ecclesial Tradition—dynamically understood—Orthodox anthropological research could help the Universal Church to speak the catholic word—that is to say, oriented to the plenitude of the divine-human mystery—this word to the community of men and women which is waiting so much for it today.[93]

The recurring themes of Behr-Sigel's reflections on men and women are here in force: rejecting the fearful reaction to modernity, affirming the rich resources of the Tradition in tackling the problem, emphasizing the humanized God and the

---

[90] Ibid., p. 90.
[91] Ibid., p. 91.
[92] Ibid., p. 92.
[93] Behr-Sigel, "Oecuménisme au Féminin: A Propos des Colloques," pp. 339–40. My translation.

deified human. She continues to distribute charisms based on gender, as in her exhortation to a "feminine ecumenism," which means an ecumenism focused on listening to and understanding the other. Behr-Sigel expects that the solidarity of women and their instinctive ability to listen could help the whole ecumenical project.[94]

After Niederaltaich, the WCC sent out a study book to participating church communities around the world to be read and discussed in small group sessions as preparation for the final meeting in the series on "The Community of Men and Women in the Church," to be held in Sheffield, England.[95] It had been developed by the WCC in 1978 and approved by Faith and Order in Bangalore, India. Circulation eventually reached 65,000 copies distributed all over the world. Behr-Sigel led the study in her own church community with two other women, MarieJoëlle Dardelin and Irene Schidlovsky, and they published the results of the conversations in *Contacts*.[96]

It was acknowledged from the outset that the French Orthodox had the peculiar experience of belonging to two communities: one French, Western, industrial, and largely secular, though with a lingering Roman Catholic presence; the other Orthodox and still colored by the memory of the Russian immigration. By and large, the activism of the former had not yet touched the latter, and feminism was met with anxiety. One subset of the working group in particular took offense at the push for the ordination of women in Western churches, perceiving it principally to be an error of modern industrialism that strives to make all things identical, denying individuals' differences. The church, by contrast, follows an anthropology that derives from the Holy Trinity, and so "reveals a community where the calls, the functions, and the positions are different—without this difference turning into subjection—a community called to express the unity of God in three persons where, without inferiority or superiority, only the Father is the source, only the Son is incarnate, only the Spirit is poured out."[97] As with Evdokimov, the only perceived alternative to making each individual identical to every other is to make all women identical to each other and likewise all men identical to each other. All the same, the group expressed universal concern over patriarchal structures, changing morés in a secular society, and the "masculinized" quality of the modern world. Not surprisingly, Evdokimov is mentioned, though principally to uplift the importance of marital love in the face of so much divorce.

Several points came out of the conversation that were thought to merit further consideration. First, no one knew how to reconcile the commonality of personhood in all humans, made in the image of the Trinity and able to transcend biological, social, and cultural determinisms, with the divinely willed differences of a sexually

---

[94]　Ibid., p. 340.

[95]　Parvey, "The Church—Women and Men in Community," in *The Community of Men and Women in the Church*, p. 15, and Parvey (ed.), *The Ordination of Women in Ecumenical Perspective*.

[96]　Behr-Sigel, "Réponse à l'Enquête du COE sur 'Hommes et femmes dans l'Eglise,'" *Contacts* 32, no. 3 (1980), pp. 246–55. All quotations are my translation. A parallel conversation was taking place among the Orthodox in the United States at the time, summarized in the report *Women and Men in the Church: A Study of the Community of Women and Men in the Church* (Syosset, NY: Department of Religious Education, Orthodox Church in America, 1980).

[97]　Behr-Sigel, "Réponse a l'Enquête," p. 247.

differentiated humanity, a fact obvious to biology and blessed by the first chapter of Genesis.[98] The connection between Trinity and anthropology was not quite as clear as desired.

Second, all agreed that it was impossible to specify psychologically the differences between the sexes with great accuracy, for stereotypes usually erupt out of such efforts. Would archetypes supply the answers where psychology fails? "The Orthodox Christian," the report states, "will say that in Christ and the Virgin Mary he discovers the revelation of these eternal archetypes. A question nevertheless is posed: is Mary not the expression of humanity entire, man and woman, the one who receives, the one in whom the God-Man must take form?"[99] Who exactly posed this question, Behr-Sigel herself, someone else, or the group as a whole? The report gives no indication. If it was Behr-Sigel, she betrays her first inkling of uncertainty on the subject. Had she followed Evdokimov strictly, she would have said that John the Baptist is the archetype for men, not Christ, though making Christ the archetype for men was not an uncommon move in Orthodox theology: Hopko had made it, for instance, in the aforementioned essay that we know Behr-Sigel to have read. To claim Mary as the archetype for all human beings, though, is certainly a move away from the strict assignation of gender roles, reemphasizing the commonality of men and women in their humanity. On the other hand, it still assumes a definition of femininity—one of reception and birth-giving—that has a fundamentally biological, even anatomical orientation to it.

A third proposed area of further discussion underscores the complexity of the issues under discussion. The importance of the body is asserted by Orthodoxy, as is its symbolism and its "possible transfiguration." Male bodies and female bodies must certainly mean *something*. Citing Hosea and St. Paul, the report says, "[M]asculinity reflects the One who man [*l'homme*] is not and will never be: the transcendent God, the Creator, the Giver. Femininity on the other hand announces the mystery of the immanent God, the God who pours Himself out, according to Grace, over all his creation, to save it, to purify it and to fructify it."[100] For all this, though, the report insists that masculine and feminine symbolism dare not obscure the fundamental evangelical message of the common call to enter the kingdom of God, to put on Christ in the power of the Spirit, as Galatians 3 proclaims.

The report ends denouncing misogynistic practices yet affirming that Orthodoxy is not essentially misogynist because of the honor accorded the Theotokos; and while the ordination of women is skirted, a creative renewal of the female diaconate is strongly recommended.[101]

Then came Sheffield and a new note of disenchantment in Behr-Sigel's writings. For one thing, she was disappointed again at the poor turnout from the Orthodox communities: only twelve members were present, nine women and three men. She wonders, in her report on the conference for *Contacts*, whether, despite understandable extenuating circumstances, it doesn't "signify equally a lack of interest, evident

---

[98] Ibid., p. 251.
[99] Ibid., p. 252.
[100] Ibid.
[101] Ibid., pp. 253–55.

among many of the Orthodox—but not at all conforming to the authentic ecclesial Tradition—in the existential implications of the great doxological affirmations of the creed of faith and for the ethical problems of a planetary scope."[102] Her presentation at the conference itself identifies the Orthodox temptation to "become enchanted by the vision [of heaven] and sometimes find in it an excuse for laziness, a justification for rigid conservatism claiming not to know about the questions that modern non-believers are asking."[103] This is, more specifically, a criticism of the neopatristic element in French and American Orthodoxy, revealing her commitments to an Orthodoxy modeled after Bukharev and Bulgakov; we will revisit this theme in Chapter 7.

Behr-Sigel was equally shocked, however, at the level of "global and unilateral" criticism and condemnation expressed by the women at Sheffield against the entire church. It is one thing to acknowledge the church's errors, but Behr-Sigel perceived that the criticisms were not entirely justified, rather edging into the ideological and throwing around the word "patriarchy" for the reaction it guaranteed. She pointed out that patriarchy does not automatically imply a lack of respect for women.[104] She also detected a tendency among the women present toward an "unhealthy masochism," detailing the church's history as nothing more than "a sad story of oppression of the weak by the strong and of women by men."[105]

In the introduction to her collection of essays, *The Ministry of Women in the Church*, written several years later, Behr-Sigel recalls Sheffield as "the provisional final stage of the study [on the community of men and women in the church], its climax, and, at the same time, its partial failure. The debates on the ordination of women took place in a highly charged atmosphere, and this question became the sore point around which crystallized many hopes and disappointments."[106] Constance Parvey, the conference's organizer, didn't intend the ordination of women to become the chief issue at Sheffield, but the plenary sessions insisted on it for fear that the issue would be smoothed over or ignored too easily.[107] There was a universal desire for women's ordination not to become an ecumenical roadblock, and Behr-Sigel in her own report spoke of the possibility of sharing communion across churches where practice differed.[108] Unfortunately, the predominance of the theme at Sheffield led to the even more highly charged "Letter to the Churches" presented to the WCC assembly in

---

[102] Behr-Sigel, "Vers une 'Communauté Nouvelle', Colloque du Conseil Oecuménique des Eglises, Sheffield 1981," *Contacts* 33, no. 3 (1981), pp. 236–40 (239). All quotations are my translation. This report is not the same as a presentation with nearly the same title that she actually delivered at the Sheffield conference, "Vers une Communauté Nouvelle," published in *Contacts* 34, no. 3 (1982), pp. 270–77. This latter was reprinted in French in the collection *Le Ministère de la Femme dans l'Eglise* with two added introductory paragraphs and translated into English for *The Ministry of Women in the Church* as "Toward a New Community," from which quotations here will be taken. It also appeared in English in *The Community of Men and Women in the Church* under the title "The Energizing Force of Tradition: Orthodox Tradition as a Resource for the Renewal of Women and Men in Community," pp. 61–68.

[103] Behr-Sigel, "Toward a New Community," in *The Ministry of Women in the Church*, p. 102.

[104] Ibid., pp. 96–97.

[105] Ibid., p. 96.

[106] Behr-Sigel, "Introduction," in *The Ministry of Women in the Church*, p. 11.

[107] See Parvey's comments, "Held Together in Hope and Sustained by God's Promise: A Personal Reflection," in *The Community of Men and Women in the Church*, pp. 177–78.

[108] Behr-Sigel, "Vers une 'Communauté Nouvelle,'" p. 238.

Dresden the following month, an attempt at a prophetic call to the churches to ordain women that was met largely with criticism and broken trust.[109]

For all this, however, Behr-Sigel, ever determined to put the best construction on everything, saw a genuine divine work in the Sheffield conference. Her report for *Contacts* concludes:

> Nevertheless, the Spirit of Pentecost, inspirer of wisdom and charity, finished by blowing over the conference. Our encounter ended with a joyous gesture that was symbolic and prophetic: the last evening, at the end of a long vigil of prayer, we offered one another, under the sign of a spoonful of honey, some tastes of the anticipated sweetness of the kingdom of heaven.[110]

The theme of a "new community" at Sheffield, already anticipated by the survey sent out to the churches, particularly captured Behr-Sigel's imagination. She notes, in her address to the assembly, that the church's ability to transfigure traditional patriarchal societies over time does not entail a responsibility to preserve those societies as such, much less in the church's own structure. Again she sees the gospel's long ferment in the West finally blowing open the old hierarchies that were never easy bedfellows with the Christian faith. She asserts:

> I recognize the authentic Tradition of the Church in a women's movement in which women express their will to be respected as free and responsible persons. It is in the dynamic of authentic Tradition, and not in the ephemeral ideologies, that we will find the source of eternal life, the source of our own true liberation. In line with and in the dynamic of this Tradition, we will invent lifestyles of community life in the family, society, and Churches.[111]

In short, Behr-Sigel could not affirm a women's movement that despised and condemned everything about the church, and in fact she saw that *that* kind of women's movement would necessarily run out of steam and collapse on itself. Rather, she inferred that the affirmation of women is really a "new awareness of the ancient baptismal faith,"[112] an inherently Christian movement that must exploit all the resources of the Tradition of the church rather than rejecting them wholesale. The church should be the sign of the desired new community where there is no discrimination of any kind.[113]

It is important to note that Behr-Sigel still assumes a gender-based distribution of qualities in her Sheffield presentation. For instance, she criticizes Western

---

[109] Behr-Sigel, "Introduction," in *The Ministry of Women in the Church*, p. 12.

[110] Behr-Sigel, "Vers une 'Communauté Nouvelle,'" p. 240. Another participant at the conference, Mercy Oduyoye, had a similar reaction: "[F]irst and most powerful . . . something happened at Sheffield. A new quality and freedom of spiritual/human life happened as we worked out our tensions, expectations, and real differences." See "Preface at Dresden to the Sheffield Recommendations," in *The Community of Men and Women in the Church*, p. 81.

[111] Behr-Sigel, "Toward a New Community," in *The Ministry of Women in the Church*, pp. 97–98.

[112] Ibid., p. 95.

[113] Behr-Sigel, "Vers une 'Communauté Nouvelle,'" pp. 236–37.

civilization as "materialist, rationalist, technological, overvaluing the qualities called 'virile'—courage, combativeness, mastery of self and world—at the expense of gifts of comprehension, of welcome of the other, of sympathy, which, considered to be 'feminine,' are suppressed as belonging to private life."[114] In her strongest affirmation of divine love and the legitimacy of women's place in the church, she is in effect a mouthpiece for Evdokimov.

> In his infinite respect and love for his creature, God wanted to associate man and woman, or *more deeply the masculine and feminine principle*, with the work of salvation. These principles are represented in the icon first by John the Baptist, "the violent one" whose violence when turned inward shows itself in the struggle against the possessive and egotistical self. Mary, the humble servant who welcomes the Spirit as a husband, represents the second principle and becomes the Theotokos, the mother of the God-Man. As an archetype of the Law in its rigor and of bitter and fertile repentance, John the Baptist prepares the way and makes level the paths. But a woman, whose *femininity is the sign of welcoming the other*, and the supremely Other, is the beginning of the new humanity in which God takes flesh . . . [T]he Church made up of women and men is essentially feminine. Nonetheless, each one of those who belong to the Church is called to assume in Christ his part as well as the part of the "other" that is also in him.[115]

Again as before, the respective masculine and feminine charisms have some proper place in persons of the opposite sex, but there is no doubt here that charisms do come in distinct masculine and feminine flavors.

An indirect critique of Evdokimov

As we have seen, this period of Behr-Sigel's work relies heavily on her friend Paul Evdokimov and largely without criticism. Yet long before Behr-Sigel was able to critique Evdokimov openly and consistently, she did in fact critique the same kinds of ideas in her 1978 review of Louis Bouyer's *Mystère et Ministères de la Femme*.[116]

Bouyer was a Roman Catholic theologian who wrote against the ordination of women for reasons strikingly similar to Evdokimov's. He employed a "vertical" rather than "horizontal" anthropology, and he wanted a third way between indifferent conservatism and the "new heresy" of the feminist type—a way for the common faith of the church to speak audaciously but as part of the living Tradition. Feminism prompted Bouyer to speak of the mystery and divine vocation of women, much as it did Evdokimov. And like Evdokimov, Bouyer was influenced by Russian sophiology and the apophaticism of the Eastern fathers, though he also claimed Thomism as an

---

[114] Ibid., p. 237.

[115] Behr-Sigel, "Toward a New Community," p. 101. My italics. Note that she refers to the Spirit as "a husband"!

[116] Behr-Sigel, review of *Mystère et Ministères de la Femme*, by L. Bouyer, *Contacts* 30 (1978), pp. 181–84. All quotations are my translation.

inspiration. Such an approach, it would seem, could hardly fail to please Behr-Sigel. But fail it did.

For Bouyer, the masculine character of Judeo-Christian priesthood is founded on the biblical revelation of the "heavenly Father" and thus a kind of masculinity of God. He qualifies it by saying that in God "sexuality is exceeded, or rather anticipated . . . in a paternity . . . that transcends the opposition of the sexes."[117] Still, he says, the man is the more apt representation of the divine paternity. Behr-Sigel objects at once that Bouyer thereby depreciates human paternity as well as the mutual experience of parenthood by the couple—a criticism she would later apply to Evdokimov. Bouyer argues that "woman" cannot signify this divine paternity because she instead signifies the "mystery of the creation, redeemed, completed, married by God."[118] In Mary the immanent presence of God is realized in humans, as anticipated by the feminine representations of Wisdom, Shekinah, the "ruah" of God. Bouyer goes so far as to attribute meaning to female physical virginity ("peu mythique," comments Behr-Sigel). Creation itself is feminine.

Behr-Sigel is swift to expose the problems with these allegories. She suggests that one ought to distinguish between masculine and feminine archetypes, on the one hand, and individual men and women who are called concretely to transcend their psychosomatic natures without denying them, on the other. The masculine priesthood may conserve a symbol from the language of revelation, but that language is the product of a historically determined culture. Could it be a sign that is relativized by a reality that has exceeded it? The sign might cease to be transparent to the reality it signifies, instead obscuring the divine reality behind it. She wonders: "In making an absolute from which one draws immutable rules, does one not pass from a theology of the image, an inexhaustible source of inspiration and meaning, to a theology of closed concepts, an instrument of oppression where one attempts to close off life and living persons in all the varied richness of their vocations and charisms?"[119] Suddenly the archetype, once the pattern for deification, becomes an "instrument of oppression." In the next stage of her thought, Behr-Sigel will take on the archetype directly.

[117] Ibid., p. 182.
[118] Ibid.
[119] Ibid., p. 184.

4

The Path to Rhodes

The disappointment that Sheffield both was and symbolized did not deter Behr-Sigel from pursuing questions about women in the church personally or publicly. Her writings on women from 1983 to 1988—which were but a small portion of her total output on a great range of theological subjects—dig deeper into the problem, both in their reach into the church's Tradition and in their growing sophistication. She shared her findings in conferences and in print; people began to take notice of her. Yet for all her prominence as an Orthodox theologian studying the question of women in the priesthood in depth, Behr-Sigel did not merit an invitation as speaker or delegate at the Rhodes consultation in 1988 devoted specifically to this concern. She came along as an observer only, and "every time she tried to speak, she was cut off and was unable to explain the whole of her thoughts."[1] It will become clear in the course of this chapter that her mature position on the subject grew out of a rejection of the very kind of theology that Rhodes embraced.

The turning point

Two years after Sheffield, seven years after Agapia, Behr-Sigel was still puzzling out "The Place of Woman in the Church."[2] Here she returns again to a recurring theme: that the world has changed. The situation of women today is not like it was before. More of them work; more of them vote; more of them share responsibilities for household and children with their husbands. The women's movement has attempted to recognize these changes and direct them for the good of women. Behr-Sigel notes that these social changes, while not apparently religious, have come about in societies that are (or were) traditionally Christian. She perceives that the church "has the vocation to

---

[1] O. Lossky, *Toward the Endless Day*, pp. 243–44.
[2] Behr-Sigel, "La Place de la Femme dans l'Eglise," *Irénikon* 58 (1983), pp. 46–53 and pp. 194–214. Reprinted in *Le Ministère de la Femme dans l'Eglise*, pp. 157–88. Quotations will be taken from the English translation that slightly (but perhaps significantly?) alters the title to, "The Place of *Women* in the Church" (my italics), in *The Ministry of Women in the Church*, pp. 149–80.

baptize this new freedom won by women so that it will not degenerate into anarchy and mere confrontation of selfishness."[3]

Behr-Sigel then records just how the church has attempted to do this through a brief history of ecumenical attention to women's issues. From the first Faith and Order conference in 1927, where only seven of the four hundred delegates were female, all the way to Agapia and Sheffield, Behr-Sigel reminds her readers of how far the church has come. She wonders if the freedom of speech at Agapia is the main reason why there has been no Agapia II, and she cites another Orthodox theologian, Metropolitan Meliton, who acknowledged the "poor quality of internal dialogue" in the Orthodox church on this issue.[4]

Alongside the historical and cultural analysis, Behr-Sigel dives into her most extensive scriptural exegesis yet. She starts with the apostle Paul's famous Galatians 3 passage: in Christ, there is no longer Jew or Greek, male or female, slave or free, but one in Jesus Christ. How does this align with his 1 Corinthians 11 concern over female prophecy in the church? Behr-Sigel notes that Paul was concerned with the order of the community and the inbreaking kingdom of God alike. He had to employ a "laborious line of argument" to keep those female heads covered. And yet he ended up interrupting himself—"Nevertheless, in the Lord woman is not independent of man nor man of woman; for as woman was made from man, so man is now born of woman. And all things are from God" (1 Cor. 11.11–12)—to assert the "reciprocity of men and women," a "principle based on God's plan." Behr-Sigel concludes, "And so we see how the Spirit clears a new path through the thick forest of human prejudices!"[5] Evdokimov had also relativized this passage but on the grounds that the veil refers to the great "mystery" of femininity. Behr-Sigel follows his lead in rejecting it as a grounds for keeping women silent in the church but for a different reason.

Behr-Sigel then analyzes Jesus' behavior with women. Following France Quéré, who warned that "we must not read the New Testament through the glasses of an American feminist," Behr-Sigel observes that Jesus does not denounce the roles or place of women in his own society. The women he knew did traditional, "womanly" things—serving at table, caring for children. On the other hand, one could equally well say that Jesus *ignored* the roles they played. He associated with women of all kinds, more and less respectable, touched them and allowed them to touch him, engaged with them and taught them. Behr-Sigel thus concludes, "Jesus did not deny the differences between the sexes. He fully assumed his own masculinity and referred to his mother as 'woman' (John 2:4). At the same time he appealed to what in each one of us is beyond sex, beyond it but raising it up to a higher order."[6] Behr-Sigel's point here is not entirely clear. What does it mean to say that Jesus "assumed his own masculinity"? Was he indeed making a point about his mother's gender in addressing her as "woman"? Has Behr-Sigel temporarily opted for Gregory of Nyssa's theological anthropology in

---

[3] Behr-Sigel, "The Place of Women," p. 158.
[4] Ibid., p. 162.
[5] Ibid., pp. 151–53.
[6] Ibid., p. 166.

appealing to a humanity "beyond sex"? This last option is unlikely, since in the very next paragraph she asserts a divinely intended single humanity in a double polarity of male and female as the patristic view. More likely it is the breakdown of her old concepts, which are weaker in this essay than they have ever been.

And this is the first place we hear Behr-Sigel criticize Evdokimov's constructions directly. In previous efforts, such as "Women in the Orthodox Church: Heavenly Vision and Historical Realities," she mentioned his mystification of women or adjusted his comments to suit her own insights, but she never before struck at the heart of Evdokimov's logic. Now, in a section advocating the restoration of the female diaconate, with all its duties and privileges and a proper ordination, she recalls the line in the Syriac *Didascalia of the Apostles* that says, "Honor the deacon as having the place of Christ; honor the deaconess as having the place of the Holy Spirit." (It is worth noting that it is not the *priest* who is honored in the place of Christ, but the male deacon. The same diaconal office is for both men and women, but each sex is honored in the place of a different Person of God.) Behr-Sigel learned about this passage from Evdokimov, who used it as proof of the special relationship between women and the Holy Spirit. Now she asks why such a distinction was made. Behr-Sigel supposes it to be the grammatical femininity of "spirit" in Aramaic. She asks whether one is then "justified in concluding with Paul Evdokimov that the Holy Spirit is somehow feminine," and whether that is also, therefore, a valid basis for excluding women from the priesthood. She answers her own question.

> This sort of speculation must be handled very carefully. There can be no question of introducing sexuality into the Christian representation of the trinitarian God and of making the distinction of the divine Persons into a sexual difference. In the same way, it seems to me at variance with Christian anthropology and soteriology to oppose the Spirit-carrying woman to the christic man-*vir*.[7]

A better trinitarian interpretation, to her mind, is to understand diaconal service as one common to men and women alike, such that their ministries "would be linked together in the distinction between the Son and the Spirit, between the Lamb and the Dove though they are eternally associated, immanent one to the other."[8] The trinitarian grounds are shifting.

As Behr-Sigel moves from the female diaconate to the female priesthood, she continues her criticism of Evdokimov. The historic arguments against women in holy orders are no longer to be considered valid, that is, arguments about the hierarchy of the sexes and the natural inferiority of women; and yet, she notices, there is a sense in which some of these arguments have been recast by contemporary theologians in a positive light when they speak of "women's spiritual charisms—which these theologians feel it is their duty to reveal to women." Evdokimov is singled out as one who wanted women not to aspire to an office at odds with their spiritual gifts. But Behr-Sigel finds now that this idea can only "confuse the matter," lacking as it does adequate scriptural

---

[7] Ibid., p. 175.
[8] Ibid.

foundation. The apostle Paul never spoke of feminine (or masculine) charisms—only of the regulation of all gifts for the good of the assembly.[9]

As Behr-Sigel works her way through the reasons for barring women from the priesthood, she finds one argument after another falling away for lack of substance. Yes, perhaps women are the "praying ones" or "religious souls," but there is no reason why that automatically excludes them from public ministry of the church—quite the contrary! Ritual impurity makes no sense in the new covenant. Jesus chose 12 apostles, but more apostles appear after the 12, and the church calls the myrrh-bearing women of Easter morning the "apostles to the apostles." Ordained women have no long-standing place in church history, but would ordaining women be a break with Tradition or merely tradition?[10]

At last Behr-Sigel comes to the heart of the Orthodox difficulty with women priests. She herself had been convinced for a long time by the iconic argument: that the priest, representing Christ to the gathered church, must be the image of Christ to the church. Now she questions the meaning of this "representation." Surely it is not meant to be crudely naturalistic. That was never the import of the theology of icons. Nor is it proper to Orthodox theology to say that the priest is "another Christ" or *in persona Christi*—which is the principal difference between the Orthodox and Roman Catholic understanding of holy orders. In fact, for the Orthodox, the priest is not the actor in the worship at all. He is only the instrument of Christ—*and* the Spirit. "The priest is thus a spokesman for the eternal Word. He lends his voice to the Word. Can this voice not be a feminine one?"[11]

If the answer is no, this cannot be on account of Christ's voice being masculine. Behr-Sigel recalls that the eucharist is not only a memorial of the Last Supper but also an "anticipation of the messianic banquet of the Kingdom and communion with the Resurrected Christ who has ascended into the heavens, that is, entered into the divine sphere where the categories of masculine and feminine are, if not destroyed, at least totally transcended."[12] And if this is still not enough—if the claims of earthly sexuality are still too great to be overcome even in anticipation of the heavenly change of status—Behr-Sigel makes her crowning argument: "[T]he priest not only represents Christ, but by saying 'we,' he also lends his voice to the Church."[13] The epiclesis is the prayer of the whole Christian church and the locally gathered assembly. At that moment, the priest represents not Christ as the bridegroom but the church as the bride. In worship, the priest lends his tongue and hands as much to the church as he does to Christ.

If anything characterizes Behr Sigel's theological style, it is the irenic serenity that she elsewhere praises in Orthodox women. It is a virtue she herself internalized; her departures from it are, at worst, into irony, but never into attacks or demands. And so, despite the strength of the argument for the ordination of women that she presents here, from an Orthodox, patristic, and biblical perspective, she does not conclude with a call for the ordination of women by the Orthodox church. This is perhaps a surprising lacuna if one is attuned to the patterns of feminist theology in (mainly) the Western

---

9 Ibid., p. 176.
10 Ibid., pp. 176–77.
11 Ibid., p. 178.
12 Ibid.
13 Ibid.

church. No good will come of blanket demands—this is Behr-Sigel's intuition. St. Paul is her guide: all things are lawful for me, but not all things are helpful (1 Cor. 6.12). She sees that not every local church is in the same place, experiencing the same changes, encountering the same problems. Demanding a change of practice of this magnitude would amount to an inexcusable lack of charity. In short, the ordination of women is not an issue of *status confessionis* but of local discipline. She suggests:

> On a problem like the ordination of women, might we not imagine different "helpful things" that the local Churches could determine for themselves? This autonomy would have to go hand in hand, however, with a concern shared by all the Churches to promote the liberty of women in the Holy Spirit and the dignity of all, men and women, inside the "new community." But would not such a pluralism of discipline in this area be compatible with the unity of faith and ecclesial communion?[14]

This concluding sentence of the essay draws the reader back to the beginning. There are two basic ecclesiological models: one hierarchical and one communal. If the church in practice is all too often the former, in essence it is the latter, after the pattern of the Holy Trinity. Church is communion. The communal essence of the church permits freedom in matters of discipline, even autonomy as she suggests, for the good order of the local community.[15] This conviction is what distinguishes Behr-Sigel from the aggressive, "prophetic" air of Sheffield and the letter presented to the WCC at Dresden, which only had the effect of alienating the unconvinced and hardening the proponents.

"The Place of Women in the Church" is the turning point in Behr-Sigel's thought. She will refine her ideas further; her sophistication will increase; her sources and criticisms will grow broader; and she will have more work to do to dismantle Evdokimov and rethink gender-based charisms. But the basic lines of her argument are already set in place.

Exploring otherness

It was quite timely that the following year, in October 1984, Behr-Sigel was invited to give a lecture at the Dominican College of Philosophy and Theology in Ottawa, Canada. Her subject was "The Otherness of Men and Women in the Context of a Christian Civilization."[16] As in the previous piece, this one is marked by two main

---

[14] Ibid., pp. 179–80.

[15] Ibid., pp. 149–50.

[16] The lecture was not published until two years later with other essays from the conference. "L'Altérité Homme-Femme dans le Contexte d'une Civilisation Chrétienne," in *L'Altérité, Vivre Ensemble Différents*, pp. 389–426 (ed. M. Gourgues and G. D. Mailhiot; Paris: Cerf, 1986). The book also includes four responses from other participants in the conference, entirely positive in their evaluation of Behr-Sigel's work. The essay was reprinted in *Le Ministère de la Femme dans l'Eglise*. Quotations here are taken from the English translation, "The Otherness of Men and Women in the Context of a Christian Civilization," in *The Ministry of Women in the Church*, pp. 25–79.

features: a deepening reflection on the biblical and patristic witness, and an increasing distance between herself and Evdokimov.

The address begins with some commonplace observations on men and women in history and culture, the current "profound cultural mutation," and the difference between the sexes from a scientific point of view. This last part is new to her thought.

> In the view of the human sciences, the otherness of men and women, the *masculine fact* as well as the *feminine fact*, shows itself as a complex and eminently "shapable" reality. Complexity and "shapability," however, leave a lot of leeway and thus allow human cultural intervention to have an influence on nature, not just to correct any eventual imperfections or to fill in gaps not covered by the instincts but also to give a *meaning* to nature, a significance and a direction that go beyond mere external sexual phenomena. Because it transcends the male-female opposition of the animal world, *the otherness of men and women belongs essentially to the realm of symbols.*[17]

This is a crucial insight. Throughout her reflections so far, Behr-Sigel has wanted to understand femininity *in se*, following Evdokimov's lead without quite accepting his particular spin on the subject. She has feared a kind of biological reductionism, one that makes femininity absolutely nothing more than a byproduct of anatomical particularities, for it seems too demeaning, too void of meaning, missing the rich language of archetypes and symbols. Even a year before this essay, she was still insisting that the wonderful sharing of parenthood between women and men does not mean that they have become "simply identical and interchangeable parts, but their differentiation has its place less in social functions than in qualitative ways of acting and reacting."[18]

Why is the shift here so important? Remember that Behr-Sigel's reason for pursuing the question of women in the church at all was the conviction that women in their femininity have distinct gifts, insights, and experiences that the church can and must take into account. If femininity as such is voided of all spiritual meaning, then the reason for Behr-Sigel's quest has been lost. Yet she now finds the idea of profound spiritual differences between men and women to be less convincing than before, without adequate scriptural and theological foundation. Thus, in "The Otherness of Men and Women," she is groping her way toward a meaning for a womanhood that is biologically grounded, culturally interpreted, and symbolically generous, yet neither oppressive nor stereotypical. It is not an easy task.

The address in Ottawa experiments a bit with the problem. Behr-Sigel decries the "reductionist tendency," even in theology, especially that of Gregory of Nyssa, to make the difference between men and women merely one of procreative function,[19] yet she asserts that "[m]otherhood is the axis around which feminine existence is built"![20] She

---

[17] Behr-Sigel, "The Otherness of Men and Women," in *The Ministry of Women in the Church*, p. 34. My italics in the last sentence only.

[18] Behr-Sigel, "The Place of Women in the Church," in *The Ministry of Women in the Church*, p. 158.

[19] Behr-Sigel, "The Otherness of Men and Women," in *The Ministry of Women in the Church*, p. 42.

[20] Ibid., p. 27.

wants to insist that "men and women do not complete each other like the parts of a whole, the parts of a mechanism" but live together in their own proper completeness as a community, after the pattern of the Holy Trinity.[21]

Behr-Sigel comes closest to an answer to her own question with an observation about Jesus' treatment of men and women.

> This total equality of everyone, of men and women called to a personal meeting with the Bridegroom who opens to them the door of the Kingdom's bridal chamber, in no way implies a negation or a rejection of the otherness of men and women. In fact this otherness constitutes a modality of encounter. It permeates the encounter like a perfume, like a melody that is unique for each person.[22]

This is a significantly different way of reading the import of sexual duality from before. It is not a gender-wide slate of characteristics but a person-specific form of expression.

And yet in this lecture there are still hints of "feminine ecumenism" and other ways of saying that women have a distinct role to play in the healing of Western society, a prophetic role at the forefront of the battle, in which they "prove their strength so as to be recognized as the equals of males and at the same time affirm their specificity which is not psychological but essentially ethical and spiritual." She has abandoned the notion of a fundamental psychological difference between men and women but the remaining ethical and spiritual difference goes unexplained. And yet, in another twist, Behr-Sigel can say that it doesn't matter whether women get their distinctive feminine features from inborn nature or cultural nurture; what matters is the quality of openness to the other.[23]

But the break with Evdokimov is definitely there, if often discreetly tucked away in footnotes. She comments, "The inferiority of women in the domain of cultural creation is artlessly proclaimed even by thinkers who try to emphasize the value of 'feminine charisms,'" citing Evdokimov's essay "Les Charismes de la Femme."[24] There is also an oblique reference to Evdokimov's denial of a paternal instinct in men corresponding to the maternal instinct in women.[25] The most important break from Evdokimov of all, though, comes in her challenge of the supposed femininity of the Holy Spirit.

The phrase "let *us* make humankind in *our* image" of Gen. 1.26 was a great source of inspiration to patristic trinitarianism: from the beginning, God is a communion of three persons, and the humans made in God's image are meant to be in communion with one another as well. Unity and plurality in this relationship are not a source of tension but the very stuff of love. Behr-Sigel notes the further development of this idea by Russian theologians of the past century, including Clément, Bulgakov, Soloviev, and Evdokimov.[26] She reviews Bulgakov's Sophia and Evdokimov's Spirit as archetypes of

---

[21] Ibid., p. 74.
[22] Ibid., p. 63.
[23] Ibid., p. 76.
[24] Ibid., p. 27. The reference can be found in Evdokimov, *La Nouveauté de l'Esprit*, p. 244.
[25] Behr-Sigel, "The Otherness of Men and Women," in *The Ministry of Women in the Church*, p. 31.
[26] See Meerson's study, *The Trinity of Love in Modern Russian Theology*.

hypostatic maternity. She also mentions Thomas Hopko, who, in his work "On the Male Character of the Christian Priesthood," identifies the male with Christ and the woman with the Holy Spirit, just like Evdokimov.

Hopko denies any common ground with Bulgakov and Soloviev, and rarely cites Evdokimov,[27] but Behr-Sigel detects the similarities all the same. She enumerates three points of convergence. First, all of them assume a "noble and generous vision of femininity." Second, they claim that sexual differences are not just a matter of God's will but of God's being. And third, they reintroduce feminine symbolism for God that, though occasionally present in the Scriptures, has been largely overlooked by the Christian tradition.[28]

But Behr-Sigel remains skeptical that Hopko, and his kindred spirit Evdokimov, have really tamed their personal *theologoumena* to the rigors of the Tradition. The fact is, their united assumption that sexual differentiation is grounded in God's eternal being is explicitly contradicted by some patristic witnesses who make sexual differentiation secondary in creation—among them particularly Gregory of Nyssa and Maximus the Confessor. The latter plainly states that sexual duality was "added later and without any relation to the divine archetype." This alternate vision is not without its dangers, chief among them "ascetical angelism." Hopko and Evdokimov are particularly keen to avoid this error and affirm the goodness of sexuality in its own right, with rich spiritual meaning.[29]

But is the cure worse than the disease? Behr-Sigel worries that, by

> grounding sexual bipolarity in a divine Person, are we not introducing sexuality into the very being of the transcendent God? Would this not be in contradiction with the biblical and patristic vision which opposed the pagan pantheons of masculine and feminine divinities? *Would not the very notion of person be obscured by a speculation that tends to confuse the ineffable distinction of persons, in God as well as in humanity, with the difference between the sexes?*[30]

Here again we see how, for Behr-Sigel, the concept of personhood increasingly displaces gender as the key issue in the debate over the ordination of women—an issue that, moreover, has tremendous trinitarian ramifications.

The Trinity is not the only doctrine rattled by Hopko and Evdokimov's ideas. Soteriology is in question too. The Son and the Spirit always work together as one, according to the trinitarian faith. To say that the spiritual vocation of men is found in

---

[27] The only two instances I have found where Hopko refers to Evdokimov on gender and trinitarian matters are in "Apophatic Theology and the Naming of God in Eastern Orthodox Tradition," in *Speaking the Christian God: The Holy Trinity and the Challenge of Feminism* (ed. Alvin F. Kimel, Jr; Grand Rapids, MI: Eerdmans, 1992), p. 161, and in "God and Gender: Articulating the Orthodox View," *St. Vladimir's Theological Quarterly* 37, nos 2–3 (1993), p. 161, and both references are just in passing. But in Hopko's own extensive development of the Son/male, Spirit/female ideas, he makes no reference to Evdokimov at all.

[28] Behr-Sigel, "The Otherness of Men and Women," in *The Ministry of Women in the Church*, pp. 45–46.

[29] Ibid., pp. 46–47.

[30] Ibid., pp. 47–48. My italics.

the Son and that of women is found in the Spirit is not only to divide Son from Spirit, but to imply that the salvation of each is somehow different.

Behr-Sigel suggests going back to the drawing board. There are two tasks to be approached afresh. The first is to understand "the spiritual significance of human sexual bipolarity." Behr-Sigel maintains that it does in fact *have* a spiritual significance. She reflects on the second creation story, the Hebrew text implying that the creation of woman is not a kind of second-best knock-off but in fact a refinement and perfection. She notes that the term for Eve, "helper," is used to describe the Lord Himself elsewhere in the Old Testament. The force of the story is toward the unity and similarity of men and women, not their difference. It is his same bone and flesh that Adam's glad cry acclaims. Behr-Sigel refers to her old friend Emmanuel Levinas in calling this relationship one of "*good distance, pure otherness,* without which there is no meeting between persons."[31]

The second task for theology is to discern whether something in God "corresponds ineffably to what we call womanhood in our human language."[32] In what respects are feminine metaphors for the transcendent God permissible, even insightful? The difficulty is obvious. If there is uncertainty about what qualifies as feminine, it is hard to assert the necessity of describing God in such terms. Yet the Scriptures themselves offer examples and the Holy Spirit is occasionally expressed with feminine grammatical terms—though of course this is what led Evdokimov into trouble.

Behr-Sigel gets help in her two appointed tasks by shifting from the creation stories to the New Testament texts about Jesus and Mary his mother. Jesus Christ, the Word incarnate, is, sure enough, a man in the sense of male. But, Behr-Sigel notes, this fact barely caught the church fathers' attention. They were far more interested in the fact of Jesus Christ as true *anthropos*, all-inclusive human, assuming all of humanity and therefore saving all of humanity, in such a way that his being male in no way excludes the salvation of females. Even more profoundly, Jesus Christ became flesh, *sarx*, the human condition afflicted by sin, and in assuming it redeemed it from its debt to death. This is the meaning of calling Christ the new Adam—not to line up one male with another male but the first creation with the new creation.[33]

And yet the fact remains—the Word took flesh as a human *male*, so Behr-Sigel asks, "[D]oes this masculinity have a theological meaning, a meaning that can enlighten the masculine-feminine symbolism in its application to concrete human persons?" She finds that, in the logic of the Scriptures, masculinity is employed as a symbol of transcendence, a transcendence that in itself possesses no sexual characteristics. The designations of Father and Son for the first two persons of the Trinity are to indicate relations of origin, but not to imply any sort of biological analogy. The term "bridegroom" referring to the Lord in Old Testament and Christ in the New Testament likewise does not intend to assign gender to the various persons involved but evokes "faithful and merciful love."[34]

---

[31] Ibid., pp. 50–51. Her italics.
[32] Ibid., p. 48.
[33] Ibid., pp. 55–56.
[34] Ibid., p. 57.

Behr-Sigel reasons that the use of a masculine rather than a feminine symbol for God in the religion of Israel was chiefly to avoid any sense of a "return to the uterine depths of divinity or a depersonalized fusion in some totality," and to emphasize the personhood of all players, divine and human, which requires true meeting, authentic relationships, genuine mutuality. Whether the implicit assumptions about men and women in this distinction are accurate or helpful she herself does not ask. What she does emphasize is the pronoun's intention to oppose a philosophy of the One and to replace it with personalistic being. When feminine metaphors convey this point, they too are used in the Scriptures: for instance, the Hebrew *rahamim* meaning "womb of mercy" to describe the Lord's tender maternity of His people, or Jesus' desire to gather up his "chicks" like a "mother hen." For that matter, the Scriptures use animal metaphors too, without any suggestion that God is a beast—the Lamb of God, for instance. Given all this, Behr-Sigel asks, "is it not especially arbitrary and at least risky to apply this theological symbolism to the human sexual differentiation so as to conclude that men and women have radically different spiritual missions?" To do so would be to misread the intent of the metaphors altogether.[35]

Behr-Sigel pushes the point further with a reflection on the Theotokos. Mary is neither an idol of biological birthgiving nor a model of passive femininity. Her *fiat* to Gabriel's proclamation is free, the Orthodox Tradition insists; God did not simply seize and use her body for His own ends. Her significance is not even so much that she bore Christ and nursed him—as someone in the crowd once suggested to Jesus (Lk. 11.27)—but that she heard the word of God and kept it. This means that Mary is not an example only for women, but for men too—in short, for people. "She is the image neither of a submissive and obedient femininity, in conformity with a certain cultural stereotype, nor of an ideally beautiful human femininity, according to the aesthetic canon of a given age. She is not to be confused with the *Eternel Féminin* of the romantics" but given her place in line with the prophetesses of the Old Testament. She is both Christ-bearer and Spirit-bearer, and as such the first sign of humanity restored by the work of Christ. The feminine symbolism of "receptivity," then, is not meant as gender commentary but as the standard for all human involvement with God, receptive to grace. "In a sense that transcends sexual differentiation, both biological and social, the historic femininity of Mary is the fundamental axis of the human vocation."[36]

Behr-Sigel wraps up her exegesis with a consideration of Paul, following the same lines she had set down in earlier essays. She chiefly notes that the exhortation of Ephesians for women to obey their husbands follows after the instruction for husbands to be Christ to their wives, which means, in short, their servants; after which Paul (or his follower who wrote Ephesians) detects the potential problems and so quickly appends a disclaimer that this is a great mystery and really refers to Christ and the church. Likewise the veil of 1 Corinthians 11 assumes that women *are* prophesying in the assembly. Behr-Sigel finds that her own concern for a Christianity capable of speaking to the problems of modernity resonates with Paul's attempts to be in but not of the culture of his own time. But most of all she notices that Paul never has the slightest

---

[35] Ibid., p. 58.
[36] Ibid., pp. 59–60.

notion of gender-based charisms. Without naming any names, her intent is clear: the "idea of feminine charisms is very dear to certain modern defenders of femininity, especially male ones, but the use of this idea runs the risk of being a mystification." And there is no basis for it in Paul, whose only concern is the regulation of gifts for the good of the church as a body.[37]

Behr-Sigel's conclusion to her essay reflects the transitional state of her mind. On the one hand, even while she rejects feminine charisms, she approvingly cites Lev Gillet's prayer of thanks for the "feminine principle." She even turns back to thank Evdokimov, along with Teilhard de Chardin and more recently France Quéré, for "calling on the energies of women to oppose the forces of dissolution and destruction." Every woman is attached to life and children, Behr-Sigel asserts with them, and to deny this fact is to deny herself. "Is not her vocation, *here and now*," Behr-Sigel asks, "to try to break the circle of solitude in which Western man has enclosed himself?" The masculine traits of virility, self-affirmation, domination, and conquest must be countered by women's "human civilization which gives priority to life, dialogue, and love: to the love-gift of self so that the other might exist."[38]

On the other hand, she argues, men and women are not respective halves trying to make a complete whole, but each man and woman is whole in him- or herself.[39] Mary's receptivity is the archetype for all humans in all relationships: "Her humility is ontological and not psychological."[40] She is the union of men and women, not their division. "Thus in the person of the Theotokos, the otherness of men and women is recognized, expressed in its spiritual meaning, and transcended. Following Mary, men and women are called upon, in the Church, to become those in whom and by whom Christ-Emmanuel, 'God with us,' comes into the world."[41] When men and women are most like Mary, they are also most like Christ.

Behr-Sigel's conflict remains unresolved. Do women have distinct qualities, by nature or by nurture, that the church and world must have to survive? Is one justified in calling qualities of self-giving and receptivity "feminine"? One half of her thought applauds these ideas; the other half deplores them.

The question internalized

Around the same time that she was preparing and delivering the address in Ottawa, Behr-Sigel read and reviewed the first edition of *Women and the Priesthood*, a collection of essays all by American Orthodox theologians save two,[42] edited by Thomas Hopko,

---

³⁷ Ibid., pp. 64–72.
³⁸ Ibid., pp. 75–76.
³⁹ Ibid., p. 75.
⁴⁰ Ibid., p. 78.
⁴¹ Ibid., p. 79.
⁴² Behr-Sigel, review of *Women and the Priesthood*, 1st edn, ed. T. Hopko, *Contacts* 36 (1984), pp. 207–14. The exceptions are Ware and Afanasiev, the latter of whom wrote on the mysterious Canon 11 of the even more mysterious Council of Laodicea, of which virtually nothing is known except its conclusion that women may not be priests. Afanasiev connects the prohibition to the threat of Montanism, in which there *were* women priests, and extrapolates to the validity of the

who, as Behr-Sigel points out, intended to "defend the status quo concerning the place of women in the church," a topic more fiercely debated in the United States than in Europe, which accounts for the "polemical" texts therein.[43]

Three essays in particular attract Behr-Sigel's attention—and ire. The first is by Kallistos Ware, better known now for his introductory works to the Orthodox church and faith. Against his use of the iconic argument, Behr-Sigel raises the same questions as in her two previous essays: what exactly the representation of Christ means; whether the priest does not also represent the church; what kind of charisms are required for priesthood; and whether they are sex-specific. Ware makes reference to Evdokimov, Behr-Sigel notes, in particular his alignment of women with the Holy Spirit. Ware calls it a "domain to explore."[44]

Thomas Hopko and his "disciple" (Behr-Sigel's term) Deborah Belonick do in fact explore this domain in their essays. Behr-Sigel pays them the ambiguous compliment of having written "the most original, the most incisive (if not the most convincing)" essays in the collection. Hopko again acknowledges no debt to Evdokimov—though he does to Bulgakov, whom Evdokimov had also read.[45] What both Hopko and Belonick are after is a "faith seeking understanding" explanation of human sexual duality and, less explicitly, an account of why the church may not ordain women. The order here is the opposite of Evdokimov's, who thought about men and women first and then concluded women could not be priests. Hopko and Belonick were convinced women may not be priests, so they went looking for answers as to why not.

Hopko begins by taking sides in the patristic discussion. He says that Maximus the Confessor and his ilk are simply wrong for placing sexuality after the first creation as a mere concession to sin. In fact, he goes much further in the opposite direction than Basil of Caesarea could ever go: sexuality "has its foundation in God, not only in his creative will, but in the very being of God such that he has revealed to us: Father, Son, and Holy Spirit."[46] In the same breath, though, Behr-Sigel notes, Hopko claims not to have introduced or identified sexuality in God, which indubitably violates the Orthodox theological tradition. He suggests instead that there are

> two "modes of divine existence" within the Trinity whose hypostatic characteristics and manner of interrelating, especially as they are revealed in the divine oikonomia of creation and salvation, bear a striking resemblance to the "mode of human

prohibition to the whole church in all time. Behr-Sigel is not convinced. See *Women and the Priesthood* (ed. Thomas Hopko; Crestwood, NY: St. Vladimir's Seminary Press, 1st edn, 1983). A significantly revised edition was published in 1999.

[43]   Behr-Sigel, review of *Women and the Priesthood*, 1st edn, pp. 207–08. All quotations are my translation. Another review similar in content to hers is by Elizabeth Moberly, who finds that "the assertions of *Women and the Priesthood* are inadequate as they stand, and must be either strengthened or repudiated." Review of *Women and the Priesthood*, 1st edn, ed. T. Hopko, *Sobornost* 6 (1984), pp. 86–89 (86). She chiefly takes issue with the absolutizing of the symbols of masculine and feminine.

[44]   Behr-Sigel, review of *Women and the Priesthood*, 1st edn, p. 209.

[45]   Ibid. Hopko mentions being influenced by Vladimir Lossky, too, although Behr-Sigel expresses reservations about the quality of the English translation Hopko read.

[46]   Ibid., p. 210.

existence" and manner of interrelating created and commanded by God for men and women in the Bible and the Church, in the Old and the New Testaments.[47]

But Behr-Sigel wonders if this does not in fact obscure the proclamation of the gospel—salvation and new life offered freely to all—and the fundamental "personalism" that goes with it.

From this point on, personalism becomes increasingly important to Behr-Sigel. Behr-Sigel does not explain the source or precise meaning of the term "personalism" in this essay. Two clues to her intention can be found, though. The first is that she was an avid reader of the journal *Esprit* founded by French personalist Emmanuel Mounier. The segment called "Woman Also a Person" in Mounier's book, *The Personalist Manifesto*, is notably compatible with Behr-Sigel's own thought. The title of her essay on the Cappadocians, "Woman Too Is in the Likeness of God," is perhaps a play on Mounier's title. The second clue to Behr-Sigel's "personalism" appears a little later in her career, when she refers to the personalism of Vladimir Lossky. This is the more important of the two for her; we will revisit the issue in the final chapter.[48]

Behr-Sigel finds gospel personalism to be threatened by the heavy insistence on men's gifts as opposed to women's gifts. She writes:

[T]he church has always affirmed the transcendence of the human person in relation to modes of existence and expression that are sexually polarized according to forms that vary with cultures and time periods. The mystery of the unique relation of each person with the living God thus cannot be reduced, in the Christian point of view, to a platonist reflection of some masculine or feminine archetype. Fr. Hopko knows it and sometimes says it. But obsessed with the preoccupation of justifying theologically the fact of the non-ordination of women in the Orthodox Church, he arrives, it seems to me, at systematizing a poetic typology, accentuating it so unilaterally that it takes a step beyond the essential kerygma. The person appears then to be absorbed in his sex, confused with it.[49]

Not only is theological anthropology at stake; so is the doctrine of the Trinity, which is implicated in this anthropology. Hopko labels the Western practice of ordaining women modalism—failing to distinguish properly between the Persons of God, making Son and Spirit (and thus masculinity and femininity) interchangeable. But Behr-Sigel thinks Hopko has failed to distinguish between divine Persons and human persons. Sexual differentiation cannot be transposed upon the divine without becoming anthropomorphic. She offers a sound rule: "The use of analogies requires prudence and restraint."[50]

---

47 Cited on ibid., p. 211. Quoted here from the original English of Thomas Hopko, "On the Male Character of the Christian Priesthood," in *Women and the Priesthood*, 1st edn, pp. 130–31. The essay was first published in *St. Vladimir's Theological Quarterly* 19, no. 3 (1975), pp. 147–73.

48 See Behr-Sigel, "L'Ordination des Femmes, Un Problème Oecuménique," in *Contacts* 42, no. 2 (1990), pp. 101–27 (122).

49 Behr-Sigel, review of *Women and the Priesthood*, 1st edn, p. 212. "Confused" (*confondue*) in the last sentence is used in the sense of the person being mistaken for the sex.

50 Ibid., p. 213.

Behr-Sigel finds Belonick even less amenable a theologian. Belonick studied under Hopko and wrote a thesis on feminism—a hostile one—and in her essay for *Women and the Priesthood* suggests that dialogue with churches that ordain women ought not even be an option for Orthodoxy. Behr-Sigel concedes that maybe some kinds of feminism deserve the harsh criticism they get, but the effect of Belonick's extreme position makes the masculinity of the priest "in a way the central dogma of the Christian faith, in the name of which one excommunicates those who think otherwise."[51] Belonick stands in stark contrast to Behr-Sigel's not only finding reasons to ordain women but even permitting local variations in practice.

Behr-Sigel concludes her review with the thought: "It is with mixed feelings, then, that I close this book. It witnesses to the vitality of American Orthodoxy ready to take up the challenges of the contemporary world"—certainly a virtue Behr-Sigel held in high esteem—"but at the same time, it seems to me, to a regrettable absence of openness to the other and, under the appearances of doctrinal fundamentalism, a lack of theological rigor."[52]

The unsatisfactory analogy between women and the Spirit is conspicuous by its absense in a rare doctrinal article Behr-Sigel published the same year as her review of *Women and the Priesthood*. A lengthy exploration of the doctrine of the Holy Spirit in Orthodox theology, she attempts a sympathetic reading of the filioque (the precedent having been set by her friend and confessor Sergius Bulgakov) and discusses the nature of trinitarian relations. She even quotes Paul Evdokimov—but not once, in her 23 pages on the Spirit, does she speak of any "feminine" quality in the Spirit or even the recurrence of this notion in contemporary Orthodox thought. Her break from that particular account of humanity through the lens of the Trinity is complete.[53]

Following the Theotokos to the priesthood

In July 1985, Behr-Sigel continued her ecumenical habit by presenting a talk on "Mary as Mother of God" at the annual Summer Seminar hosted by the Institute for Ecumenical Research, an affiliate of the Lutheran World Federation located in Strasbourg, France.[54]

Behr-Sigel begins by contrasting the "lyrical exuberance of the liturgical glorification of Mary" with the "sobriety of the dogmatic statements about her" in the Orthodox church. The only "official" statements in Orthodoxy on Mary are the phrase about her in the Nicene Creed—that Jesus Christ took flesh from the Virgin Mary—and the

---

51 Ibid., p. 214.

52 Ibid.

53 "Quelques Aspects de la Théologie et de l'Expérience de l'Esprit Saint dans l'Eglise Orthodoxe Aujourd'hui," *Tantur Yearbook* (1982–83), pp. 129–50.

54 The essay was published first as "Marie, Mère de Dieu. Mariologie Traditionelle et Questions Nouvelles," *Irénikon* 58, no. 4 (1985), pp. 451–70 and 59, no. 1 (1986), pp. 20–31. It was reprinted in *Le Ministère de la Femme dans l'Eglise*, pp. 189–224. Portions of the French article were reprinted as "Marie, Visage de l'Humanité Nouvelle," in *Unité des Chrétiens* 69 (1988), pp. 20–21 and again in *Unité des Chrétiens* 95 (1994), p. 37. Quotations here are taken from the English translation, "Mary, the Mother of God: Traditional Mariology and New Questions," in *The Ministry of Women in the Church*, pp. 181–216.

title awarded her by the third ecumenical council in Ephesus, Theotokos.[55] There is no systematic mariology in the East like there is in the Roman Catholic West. Behr-Sigel praises Orthodoxy for this, "neither a restrictive dogmatization going hand in hand with a heavy intellectual elaboration, nor a rejection or neglect."[56] She prizes the resulting freedom in the church. That freedom allowed Bulgakov and Soloviev to develop their ideas of Mary as Sophia, divine wisdom, and the human face of God.[57] At the same time, Behr-Sigel makes it perfectly clear to her mostly Protestant audience that everything said about Mary witnesses to her Son, keeping the Orthodox dogmatically in the clear. The freedom she praises simply permits "persons and communities to interpret and appropriate the mystery according to times and places."[58]

But it is not only a love of Mary and the fittingness of Orthodox church practice about her that interests Behr-Sigel here. She is still wrestling with femininity. A reflection on Mary, Behr-Sigel proposes, might just "enlighten our contemporary research on the image of woman that is projected by the Church's teaching. Beyond that, light may also be shed on the place of the feminine principle in the history of salvation."[59] So after a discussion of the conciliar pronouncements about Mary, and the meaning of the liturgical feasts associated with her in the Orthodox church, Behr-Sigel turns to the question of Mary's humanity and femininity. The Theotokos is "the image and personification of the *Spirit-bearing* Church, the womb of the new humanity."[60]

What does femininity have to do with it? The Seminar's theme was on "Mary and the Role of Women in the Church," implying a connection between them. But in Behr-Sigel's thought, one thing is immediately clear: Mary is "neither a guardian goddess nor the model for women." She is the archetype for *every* person desiring to give birth to Christ spiritually, a desire clearly not restricted to women. Behr-Sigel cites St. Seraphim of Sarov who said that both men and women are "of her race," and Maximus the Confessor who taught that since Christ is born of a Virgin, "the separation of human nature into males and females is overcome." Even the "ascetic symbolism" employed in icons is meant to direct attention away from femininity in Mary—quite the opposite of, say, Renaissance madonnas in the West.

The acclaim of Mary's holiness, perfect openness to God, is not intended to alienate sinful men or women from her. Behr-Sigel sees here as elsewhere a danger of angelism, which she calls the mariological equivalent of docetism. The "feminine" in Mary, as such thinkers as Bulgakov, Soloviev, and Evdokimov saw it, was to be finally the principle of relationality and self-giving love.[61] Behr-Sigel points out that for Evdokimov this principle is even more powerfully found in the feminine Spirit. But now Behr-Sigel is aware of the pitfalls, so she asks, "Is it not dangerous to turn the masculine and feminine principles into personal realities to the detriment of the basic

---

[55] Behr-Sigel, "Mary, the Mother of God," in *The Ministry of Women in the Church*, p. 182.
[56] Ibid., p. 183.
[57] Ibid.
[58] Ibid., p. 184.
[59] Ibid.
[60] Ibid., p. 204.
[61] Ibid., p. 208.

category of *person* as the image of God in man (*anthropos*)?" Personhood displaces gender as constitutive of individual human beings.[62]

And this finally brings Behr-Sigel to make the distinction she has been after for a long time. She writes:

> Beyond its meaning for women, Mary's womanhood can have a meaning for *anthropos*, all mankind [*l'humanité*]. In their relation to God, the source and giver of life, all persons and mankind in general are called upon to adopt an attitude of openness and altruistic self-abandonment which makes them transparent to the radiance of the Other. Our language calls this attitude "womanly" because women perhaps are more spontaneously disposed to it. It is of little importance whether this attitude comes from nature or culture or is related to their maternal vocation or to their centuries-old standing. It is often the case, however, that a man (*aner*) does not discover this openness to the Other and to others except through a woman: mother, sister, wife, lover. The femininity of the Mother of God shows us the basic structure of humanity in its highest vocation, the call to holiness. As a result, women have their proper responsibilities in the Church, but it seems to me that there is not a proper distribution of roles and ministries based on sex. As St. Paul taught, this distribution is based on charisms, which though they may be colored differently by sex, are essentially gifts from God to a *person* for the building up of the community.[63]

Notice her nuance here. "Perhaps" women are more spontaneously self-giving. "Often" men experience openness better due to the love of a woman. The source of female openness is beyond certain analysis—there is any number of possibilities for it. But it turns out that what we call "femininity," for various reasons, really just means "humanity," *holy* humanity, to be exact. In this light, it is not more appropriate to identify the feminine with the holy than the masculine. But the fact that holy humanity was expressed superlatively by a woman, the Theotokos, has been a source of strength and inspiration for women in the "more or less patriarchal societies in which the historical Orthodox Churches have their roots."[64] It is a pragmatic issue, then, more than a dogmatic one.

The following year, Behr-Sigel had the pleasure of reviewing an article that expressed her developing views quite nicely.[65] Anne Jensen in a journal article had asked "How Patriarchal Is the Eastern Church?" and concluded that, all things considered, it is *less* so than the Western churches.[66] The ordination of women is a red herring, because it has still not become a properly internal question in the East. But the ecclesiology of communion, the stress on the koinonia of the Trinity, and

---

[62] Ibid., p. 209.

[63] Ibid., p. 212. Her italics.

[64] Ibid., p. 211.

[65] Behr-Sigel, "L'Eglise d'Orient Est-Elle Patriarcaliste!" *Contacts* 38, no. 3 (1986), pp. 235–37. The exclamation mark is a typographical error; it should be a question mark.

[66] Anne Jensen, "L'Eglise Orthodoxe: Est-Elle Patriarcaliste?" *Una Sancta* 40, no. 2 (1985), pp. 130–45.

the overall emphasis on God's love for humanity make Orthodoxy a generally more welcoming place for women.

Jensen also discusses Evdokimov at some length. She finds him, as Behr-Sigel did, remarkably affirming of women but misguided in his conclusions. Jensen concludes (here in Behr-Sigel's words) that Evdokimov's trinitarian speculations

> don't hold up to critical examination despite their generous intentions. The patristic trinitarian vision concerns the distinction of the divine Persons. It is not transposable onto the biological differentiation of the sexes. The Logos, in the thought of the Eastern fathers, is not the archetype of the human male [*l'homme-mâle*]—an idea borrowed from the psychoanalysis of C. Jung. It is the celestial man (*homme*) in the image and according to the likeness of which all of humanity, men and women, is created.[67]

Jensen extends the critique to Hopko and Belonick as well. And Behr-Sigel has cut the Gordian knot: the distinction among the Persons of the Trinity "is not transposable onto the biological differentiation of the sexes."

1987 was a signal year for Behr-Sigel. Her first essay devoted entirely to the ordination of women was published in a German-language collection published by the Catholic Academy of Freiburg, "Why No Ordination of Woman? Different Attitudes in the Christian Church."[68] Here Behr-Sigel pushes a little further back than her own involvement in the ecumenical women's movement and discovers Orthodox reflection on the ordination of women dating to the early 1960s in two short articles by Nicolae Chitescu and George Khodre. Chitescu's piece argues simply from tradition and the usual scriptural texts, to which he adds an allusion to women's "psychological weakness" and an outright reference to their monthly "ritual impurity."[69] Khodre, for his part, emphasizes the goodness of women—even a "mystery of woman"—which explains their exclusion from the priesthood. Woman is a "symbol of the religious soul." Khodre invokes the "order of creation" that grace does not destroy but redeems and leads to its goal. Because men and women are different and not interchangeable in their bodily sexuality, neither are they in vocation.[70]

From this review of early efforts on the ordination of women Behr-Sigel turns, not surprisingly, to Evdokimov. "He deepens the ideas," she writes,

> which George Khodre only quickly touched upon, develops them further in the light of C. G. Jung's psychoanalysis and works them finally into arguments against the ordination of women to the priestly office. But actually Paul Evdokimov was

---

[67] Behr-Sigel, "L'Eglise d'Orient Est-Elle Patriarcaliste!" p. 236. My translation.

[68] Behr-Sigel's contribution is "Ordination von Frauen? Ein Versuch des Bedenkens einer aktuellen Frage im Lichte der lebendigen Tradition der orthodoxen Kirche," in *Warum keine Ordination der Frau? Unterschiedliche Einstellungen in den christlichen Kirchen*, pp. 50–72 (ed. Elisabeth Gössmann and Dietmar Bader; Munich: Verlag Schnell und Steiner, 1987). No translator is listed, so one must assume she composed the essay in German herself, which is not improbable, as German was her first language and she taught it professionally during her years in Nancy. All quotations are my translation.

[69] Ibid., pp. 52–53.

[70] Ibid., pp. 53–54.

little interested in this problem. His main interest was in a Christian humanism as
the fulfillment of all that is human in Christ.[71]

This includes sexual love between men and women as a good in itself, a mystery and
sacrament, not just as a means to procreation.[72] Thus Evdokimov clarifies and defines
the meaning of woman's call, a high calling, in his view. But Behr-Sigel finally observes
that "Man" and "Woman"—always in the singular—are for him chiefly "individuations
of complementary ideas."[73]

Behr-Sigel's newfound conviction that personhood, not gender, is the key to
patristic and biblical anthropology alienates her further from Evdokimov. She asks,
"[D]oesn't this idealization mean at the same time an impoverishment of the concrete
person—man and woman—in whom masculinity and femininity are always only a
modality, a polarization of what is collectively human? A polarization, which does not
exclude the *other* pole—in each of us."[74] From there she repeats her previous concerns
about Evdokimov's introduction of sexuality into the Trinity and the shaky ground for
speaking of male and female charisms. She notes that in his own essay, "La Saint Esprit
et la Mère de Dieu," Evdokimov makes the apparent mistake of saying that "[f]or the
Eastern tradition, tender maternal love is the essential charism of the priesthood!"[75]
Despite these troubling features, Evdokimov is taken by many as the standard for
Orthodox thought on the subject, which does not please Behr-Sigel. Similar troubling
features in Hopko and Belonick are explored and dismantled here, in much the same
language as in Behr-Sigel's review of *Women and the Priesthood*.

At the end of the essay, Behr-Sigel states, "I have felt myself called here and there
to be a word-bearer of this minority" opinion about women and priesthood. "I know
that I am not alone. Encouragement to humble but fearless further-thinking on the
problem" comes from Metropolitan Anthony Bloom, who wonders whether the
"ontological difference" between men and women, which he himself doesn't doubt,
really is an adequate reason for barring women from the priesthood. And Behr-Sigel,
ever gracious, makes a point of thanking Evdokimov for helping her think through the
issue; she just believes it requires more thinking. Would the ordination of women to
the priesthood really result in the loss of distinctly feminine gifts, as Evdokimov feared?
She doubts it. "Is this concern not grounded in a monolithic-masculine conception of
the ecclesial office? Couldn't one hand the office over to women, to shape it in such a
way that meant no loss, but rather a clarification of the feminine-motherly?"[76] Until
the matter is decided by the universal church, she pleads again for it to be treated as a
matter of discipline rather than doctrine.[77]

The aforementioned Anthony Bloom publicly supported Behr-Sigel in her signal
year of 1987. It was the year of publication for her first collection of essays on the

---

[71] Ibid., p. 54.
[72] Ibid.
[73] Ibid, p. 55.
[74] Ibid.
[75] Ibid., p. 57. The Evdokimov reference is to *La Nouveauté de l'Esprit*, p. 264.
[76] Behr-Sigel, "Ordination von Frauen?" in *Warum keine Ordination der Frau?* p. 69.
[77] Ibid., pp. 70–71.

subject that had become so dear to her heart in the past decade. In the preface to *Le Ministère de la Femme dans l'Eglise*, Bloom writes:

> With great joy I recommend this book to all serious readers, to those who are ready to put aside their prejudices. May it be the "first swallow that announces the coming of spring." It will, I hope, open a new horizon for many Churches, for many fearful spirits that are afraid of rethinking ideas that have been accepted without reflection.[78]

He reflects on the fullness of Christ's humanity and the patristic rule that what is not assumed is not healed. He even suggests that Mary herself twice exercised a properly "priestly" ministry: in the presentation of her son to the Lord in the temple and in her vigil at the foot of the cross. This is certainly a reversal of the usual Orthodox reading of marian texts. But it is perfectly in keeping with Behr-Sigel's insight that Mary does, in fact, point the way toward women in the priesthood.[79]

The essays published in *Le Ministère de la Femme dans l'Eglise* have already been discussed in these pages. What is new is Behr-Sigel's introduction.[80] She summarizes the brief history of Orthodox involvement in ecumenical questions about women, and her part within it, adding a bit of background on her own childhood and young adulthood. Amidst abstracts of the essays in the book, she repeats arguments by now familiar about supposed feminine charisms, Evdokimov and Hopko's places in the debates, and her ultimate dissatisfaction with the iconic argument.

A theme that has been with her all along gets a little more attention now, though: that of Tradition and tradition. Behr-Sigel observes that the instinctive Orthodox reaction to the matter of women in the priesthood is to recite tradition: it has never been done before, therefore it cannot and will not be done now. What exactly qualifies as the true Tradition—which Vladimir Lossky called the "critical spirit of the church"[81]—was the question of Agapia. The women who gathered there desired to "rediscover, under the deposits of the past, the authentic ecclesial Tradition about women, as it sprang forth from the liberating Gospel of Christ," but even more, to take and "apply that Tradition creatively to new situations."[82] Tradition does not exist chiefly to repristinate but to create anew and give new life. Tradition and gospel go hand in hand. In the very question of the status of women, in the study of the past and affirmation of its wisdom

---

[78] The quotation here is taken from the English translation of the "Preface to the French Edition," in *The Ministry of Women in the Church*, p. xiii.

[79] Ibid., pp. xiii–xiv. The English edition also includes a "Preface to the English Edition" by Thomas Hopko, in which he calls her "Eastern Orthodoxy's premier woman thinker" who willingly "opens herself to various questions and criticisms. She can and will—and of course even *must*—be challenged about her choice of sources and references in dealing with her questions, as well as about her interpretations of biblical, liturgical, and patristic texts, her theological conclusions and her practical applications," pp. ix–x. Given her criticism of his own work, it is a mighty gracious way of expressing his doubts!

[80] Quotations here are taken from the English translation in *The Ministry of Women in the Church*, pp. 1–24.

[81] Ibid., p. 9.

[82] Ibid., p. 11.

alongside the removal of its false accretions, Behr-Sigel discerned "above all a call, in a new historical form, to be converted to the Gospel."[83]

The Interorthodox Consultation at Rhodes

By the late 1980s, the distance between tradition and Tradition caught up with the Orthodox church. The ecumenical issues and Behr-Sigel's own contributions convinced the Orthodox that they did, after all, need to make the question an internal one. In 1988 they did just that.[84]

It was an auspicious year for theological reflection on women. The WCC had declared an ecumenical decade of churches in solidarity with women to begin in 1988, complete with conferences, celebrations, and visits from WCC staff to local churches around the world to hear reports on the status of women in them. Behr-Sigel was to be involved in many such activities over the next ten years: three seminars held at the Ecumenical Institute in Bossey in 1992, 1994, and 1997 on the subject of "Feminine Images and Orthodox Spirituality," and two gatherings for Orthodox women in Damascus and Istanbul in 1996 and 1997 respectively.[85] Behr-Sigel became ill and was unable to attend the Damascus gathering, though she still contributed a paper to the conference proceedings. But the most important event for the theology of women and the priesthood in the Orthodox church happened at the very beginning of the Women's Decade, in 1988.

From October 30 to November 7, Orthodox delegates from all over the world gathered on the island of Rhodes in the Aegean Sea to discuss the place of women in the church.[86] All the autocephalous churches (except Jerusalem) were represented by bishops, priests, and laypeople. It was the highest level of church gathering in which Orthodox women had ever participated.[87] The Rhodes assembly grew out of the third pan-Orthodox "preconciliar" conference in Chambésy, Switzerland that took place from October 28 to November 6, 1986. The assembly there desired an official Orthodox statement explaining its refusal to ordain women—assuming that refusal would be the inevitable Orthodox position. Such a statement was to have chiefly an ecumenical and defensive purpose.

---

[83] Ibid., p. 14.

[84] Olga Lossky reports that it was the American Orthodox theologians Alexander Schmemann and John Meyendorff, in conversation with the ecumenical patriarch, who made the Rhodes Consultation happen. *Toward the Endless Day*, p. 242.

[85] See the reports by Amal Dibo, "Discerning the Signs of the Times: Women in the Life of the Orthodox Church. WCC Ecumenical Decade of Churches in Solidarity with Women, Damascus, Syria 1996," *MaryMartha* 5, no. 2 (1997), pp. 36–42, and "Discerning the Signs of the Times: Women in the Life of the Orthodox Church. WCC Ecumenical Decade of Churches in Solidarity with Women, Second Regional Conference, Istanbul, Turkey. May 1997," *MaryMartha* 5, no. 2 (1997), pp. 45–53.

[86] The conference's conclusions alone were published as *Conclusions of the InterOrthodox Consultation on the Place of the Woman in the Orthodox Church and the Question of the Ordination of Women, Rhodes, Greece, 30 Oct.–7 Nov. 1988* (Minneapolis: Light and Life, 1990). The conclusions and all the presentations were published together in *The Place of the Woman in the Orthodox Church and the Question of the Ordination of Women: Interorthodox Symposium, Rhodos, Greece, 30 October–7 November 1988* (ed. Gennadios Limouris; Katerini, Greece: Tertios Publications, 1992).

[87] Behr-Sigel, "L'Ordination des Femmes: Un Problème Oecuménique," p. 113.

The consultation quickly opened up to more concerns than those of women in the priesthood, addressing women's issues in the church across the board, almost a new Agapia with more participants all around and more men in particular. Behr-Sigel comments, "For an attitude purely negative and defensive in the face of the interpolations of modern feminism was substituted—let us hope—a will to common research according to the spirit of a 'creative fidelity' to the gospel and to the authentic *holy Tradition*, concealed too often by human traditions." Furthermore, as a mere "consultation," the Rhodes gathering would have no binding status on any Orthodox church, which had the happy effect of allowing a little more freedom in the discussions.[88]

Noting the irony of the most traditional church on earth gathering to discuss a burning modern question in an "ultra-modern hotel with seventeen floors. A tourist tower of Babel," Behr-Sigel was pleased to see Orthodoxy emerging from its "Byzantine-Slavic and Middle Eastern cocoon."[89] But her perception of its results changed either with time to reflect or the audience she addressed, most likely both. Her first published report on the conference appeared in *Irénikon*, a Belgian ecumenical journal based at the monastery in Chevetogne with the purpose of encouraging "Christians of various traditions to better understand each other, and thereby to grow in mutual respect and esteem, as a first step to serious dialogue."[90] For this readership, Behr-Sigel focuses on the ecumenical potential of the consultation.

For one thing, she emphasizes that no view of the ordination of women enjoys unanimous status even in the Orthodox church. She writes:

> The revelation of this pluralism in the interior of the unity of faith seemed to me to be one of the most positive aspects of this consultation. A source of dynamism, it is opposed to a sclerosis of thought and dogmatic slumber in the face of the questions of the modern secularized world. But the revelation of pluralism in relation, in particular, to the problem of the ordination of women has also surprised and scared a certain number of bishops and theologians. It also appears little in the official text of the conclusions. It is only discernable as a watermark.[91]

She specifies other theologians present who were not so sure that women could never be priests, namely John Erickson[92] and Nicholas Lossky, along with their reasons for thinking so—quite similar to her own. In fact, there was concern that the excessive emphasis on Christ's masculinity signifies, or could lead to, a kind of Nestorianism.[93] The "conclusions" of the consultation came out against the ordination of women but did not call the practice a heresy—for which Behr-Sigel was grateful—and included, to her mind, a good theological anthropology but a faulty Adam/Christ, Eve/Mary typology.

---

[88] Behr-Sigel, "Les Eglises Orthodoxes s'Interrogent sur la Place de la Femme dans l'Eglise," *Irénikon* 61, no. 4 (1988), pp. 523–29 (524). All quotations are my translation.

[89] Ibid., pp. 524–25.

[90] Monastère de Chevetogne website about its journal *Irénikon*, <www.monasterechevetogne.com/index.php?taalkeuze=3> [accessed December 10, 2012].

[91] Behr-Sigel, "Les Eglises Orthodoxes s'Interrogent," p. 526.

[92] See John H. Erickson, "The Priesthood in Patristic Teaching," in *The Place of the Woman in the Orthodox Church*, pp. 103–15.

[93] Behr-Sigel, "Les Eglises Orthodoxes s'Interrogent," p. 527.

Nevertheless, Behr-Sigel's judgment on Rhodes is positive here. The conference opened up the debate and broke the ice. She comments, "Without being too optimistic, I believe that it has contributed to liberating Orthodox theological thought from the neopatristic straitjacket in which it has risked shutting itself away, cut off from the concrete life of men and women of our time."[94] These are strong words for Behr-Sigel, but they are consistent with her constant drumbeat that Orthodoxy must address the questions of the modern world. Whatever else happened, Rhodes proved that Orthodoxy was not as monolithic as previously thought—an important point to make in an ecumenical journal.

In-house, though, Behr-Sigel had a different audience to face and a different attitude to voice. In her report for *Contacts*, she repeats the material from the *Irénikon* piece, but adds a significant amount of editorial commentary.[95]

The delegates at Rhodes, she explains, were divided into three camps. The first group thought that the ordination of women was self-evidently impossible, and that was that. The second group thought it was quite possible indeed. The third group, which Behr-Sigel calls "neo-conservative," agreed with the first group that it wasn't possible but, being acclimated to the Western world, feared to appear misogynist. This third group genuinely desired to eliminate any misogynist practices clinging to the church but also wanted to provide adequate theological reasons for barring women from the altar.

The members of this last group spoke most forcefully, and they carried the day. Unsurprisingly, Evdokimov and Hopko were the leading theological lights for them, although Evdokimov had died 18 years earlier and Hopko was not personally present. For example, Metropolitan Chrysostomos of Myra verges on plagiarism in his use of Evdokimov's *Woman and the Salvation of the World*, lifting phrases right out of the book with only the most meager of citations.[96] His usage of Evdokimov isn't even entirely consistent with his own points. As he develops his anthropology, he writes:

According to the Orthodox Tradition, man and woman are at once *the same* and *different*. They are the same in that both were formed "in the image and likeness

---

[94] Ibid., p. 528.

[95] Behr-Sigel, "La Consultation Interorthodoxe de Rhodes: La Femme dans l'Eglise," *Contacts* 41, no. 2 (1989), pp. 81–93. All quotations are my translation. See also her comments in "The Ordination of Women," in *The Ordination of Women in the Orthodox Church*. Liveris discusses the conference in *Ancient Taboos*, pp. 118–27, and although she does not specify the three "camps," she does notice the heavy emphasis on femininity and masculinity in the proceedings. Kyriaki Karidoyanes FitzGerald's insightful essay, "The Eve-Mary Typology and Women in the Orthodox Church: Reconsidering Rhodes," *Anglican Theological Review* 84, no. 3 (2002), pp. 627–45, demonstrates the intrusion of Western scholastic concepts, which is referred to as "manual theology" or "pseudomorphosis," into the Rhodes conclusions, and highlights how recent the Eve/Mary typology really is—certainly not a venerable old Orthodox maxim. FitzGerald's report, "The Inter-Orthodox Theological Consultation on Women in the Church," *Ecumenical Trends* 18, no. 3 (1989), pp. 33–36, is journalistic rather than theological in nature. She also delivered a paper at the Rhodes consultation, "An Orthodox Assessment of Modern Feminist Theology," which can be found in *The Place of the Woman in the Orthodox Church*, pp. 287–318.

[96] Chrysostomos of Myra, "Priesthood and Women in Ecclesiological Perspective," in *The Place of the Woman in the Orthodox Church*, pp. 117–32.

of God". They are different in that they are endowed with different physical characteristics. This means that they are differentiated as to their male or female physical qualities or properties, which can be neither changed nor exchanged.[97]

Here, and in the paragraphs to follow, Chrysostomos emphasizes the *biological* difference between men and women. But two pages later, when Evdokimov begins to be cited, we suddenly read, "Scripture as a whole raises woman to the rank of a principle." (Behr-Sigel would hardly consider this move an elevation!) The next few pages rely heavily on Evdokimov: women betray their natures in becoming priests, man as priest "penetrates sacramentally," woman's charism is "giving birth" to Christ in the human soul, and so forth.[98] Another speaker, Vlassios Pheidas, rejects the Evdokimov-Hopko ontological connection between women and Spirit but accepts it functionally and typologically.[99]

Accordingly, the third group pushed for the reinstitution of the female diaconate (though with blessing, not ordination), the admission of women to the minor orders of reader, chanter, and subdeacon, and the creation of new offices for women, such as teacher of theology. They decried any persisting taboos attached to "ritual impurity" and recommended careful study of inclusive language and of pauline texts on the submission of women. Discrimination on the basis of sex was categorically condemned. All of this, of course, met with Behr-Sigel's delighted approval; and yet, at the same time, she suspected that underneath the admission of women to the lower orders was "a certain naivete and the persistence in the unconscious—despite solemn denials—of the idea of the *natural* inferiority of women."[100]

In the end, the very arguments Behr-Sigel had been slowly and carefully dismantling over the past dozen years were embraced in the conclusions of the consultation. The noticeably unparallel typological parallel of Adam/Christ, Eve/Mary justified the exclusion of women from the clerical office. The conclusions explain, "The central person in the special ministry of women in the divine plan of salvation is the Mother of God, the Theotokos." It was her *fiat* that released Eve from the bonds of obedience. In Behr-Sigel's judgment, the result is a "banal, naturalistic" mariology that is a model only for women, not for all of sanctified humanity. Such a view of Mary devolves into an instrument of sexual discrimination in the church, splitting men and women up into beings so profoundly different that the resulting vision looks more like the fall than creation.[101]

Furthermore, on trinitarian grounds, Behr-Sigel demurs. She objects:

These *theologoumena* (for it is not a matter of dogmatic verities!) raise nevertheless questions and objections: from the soteriological point of view, far from equalizing them, do they not separate too radically—beyond the distinction

---

[97] Ibid., p. 127. His italics.
[98] Ibid., pp. 130–31.
[99] Vlassios Pheidas, "The Question of the Priesthood of Women," in *The Place of the Woman in the Orthodox Church*, pp. 157–96, especially pp. 175–81.
[100] Behr-Sigel, "La Consultation Interorthodoxe de Rhodes," p. 88.
[101] Behr-Sigel, "L'Ordination des Femmes, un Problème Oecuménique," pp. 115–16.

of the Persons—the economy of the Son from that of the Spirit? In the Orthodox perspective, always trinitarian, the Son and the Spirit are distinct but always act together in a relation of mutuality and reciprocity. It is in the power of the Spirit who reposes upon Him that Christ is the Unique High Priest according to the order of Melchizedek. The Spirit comes upon Mary, but it is to form Christ in her, as He makes Christ, in a different fashion but analogously, in each baptized person, man or woman. The priestly ministry as a representation not crudely realistic but "iconic" of the ministry of Christ is a charism of the Spirit who is invoked in the prayers of ordination. And yet the Spirit "blows where he wills" (John 3:8) without being limited by barriers of race, social condition and sex. He transfigures the differences that are neither erased nor annihilated but that, in the radiance of the Trinitarian Mystery, should be able to express themselves freely, in the same service as well as in different services. Should not the church situate itself in this same liberty of the Spirit that is not anarchy?[102]

Since she had moved away from the Evdokimov-based constructions of gender in the church, Behr-Sigel also had to object to the way femininity was handled in the conclusions. She suggests that the alignment of the Spirit with women and all the implications the "third group" draws from it rest

> upon a confusion between a biological characteristic of which science today has discovered the complexity, and the spiritual reality of which this biology, in the language of a historically given culture, has become the symbol: femininity as signifying the capacity of welcome, openness to others and the Other, openness to the transcendence of a humanity wholly *capax Dei*. Of this spiritual femininity that belongs to the image of God the human male is not deprived, no more than the woman is deprived of the virility of "the violent who seize the kingdom of heaven." (Mt. 11.12)[103]

What is called "feminine" or "masculine" is finally symbolic, not ontological, and both kinds of virtues, if one continues to identify them in this way, are to be practiced by both kinds of humans.

But the femininity-masculinity distinction won at Rhodes all the same; it was the most solid rock available. The historical proofs against women's ordination, by contrast, were decidedly weak. The only three cited in the conclusions are: (1) a brief comment in the obscure Council of Laodicea (*Apostolic Constitutions* III.6.1–2 and III.9.1–4), which was discussed in Afanasiev's essay in *Women and the Priesthood*; (2) a fragment of Tertullian (*De Virginibus Velandis* 9), hardly a favorite thinker among the Orthodox otherwise; and (3) St. Epiphanius's remark, "Since the beginning of the world, no woman has ever served the Lord as priest" (Epiphanius, *Adversus Haereses* 79). If anything, the poverty of the sources testifies to how little the Christian tradition has thought about the subject at all. The conclusions even indirectly acknowledge that the

---

[102] Behr-Sigel, "La Consultation Interorthodoxe de Rhodes," pp. 90–91.
[103] Ibid., p. 91.

biblical witness is not adequate to argue against women in the priesthood.[104] The iconic argument remains decisive: liturgical symbolism demands a male priest. Yet even that decisive argument could not be made quite decisively enough. The conclusions resort to saying:

> We are not simply dealing with theological concepts and ideas. We are in a sphere of profound, almost indescribable experience of the inner ethos of the world-saving and cosmic dimensions of Christian truth. The iconic and typological mode of dealing with the issue tells us that rational constructs will not be adequate to describe and express it fully. Like all of the mysteries of the Faith as lived in Orthodoxy, this one too, is articulated with the fear of God and with a sense of reverence. Yet, *deep in the inner workings of the ethos and Tradition of the Church, we sense that our words are words of truth and not mere apologetics*, and that ignoring the reality of which they speak will not only deny the past reality of the Church, but will deprive all who do so of foundational and essential dimensions of the full Christian experience of life in Christ.[105]

Behr-Sigel is not impressed. Yet she does her best to rein in her own disappointment. She observes:

> It is known that one can say that the same glass of water is either half empty or half full. This image can be applied to the value judgments carried by the Rhodes Consultation. They will be different according to what one expected from it but also according to the static or dynamic perspective where this event is situated. One can hold on to the "conclusions" as they were formulated and consider that they put an end to the debate. One can also, on the contrary, see in the unfolding of this consultation, with its passionate discussions and its provisional conclusions, the first stage in a process of "conscientization" that is only just beginning. It is in this second point of view, consciously, that I would put myself, holding out hope. As its name indicates, the "consultation" of Rhodes was not called upon to make decisions. In its conclusions, it formulated some opinions.[106]

And it is very fortunate, from her point of view, that the conclusions could never be more than mere opinions. There is no denying the improvements that came with Rhodes, but more and better things could still happen. "Some of us," she notes at the end, "believe that in fidelity to the Tradition as the living transmission of the Word of the Living God, creative evolutions are possible."[107]

---

[104] Roman Catholics have admitted the same; see the Pontifical Biblical Commission report, "Can Women Be Priests?" in *Women Priests: A Catholic Commentary on the Vatican Declaration*, pp. 338–46 (ed. Leonard Swidler and Arlene Swidler; New York: Paulist Press, 1977). The Old Catholic-Orthodox dialogue also came to the same conclusion; see the collected papers in *Anglican Theological Review* 84, no. 3 (2002).

[105] "Conclusions of the Consultation," in *The Place of the Woman in the Orthodox Church*, p. 27. My italics.

[106] Behr-Sigel, "La Consultation Interorthodoxe de Rhodes," p. 89.

[107] Ibid., p. 92.

This implies a reform of ecclesiology, based on the koinonia of the Trinity, the living Tradition throughout the years of the church, a vision which is "more historical, less unilaterally platonic, ideal, and idealistic."[108] Behr-Sigel is no longer an idealist. Along with her loss of idealism went the loss of the "new community" motif that had once inspired her so much in ecumenical and feminist conversation.[109] Altogether, Behr-Sigel has come a long way from the ecclesiology that first brought her into the Orthodox church—and into ecumenical dialogue as well.

---

[108] Ibid., p. 89.

[109] In this light, one may wonder whether Behr-Sigel herself gave the title "L'Oecuménisme au Féminin" to a report she wrote for *Oecuménisme Information* 334 (2003), pp. 8–9, long after she had abandoned this kind of language. This very short report is about a conference sponsored by Elisabeth Parmentier on the theme of feminist theology and its challenge to the church, encouraging deeper theological reflection but not the sort of gender-based charisms or new community that characterized Behr-Sigel's early thought. She doesn't use the phrase "feminine ecumenism" in the article itself.

5

After Rhodes

By this point, Behr-Sigel had reached her mature position on the ordination of women. Over the next 15 years or so, her essays on the subject were built of the same blocks, sometimes even using the same phrases and paragraphs, with little additions or deletions here and there depending on her audience. She kept at it until the end of her life, when she "fell asleep in the Lord" at the age of 98 on November 26, 2005.[1]

A momentary lapse in serenity

After Rhodes, Behr-Sigel appeared in public a number of times to speak directly to the issue of the ordination of women, and for these events her most sophisticated essays developed. The first occasion was a colloquium held during November 1989 in Palermo, Sicily, on "Women and Ministry," organized by l'Instituto Costanza Scelfo Barberi of the Catholic Theological Faculty, followed swiftly by the second, the Orthodox Academy of Crete in January 1990 on the subject of "Church and Culture." Her presentations were identical aside from some slight reworking, and a French version with the title "L'Ordination des Femmes: Un Problème Oecuménique. Développements Récents dans la Sphère de l'Eglise Orthodoxe," appeared in *Contacts* in 1990.[2] It covers familiar

---

[1] See the various memorials written about her at <www.pagesorthodoxes.net/saints/behr-sigel/behr-sigel-intro-hommage.htm> [accessed December 10, 2012].

[2] Her French essay, "L'Ordination des Femmes, un Problème Oecuménique," which appeared in *Contacts* 42, no. 2 (1990), pp. 101–27, owes a substantial amount of its content to her German article "Ordination von Frauen?" discussed in ch. 3. Quotations in this section are taken from the *Contacts* article, which was also reprinted in *Kirchen im Kontext unterschiedlicher Kulturen: Auf dem Weg ins dritte Jahrtausend*, pp. 275–94 (ed. Wolfgang Heller; Göttingen: Vandenhoeck und Ruprecht, 1991), and again in *Discerner les Signes du Temps*, pp. 131–52, under the title "Femmes et Sacerdoce: Un Problème Oecuménique, Développements Récents dans la Sphère de l'Eglise Orthodoxe." It was also published in Italian as "Li Ordinazione delle Donne, un Problema Ecumenica," in *Donne e Ministero*, pp. 119–49 (ed. Cettina Militello; Rome: Dehoniane, 1991). An English translation of it, following further reworking by Behr-Sigel, appeared in *Sobornost* 13, no. 1 (1991), pp. 25–40, and was reprinted in *Theology* 97 (1994), pp. 9–26. A much, much shorter version of the English article shows up later as "The Ordination of Women, an Ecumenical Problem," *MaryMartha* 2, no. 2 (1992), pp. 9–11. For more on the Orthodox Academy of Crete in 1990, see Elaine Gounaris

territory. She identifies a need to rethink the issue of women's ordination. Then she recites the history—always reminding the Orthodox of where they have been, since no one besides her was present at every major event—from Chitescu and Khodre's presentations in 1963 at the Commission on Faith and Order in Montreal to the theological triumph of Evdokimov and Hopko at Rhodes in 1988. Throughout, she identifies the same theological problems.

At the end of her essay, she proposes three tasks for Orthodoxy to take on. The first—this one endorsed by Rhodes—is to make a clean sweep and eliminate all the lingering practices based on impurity taboos. The second task is to develop the theology of personhood. This motif, as we have seen, had growing importance in Behr-Sigel's thought. Several times in this essay she cites the explicit, public support she has received for her defense of the ordination of women from Metropolitan Anthony Bloom. The basis for their shared conviction is the "personalism of the Fathers of the Church creatively renewed by the great Franco-Russian contemporary theologian Vladimir Lossky." In Lossky's thought, as Behr-Sigel reports, each person is a

> mysterious totality, unique, unclassifiable, free . . . irreducible to any category— such as sex—in which one would be tempted to enclose him. To affirm this is not to return to denying or devaluing sexuality once again, as was sometimes the temptation of certain Greek Fathers. The person transcends sex without annihilating it on the level of the creature, that is to say, on the level of the concrete human being.[3]

And this leads to the third task—to ask, what kind of priesthood is the Christian priesthood? It must bear some connection to personhood, especially when the priest is said to "represent" the person of Christ. As usual, Behr-Sigel rejects a naturalistic kind of representation, which doesn't do justice to this rich Losskyian vision of

---

Hanna, "Crete Consultation Report," *MaryMartha* 1, no. 1 (1991), pp. 3–4; the consultation's own report, "Orthodox Women's Consultation, Orthodox Academy of Crete, January 1990. Church and Culture: Ministry, Human Sexuality, Participation and Decision Making," *MaryMartha* 1, nos 1–3 (1991–92), pp. 3–7; and the discussion by Liveris in *Ancient Taboos*, pp. 140–45. Liveris in particular praises Behr-Sigel for her work. "[H]er papers written since Agapia indicate a development in her scholarship, theologically, anthropologically and sociologically, that is of considerable assistance to any scholar wishing to investigate the issue of women's ministry in the Orthodox churches. She has provided a resource, unusual for the Orthodox layperson, that is readable and accessible especially by those not theologically educated. Her work is certainly not the definitive statement on women's ministry, but she goes much further and is much bolder than writers from America, for instance, in raising the issue of ministry and participation of women to that of the 'royal priesthood equal to that of laymen,'" p. 143. Hopko was the only male delegate at Crete, presenting his paper "God and Gender: Human Sexuality from an Orthodox Perspective," which was later published as "God and Gender: Articulating the Orthodox View."

[3] Behr-Sigel, "L'Ordination des Femmes, un Problème Oecuménique," p. 122. All quotations are my translation. Behr-Sigel's appreciation of the personalism of Vladimir Lossky has its roots, at least in part, in Clément's book, *Orient-Occident—Deux Passeurs*. Cf. Behr-Sigel's "Developments in Orthodox Theology in Western Europe" (unpublished), delivered at the Prague conference on "Doing Theology in Different Contexts" in 1988, published in French as "Développements de la Théologie Orthodoxe en Europe Occidentale," *Supplément Service Orthodoxe de Presse* 131-C (1988), pp. 1–5.

personhood, in favor of one that can recognize the face of Christ in women as well as in men.[4]

This article drew the fire of one M.-J. Monsaingeon.[5] A recent convert to Orthodoxy, he was distressed at the suggestion of women priests coming not only from Behr-Sigel but from Metropolitan Anthony Bloom as well. An Orthodox priest is not like a Protestant pastor, he argues: the priest is not only the *representative* of Christ but also the *representation* of Christ. "This uncontested fact," he writes, "is the incontrovertible reason against the ordination of women to the priesthood."[6] Furthermore, he writes, young men don't seek out the priesthood but are tapped for it by spiritual fathers, who persuade them to the office despite their initial resistance. A woman who feels herself called, without anyone to call her, is automatically suspect. Women priests would also be an insurmountable block to ecumenical rapprochement with Rome (he assumes, evidently, that Rome will never change its mind either). However, Monsaingeon finds women eminently suitable as deacons, who could quite happily and beneficially live out their Christian vocations in such works of mercy, especially in bringing the consecrated bread and wine to invalids after the parish liturgy.

Behr-Sigel's response to Monsaingeon is the angriest one she ever commits to paper. Apparently even Orthodox serenity has its limits!

She begins with a note of skepticism about the "idyllic vision" of "always humble" men who "would only accept access to this holy ministry under constraint and force."[7] From there she moves to a clarification of her own position—that she has "never affirmed that women have the *right* to 'demand'" access to the priesthood. As we have seen, Behr-Sigel never actually petitioned the Orthodox church to ordain women, even while she methodically dismantled the arguments against excluding them. Nor did she ever endorse feminist "aggression," as her comments about Sheffield reveal. Time and again she suggested the practice be treated as a matter of local discipline to be solved by the churches as need and desire allow.

The theological basis for her practical stance is that priesthood ultimately belongs to God, to Jesus Christ, the "unique High Priest, the unique mediator between God and humanity." It is the grace of the "Christ *philanthropos . . .* to associate people [*les hommes*], human persons [*les personnes humaines*], with his redemptive and sanctifying work." The association is extended first and foremost to all the baptized (1 Pet. 2.5), "the *common* priestly vocation of the people of God."[8] From there, a "specific ministry" is extended to "*some people*" in organic continuity with the royal priesthood.[9] She rallies to her defense Lev Gillet, who taught that clerical priesthood "is not of an essence other than the priesthood of all the faithful, but [the priests] have a special mission of the Church to express and exercise the universal priesthood," a citation taken from

<hr>

4 Behr-Sigel, "L'Ordination des Femmes, un Problème Oecuménique," p. 122.
5 M.-J. Monsaingeon, "A Propos du Rôle de la Femme dans l'Eglise," *Contacts* 42 (1990), pp. 224–25.
6 Ibid., p. 224. My translation.
7 Behr-Sigel, "A Propos de l'Ordination des Femmes (Réponse à Monsieur Monsaingeon)," *Contacts* 42, no. 4 (1990), pp. 299–303 (299). All quotations are my translation.
8 Ibid., pp. 299–300. Her italics.
9 Ibid., p. 300. Her italics.

his book *L'Offrande Liturgique*.[10] Though she doesn't cite it by name, another of Gillet's books, *Sois Mon Prêtre*, is likely also in the background of her remarks. In her review of this second book in 1963, she particularly praised its emphasis on the continuity of the royal and clerical priesthoods, and their mutual distinction from the unique high priesthood of Christ, as well as the rich description of the gifts and calling of priests. In this review she sees the ecumenical potential of defining priesthood this way rather than through classic dogmatic disputes, but it is also clear that everything she and Gillet mention could apply equally well to women in the priesthood, and it is likely that this basic understanding of the priesthood is in the background of her later writings on the ordination of women.[11]

The spiritual leaders of the church, then, discern other likely candidates for this public priesthood, especially seeking "the charisms which predispose one to the exercise of these specific ministries, to verify the authenticity of an interior call that could be an illusion."[12]

Here now is the nub of the question. Behr-Sigel asks,

> [I]s one entitled to declare in advance, on account of the single criterion of sex, that a woman, a mysterious human person, a baptized person who, in baptism, has "put on" Christ (according to the ancient baptismal hymn of the epistle to the Galatians), who being chrismated has received the seal of the gift of the Holy Spirit, could not, in any case, receive the call from God to the specific sacerdotal ministry? Why would this ministry, distinct according to the function but of the same essence as the common sacerdotal ministry, be reserved solely to humans of the masculine sex?[13]

Monsaingeon, in keeping with the one remaining argument against female priesthood universally invoked by its Orthodox opponents, says that women are not in the image of Christ, which is essential for the exercise of priestly ministry, especially at the eucharist. For the first time Behr-Sigel, in denying the naturalistic aspects of icons and images, suggests that the same principle would require a circumcised Jew to celebrate the eucharist; or even that only circumcised Jews could *receive* the

---

10   Ibid., p. 300, quoting A Monk of the Eastern Church [Lev Gillet], *L'Offrande Liturgique* (Paris: n.p., 1988), pp. 72–73. Around the same time, Behr-Sigel wrote a review of *Myriam et Israel: Le Mystère de l'Epouse* by Marie-Thérèse Huguet, a Catholic thinker, in *Paix* 63, no. 3 (1990), pp. 72–73. In the light of Jewish-Christian dialogue, the book rings familiar notes from Evdokimov's theology, proposing different kinds of Christian being for women and men, the former being charismatic and the latter institutional. Behr-Sigel traces this line of thought to Louis Bouyer, whose work she had criticized many years earlier. Her characteristically gentle concluding judgment is: "Even if for reasons of a theological order, in particular the theology of the priesthood and theological anthropology, I cannot follow her in a line of argumentation that opposes the access of women to a public ordained ministry in the church, I appreciate her rich and nuanced thought." My translation, p. 73. Once again it is the underlying theology of the priesthood that troubles her as much as the specific denial of it to women.

11   Behr-Sigel, review of *Sois Mon Prêtre*, by A Monk of the Eastern Church, *Contacts* 15 (1963), pp. 69–71.

12   Behr-Sigel, "A Propos de l'Ordination des Femmes," p. 300.

13   Ibid., pp. 300–01.

eucharist. Of course, this is absurd. And in any event, there already *is* a circumcised Jewish male presiding at the eucharist: Jesus Christ, himself truly present, who did not qualify for the priesthood under Jewish law but rather became "High Priest according to the order of Melchizedek . . . also the God-Man who, assuming the totality of the human, has elevated it with himself to heaven, introduced it in the divine sphere, there where there is no more separation but only communion of persons in the communion of the *agape* of the divine Persons."[14]

A better and more accurate image for the celebrating priest, then, is not Christ the bridegroom, but the friend of the bridegroom (Jn 3.29) whose role is joy, fidelity, and devotion to the bridegroom. Here is a fine example of Behr-Sigel's positioning herself within the Tradition, invoking the imagery of Scripture to challenge a tradition that no longer witnesses accurately to the Orthodox faith. She writes, "To respond to the great challenges of modernity and to its profound spiritual needs means that we Christians must not barricade ourselves behind formulas and symbols literally but superficially interpreted, but to re-root ourselves creatively in the Gospel and in the authentic Tradition."[15]

Other Orthodox women respond

By now Behr-Sigel had gained some allies of her own. She was active in organizing official conversations among the Orthodox in France regarding the status of women. She got a chance to share her findings along with her friend Nicole Maillard when the WCC undertook a project to examine the world religions' attitudes toward women.[16] The WCC's Sub-unit on Women solicited reports from representatives of eight countries. These initial studies examined only the scriptural documents and beliefs accepted by the faithful of each religion with reference to what they said about women. They did not report upon actual practice or women's experience.

Thus, when the results were in, a desire grew to find out what women actually experienced, how much they were a part of the interpretation of their own Scriptures, and the emotional impact of the religion on women's attitudes toward their bodies and their sexuality. Behr-Sigel and Maillard, therefore, were invited to respond to the original paper written by an Orthodox scholar from Romania, Anca-Lucia Manolache. Manolache mainly discusses Romanian state and canon laws regarding women, nearly all of which are negative. She suggests the time is ripe for a change, though she considers it unfair to say that Christianity has done nothing to improve the status of women in society.[17]

---

[14] Ibid., pp. 301–02.

[15] Ibid., p. 303.

[16] The study was the result both of reflection on the "Community of Women and Men in the Church" series discussed in ch. 2 and the United Nations Decade for Women (1976–85). The WCC sponsored its own decade for women in response to the UN's under the name "Ecumenical Decade 1988–1998: Churches in Solidarity with Women." See the "Introduction" by Marie Assaad in *Women, Religion and Sexuality*, pp. ix–xii. Behr-Sigel reviewed the book in *Contacts* 43 (1991), pp. 76–77.

[17] Anna-Lucia Manolache, "Orthodoxy and Women: A Romanian Perspective," in *Women, Religion and Sexuality*, pp. 172–83.

Behr-Sigel and Maillard, interestingly, are not impressed with what Christianity has managed in society so far. They take Manolache's supposition that society *first* has to ripen for change first to be too generous. They write:

> We believe there is no genuine inner conversion unless it is also translated into a new way of being and acting, that is, into new outward attitudes. The question of whether Jesus came to change hearts or to overturn unjust social relations strikes us as a non-issue. The church does not have to wait for *"the proper moment in history"* as though structures ripened of their own accord. The Holy Spirit is at work yesterday, tomorrow . . . and today![18]

Certainly, inadequate scientific knowledge had something to do with the low regard in which women were held—as mere auxiliaries to procreation, made impure by their flow of blood—but Jesus and the patristic witness provided ample material for overcoming such attitudes. Behr-Sigel and Maillard admit that the situation is quite a bit better in France than in Romania, from personal relationships to theological education. The latter especially is a vital deterrent to distorted exegesis, such as the kind of mariology that becomes "a straitjacket of the worst kind for women, as when 'Mary, humble servant of the Lord' is all too quickly interpreted to mean 'women, be humble servants of your husbands or of men in general!'"[19] Behr-Sigel's usual mariological point comes out by contrast: the Theotokos is active, not passive, in welcoming the Spirit, and as such is a model for women and men alike.

In response to Manolache's distressed report that Romanian women have often internalized and therefore perpetuated their secondary status, Behr-Sigel and Maillard bring to light a French version of such women whom they call "elegant intellectuals." These women "do in fact exercise power of a more or less hidden sort, using charm and seduction. These women would feel they were denying their 'femininity' if instead they could play an officially recognized role—which would then, of course, be open to scrutiny by everyone."[20] Perhaps it is more Maillard's insight than Behr-Sigel's, since this theme appears nowhere else in the latter's work. But it does introduce another angle on the ordination of women question. Although women's constant presence in church, often in greater numbers than men, is cited as proof enough of their welcome, their *unacknowledged* power may be, in reality, a detriment to church life. Such power cannot and should not be eliminated, but it ought to be acknowledged and regulated.

However much better the situation is compared to Romania, even the French Orthodox still endure ritual taboos perpetuated, for instance, in the churching of women. The authors admit that there *may* have once been a sensible rationale, such as assuring women that they are not unclean after the blood of childbirth or even acknowledging the tremendous act of giving birth. Whatever the meaning once was, though, it is no longer interpreted correctly in modern French culture. And there is

---

[18] Behr-Sigel, "Orthodoxy and Women in France," p. 185.
[19] Ibid., p. 187.
[20] Ibid., p. 188.

even less justification for the different treatment of baby boys and girls presented in church. The two women are astonished:

> How is one to explain the existence in the church of all these discriminations, taboos and rites? Is it not true that in Christ there is neither male nor female? That everything without exception is renewed in Christ and illuminated by Christ? Why, then, do so many grey areas remain among us, as though we somehow wanted to withhold them from God's infinite love?[21]

Then comes a fresh critical insight into the underlying theology. "In fact," they write,

> it is as though the Orthodox continued to believe that there are two orders of the Holy, even after Jesus Christ: the cosmic, natural holy order which is supposed to include eros, and the holy order of God's kingdom, the eschaton, life in Christ through the Holy Spirit. Woman is unconsciously assimilated in the cosmic, natural order of the Holy. At most she may participate in the holy order of Christ's kingdom if she is consecrated and a virgin, or humble and submissive in the extreme.[22]

If this is the case, then the churching of women, for instance, is not meant to indicate "moral contempt" for the woman but to return her from the cosmic sacred to the eschatological sacred. It is an "unconsciously dualistic approach to reality and life. Orthodox Christianity, like all popular religions, is syncretistic in character. It is a mixture of gospel and ancient beliefs."[23]

Behr-Sigel and Maillard's conclusion, then, is that the priests and bishops must teach the faithful what is truly of the gospel and what is not. The inculturation of the gospel inevitably means collecting some syncretistic elements along the way, but the call always remains to return to the purity of the gospel.[24] Even the church fathers, who were not above making misogynistic remarks, surprise with their unexpected praise of women or exhortations of husbands to love their wives tenderly without abuse.[25]

Starting in 1992, Behr-Sigel established a relationship with the Orthodox women's journal *MaryMartha*.[26] Leonie B. Liveris, the editor, received a grant from the WCC to publish the journal, more like a newsletter, collecting articles in English and French from around the world pertaining to Orthodox women's issues. Liveris herself had a choppy relationship with the Orthodox church: she was a convert, unprepared for the second-class status she would find there, a perpetual outsider since her Orthodox community in Australia was composed largely of Greek immigrants, and frequently

---

[21] Ibid., p. 189.
[22] Ibid., pp. 189–90.
[23] Ibid., p. 190.
[24] Ibid.
[25] Ibid., p. 191.
[26] The issues are now archived online at <http://members.iinet.net.au/~mmjournl/MaryMartha/> [accessed December 10, 2012].

dismissed for her outspokenness on the grounds that she wasn't Orthodox enough. Nevertheless, for about six years, *MaryMartha* was the clearinghouse for all things pertaining to Orthodoxy and women, and that put Liveris in good stead for writing a history of feminism in the Orthodox church.[27]

Behr-Sigel and Liveris had the opportunity to meet in person at the first of four conferences on "Feminine Images and Orthodox Spirituality" held at the Ecumenical Institute in Bossey in May and June of 1992.[28] Part of the WCC's Ecumenical Decade of Churches in Solidarity with Women, at each event "Orthodox, Protestant and Roman Catholic women spoke about their own vocation in the church."[29] As Behr-Sigel saw it, the seminar helped non-Orthodox understand the role women play in the Orthodox church, which is often assumed to be "patriarchal," indeed "misogynist," and they achieved genuine dialogue about divisive issues between Orthodox and Protestants in particular. The Protestants gained a better understanding of the veneration of Mary and the saints, the role of nuns, priests' wives, female iconographers and theologians, and "simple mothers of a family." The Orthodox women, for their part, were open to hearing feminist questions and concerns, sometimes even sharing them, and learned about feminist hermeneutics. It is noteworthy here that Behr-Sigel basically equates Protestant with feminist. The "diaspora" Orthodox played the vital role of translation between those from traditionally Orthodox countries and those who were theologically and geographically Westerners.[30] Interestingly, among those present was George Khodre, who wrote one of the first essays against the ordination of women for the Faith and Order conference in 1963.

Behr-Sigel's presentation at Bossey opens with a trinitarian vision:

> What I want to give you is a sort of testament, an evaluation of fifteen years of struggle for the church to become a little more of what it is in the mind of our God, One in three persons: a community, or rather a communion of persons in his likeness, men and women ineffably different but equal in dignity, free and responsible, under the inspiration of the Holy Spirit.[31]

She goes on to speak of her own experiences in the Orthodox church, admitting that even in her twenties when she joined she knew she "could hope for no sacramental, public ministry. I regretted this, but accepted the rule without finding complete

---

[27] Liveris, *Ancient Taboos*. Behr-Sigel figures as something of a hero in the book, along with American scholar Eva Catafygiotu Topping.

[28] See Liveris, "Seminar Report: Feminine Images and Orthodox Spirituality Seminar, Ecumenical Institute, Bossey May 1992," *MaryMartha* 2, no. 2 (1992), pp. 12–13.

[29] Terry Pirri-Simonian, "Guest Editorial," *Ecumenical Review* 60, nos 1–2 (2008), pp. 1–6 (2).

[30] Behr-Sigel, "Images Féminines et Spiritualité Orthodoxe: Institut Oecuménique de Bossey: 24 Mai au 3 Juin 1992," *Bulletin de la Crypte* 205 (1992), p. 17; reprinted as "Institut Oecuménique de Bossey: Seminaire sur 'Images Féminines & Spiritualité Orthodoxe,'" *L'Alliance* (new series) 9 (1992), pp. 24–25. Note that this French report is *not* the same as the English essay with the same title, "Feminine Images and Orthodox Spirituality," first published posthumously in *Ecumenical Review* 60, nos 1–2 (2008), pp. 7–15, which is Behr-Sigel's keynote address at the Bossey seminar.

[31] Behr-Sigel, "Feminine Images and Orthodox Spirituality," p. 7. The introductory note stating that Behr-Sigel "joined the Orthodox Church on marriage" is incorrect. In fact, she met André Behr for the first time on the day she was received into the Orthodox church!

justification for it."[32] Contrary to outsiders' general views, though, Behr-Sigel reports that she found the Orthodox church a place welcoming and affirming to women. She compliments Evdokimov for his role in opening up the discussion about sexuality, even if she "had to criticize certain views concerning the 'Eternel féminin' put forward by my friend Pavlik, views that seemed to me to be marked by a somewhat mystifying romanticism."[33] She also expresses regret at the stalemate in the conversation over the ordination of women.

> The chance to institute a real dialogue between the Orthodox and spokeswomen for western feminism seems to me to have been lost, except in some individual cases such as mine, and this through the fault of both sides: a lack of preparation, and above all a lack of interest on the part of Orthodox theologians who came from countries where research and theological debate have, for decades, been frozen or non-existent; passion, impatience and sometimes complacency on the part of western feminists who reckoned to impose their views, presenting as a work of the Holy Spirit an ideology of the rights of men and women elaborated without any real participation on the part of the Orthodox and felt by them as offensive; their church being denounced as archaic and misogynist.[34]

She then reviews various attempts within Orthodoxy to deal with questions about women, such as those by Olivier Clément and Eva Catafygiotu Topping, and concludes with her by-now standard inclusive reading of the significance of the Theotokos: Mary is "the sign of a vocation to spiritual maternity—the birth in each man and woman of the new man in Christ, which is the vocation of the whole of humanity, called to become the whole Christ."[35]

Two years later, Behr-Sigel (along with another French Orthodox, Nicolas Lossky) gave a brief interview reprinted in *MaryMartha* on how "women-priests" were viewed by the Orthodox. Behr-Sigel's comments were more distilled than usual. "What shocks me," she says, "in the refusal of female priesthood is that it is disputed whether a woman could receive the gifts of ordination. For, after all, priesthood comes from Christ!"[36] One would not want to suggest that a female body somehow repels the gifts of the Spirit. The iconic argument is mentioned, of course, and Behr-Sigel challenges the analogy again.

> This concept is inspired by the idea of the carnal relation where the man sows the seed and the woman receives it. This symbol of the Christ-Spouse is an image that says that the Church is totally dependent and receptive in relation to Christ; this is true. That being said, this symbol is not to be taken as a biological or

---

[32] Ibid., p. 8.

[33] Ibid.

[34] Ibid., pp. 11–12.

[35] Ibid., p. 15.

[36] Jean Mercier, "Interviews d'Elisabeth Behr-Sigel et de Nicolas Lossky: Les Femmes-Prêtres Vues par des Orthodoxes," *MaryMartha* 3 (1994), pp. 24–25. All quotations are my translation.

anthropological reality. What is more, the priest does not represent Christ but the Church.[37]

That is to say, the epiclesis expresses more solidarity between priest and people than between priest and Lord. As always, Behr-Sigel is unwilling to deny genuine differences—of psychological and biological kinds, to be specific—but these differences do not prevent men and women from exercising the same function; they only mean that men and women will exercise it in a different manner. "It is necessary to guard against enclosing man and woman in ontological definitions: happily, the defects and human qualities are equally distributed!"[38] This is the heart of the debate about priesthood where theological anthropology is concerned. For herself, Behr-Sigel only hopes that her ideas will not be labeled heretical, even if they are not accepted, and she proposes disciplinary pluralism once again.

Alongside the enthusiastic acclaim she received from Liveris and company, Behr-Sigel had her critics too, generally more sophisticated in their critiques than the aforementioned Monsaingeon. It *is* something of a surprise, though, that among them was Verna F. Harrison, a leading female Orthodox patristics scholar.

Harrison's essay, "Orthodox Arguments Against the Ordination of Women as Priests," which was later to be published in the revised edition of *Women and the Priesthood*, first appeared in *Sobornost* and included some observations about internal issues in the Orthodox church omitted from the book version.[39] Harrison mentions *MaryMartha*, the Rhodes Consultation, the Orthodox Academy of Crete, and a week-long summer institute at St. Vladimir's in the United States on the subject of women in the church in June 1991: all evidence of the pertinence of her subject and the plethora of Orthodox attention being given to it. Harrison agrees that not only more attention but better and deeper thought on the subject are required, and asserts that what is being discussed is not, finally, the practice of ordaining women but deeper matters of theological anthropology and the trinitarian nature. She regrets the polarization already developing: some people thought it was outrageous that St. Vladimir's should have a conference on the subject at all—without even knowing what position would be taken on any issue—while at the other extreme Eva Catafygiotu Topping's feminist stance has, in Harrison's view, simply alienated most of the faithful.

Furthermore, with a historical rigor that exceeds Behr-Sigel's own work (Behr-Sigel generally relied on secondary sources for her patristic material), Harrison demonstrates that the Christ/male, Spirit/female connection proposed by Evdokimov and uplifted by Hopko is utterly without patristic grounding. She calls attention to Hopko's poor use of sources (a bad dissertation on John Chrysostom, for instance) as well as some of his earlier comments commending the natural subordination of women and suggesting that female sainthood itself is a compromise for a fallen world. By contrast, Harrison says, gender plays no part in patristic thinking; the apophatic principle prevents its

---

[37]   Ibid.

[38]   Ibid.

[39]   Verna F. Harrison, "Orthodox Arguments against the Ordination of Women as Priests," *Sobornost* 14, no. 1 (1992), pp. 6–24. A slightly shorter version appears in *Women and the Priesthood*, rev. edn, pp. 165–87. Quotations here are taken from the *Sobornost* version.

introduction into the divine. Gender is not central to humanity, either. The irony is that both feminist theologians who want a female Person of God to promote women's power in the church, and their conservative opponents who want a feminized Holy Spirit to keep women out of the clerical office, have inadvertently joined forces—and are equally mistaken.[40]

Curiously, when Harrison considers the question of women in the priesthood, she concludes that it is impossible; but the wind goes out of her sails as she does so. She notices that the priest in the epicletic orans position is more like the classic image of woman than man; she suggests that the priest most of all resembles the Theotokos; and she recalls that the church is not only the bride of Christ (apparently feminine) but also the body of Christ (apparently masculine). All of these points drive toward Behr-Sigel's position, but Harrison draws back at the last second. The best explanation she can muster is that the priest allegorically represents the body of Christ (note: not Christ as such, nor is it the congregation that allegorically represents the body of Christ), and this requires male symbolism. Harrison, then, was no friend of the Rhodes Consultation's theological rationale for prohibiting the ordination of women. It appears that she took up the issue in this article precisely to counter the endorsement of women's ordination by Metropolitan Anthony Bloom in Great Britain and Behr-Sigel herself in France. Or perhaps her weak comments were the closest she could get to commending Behr-Sigel's position without calling down the fire on her own head.

Behr-Sigel was swift to answer the challenge, one she considered "intelligent and thoughtful," "irenic" and "serious."[41] In many respects, in fact, she finds Harrison a helpful ally, especially in countering the theological anthropology undergirding the usual arguments against ordaining women. "But then," Behr-Sigel notes with some surprise, "suddenly [Harrison] performs a volte-face." Harrison opposes Behr-Sigel's arguments *for* the ordination of women "with two 'Orthodox arguments'" *against* it, the apparent implication being that Behr-Sigel's own arguments are not quite Orthodox enough—a common enough move in this debate. The two winning Orthodox arguments for Harrison are Tradition and liturgical symbolism. Behr-Sigel appreciates at least that Harrison has successfully shown that Orthodox opposition to women in the priesthood need not be the reflexive reaction of "obscurantism, archaism, and misogyny." But in the end Behr-Sigel still finds Harrison's arguments wanting.[42]

The first problem is in how Harrison defines Tradition: at once "too wide, too vague, and yet too narrow." Harrison speaks of Tradition as the communion of love and prayer of the church through time and space, but Behr-Sigel wonders where the objective grounding of this psychological description of the church lies. Harrison uplifts the continuity of the liturgical tradition, and the way in which all its minute details have significance, and yet Behr-Sigel wonders again where the Scriptures belong in this tradition; Harrison does not mention them. What it comes down to is this: is the maleness of the priest a matter of the *catholic* Tradition of the church, on the level

---

[40] Harrison, "Orthodox Arguments against the Ordination of Women as Priests," p. 13.
[41] Behr-Sigel, "'The Ordination of Women: An Ecumenical Problem': A Reply to a Reply," trans. Anthony Greenan, *Sobornost* 15, no. 1 (1993), pp. 20–26 (20).
[42] Ibid., p. 20.

of doctrine? Or is it a matter of local church practice, a tradition within the Tradition? Behr-Sigel finds that Harrison provides no criteria for distinguishing between Tradition and traditions. And if the Scriptures are missing from this description of Tradition, the Holy Spirit is even more so—specifically the "life-giving power of the Spirit which breathes reality into what might otherwise become an obsession with the letter, ritualism and a simple repetition of the past."[43] Behr-Sigel worries that Harrison's model of Tradition preserves the past for its own sake and in the process forgets Jesus' promise to lead his followers into all truth, into the future (Jn 16.12–14). For Behr-Sigel, as for Evdokimov, the women's movement is a "sign of the times," a call to the church to enact, at long last, the proclamation of Gal. 3.28.

As for liturgical symbolism, Behr-Sigel again agrees with Harrison that many things happen on many levels: the priest symbolizes both the people and Christ, and in his role he exercises not only these symbolic functions but also pastoral responsibility and authority. Thus women are excluded from the latter as much as the former in denying them the priesthood. The reason the priest, that is, the local pastor, celebrates the eucharist is because of his calling to guide and protect the flock and its unity, following Christ's example in washing their feet. "What is important," Behr-Sigel says, "is the reality of this service, and not the gender of the person who is charged to do it. Shall a woman be declared in advance incapable of carrying it out because she is a woman? If this is what we claim, are we not falling into the functional stereotypes, male and female, so rightly criticised by Verna Harrison?"[44]

If anything, Behr-Sigel is perplexed by the about-face on Harrison's part. There is nothing in the New Testament to suggest that charisms are distributed according to gender, or that offices are linked to gender imagery; with which Harrison agrees. The priesthood itself is damaged when its *sine qua non* is masculinity.

> If we are not to impoverish the meaning of the priesthood and risk turning it into a disincarnate symbol, a simple role in a liturgical drama, without any relationship to the reality of church life, it is vital to make clear the link between the celebration of the Eucharist and the function of the pastor of the community, a humble and great service, which—as Verna Harrison states—is often performed by women today.[45]

In short, the reductive insistence on the liturgical symbolism (which is a recent emphasis, Behr-Sigel adds) ends up shortchanging the priesthood itself. The connection between the priest's love for the parish and his place in the celebration of the liturgy is much more vital to the communication of the gospel than his gender.

What then does the maleness of the priest liturgically convey? Interestingly, Harrison herself rejects the connection between the maleness of Christ and the maleness of the priest, and does so on Cappadocian grounds—it is too threatening to the anthropological unity required by "what is not assumed is not healed." Instead,

---

[43] Ibid., p. 21.
[44] Ibid., p. 23.
[45] Ibid., p. 24.

maleness is a symbol, whose meaning is transcendence, best expressed in nuptial images. As Behr-Sigel describes Harrison's view, we should see in

> the Father (of whom the Son is the image) the absolute donor and the bridegroom, from whom the creature, the bride, receives all that she is—all her life . . . In this perspective, all creation, all mankind, men and women, is symbolically female in its relationship to God, as some Fathers of the Church would hold. As far as the spiritual message is concerned, I agree completely. However, if taken literally, does not this symbolism of the marriage appear to be tied to an interpretation of the biological process of procreation, which is now out-of-date and known to be incorrect? The female, as we now know, is not merely the soil in which the male plants the seed. She makes her own contribution, without which the child, the fruit of both, cannot come about. If we wish to preserve, as I do, the ancient biblical symbolism of the marriage between God and his people, we must see in it, without interpreting the terms too rigidly, the symbol of the communion, through grace, with the God of Love, which is the vocation of mankind, and thus of every man and every woman.[46]

Thus Behr-Sigel gladly grants the *meaning* of the symbolism. The problem is with the symbol itself—it no longer conveys what it used to convey. Not only has improved science altered its meaning, but cultural conditions have changed so drastically that, increasingly, the male-only priesthood conveys quite the opposite of what it once intended to.

It is vital to recognize the specificity of Behr-Sigel's objection here. She is not launching a hermeneutical attack on *all* symbols, as other theologians such as Sallie McFague have done. It is a specific critique of cultural assumptions about femininity, not a general critique of the ability of symbols and metaphors to convey truths about the divine. Her concerns are analogous to those of Paul Evdokimov in his critique of certain uses of the Ephesians 5 marital imagery, which assumes a good and loving marriage, not just any marriage in general (and certainly not a bad one). The details make a difference to the import of the symbol. If the details of femininity in an ecclesial symbol are wrong—assuming a passive reproductive role and mutable personal qualities—then the whole intent of the symbol can falter and even fail. Behr-Sigel judges that feminine and masculine imagery in the clerical and royal priesthoods has, indeed, failed.

Final thoughts on the matter

Behr-Sigel's thorough and most mature essay on the subject, "The Ordination of Women: Also a Question for the Orthodox Churches,"[47] follows much the same order

---

[46] Ibid.

[47] The essay first appeared in French as "L'Ordination des Femmes: Une Question Posée Aussi aux Eglises Orthodoxes," in *Communion et Réunion: Mélanges Jean-Marie Roger Tillard*, pp. 363–87 (ed. Gillian R. Evans and Michel Gourgues; Leuven: Leuven University Press, 1995). Portions reprinted

and logic as her previous piece, "The Ordination of Women: An Ecumenical Problem." The new one includes considerably more detail and discussion of the theological puzzles posed and also incorporates previous studies, such as her review of *Women and the Priesthood*.

What stands out in this new essay? Taking up her insights from the exchange with Verna Harrison, Behr-Sigel penetrates the problem of gender-based anthropological arguments about the priesthood's liturgical symbolism. Women, in this line of thought, are not degraded but honored as paragons of holiness to which all people (thus men too) should aspire, but the sideways result is that priesthood, divorced from this particular concern for holiness of being, becomes "essentially symbolic and risks being reduced to a formal ritual function."[48] She mentions John Erickson's presentation at the Rhodes Consultation. He found that in patristic thought, the clergy played not only the part of *hiereus* ("priest") but also "*proestos, prostamenos, didaskalos, mystagogos, latrostes psyches*" ("presider, superior, teacher, initiator into mysteries, physician of souls").[49] One would hardly say that women are naturally incapable of exercising any of the latter offices. It turns out that excluding women from the priesthood on the grounds that priesthood is chiefly a matter of liturgical symbolism results in a terrible impoverishment of the priesthood—for *male* priests!

It is no surprise, of course, that Behr-Sigel traces the valuation of women's holiness and simultaneous exclusion from priesthood to Paul Evdokimov. But her critique of him here is at its most nuanced and precise. She writes:

> Evdokimov was a married theologian and he was haunted by the enigmatic figure of one of the great 19th century Russian theologians, Alexander Bukharev, an early example of a "monk returned to the world" there to live out an "inward monasticism." Evdokimov was attempting to rehabilitate the sexual dimension of the human person. It was, according to him, a neglected dimension, indeed, a dimension despised by certain forms of "inhuman asceticism," underlaid by the Platonic dualism of body/spirit which has infected Christianity. This preoccupation

---

as "L'Ordination de Femmes: La Consultation de Rhodes," *Unité des Chrétiens* 107 (1997), pp. 12–13. Translated into Russian in *Strantsi* 4, no. 1 (1999), pp. 24–32 and 4, no. 2 (1999), pp. 190–200. It was reprinted in French in a book jointly authored by Behr-Sigel and Kallistos (Timothy) Ware, entitled *L'Ordination de Femmes dans l'Eglise Orthodoxe*, pp. 17–50 (Paris: Cerf, 1998), along with another essay by Behr-Sigel, "Les Femmes dans l'Eglise Orthodoxe," pp. 7–16. This book was published in English as *The Ordination of Women in the Orthodox Church*. Behr-Sigel's two essays therein are entitled, "The Ordination of Women: Also a Question for the Orthodox Churches," pp. 11–48, and "Women in the Orthodox Church," pp. 1–10, which latter was also published in *The St. Nina Quarterly* 2, no. 2 (1998), pp. 1, 8–11. An essay extremely similar to "L'Ordination des Femmes: Une Question Posée Aussi aux Eglises Orthodoxes" was published as "L'Ordination des Femmes: Un Point Chaud du Dialogue Oecuménique," in *Contacts* 53, no. 3 (2001), pp. 236–52; it will be discussed below. To the book he coauthored with Behr-Sigel, Ware contributed "Man, Woman, and the Priesthood of Christ," a revision of the essay he first published in the 1984 edition of *Woman and the Priesthood*. It is this same revision that shows up in the revised edition of *Woman and the Priesthood* in 1999; it is substantially different from his essay in the first edition, which does not appear at all in the revised edition.

48 Behr-Sigel, "The Ordination of Women: Also a Question for the Orthodox Churches," in *The Ordination of Women in the Orthodox Church*, p. 15.

49 Ibid., p. 42.

causes him to tend in places towards a view of all persons as being determined by their sex, which stands in contradiction to the patristic and biblical idea of the human person as created in the image of God to grow into God's likeness, i.e., as Gregory of Nyssa states, marked by a mysterious freedom. This freedom transcends sex, but without denying it. This tendency is particularly evident in Evdokimov's dealing with the problem of the ordination of women.[50]

Again, Behr-Sigel takes care to state that the ordination of women was not Evdokimov's issue, so he should be neither blamed nor claimed by either side. What he cared about was the priesthood of all believers. His interest in the spiritual aspect of sexuality led him to posit feminine and masculine charisms, from which his passing thoughts on the ordination of women were derived. The problem is in his conception of charisms, prior to the question of ordination. After quoting a typically flowery bit about man's action in the world, complemented by woman, "mirror" and "wellspring" to his soul, Behr-Sigel comments,

> In reality, this dichotomy is a repetition, dressed out in romantic rhetoric, of age-old stereotypes which see women's destiny as being called to a holiness of "being"—a holiness to an extent passive—in the service of men, who are active and creative. That provides the framework in Evdokimov's anthropological scheme for the vocation of men to be priests—thus enabling them to express their male creative energy—and the vocation of women to a supporting but passive holiness, paradoxically related to the Holy Spirit, who is, however, designated as "Creator" in Christian Tradition.[51]

Elsewhere Evdokimov supplements this with the idea, derived from Bulgakov, of the "hypostatic maternity of the Spirit," best exemplified in the Theotokos, and the ideal for all spiritually reborn Christian women. But, Behr-Sigel asks,

> Would it not be possible for the Church to acknowledge and bless a ministry of women as an expression of this maternal charism? Strangely, that possibility is not envisaged by Paul Evdokimov, who sees a radical difference between charismatic ministry and institutional ministry. But is not such a radical difference a contradiction of the apostle Paul's teaching on ministries and its continuation in the Church Fathers?[52]

Behr-Sigel doesn't want to maintain the feminine-masculine charism distinction. But if someone else does—and there are certainly those who do—she tries to demonstrate that it is still not a valid basis for excluding women from the priesthood.

Behr-Sigel is more critical of Hopko, wondering if he could be identified as part of a "current sometimes described as 'panerotic' running through modern Russian religious

---

[50] Ibid., p. 17.
[51] Ibid., p. 18.
[52] Ibid., p. 19.

thinking from Vladimir Soloviev to Fr. Serge Bulgakov, of which Paul Evdokimov is one of the heirs."[53] According to Behr-Sigel, Hopko denies any connection, but the similarities are indeed striking. Just like Evdokimov, Hopko sees in the anthropological division into male and female a reflection of the divine Trinity itself. Behr-Sigel sees in Hopko an "extrapolation from the concept of the mysterious otherness of divine and human persons to the concept of absolutized and, in a way, sacred difference between the sexes . . . this entails radically different vocations and roles in relationships, for women in the 'economy of the Spirit,' and for men in the 'economy of Christ.'" Women must submit to men as the Spirit does to the Son, a submission that Hopko still insists is "dynamic, active, and powerful," yet does its work "silently, hiddenly and invisibly." Behr-Sigel concludes: "In that way the patriarchal understanding of the 'natural' roles of men and women is projected onto God, exalted and assimilated to the eternal divine order."[54]

Hopko, of course, is wise enough to realize how sin regularly messes up the proper expression of the divine order. His solution is to express it perfectly in the divine liturgy. There the priest can be the objective male presence of Christ. Behr-Sigel writes:

> In the sacramental presence of the ordained priest in the celebration of the mystery of the eucharist, his maleness belongs in a way to the substance of the sacrament— an essential, indispensable and indeed determinative element. In this perspective, according to Fr. Hopko, his "specific charisms, talents, and skills may vary" and are of little importance. What is important is "his objective image," which must be "vivid and firm." He must be "a male member of the church community," so as to make sacramentally present the Christ/Logos, "the head and bridegroom of the Church," whose characteristics as a Person in the Godhead are "male."[55]

So Hopko finds common ground here with Verna Harrison (even though she thoroughly rejects the "male" qualities of the Son!) in defining the priesthood, a definition that Behr-Sigel finds increasingly disturbing. The priest as shepherd of the flock means less and less, and his own gifts and charisms must be irrelevant, otherwise (one supposes) women would have far too much claim on the office. The priest is reduced to what he *appears* to be *symbolically*, as a male in the liturgy. The othering of men from women must stand as an absolute fact; so the Son and the Spirit are also made drastically other, even though the early church battled heretics who denied the *homoousios* of the Spirit with the Father and the Son! Either the spectacle of women at the altar is so horrifying as to deprive Orthodox theologians of their trinitarian wits or the ontological status of gender stands in need of serious reassessment.

At the end of the essay, Behr-Sigel reiterates her own view, one she asserts is best in keeping with the true Tradition of the church. Sexual differentiation is a real, indisputable fact, but the way the differentiation is used to deny priesthood to women

---

[53]   Ibid., pp. 46–47.
[54]   Ibid., pp. 25–26. Behr-Sigel is quoting from Hopko's essay in the first edition of *Women and the Priesthood*, pp. 111–12.
[55]   Ibid., pp. 26–27.

contradicts the anthropology, christology, and soteriology of the church fathers. Maleness is simply not a feature of Jesus' personhood interesting to the church fathers; all their energy is devoted to expounding how he is true *anthropos*. The accent on Christ's maleness for a male priesthood ends up losing the soteriological inclusion of males and females alike. It even mistakes what is meant by representation and ignores the priest's solidarity with the faithful. And if the church fathers would not bother with the maleness of Jesus per se, much less would they permit a projection of sexual differentiation onto the eternal Son and Spirit.[56] Even if the church fathers' attitude toward sexuality was not as positive as one might like it today, the situation is not corrected by the apparently more positive modern view of sexual differentiation that is then used to

> justify a dichotomy contrasting male human beings linked to Christ, and thus called to represent him, over against women, linked with the Holy Spirit, and for that reason paradoxically excluded from representing, icon-like, him who is par excellence the Anointed One (which is the meaning of the word "Christ"), anointed by the Spirit, an anointing in which all Christians, male and female, are called to participate.[57]

Behr-Sigel points out again that she has never asked for the Orthodox church to ordain women.[58] She has simply raised questions and suggested possibilities but never pursued any course of action. Her proposal for "disciplinary pluralism" on the issue is for a specific reason. She writes:

> As in the early days of the Church, those who feel that they are free in Christ and freed by Christ from certain stereotypes and taboos must avoid scandalizing the "weak," who in other areas may be the spiritually "strong". But we must never give way to threats from obscurantist fundamentalists, who are often Westerners who are recent converts to the Orthodox Church. It must, however, be admitted that in its present state any decision to ordain women to the priesthood would almost inevitably give rise to schism in the Orthodox Church. In view of this risk, we must be patiently impatient. The greatest gift of the Spirit, to which we are all called to aspire, is the gift of agape, the love which "is patient" and "always hopes." (1 Cor. 13.4, 7)[59]

Was anyone listening? Leonie B. Liveris of *MaryMartha* certainly was. Over the next two years several items of Behr-Sigel's were published. Two in 1995 were brief reports. One asks to what extent the Orthodox have participated in the WCC's decade for women. Happily, the answer is: in a good number of events. There have been meetings; conferences in New York at St. Vladimir's (mentioned above), Denver, Dallas, and

---

[56] Ibid., pp. 38, 40.
[57] Ibid., p. 39.
[58] Ibid., p. 35.
[59] Ibid., p. 44.

Montreal; and the "Church and Culture" conference in Crete.[60] A second report in the same volume of *MaryMartha* discusses the international conference held in Levadia, Greece on "Orthodox Women in a United Europe." Behr-Sigel expresses her usual optimism—rather astonishing, given the amount of travel she was doing and her 87 years of age—though she is unimpressed with a hint of "self-satisfaction" here and there. But she is glad to see Orthodox women taking seriously the question of how they can contribute outside of their immediate church and national communities to the good of the whole European continent. There was little said about specific church matters, but the question of the ordination of women did come up—with the assertion that it is still an open question, according to Kallistos Ware—as well as some regret that the Rhodes recommendation for deaconesses has been thus far ignored.[61]

Theological matters came back to the center at the second ecumenical gathering for women at Bossey in 1994.[62] Behr-Sigel delivered a paper on the subject, "The Community of Women and Men: What Does This Mean for a Prophetic and Sacramental Church?" The title was not her own; it was given to her, and her presentation begins with curiosity at it. Are "prophetic" and "sacramental" here distinct terms because they are fundamentally disconnected from one another? To Behr-Sigel, even if this happens in actual historical churches, it is a mistake. Prophecy and sacraments belong together. In Christ, "the prophetic word . . . teaches, exhorts, and reveals the meaning, the significance and direction, of God's plan on the one hand, and on the other, the sacramental sign of baptism . . . confirms and actualises the gift of new life to all."[63] The three basic sacraments of the Orthodox church, namely baptism, chrismation, and the eucharist, give rise to the other four (marriage, holy orders, anointing of the sick, confession) and empower the believer in the prophetic work of the church. Behr-Sigel notes with interest that women have always, from the very beginning and without a break, participated in the three primary sacraments. Baptism abolishes the separation and hostility between the sexes by the greater unity that comes of being clothed in Christ. Chrismation "christifies" each person by the anointing of the Holy Spirit, uniting each to Son and Spirit. Although Behr-Sigel doesn't say so here, the implication for her adversaries is clear enough—it makes no sense, in the light of the sacrament of chrismation, to speak of men's affinity to the Son and women's to the Spirit, or of distinct masculine and feminine charisms. The eucharist, too, binds every member of the church into the one body of Christ, making one offering of thanksgiving to the Father, praying one epiclesis to the Spirit. The implications of the sacraments are clear enough—men and women possess an equal dignity and a common vocation toward deification.

---

[60] Behr-Sigel, "Women's Decade: Orthodox Participation," *MaryMartha* 4, no. 1 (1995), pp. 23–24.

[61] Behr-Sigel, "International Conference 'The Orthodox Women in a United Europe,'" trans. Colin Williams, *MaryMartha* 4, no. 1 (1995), pp. 15–17.

[62] See Liveris, "Seminars at Bossey 1994," *MaryMartha* 3, nos 3–4 (1994), pp. 42–46, which covers both "Women in Dialogue—Wholeness of Vision Towards the 21st Century, 29 April–8 May 1994" and "Feminist and Orthodox Spiritualities, Bossey, 9–19 May 1994."

[63] Behr-Sigel, "The Community of Women and Men: What Does This Mean for a Prophetic and Sacramental Church?" trans. Maria Rule, *MaryMartha* 4, no. 2 (1996), pp. 22–30 (24).

MaryMartha continued its publication of essays by and about Behr-Sigel through its last volume and year, 1998. On the occasion of her ninetieth birthday in 1997, an interview with her friend Lyn Breck was published, highlighting Behr-Sigel's youthful spirit, big heart, and petite frame (4'9"!). Behr-Sigel admitted to her terror at being invited to Agapia two decades previously and, when asked what her advice for Orthodox women would be, answered, "They should be conscious of their dignity and responsibility as baptized, chrismated Christians; conscious of their royal priesthood—in fact, this is for everyone, not only for women."[64] Her thought has matured to the point that it strikes her as basically misleading to tell Christian *women* how to behave rather than simply Christian *people*. And, she adds, Christian people should think freely, not accepting weak arguments—especially where matters of women and priesthood are concerned.

Behr-Sigel continued to be active at home. For instance, with her daughter Nadine Arnould and her friend Véronique Lossky, she sponsored two sessions at the Orthodox Fraternity conference in 1996 to discuss "Men and Women in the Church," both of which gatherings were well attended.[65] By then a small group had been meeting in Paris for eight years to discuss the situation of women in the church.

However, as is common for theology in the modern world, the principal occasions for Behr-Sigel's work continued to be international conferences, both ecumenical and Orthodox. In 1996 she attended a conference on Mary hosted by the University of Lyon where she presented a reflection on Mary and women.[66] Her opening thoughts are emblematic of how far she had come since her first foray into women's issues at Agapia.

> A year ago, when I was asked to speak at this colloquy, the theme proposed for my presentation was "Mary and Women." Several months later, when I received the program, I noticed that the title had been changed to "Mary and Woman." The substitution of the singular collective for the plural, a substitution that seemed obvious and one which must have been made without thinking that anyone would notice the difference—well, this substitution gave me something to ponder.[67]

Despite the trend to exalt women, seemingly, in lofty language of their charisms and vocations, Behr-Sigel detects in the grammar a habit of seeing women not as persons,

---

64 Breck, "Elisabeth Behr-Sigel—Entretien," pp. 13–14. My translation.
65 Véronique Lossky, "Men and Women in the Church: Report of the Workshop, Vendee," trans. Colin Williams, *MaryMartha* 5, no. 2 (1997), pp. 33–35. See also Véronique Lossky's articles, "La Femme dans l'Eglise Orthodoxe," *Contacts* 44 (1992), pp. 221–32; "Le Ministère des Femmes d'un Point de Vue Orthodoxe: Une Relecture," *Contacts* 48 (1996), pp. 101–18, reprinted in *MaryMartha* 5, no. 2 (1997), pp. 54–68, and also translated into English as, "Women's Ministry—From an Orthodox Point of View. A Re-reading," trans. Colin Williams, *MaryMartha* 5, no. 2 (1997), pp. 69–82; and "La Place de la Femme dans l'Eglise Orthodoxe," *Contacts* 55 (2003), pp. 104–08.
66 The conference papers were published the following year in *Théologie, Histoire et Piété Mariale: Actes du Colloque de la Faculté de Théologie de Lyon, 1–3 Octobre 1996*, pp. 309–24 (ed. Jean Comby; Lyon: Profac, 1997). Behr-Sigel's was entitled "Marie et les Femmes" and was subsequently reprinted in *Discerner les Signes du Temps*, pp. 21–33. Quotations here are taken from the English translation, "Mary and Women," in *Discerning the Signs of the Times*, pp. 101–13.
67 Behr-Sigel, "Mary and Women," p. 101.

"singular and unique, but simple specimens or samples of a species defined essentially by its sex."[68] To her, this loses the whole Judeo-Christian insistence on the *anthropos*, who is sexual and yet transcends sexuality, who is a member of a group and yet always individual, "colored by sex," as Behr-Sigel says, "but not reducible to sexual difference."[69]

In that light, Behr-Sigel thinks it is worth asking: what is the reason for reflecting on Mary and women at all? Is it to be assumed that Mary and women have a "privileged relation" because of their sex? Behr-Sigel notes that men have always been at the forefront of marian theology, from Cyril of Alexandria's proposed title of Theotokos to the recent popes propounding marian dogma *ex cathedra*. And, as Evdokimov noticed long ago, all too often the exaltation of Mary has been matched by scorn for her ordinary sisters. An infelicitous dynamic emerges: for the "guilty" woman, "it remains only to implore the intercession of the 'most pure Mother of God' with a wrathful God, depicted in masculine characteristics."[70] If a woman is not to be perceived as guilty, she must compensate by being submissive: "As Mary has submitted to the divine will, so her sisters should in their turn submit to all those who represent God, who always seem to possess masculine identities and traits: their fathers, brothers, husbands, and priests."[71]

With feminism—more often the work of Protestant or agnostic women than Roman Catholics or Orthodox—a new perspective on the mother of God has come to the surface. "Christian feminists are reclaiming Mary not only to affirm the dignity of women as human beings but in order to promote specifically feminine values, the particular identity of women as opposed to the values and identity of men." It should be no surprise by now that Behr-Sigel cannot embrace this shift with unmitigated enthusiasm. "To what extent such an aspiration is within the lines of the personalism of the Gospel and the theological anthropology of the Fathers is a question that must be raised."[72]

Behr-Sigel sees an instance of such Christian feminism in the papal document *Mulieris Dignitatem*.[73] Femininity itself is exalted on account of the Mother of God; it means "plenitude." And it is again grounds for excluding women from the priesthood. "The impossibility of ordaining women results precisely from the sublimated femininity that defines women, that was magnified in Mary and through her in all women."

---

[68] Ibid. In the same vein, see her critical review of *L'Oeuvre du Sixième Jour–Creation de l'Homme*, by D. M. Debuisson, *Contacts* 49 (1997), pp. 366–70.

[69] Behr-Sigel, "Mary and Women," p. 101.

[70] Ibid., p. 103.

[71] Ibid., p. 104.

[72] Ibid.

[73] An essay by Léonie Caldecott about *Mulieris Dignitatem* discusses Behr-Sigel's work and identifies its similarities to the papal document—that is, Behr-Sigel's early work. An endnote comments: "I am quoting with approval from her earlier writing, but I emphatically part company with Behr-Sigel in her later stages, where she gravitated towards accepting female ordination. This evolution seems to me to show up, among other things, a certain weakness in her style of reasoning about tradition and adaptation." The exact nature of the weakness is left unexplained. In short, Caldecott approves in Behr-Sigel exactly what Behr-Sigel came to reject. "Sincere Gift: The Pope's 'New Feminism,'" in *John Paul II and Moral Theology*, pp. 216–34 (ed. Charles E. Curran and Richard A. McCormick, S. J.; Readings in Moral Theology, 10; New York: Paulist Press, 1978).

A woman who becomes a priest essentially also becomes masculine, rejecting her femininity, her "richness" and "originality," in the words of the document. Behr-Sigel wonders whether John Paul II had read Evdokimov's works; *Woman and the Salvation of the World* had been published in Italian ten years before *Mulieris Dignitatem* was released.[74] The same emphasis on the goodness of femininity, feminine charisms, and the essential nature of womanhood that is betrayed by claiming priesthood are all there, though the suggestion of femininity in the Holy Spirit is not.

At last Behr-Sigel reaches the heart of the matter. Some women as well as men may like the exaltation of femininity or the privileged relation between Mary and women.

> But is this not a misunderstanding? To make of femininity something of the essence of Mary, to see in her only the archetype of the feminine, is this not to diminish it? She is a woman, but above all a human being in fullness, in whom, as Maximus the Confessor very powerfully says, "the division between man and woman is surpassed." To perpetuate and even sacralize this separation in placing Mary above all other women, next to the Holy Spirit, with men at the side of Christ: such speculation is in utter contradiction with the baptismal hymn in the epistle to the Galatians (3:26–28) and has no scriptural foundation whatsoever. In practice, feminists point out, such thinking only serves to separate idealized women from any functions which in the Church would imply authority and decision-making.[75]

In short, Behr-Sigel rejects the subject of her paper altogether. The rest of it is exegesis of marian texts demonstrating Mary's freedom, faith, and relationships to others— all that makes her a person, in other words, rather than an archetype of incarnate femininity. Even her maternity is emphasized for its spiritual rather than physical meaning; "[o]therwise men would be deprived of the symbolic richness that Mary offers them."[76]

The very day after the Lyon conference ended, the Damascus gathering for Orthodox women began, on the happy theme of "Discerning the Signs of the Times."[77] Behr-Sigel's contribution was a short reflection on "The Meaning of Ministry."[78] As it

---

[74] Evdokimov was present at portions of the Second Vatican Council as an Orthodox observer. It is possible that he met the future Pope John Paul II. It would be very interesting to see if any definite correspondence between the two theologians could be established.

[75] Behr-Sigel, "Mary and Women," pp. 107–08.

[76] Ibid., p. 109.

[77] The papers delivered at Damascus and the following year at Istanbul are all collected in *Orthodox Women Speak: Discerning the "Signs of the Times"* (ed. Kyriaki Karidoyanes FitzGerald; Geneva: WCC, 1999). The dedication states: "With profound appreciation and respect for a woman who has been faithfully bearing witness to the fullness of the 'life in abundance' (John 10:10) extended to both women and men, this volume is lovingly dedicated to Elisabeth Behr-Sigel." Behr-Sigel reviewed the collection in *Bulletin de la Crypte* 286 (2000), pp. 21–22, which was reprinted in *Contacts* 52 (2000), pp. 271–74.

[78] She had already published this essay in French as "Réflexions sur le Ministère et les Ministères dans l'Eglise: Une Voix Orthodoxe," *Trajets* 2 (1993–94), pp. 53–57. It was later published in English as "The Meaning of Ministry," in *Orthodox Women Speak*, pp. 93–97, and then re-translated into French by Valère de Pryck and published as, "La Signification du Ministère," *Lumière du Thabor* 28 (2006), pp. 22–25.

turns out, she became ill and missed the conference, but her essay was included in the conference proceedings all the same.

Two items stand out. First, Behr-Sigel demonstrates a deep sympathy with Evdokimov, however far she has traveled from his thoughts on women, in his uplifting the ministry of all the baptized, the royal priesthood, within which the clerical priesthood exercises a particular task. And out of that, second, she further emphasizes the particular gifts needed by priests through the blessing of the Spirit. Clerical priesthood is ultimately about these gifts of the Spirit for the task of nourishing and strengthening the whole body of priests and ministers, that is, the baptized. The unspoken corollary: it is not about liturgical symbolism and gender.

Half a year later, Orthodox women gathered again, this time in Istanbul, and Behr-Sigel spoke on "Women in Jesus' Earthly Life."[79] In its structure and theology, this essay parallels her paper in Lyon on Mary and women. Is there a particular kind of relationship between Jesus and women on account of their differing sex? What Behr-Sigel finds is that Jesus never addresses women *qua* women, as if they collectively shared certain vices (as Christian tradition has often asserted), nor does he assume they share certain virtues, either (as Evdokimov did). "Jesus does not exhort women to be obedient and submissive, as is proper for them. He does not speak of feminine tenderness as opposed to masculine toughness. Dare I say that Jesus is not interested in *Woman*, but rather in *women*, in each of them as he meets her personally." Women, in fact, are persons.[80]

In light of that insight, Behr-Sigel discusses the various gospel stories of Jesus' encounters with women. She concludes by considering the woman who anointed Jesus with nard, of whom Jesus said this act would be told along with the gospel "in remembrance of her." She notes the similarity in language here with the eucharistic institution. Behr-Sigel asks, "Have the churches preserved this exhortation and meditated on it sufficiently? Has the perfume of this gesture filled our entire house, as the gospel of John says it did in the house of Martha, Mary, and Lazarus?"[81]

The third of the Bossey conferences took place from June 23 to July 3, 1997. When Teny Pirri-Simonian wrote to invite Behr-Sigel to attend, she suggested that they should "revisit Sheffield." In her keynote on the theme "The Bible, Tradition, the Sacraments," Behr-Sigel retells the history and then exhorts the participants to pick up the thread once again, this time "avoiding the mistakes and sins of their predecessors: self-sufficiency and ignorance of the other that is so often a form of disdain."[82] She

---

[79] Behr-Sigel, "Women in Jesus' Earthly Life," in *Orthodox Women Speak*, pp. 51–55. The essay was first printed as "Jesus and Women," *MaryMartha* 6, no. 1 (1998), pp. 35–36. A version of this essay, again with the title "Jesus and Women," appears in *Discerning the Signs of the Times*, pp. 95–99, as well as in the French version of the book, pp. 15–19. Liveris records her impressions of both Istanbul and the third Bossey seminar in "Consultation Report: MaryMartha Editorial—Istanbul and Bossey," *MaryMartha* 5, no. 2 (1997), pp. 3–7.

[80] Behr-Sigel, "Women in Jesus' Earthly Life," p. 52.

[81] Ibid., p. 55.

[82] "La Bible, la Tradition, les Sacrements, Sources de l'Autorité dans l'Eglise," *Contacts* 50, no. 3 (1998), pp. 204–14; reprinted in *Discerner les Signes du Temps*, pp. 111–19. Quotations taken from "The Bible, Tradition, the Sacraments," in *Discerning the Signs of the Times*, pp. 81–94.

meditates first on ecclesiology, then on theological anthropology—which she insists is theocentric, not androcentric, in patristic thought. She compares the many female saints and leaders of church history to the rare and rather obscure prohibitions against their leadership. She concludes that Scripture and Tradition contain not only one stream of thought about women but two, and the two have always been in tension, one affirming and uplifting women as full persons, the other silencing and suppressing them, often in the gentlest and most protective of ways.[83] The Orthodox church takes seriously both Bible and Tradition, but it is faced now with the puzzle of a genuine disagreement within Bible and Tradition alike about how women are to be regarded. That in itself is a shocking fact to many. Behr-Sigel is less distressed because of her conviction about the nature of Tradition itself: it is not an "ossified" deposit but "new life with Christ and in Christ, guided by the Spirit."[84]

In 1998, Behr-Sigel together with her friend Bp. Kallistos Ware published a little book entitled *L'Ordination des Femmes dans l'Eglise Orthodoxe*. The one essay by Ware was also published the following year in the second edition of *Women and the Priesthood*. It expresses his growing doubts about traditional and contemporary arguments excluding women from the priesthood, though he stops short of actually recommending the practice of ordaining women. Along with her previously published piece, "The Ordination of Women: Also a Question for the Orthodox Churches," Behr-Sigel contributes a new and much shorter essay entitled, "Women in the Orthodox Church." This latter piece is a very compact overview of patristic and modern thought on women, women's experiences in the church, and how those experiences diverge across traditionally Orthodox countries and in the so-called Diaspora. It is more like her original piece for Agapia, based on observation rather than theological explorations.[85]

The new millennium saw Behr-Sigel (already well into her 90s) write another variation on her mature essay for *Contacts*, this one entitled, "L'Ordination des Femmes: Un Point Chaud du Dialogue Oecuménique."[86] Although it omits the careful detail that built up her previous versions, this essay again uses the same structure as before: the fast and violent changes of the modern world; the Orthodox first facing the question of women's ordination in the work of Khodre and Chitescu; Evdokimov and Hopko's further development of the ideas; the entrance of Orthodox women into the debate from Agapia onward; Rhodes and its aftermath; and finally Behr-Sigel's own position, as she has argued before.

Two significant events took place in 2003. First, a festschrift was published in her honor, *"Toi, Suis-Moi": Mélanges Offerts en Hommage à Elisabeth Behr-Sigel*. It includes only one essay on women in the church, by the Orthodox priest at Behr-Sigel's francophone parish who was also a professor at Saint-Serge, Boris Bobrinskoy.

---

[83] Behr-Sigel, "The Bible, Tradition, the Sacraments," p. 89.

[84] Ibid., p. 92.

[85] See fn. 47 above. With some modifications, the same essay appears as the entry for "Women," in *The Blackwell Dictionary of Eastern Christianity*, pp. 515–19 (ed. Ken Parry et al.; Oxford: Blackwell, 1999).

[86] Behr-Sigel, "L'Ordination des Femmes: Un Point Chaud du Dialogue Oecuménique," first in *Contacts* and later reprinted in *Discerner les Signes du Temps*, pp. 153–66. She originally delivered the paper at a gathering of the Institut Supérieur d'Etudes Oecuméniques in Paris on February 14, 2001.

Regrettably, the essay is something of an embarrassment. It sounds as though Bobrinskoy never read a word of Behr-Sigel's but absorbed all of Evdokimov's ideas. For instance, Bobrinskoy speaks of a "paternity" in God the Father, a "masculinity" in God the Son, and a "femininity" in the Spirit, the last of which is matched by a "total femininity of human nature in its relationship to God," and all of these gender ideas are attributed to St. Paul![87] Further, Bobrinskoy writes, it is necessary for the priest to have a iconic masculine character while the "ministry of the woman is a necessary, spontaneous, constant ecclesial diakonia"[88] marked by self-effacement, modesty, the most humble everyday service, silence in hearing the Word, and interior reception of it. He concludes that it is because Christ was male, thus the husband and not the wife of the church, that a priest must be masculine too. One can only imagine how Behr-Sigel reacted when she read it.

The other big event was Behr-Sigel's final trip out of the comforts of Paris into the wide world to present her argument in "L'Ordination des Femmes: Un Point Chaud du Dialogue Oecuménique" to an American audience. An American Orthodox women's publication, *St. Nina Quarterly*, that in some respects picked up where *MaryMartha* left off, sponsored her trip abroad. She presented her essay, called in English "The Ordination of Women—A Point of Contention in Ecumenical Dialogue," for the Fr. Georges Florovsky Lecture hosted by St. Vladimir's Orthodox Theological Seminary in Crestwood, New York, on May 30, during the annual meeting of the Orthodox Theological Society in America, which was followed by a day-long conference with Behr-Sigel sponsored by the *St. Nina Quarterly*. On June 3, she presented the material from her article "Women in the Orthodox Church" in Brookline, Massachusetts, on the premises of Holy Cross Greek Orthodox Seminary, for an event also sponsored by *St. Nina Quarterly*. Behr-Sigel's voice was too weak to read the papers herself. Bonnie Michal read for her at Holy Cross, and Susan Ashbrook Harvey did at St. Vladimir's. Ironically enough, her Florovsky lecture on women's ordination was essentially the same essay that St. Vladimir's Seminary Press deleted from the original manuscript of her essay collection *Discerning the Signs of the Times* when it was acquired with the purchase of Oakwood Publications. Because of its status as the Florovsky lecture, though, the essay found its way into print under the St. Vladimir's flag anyway, in its quarterly theological journal.[89]

After the lecture at each location there was a question-and-answer session, the details of which were recorded by the St. Nina's staff sponsoring her visit. Her comments about her life and relationships—especially during the Second World War—are both delightful and illuminating. For our purposes here, though, her answers to two particular questions stand out.

---

[87] Boris Bobrinskoy, "La Place de la Femme dans la Vie de l'Eglise," in *"Toi, Suis-Moi,"* pp. 397–98. All quotations are my translation.

[88] Ibid., p. 400.

[89] Behr-Sigel, "The Ordination of Women—A Point of Contention in Ecumenical Dialogue," *St. Vladimir's Theological Quarterly* 48, no. 1 (2004), pp. 49–66. The French version of the article, however, did appear in the French edition of *Discerner les Signes du Temps*, pp. 153–66.

In the first instance, someone at St. Vladimir's asked Behr-Sigel why she had "chosen to spend so much of [her] time focusing on women in the church." Her prompt reply:

This is a false impression. In fact I have spent a lot of time [on other subjects]; people have not read the other books I have written. Exploring the images of sanctity in Russia was my first published book. It happened in fact when I was, to my surprise, invited to the meeting at Agapia. At that time there were so few women with theological education. This is what drew me into the issue and in fact changed my life. First of all it brought me to contact with other Orthodox women, which led me to realize the importance of the subject, especially since this is such a burning issue on the ecumenical scene. Maybe I am wrong, but I felt that God asked me to do this thing.[90]

Her work on women began very late in her life—and in a life rather longer than the usual—and it is a piece of her larger theological project, not the center of it.

Another person, this time at Holy Cross, asked her, "How do you see your work as a blessing to men as well as women?" Her response expresses where she finally arrived on the issue of theological anthropology. She replied,

It is because of my sense of the church as being catholic and universal, where men and women are both created in the image and likeness of God, in the image of the Holy Trinity, and so they must work together. They are all together and they can live only by mutual respect and working with one another. You cannot separate the issue of women from men.[91]

It is as Gregory of Nazianzus said: "The same birth for men and women, the same clay, the same death, the same resurrection."

---

[90] Interview with Elisabeth Behr-Sigel [transcript], b. 1907, *St. Nina Quarterly*, on May 30, 2003 at St. Vladimir's Orthodox Theological Seminary and June 3, 2003 at Holy Cross Greek Orthodox School of Theology (unpublished).

[91] Ibid.

6

The Female Diaconate

All of our attention so far has focused on Behr-Sigel's theological arguments in favor of the ordination of women to the priesthood. It is time now to pause and consider how she viewed the diaconate, the only ecclesial office to which women were ever ordained in the Orthodox church.

Behr-Sigel discusses the female diaconate right at the beginning of her work on women in her keynote at Agapia. She notes that it was a lively office in the first millennium of the church, involving a genuine ordination with the laying-on of hands and the wearing of a stole (*orarion*). These deaconesses "received communion from the eucharistic cup and placed it on the altar." They prepared women for and attended them during baptism, provided spiritual and material help to those in need, and taught the faith, although they did not baptize or preach. In the early twentieth century, Russia saw a resurgence of interest in the female diaconate, but the Revolution put an end to any plans for a fresh start.[1] A college for deaconesses was founded in Greece in 1957, though the women trained there are not ordained and their ministry is charitable and social rather than educational or spiritual. A lively order of deaconesses exists in the Coptic church now, too, as a fresh attempt to engage contemporary problems.[2]

In her article directly following upon Agapia, Behr-Sigel has a little more history in her arsenal. The Council of Nicea mentions the ordination of deaconesses by the laying-on of hands, and Chalcedon uses both the terms *cheirothesis* and *cheirotonia*, the first of which means "consecration" and the latter of which means "ordination."[3] Here Behr-Sigel explicitly commends the reinstitution of the diaconate for women, not a rigid imitation of the old ways but a re-creation for a new situation. "We need to rethink it in terms of a new and original ministry," she writes, as a "sign of the presence of the comforting Spirit at the side of the Bride who is looking for the Bridegroom."[4] Note the implied alignment of women deacons with the Holy Spirit,

---

[1] It was even on the agenda for the pan-Russian church council of 1917/18 and personally patronized by Grand Duchess Elisabeth of Russia, who was martyred in the revolution. See Behr-Sigel, "An Orthodox Diaconate for Women?" *Sobornost* 23, no. 1 (2001), pp. 60–63 (61).

[2] Behr-Sigel, "Keynote," in *Orthodox Women*, pp. 26–27. All of Behr-Sigel's details on the diaconate here come from the article by Militza Zernov, "Women's Ministry in the Church."

[3] Behr-Sigel, "Women in the Orthodox Church: Heavenly Vision and Historical Realities," p. 146.

[4] Ibid., p. 147.

along the lines suggested by Evdokimov; later Behr-Sigel would emphasize the christological source of the diaconate for women and men alike. In her open letter of 1979, signed by many friends and colleagues, Behr-Sigel proposes, among other changes like the removal of purity taboos, a renewed female diaconate: her first public act on its behalf.[5]

More historical details emerge in her 1983 essay on "The Place of Women in the Church," accompanied by an extended list of sources on the female diaconate.[6] Despite current disputes over *cheirothesis* as consecration versus *cheirotonia* as ordination, Behr-Sigel finds that the distinction did not exist when women were entering the diaconate centuries ago. She also reports that the deaconesses took communion around the altar with the male clergy and helped in the baptismal unction of women.[7] For the first time, though, Behr-Sigel sees a danger in advocacy for the female diaconate. She writes that it "should in no way be seen as a substitute for their participation in the presbyteral ministry. Nor should it serve as an alibi for avoiding a serious theological reflection about the ordination of women to the priesthood."[8]

Behr-Sigel deepens her thoughts on the issue in a 1987 review of *Des Femmes Diacres. Un Nouveau Chemin Pour L'Eglise* by Marie-Josephe Aubert.[9] The author is a Roman Catholic woman who laments how the church publicly ignores women's gifts while still using women to do a great number of things unofficially when no men are available to do them. Behr-Sigel is more or less sympathetic to her desire to see the ancient female diaconate re-created in order to give these women a proper standing in the church.

But at the end of the review Behr-Sigel expresses a "regret." Though the historical and phenomenological account of the diaconate is excellent, Aubert isn't up to par in the realm of theological and anthropological reflection. A "structural opposition" between man and woman is simply assumed, making the diaconate a feminine ministry of which Mary is the prototype. Behr-Sigel certainly has no objection to service as such, or to women serving. But she fears that identifying Mary with the diaconate, and both with women, ends up enclosing women in the diaconal ministry—a ministry whose sacramental character is simply left hanging, unresolved—and opposing that

---

[5] Behr-Sigel, "Questions about Women and Men," p. 225.

[6] See Behr-Sigel, "The Place of Women in the Church," in *The Ministry of Women in the Church*, p. 171, fn. 30 for the list of sources. The two most extensive studies on the issue are a thesis by Evangelos Theodorou, *Hè "Cheirotonia," hè "Cheirothesia" tôn Diakonissôn* (Athens: n.p., 1954) and a book by Kyriaki Karidoyanes FitzGerald, *Women Deacons in the Orthodox Church: Called to Holiness and Ministry* (Brookline, MA: Holy Cross Orthodox Press, 1998). Theodorou was present at the WCC gathering at Klingenthal and publicly supported the ordination of deaconesses there; he also gave a presentation at the 1988 Rhodes Consultation on "The Institution of Deaconesses in the Orthodox Church and the Possibility of Its Restoration," in *The Place of the Woman in the Orthodox Church*, pp. 207–38. See also the study by Sebastian Brock, "Deaconesses in the Syriac Tradition," in *Woman in Prism and Focus*, pp. 205–17.

[7] Behr-Sigel, "The Place of Women in the Church," p. 173.

[8] Ibid., p. 174.

[9] Behr-Sigel, review of *Des Femmes Diacres. Un Nouveau Chemin pour l'Eglise*, by M.-J. Aubert, *Contacts* 39 (1987), pp. 316–19.

ministry to the presbyteral ministry, which is said by contrast to be masculine. She writes,

> This authentic diaconate, service to the poor (whatever may be the nature of their poverty) and not ministry "for the women," is a matter open to all those, women and men, whom the Lord calls and whose personal vocation and charism the church, in sending them, authenticates. The model of the deacon but also of the deaconess… is Christ, the supreme Servant. In granting them to the gift of his Spirit that shines in Mary, Christ associates men and women with His Diaconate.[10]

The similarity to Behr-Sigel's arguments about the ordination of women to the priesthood is unmistakable. Just as both the Son and the Spirit bestow gifts in ordination to the priesthood, they also bestow gifts in ordination to the diaconate—to men and women without distinction. Behr-Sigel, then, wants a better theology of the diaconate and sees it as a corollary of a better theology of the priesthood. The desire of women to enter both is an occasion to rethink both.

While these explicit comments on the diaconate reveal Behr-Sigel's conclusions on the subject, her opinions were in reality formed prior to any explicit theological considerations by her friendship with Mother Maria Skobtsova, a Russian nun in Paris who died in Ravensbrück in 1945 and was canonized by the ecumenical patriarchate in 2004. Mother Maria's peculiar kind of sainthood—complete with a pair of divorces, pleasure in smoking and drinking, and boredom during long Byzantine liturgies—very likely undermined Behr-Sigel's assumptions about "feminine" charisms, too. It would be a serious lacuna, in any event, to talk about Behr-Sigel's work on women without discussing this friend of hers on whom she wrote so much.[11]

Mother Maria, born Elisabeth Pilenko, came from a well-to-do Ukrainian family in Riga, Latvia. Most of her childhood was spent in a family estate on the Black Sea among her father's vineyards. But when her father died early, the young Skobtsova and her mother moved to St. Petersburg, and the girl had a crisis of faith: an unjust death means no justice, no justice means no God. Already a talented poet in her early teens, Skobtsova moved among the intellectual circles of the city and listened to their revolutionary talk, but was unimpressed by their unwillingness to commit themselves

---

[10] Ibid., p. 319. My translation.

[11] Behr-Sigel's writings on Mother Maria Skobtsova are as follows. "Pour le Vingtième Anniversaire de la Mort de Mère Marie Skobtzoff [sic]," *Contacts* 17 (1965), pp. 178–93. Review of *Pearl of Great Price: The Life of Mother Maria Skobtsova*, by S. Hackel, *Contacts* 17 (1965), pp. 260–61. "Une Religieuse Russe à Paris: Mère Marie Skobtsov (1891–1945)," *Unité des Chrétiens* 58 (1985), pp. 21–23. "Mère Marie Skobtsov," *Le Messager Orthodoxe* 111 (1989) pp. 56–70, with portions reprinted in *Bulletin de la Crypte* 171 (1989), pp. 14–15 and again in 224 (1994), pp. 6–11; an English translation appeared as "Mother Maria Skobtsova, 1891–1945," in *Discerning the Signs of the Times*, pp. 41–53, followed by the publication of the original French in *Discerner les Signes du Temps*, pp. 51–64. "Marie Skobtsova 1891–1945," in *Ecumenical Pilgrims*, pp. 216–20; adapted as "An Orthodox Nun: The Life of Elisabeth Skobtsova," *One World* 208 (1995), pp. 14–15; original reprinted as "The Life of Elisabeth Skobtsova—An Orthodox Nun," *MaryMartha* 4, no. 2 (1996), pp. 16–21. Review of *Mère Marie*, by L. Varaut, *Bulletin de la Crypte* 289 (2001), p. 26. "Mère Marie Skobtsov et le Père Lev Gillet," *Contacts* 56 (2004), pp. 361–64; reprinted in *Bulletin de la Crypte* 322 (2004), pp. 24–25; revised and amended (but still virtually identical) in *Contacts* 57 (2005), pp. 315–18.

to the point of physical death. She herself got caught up in a mysticism of the Russian land and peasant. In time she married Dmitrii Kuzmin-Karavaev, with whom she had a daughter, Gaiana, but the marriage quickly failed. After the Revolution, Skobtsova returned to her family estate and found herself named mayor of the town, a difficult job that ended with her being put on trial for collaboration. Luckily, one of the judges, Daniel Skobtsov, fell in love with her and they married. Together they had two children, Yuri and Anastasia. But again, after the family fled to Paris for safety, the marriage fell apart and ended in an amicable divorce.

So far there is little to foreshadow Skobtsova's eventual canonization. It was the death of little Anastasia that wrought the change: an enormous grief that brought with it an acceptance, even an embrace, of suffering. It also illumined to Skobtsova her reprehensible past life, which in turn provoked the desire to lead a new life of limitless love. She became the traveling secretary for ACER, the Russian Christian youth movement, first visiting universities but in time factories, too, where Russian immigrants were dying of tuberculosis and alcoholism. She found still others who were institutionalized for mild psychological conditions simply because French officials couldn't understand them. Through these experiences, Skobtsova's calling became clearer to her, and in 1932 she took monastic vows. The local metropolitan Evlogy even "authorized her to preach during the liturgy."[12] Her organization of Orthodox Action and her work in Paris on behalf of the homeless, the unemployed, ex-prostitutes, and finally persecuted Jews led to her arrest and deportation by the Nazis. She died in Ravensbrück, probably of untreated dysentery, in 1945.[13]

Behr-Sigel knew Skobtsova personally; they were introduced by their common friend Lev Gillet.[14] Behr-Sigel appears to have been a little in awe of the bustling energy of the nun and her fearless advocacy on behalf of others. There certainly were feelings of kinship. Behr-Sigel reports that Skobtsova was one of the first women, if not the very first, to pursue theological studies in St. Petersburg, much as Behr-Sigel herself did in France. In several places Behr-Sigel reports about her last contact with Skobtsova, who begged Behr-Sigel to look after the child of some Jewish friends who had just been arrested. But what seems to have impressed Behr-Sigel most was—not surprisingly— Skobtsova's discernment of the "signs of the times."

The monastic office, as much as Skobtsova wanted it, didn't rest altogether comfortably on her. There was some trouble about getting her consecrated, since she was twice divorced. The business was managed only through the discovery of an old canon permitting divorce when one spouse wished to enter the monastic life. Daniel Skobtsov willingly granted her ecclesial divorce on those grounds. Still, Lev Gillet warned Skobtsova against taking vows, fearing they would only hold her back.[15] As Behr-Sigel herself observed, there was something about Skobtsova that made her constitutionally uncomfortable with rules, regulations, and institutions. She was an eschatological, apocalyptic spirit; she sensed the arrival of "a 'kairos' that

---

[12] Behr-Sigel, "Feminine Images and Orthodox Spirituality," p. 9.

[13] Behr-Sigel reports this story in most of her writings on Mother Maria. Her most thorough article is the one in *Discerning the Signs of the Times*, "Mother Maria Skobtsova, 1891–1945."

[14] Behr-Sigel, "Mère Marie Skobtsov et le Père Lev Gillet," *Contacts*, p. 361.

[15] Behr-Sigel, "Mother Maria Skobtsova, 1891–1945," p. 46.

would demand not only the renewal of old ecclesial structures but the renunciation, maybe temporary, of all structure, or at least of all identification of the Christian faith with an exterior order, indeed with a culture." The potential idolatry of one's own family, art, creativity, even the Russia that Skobtsova once adored, is all too strong.[16]

In her first piece on Skobtsova, Behr-Sigel sounds a tiny bit scandalized by, or at least tentative about, Skobtsova's indifference to institutions. Skobtsova had little patience for long Byzantine liturgies, which frankly bored her; she was too busy serving her neighbor for that. But there is no doubt that Skobtsova's service was entirely the fruit of her passion for Christ. And she not only served—she also preached.[17] It was her love of Christ that prompted Skobtsova to ask: what should the relationship be between monasticism and the world? Can traditional monasticism be adapted to modern needs, or does an entirely new way of life need to arise?[18] After taking her vows, Skobtsova returned to her birthplace to tour monasteries in Latvia and Estonia. She was not impressed with what she saw. As Behr-Sigel describes her reaction:

> She returned from these travels more aware than ever that these traditional forms of monasticism were not appropriate for the situation of the Russian emigration in western Europe. She experienced these traditional forms of monasticism as being antiquated and contaminated by a bourgeois spirit, something that was for her antithetical to the true radical monastic vocation. For many women, Mother Maria believed, monasticism was a means of founding a spiritual family that offered refuge, security, and "high walls of protection against the ugliness and misery of the world." . . . Mother Maria dreamt of a creatively renewed monasticism that would be a response to the vocation discerned in the "signs of the times."[19]

The language here is remarkably similar to that Behr-Sigel herself uses early in her career on women's issues—desiring to find a new community, addressing the needs of contemporary life, wisely discerning the signs.

The phrase "creatively renewed monasticism" is key here, too. It is for a creatively renewed diaconate that Behr-Sigel became an advocate, and it is clear enough that her model was Mother Maria. In the essay she wrote for her course on "Formation Oecuménique Interconfessionelle," Behr-Sigel describes Skobtsova's work explicitly as a diaconal ministry. Despite the lack of the title, Skobtsova was one "exercising the ministry of a deaconess," as Behr-Sigel says twice here,[20] and elsewhere she explicitly calls her a "diaconal minister."[21] She was an "authentic social worker" who nevertheless

---

[16] Behr-Sigel, "Pour le Vingtième Anniversaire de la Mort de Mère Marie Skobtzoff," p. 188. My translation.

[17] Behr-Sigel, "Mother Maria Skobtsova, 1891–1945," p. 46.

[18] Behr-Sigel, "Pour le Vingtième Anniversaire de la Mort de Mère Marie Skobtzoff," p. 189.

[19] Behr-Sigel, "Mother Maria Skobtsova, 1891–1945," p. 47.

[20] Ibid., pp. 46, 49. It is likely Behr-Sigel got the idea of Mother Maria as deaconess from Sergei Hackel, *Pearl of Great Price: The Life of Mother Maria Skobtsova 1891–1945* (Crestwood, NY: St. Vladimir's Seminary Press, 1981), p. 71.

[21] Behr-Sigel, review of *Mère Marie*, pp. 239–40.

was well-versed in theology and philosophy and could hold her own in any debate.[22] If monasticism was perhaps not the best fit for Skobtsova, there's little doubt that a creatively renewed diaconate would have fit the bill perfectly.

Nor is it any surprise that Skobtsova is the first person Behr-Sigel mentions in her report on the Crete consultation on the diaconate.[23] This inter-Orthodox gathering in 1978 was structured around the theme of "Church and Service: The Orthodox Approach to the Diaconate," a title that Behr-Sigel found a bit vague. A "ministry of the church alongside people who live and suffer in the world" would be a more precise definition.[24] Either way, attention to the diaconate was long overdue. Historical circumstances in part account for the lapse of interest, though Behr-Sigel does not hesitate to lay some blame also at the door of the "representatives of a neopatristic current, historical, speculative and mystical, little interested in the problems of social ethics and action in the world *here and now*."[25] The Crete consultation held promise insofar as it recognized the "richness and variety of Orthodox diaconal actions in different regions."[26] The diaconate ought to be dealing with problems of hunger, illiteracy, injustice, economic underdevelopment, and torture: expressions of a basic hatred for all things human. If the Orthodox church ignores these problems, she asks,

> [i]sn't our inattention to the calls of the Spirit to a prophetic witness in the world equally incriminating, joined to a form of practical heresy where, while confessing with the lips a strict Orthodoxy, we often stumble? A heresy of a dualistic pseudo-spiritualism, denounced in the colloquium in Crete by the Greek theologian Alexander Papaderos, a heresy that consists in affirming that the *secular*, meaning the battle against the aforementioned plagues, has no relationship to the *salvation* announced by the Gospel. To combat this idealism inherited from pagan philosophy, an idealism absolutely contrary to all biblical anthropology, for which the human in his psychosomatic and spiritual totality is created in the image of God and thus called to salvation: would this not be one of the actual, urgent tasks of Orthodox theology?[27]

There is no mistaking the voice of Mother Maria Skobtsova behind these words.

To this Behr-Sigel adds her own christological justification of the diaconate.

> The image of Christ the Servant inspires the diaconate of the Church. As the service of God among people, it is not an appendix added on to ecclesial life but the radiance of that which constitutes its heart: the eucharist, communion—under

---

[22] Behr-Sigel, "Mother Maria Skobtsova, 1891–1945," p. 49.

[23] Behr-Sigel, "Après le Colloque de Crète sur la Diaconie," *Service Orthodoxe de Presse* 34 (1979), pp. 7–11 (7). All quotations are my translation. Not to be confused with the Crete Consultation on "Church and Culture" discussed in ch. 4.

[24] Ibid.

[25] Ibid.

[26] Ibid., p. 8.

[27] Ibid.

the form of bread and wine offered and shared—in the sacrifice of "the Lamb immolated from the beginning . . ." "in all and for all." If it is not extended to a life given and shared, the sacramental communion in the Body and Blood of Christ, isn't it for the Christian "judgment and condemnation"?[28]

Diaconal service is itself the Christian way of life. Behr-Sigel was pleased with the commitment that came out of the conference to "reactualize" the ministry of deacons *and* deaconesses in keeping with their scriptural basis, along with integrating all laypeople, men and women, into the diaconal service of the Church.[29]

And here at last Behr-Sigel found herself not entirely alone in her hopes for women's ministry in the Church. There was and is great interest among Orthodox communities around the world in reinstating and re-creating the female diaconate, though whether the office would be conferred with a "consecration" or an "ordination" remains unresolved. Ten years after the Crete gathering, the conclusions of the Rhodes Consultation in 1988 called unanimously for a renewed female diaconate (though with consecration, not ordination); the Orthodox Academy of Crete did the same in 1990;[30] so did the Damascus and Istanbul gatherings of Orthodox women in 1996 and 1997.[31] To date, however, no concrete action has been taken.

At the turn of the new millennium, and on the basis of the conversations of the ongoing Paris Orthodox group discussing women and men in the Church, Behr-Sigel composed[32]—and again gathered signatures for—a letter, this time to Bartholomew I, the ecumenical patriarch in Constantinople, requesting the reconstitution of the female diaconate.[33] Versions of the letter were eventually submitted to all the heads of Orthodox autocephalous churches and the patriarchates of Moscow and Antioch. Bartholomew seemed a likely ally, as he stated in an interview that "no obstacle in canon law stands in the way of ordination of women to the diaconate. This institution of the early Church deserves to be revitalised."[34] Behr-Sigel likes the patriarch's choice of words. She writes that the desire is for "more than a simple and archaeological reconstitution of the ancient ministry of deaconesses. In accordance with the term used by your All-holiness, it is a question of its revitalisation, in other words its realisation in the context of the culture and requirements of the present day, while yet remaining faithful to its original and its essential aims."[35] She is especially careful to say that since modern society does not perpetuate the same level of segregation of the sexes as in early Christianity, deaconesses should serve the whole community of the church and world, not just other women. As it is, women already serve in a

---

[28] Ibid., p. 9.
[29] Ibid., p. 10.
[30] See "Orthodox Women's Consultation, Orthodox Academy of Crete, January 1990."
[31] Behr-Sigel, "An Orthodox Diaconate for Women?" p. 61.
[32] Interview with Behr-Sigel, 2003.
[33] Behr-Sigel, "Vers une Restauration Créative du Diaconat Féminin?" *Contacts* 53, no. 3 (2001), pp. 253–58. This article includes both Behr-Sigel's prefatory text and the letter to the ecumenical patriarch. The letter alone, which Behr-Sigel herself composed, appears in English in the aforementioned "An Orthodox Diaconate for Women?"
[34] Behr-Sigel, "An Orthodox Diaconate for Women?" p. 61.
[35] Ibid., p. 62.

"semi-diaconal capacity," so the "epiclesis of their diaconal ordination would fortify these women in their ministry." And it is not at all surprising that Behr-Sigel suggests a need to revitalize the male diaconate as well.[36]

But again, the call for a female diaconate was neglected. In her lecture at Holy Cross and St. Vladimir's in the United States in 2003, Behr-Sigel sadly observed that despite the Rhodes mandate there was no sign yet of women deaconesses on the horizon. Instead, the question had been met "with an institutional opposition fed mostly by obscure fears," most likely pertaining to the question of presbyteral ordination.[37] It seems likely now that the female diaconate will not be reinstituted until the question of the female priesthood is resolved, along with all the theological questions trailing in its wake.

Behr-Sigel never suggested, despite all her arguments in favor of ordaining women, that she herself desired to enter the Orthodox priesthood. Even though she had very happy memories of her eight-month stint as a lay preacher in a rural Reformed congregation, the priestly office seems not to have held any personal allure for her. And yet throughout her life she was a public speaker for the church, a theologian, a professor at Orthodox, Catholic, and ecumenical schools, the lay president of her French-speaking parish, and an activist for l'ACAT. Behr-Sigel may never have held a formal office in the church, but she was, in her own distinctive way, a deaconess. Her colleague at *Contacts*, Michel Stavrou, says of her and Nina Pécheff-Evdokimov (Paul Evdokimov's daughter): "In a certain fashion, they exercised the social role of 'deaconessses' in their parish."[38] And this diaconate was certainly of the "creatively renewed" kind she wished to see embodied in the Orthodox church of today: one that seeks out the sorrows, needs, and questions of the world and tries to satisfy them. Her demeanor, even in the midst of divisive issues, was always one of service, always diaconal.

[36] Ibid., p. 63.
[37] Behr-Sigel, "The Ordination of Women: A Point of Contention," p. 62.
[38] Stavrou, "La Question du Diaconat Féminin," p. 483. My translation.

7

Feminist, Protestant, Orthodox?

Elisabeth Behr-Sigel was nothing if not a bridge-builder. She was among the first women to enter the male-dominated field of theology. She was raised and educated Lutheran but as an adult professed the Orthodox Christian faith without repudiating her past. She was brought up to speak German, later embraced the French language and culture, and kept company with Russian émigré thinkers, writing her dissertation on the little-known Russian theologian Alexander Bukharev. She was a cultural Westerner in a theologically Eastern setting. She was an ecumenist in a church that has often resisted or even departed from ecumenical dialogue. She defended the ordination of women in the church most unanimously opposed to it.[1] Despite her unconventional views, she has been proclaimed "the grandmother of Western Orthodoxy," "Eastern Orthodoxy's premier woman thinker,"[2] and even "a father in the faith,"[3] and accordingly she has been fêted with a festschrift sponsored by the community of Saint-Elie and with commemorative events at St.-Serge in Paris in June 2007, the Lebanese Academy of Fine Arts in Beirut in January 2009, and the Institute for Ecumenical Research in September 2011.[4]

This set of unusual combinations in an exceptionally long life raises three interpretative questions regarding Behr-Sigel's theology. The first question is: how "feminist" was she? Feminism is largely responsible for calling attention to women's place in the church and ecclesial offices, and Behr-Sigel herself knew and read feminist

[1] Interestingly, I have yet to find a single open attack on her person or ideas from other Orthodox, though silence is its own kind of comment.

[2] Hopko, "Preface to the English Edition," in *The Ministry of Women in the Church*, p. ix.

[3] Christopher D'Aloisio, president of Syndesmos, the Orthodox youth organization, gave her this title in his piece, "Elisabeth Behr-Sigel, a Father in the Faith," *Syndesmos News* 19, no. 1 (2006), pp. 1, 3–4.

[4] A colloquium entitled "Elisabeth Behr-Sigel, un Siècle d'Engagement dans l'Eglise," was held on June 23, 2007 at Saint-Serge in Paris to discuss her life and work, with more than 60 people participating. The papers are collected in *Contacts* 59, no. 4 (2007). The event in Lebanon is reported in "Beyrouth: Rencontre Commémorative à la Mémoire d'Elisabeth Behr-Sigel," *Service Orthodoxe de Presse* 337 (2009), pp. 9–10. The papers of the Strasbourg conference are collected in "*A Communion Lived in Faith and Love*": *Reflections on Elisabeth Behr-Sigel's Ecclesiology* (ed. Eleni Kasselouri-Hatzivassiliadi and Sarah Hinlicky Wilson; Doxa and Praxis; Geneva: WCC Publications, 2013).

theology. To what extent did it influence her convictions? The second question, which relates to the first one, is: how "Protestant" was she? Did her baptism, confirmation, and education in the Lutheran church carry over into her work as an Orthodox theologian? Did her ecumenical involvements influence her back toward Protestant theology? More to the point, was her defense of the ordination of women—a practice that exists so far only among Protestants—grounded in Protestant rather than Orthodox theology? Finally, what kind of an Orthodox theologian was she? It has been recognized for some time now that there are two principal streams of modern Orthodox theology in the West, both deriving from prerevolutionary Russia and the emigration that followed. Where does Paris-based and Russian-influenced Behr-Sigel fit within the larger story of Orthodoxy in the twentieth century?

How feminist?

Behr-Sigel always maintained a great respect for the secular expression of feminism.[5] She found herself sympathetic to it in her early adulthood, as her husband helped with childcare and housework, and then during the Second World War when the lack of men to do work outside the home meant that she and other women took up the duties—and performed them well.[6] From Paul Evdokimov, Behr-Sigel gained an appreciation for feminism, especially the "feminine" values it promoted. He taught her to regard it as a "sign of the times." She admits, "This movement is certainly an ambiguous and sometimes irritating sign, written in clumsy letters and spoken of in consciously provocative terms, a sign of 'a Christian idea gone haywire' in our Far West that finds itself submerged by a nihilistic tidal wave." Its violence, however, also carries the hope that people will earn "the *right to be different*, whether on the ethnic, cultural, or sexual level. The women's movement participates both in the violence and in the noble hope that is the divine image in man."[7] At the same time, Behr-Sigel believed that feminism couldn't sustain its own momentum without the wisdom of the Christian faith, from which she believed feminism ultimately to derive. As she wrote in the early 1980s, "The Church has the vocation to baptize this new freedom won by women so that it will not degenerate into anarchy and mere confrontation of selfishness."[8]

Her attitude toward feminism within the church, however, was a little more complex. She was certainly not pleased with militant feminist movements that simply demanded the ordination of women, a position she found to be lacking in the necessary charity and serenity it takes to work through such a contentious issue. But Behr-Sigel was still willing to participate in ecumenical gatherings with a feminist presence—for instance, the Bossey seminars on "Feminine Images and Orthodox Spirituality." She also regularly

---

[5] Late in life she could still jokingly refer to herself as a "militant feminist," though this likely refers to how others perceived her than how she perceived herself. Olga Lossky, *Toward the Endless Day*, p. 257.

[6] Interview with Elisabeth Behr-Sigel. Though her husband did say, "anything but the diapers."

[7] Behr-Sigel, "Women in the Orthodox Church: Heavenly Vision and Historical Realities," in *The Ministry of Women in the Church*, p. 107.

[8] Behr-Sigel, "The Place of Women in the Church," in *The Ministry of Women in the Church*, p. 158.

reviewed books by feminists scholars for *Contacts*, which journal altogether published around 115 of her reviews. These are an important source for tracking Behr-Sigel's developing views on feminism.

Her earliest foray into reviewing a "feminist" kind of book was with Elisabeth Schmidt's *J'étais une Pasteur en Algérie*. Behr-Sigel praises the book and its author. She writes:

> Called to assume responsibilities reserved, in our society, generally to men, Elisabeth Schmidt shows herself at their level with simplicity and courage. At the same time, she remains a woman; and it is precisely this being female that facilitates her bypassing of certain obstacles and permits the opening of doors that would remain shut to her male colleagues, in particular in relation with Arab women. The book includes no apology for female pastoral ministry. But it is a witness that lends itself to reflection.[9]

It is not surprising that Behr-Sigel is sympathetic, as she herself once exercised a (lay) pastoral ministry; nor is it surprising that she doesn't miss any "apology" for Schmidt's work. The review is from 1976, the same year as the Agapia gathering in Romania and the very beginning of Behr-Sigel's own work on women in the church.

The next year she reviewed *La Femme Avenir* by France Quéré, a Protestant theologian whom Behr-Sigel continued to cite throughout her career. Behr-Sigel admires Quéré's emphasis on the particularity of female gifts over against male ones, since at this stage Behr-Sigel is still thinking chiefly along the lines set down by Evdokimov. The question here, Behr-Sigel writes, is about "the destiny of humanity in man [*l'humanité en l'homme*]. A destiny of which the woman could possess the key. But will she help him open the way to a 'new humanism'?"[10] Quéré's intention, Behr-Sigel reports, is to "promote feminine values, love and care for life, a sense of the reciprocity and symmetry in service, in order to teach humanity 'to live in the plural' and to establish 'an art of conversation in that place where perpetual affronts and the instinct to dominate reign.'"[11] Behr-Sigel is attracted by the idea of feminine charisms challenging male vices, namely conquest, domination, exploitation, and solipsism. Quéré herself speaks of a "profound, confused, multiform, wild or sublimated" instinct that attaches women to life, children, and nature. Woman is open to the other; woman can offer a prophetic critique of life today. Woman must both address man and affirm her own female nature. The task, Quéré writes, requires both struggle and conversion.[12]

Behr-Sigel wonders if the latter term is a merely accidental upsurge of religious language in what is purely a secular fight, or if feminism is an authentic encounter with the gospel. She decides it to be the latter. She likes Quéré's suggestion of a

---

[9] Behr-Sigel, review of *J'étais une Pasteur en Algérie*, by E. Schmidt, *Contacts* 28 (1976), p. 172. My translation.

[10] Behr-Sigel, review of *La Femme Avenir*, by F. Quéré, *Contacts* 29 (1977), pp. 348–51. All quotations are my translation.

[11] Ibid.

[12] Ibid., p. 349.

correspondence between women's forms of service and the revelation of God as servant. Further, the "total feminism" that Quéré advocates is in fact a "total humanism" or even a "total divino-humanism," open to the divine mystery. Without consciously realizing it, Behr-Sigel has begun to identify the supposedly distinctive charisms of women with the charisms that all people—thus men too—ought to have, though she doesn't yet have the intellectual framework to reconcile the apparent paradox.[13]

Characteristically, Behr-Sigel asks: how are we Orthodox going to respond to this? Feminism that asks for equal rights doesn't go far enough and doesn't really excite Behr-Sigel, either, though she acknowledges its value. What really matters is to embrace values other than those that reign in a civilization masculinized to the excess, evangelical values of service, reciprocity, and respect for the other. Without the evangelical corrective, feminism risks creating women who are no better than men or the "old man" Adam, sinful and egotistical. Women do better to see a sign of hope in the Theotokos, the New Eve and humble servant of the Lord, in whom humanity has crushed the head of the serpent. Here Behr-Sigel still takes Mary to be a model specifically for women.

The review of Quéré's book demonstrates that as long as Behr-Sigel thinks about *feminine* charisms as opposed to the *common* charisms of men and women, ecclesial and other kinds of feminism make a good deal of sense to her. They reclaim and uplift those values that women have (supposedly) always carried with them despite their social oppression. And they reveal a deep structural sympathy between feminism and thinkers like Evdokimov and Thomas Hopko, who argued along similar lines.

Behr-Sigel didn't restrict herself to constructive feminist volumes. She also enjoyed books like Monique Hébrard's *Les Femmes dans L'Eglise*, a collection of interviews with various women in the church.[14] A similar kind of book was Jeanne Becher's *Women, Religion, and Sexuality*, to which Behr-Sigel made a contribution with her friend Nicole Maillard.[15] Behr-Sigel's review of this volume in *Contacts* is noteworthy in that she endorses Rosemary Radford Ruether's argument that the rejection of women by men is really about rejecting mortality: in other words, Behr-Sigel explicitly commends an explicitly feminist theologian. Similarly, in her review of *L'Incontournable Echange* by Elisabeth J. Lacelle, Behr-Sigel reports fearlessly on Lacelle's reading and appropriation of North American feminists like Ruether, Schüssler-Fiorenza, and Russell.[16] While admitting that Lacelle's work will invite questions, reservations, and critiques, she believes all the same that the book could serve as "an invitation to explore the territory that up till now has been poorly known by the majority of our theologians."[17] Behr-Sigel read historical studies, too, like Ruth Albrecht's *Das Leben der Heiligen Makrina auf dem Hintergrund der Thekla-Traditionen*,[18] which carefully analyzed the mixed patristic

---

13   Ibid., p. 350.

14   Behr-Sigel, review of *Les Femmes dans L'Eglise*, by M. Hébrard, *Contacts* 37 (1985), pp. 74–76.

15   Behr-Sigel, review of *Women, Religion and Sexuality*, ed. Jeanne Becher, pp. 76–77.

16   Behr-Sigel, review of *L'Incontournable Echange*, by E. J. Lacelle, *Contacts* 48 (1996), pp. 63–65. Lacelle later wrote about Behr-Sigel; see "Elisabeth Behr-Sigel," in *Penseurs et Apôtres du XXᵉ Siècle*, pp. 375–86 (ed. Jean Genest; Montreal: Fides, 2001).

17   Behr-Sigel, review of *L'Incontournable Echange*, p. 65. My translation.

18   Behr-Sigel, review of *Das Leben der Heiligen Makrina auf dem Hintergrund der Thekla-Traditionen*, by R. Albrecht, *Contacts* 39 (1987), pp. 77–79.

messages on women and documented the roles that women played in developing their own monastic tradition.

Behr-Sigel's mature judgment on feminism appears most clearly in two reviews, ten years apart. The first is of *Gottes Selbstbewusste Töchter: Frauen-Emanzipation im Frühen Christentum?* by Anne Jensen, a theologian who some years earlier had written an article concluding that the Eastern church is less patriarchal than the Western church.[19] Jensen asks whether Christianity started out pro-woman or was always basically anti-woman. She concludes that the former is the case, and then asks why, by the Middle Ages, the church had become more misogynist. She suggests three reasons. First, it was the result of the hierarchical priesthood replacing the charismatic authority of an earlier era; second, it was the distrust of sexuality that goes with monasticism; and third, it was a certain contempt for intellectual culture as Greco-Roman civilization died out, coupled with eschatological expectation. Behr-Sigel challenges the second reason, on the grounds that, even if the monastic ideal sometimes did include a morbid fear of women, it equally contributed to their liberation and independence from males.[20] But there is general sympathy here between Behr-Sigel and Jensen's thesis that Christianity is not fundamentally anti-woman. The book prompted Behr-Sigel to recommend further reflection on the relation between the masculine and the feminine as it concerns the "representation of Christ."

The second relevant book that Behr-Sigel reviewed is *L'Eglise et les Femmes* by Xénia Iouriev, a Greek theologian. Iouriev's self-appointed task is not to ask the church to change its practice to fit changing modern conditions but rather to ask whether the church's practice reflects its own theology. The study is a trinitarian examination of theological anthropology and related doctrines. In the end Iouriev concludes that the church has *not*, in fact, acted consistently with its own beliefs. She suggests that the excessive "masculinity" of the church is the cause of its schisms and general rigidity. Worse yet, the church's denial of the basic unity of men and women is the anthropological version of the Arian heresy, which denies the unity of God and human in Christ.

To this point Behr-Sigel is sympathetic. However, she regrets what she calls the "aggressive and simplistic feminist rhetoric" in the book that assumes "unilateral victimization of the woman, along with making the male guilty in an equally unilateral way." This is a "disastrous reaction" that simply reverses the traditional treatment of Eve as the eternally culpable temptress. She adds, "I cannot, in conscience, subscribe to the affirmation of the author according to which, after the primitive charismatic epoch, the Church became 'an institution organized by men and for men.'"[21] Behr-Sigel asks whether the Spirit abandoned the church, contrary to Christ's promises. She answers no. Whatever else its errors, the church continued to baptize women, chrismate them, and call them to holiness. These are not minor matters. The constitutive elements of

---

[19] See Behr-Sigel's discussion of this earlier article in "L'Eglise d'Orient Est-Elle Patriarcaliste!" pp. 235–37.

[20] Behr-Sigel, review of *Gottes Selbstbewusste Töchter: Frauen-Emanzipation im Frühen Christentum?* by A. Jensen, *Contacts* 45 (1993), pp. 153–56 (155).

[21] Behr-Sigel, review of *L'Eglise et les Femmes*, by X. Iouriev, *Contacts* 55 (2003), pp. 136–41 (140). My translation.

the church do conform to the baptismal hymn of Galatians 3. In any event, Behr-Sigel always dislikes laying blame with any one party. Her lifelong praise of "serenity" or, in philosophical language, "apatheia" leaves her little room for sympathy with feminism of this sort.

To the question, then, of how much of a feminist Behr-Sigel was, the answer will vary depending on the definition of feminism given. She was generally affirmative of feminist goals in secular life, but her criticisms of church practice stemmed from the Orthodox Tradition itself. She did not view the Tradition as fundamentally flawed; exclusion of women from the priesthood was finally a matter of denying the soteriology and theological anthropology that the Scriptures and church fathers professed, not a fundamental flaw in the soteriology and theological anthropology themselves. Nor was it chiefly a matter of the marginalization of one group by another. The moment the latter issue defined the whole theological debate, Behr-Sigel was likely to withdraw her support. But if the Orthodox dared to learn from feminist research and critiques, she hoped, they could "assimilate them in order to be able, eventually, to evangelize them and also, thanks to them, to evangelize the historical social dimension of our church."[22]

This is not to say that Behr-Sigel was at all sympathetic to ongoing misogynist practices in the Orthodox church. She continuously spoke against the exclusion of baptized baby girls from the altar, the churching of "impure" new mothers, and the silencing of women's voices in the church. But she believed that the call to address women's issues was a call to be converted again to the gospel.[23] To refuse the call was not simply to neglect a particular oppressed group but to fail the charge to "discern the signs of the times" and "test the spirits."[24] The question about women, she argued, is as old as the gospel itself, and it reasserts itself today as a "new awareness of the ancient baptismal faith."[25] When feminist theologians thought along these lines; she was with them. When they departed, she left their company, too.

How Protestant?

In contemporary Orthodoxy, converts play nearly as vital a role in the theological and ecclesial life of the church as "cradle Orthodox." Behr-Sigel was just one of many converts. Included among them are Lev Gillet, the "Monk of the Eastern Church"; Kallistos (Timothy) Ware, author of the best-known introductions to the Orthodox faith; Leonie Liveris of *MaryMartha*; patristic scholar Susan Ashbrook Harvey; Frederica Matthewes-Green, an American popularizer of all things Orthodox; and such theologians as Olivier Clément, John Erickson, and Michael Plekon.

---

[22] Behr-Sigel, "Feminine Images and Orthodox Spirituality," p. 14.
[23] Behr-Sigel, "Introduction," in *The Ministry of Women in the Church*, p. 14.
[24] Ibid., p. 23.
[25] Behr-Sigel, "Toward a New Community," in *The Ministry of Women in the Church*, p. 95.

The dynamic between the two groups is not always an easy one.[26] This is especially the case where women's issues are concerned. In some cases, converts are eager to adopt all Orthodox customs wholesale without any distinction between what is "ethnic" and what is "evangelical,"[27] while in other cases converts bring along their feminist convictions that they believe to be *not* ultimately at odds with the Orthodox Christian faith.[28] The former category fares better than the latter in the United States. Paris is a bit more progressive, a friendlier place for the latter, and probably less representative of worldwide trends. There is a tendency, at any rate, to chalk up advocacy for the ordination of women or related issues to undue Protestant or ecumenical influence—it is, after all, only Protestants who are ordaining women at the moment—or to an incomplete mental conversion to Orthodoxy.

Behr-Sigel seems not to have been subject to such accusations, perhaps because she took up the issue after she'd been a member of the Orthodox church for more than 50 years. Nevertheless, it is a question well worth pursuing. She was baptized and confirmed in the Lutheran church and theologically educated at the Protestant faculties in Strasbourg and Paris, studying with Oscar Cullmann and graduating at the top of her class. Reformed pastors were her most important early mentors. She also spent eight months as the lay pastor of a tiny Reformed congregation in Alsace, though, curiously, this was after she had already converted to Orthodoxy.[29] Of this ministry she made the telling remark, "I keep the memory of a time of grace and, pinned to my heart, the hope that one day women, responding to new needs, will be able to exercise a ministry analogous to mine—whatever the title may be—in the heart of the Orthodox Church."[30] When she did enter the Orthodox church, Lev Gillet chrismated but did not "rebaptize" her, nor did he require her to repudiate her previous church home, as Gillet himself had not been required to do.[31]

Long before Agapia, Behr-Sigel had been actively involved in ecumenism. She reports that her most profound ecumenical experience was in a solidarity group during the Second World War, some members of which were deported and killed for their efforts.[32] She was certainly open to the insights of the "Christian other," with eight

---

26. See the discussion by Demetra Velisarios Jaquet, "Women in Orthodox Christian Traditions," in *Encyclopedia of Women and Religion in North America*, pp. 510–11 (ed. Rosemary Skinner Keller and Rosemary Radford Ruether; vol. 2; Bloomington and Indianapolis: Indiana University Press, 2006). Elisabeth Behr-Sigel herself is pictured on p. 510. A careful comparison of this article by Jaquet from 2006 with my "Epilogue: Orthodoxy, Modernity, and Feminism Recovered" in *Discerning the Signs of the Times*, pp. 137–48, which was published five years earlier in 2001, will show that a great portion of my text, unquoted and uncited, has been reproduced in Jaquet's article.

27. Such as Frederica Matthewes-Green. Jaquet, "Women in Orthodox Christian Traditions," p. 511.

28. Such as Leonie B. Liveris.

29. Behr-Sigel's Orthodox bishop, Metropolitan Evlogy, gave his express permission for her to do this work because of the great shortage of pastors at the time. See Behr-Sigel, "My Journey to the Orthodox Church," trans. Deno Takles, in *Discerning the Signs of the Times*, p. 7.

30. Ibid., p. 8.

31. Ibid., p. 7. Behr-Sigel was chrismated on December 13, 1929. See also Behr-Sigel's biography, *Lev Gillet: "A Monk of the Eastern Church,"* p. 120 (trans. Helen Wright; Oxford: Fellowship of St. Alban and St. Sergius, 1999).

32. Interview with Behr-Sigel, 2003.

published articles on ecumenical topics from the late 1950s to the early 1970s.[33] She was a "faithful reader" of the Protestant journal *Réforme* from its inception.[34] It was through the interventions of the WCC that she got into the question of women in the church, and during the last 30 years of her life she attended numerous ecumenical conferences on the issue as well as writing 23 articles on ecumenical topics (not including pieces about women in the church) and reviewing books by Roman Catholic and Protestant theologians.[35] So it stands to reason that Behr-Sigel may have either retained or absorbed, so to speak, a Protestant outlook on matters pertaining to church and priesthood.

Some of her scholarly interests seem to point in that direction. Her doctoral dissertation was on the Russian theologian Alexander Bukharev, who among other things was famous for leaving his monastic vows and marrying. Bukharev envisioned a monasticism not within cloistered walls but in the city, in the thick of life, even in

[33]   For instance, in the 1950s, "Vers l'Unité Chrétienne," *Contacts* 11, no. 2 (1959), pp. 121–26, and "Du Phanar au Vatican," *Contacts* 11, no. 4 (1959), pp. 257–59; in the 1960s, "Les Orthdoxes et le Pèlerinage de Paul VI," *Le Messager Orthodoxe* 24–25 (1963–64), pp. 31–33, "Repenser la Theologie du Mariage?" *Contacts* 16, no. 4 (1964), pp. 291–301, and "Inauguration d'un Centre d'Etudes Oecuméniques (Strasbourg, 31 Janvier et 1er Fevrier 1965)," *Contacts* 17 (1965), pp. 73–76; in the 1970s, before her work on women led her into greater ecumenical involvement, "A Propos du Débat sur le Célibat Sacerdotal dans l'Eglise Latine," *Contacts* 22, no. 1 (1970), pp. 54–60; "Charles Westphal (1896–1972)," *Contacts* 24 (1972), p. 214, about a pastor of the Reformed Church in France; "Questions à Propos d'une Célébration Oecuménique," *Bulletin de la Crypte* 13 (1973), p. 8; and "Des Orthodoxes Oeuvrent au Sein de la CIMADE," *Contacts* 27 (1975), pp. 209–11.

[34]   Behr-Sigel, "Porteur de Valeurs," *Réforme* (October 10–16, 2002), p. 11. She also wrote for *Réforme* a brief article defending infant baptism and communion, the latter especially not a position normally associated with Protestants. "Offert à Tous, le Triple Sacrement," *Réforme* (June 6, 1981), p. 7.

[35]   Her articles of ecumenical import after 1975, not related to women's issues, include the following. "Après la Semaine des Prières pour l'Unité des Chrétiens," *Service Orthodoxe de Presse* 15 (1977), p. 7; "Conférence Jubilaire du Fellowship Saint Alban et Saint Serge," *Bulletin de la Crypte* 57 (1977), pp. 11–12; "La Cimade Fête Son 40ᵉ Anniversaire," *Bulletin de la Crypte* 87 (1980), p. 12; "In Memoriam: Pasteur Henri Roser, Suzanne de Dietrich," *Contacts* 32, no. 4 (1980), p. 342, about Protestant resisters during the Nazi regime who were personal friends of Behr-Sigel's; "A Propos de l'Affaire Kung: Une Crise, Mais l'Espérance Est Indéfectible," *Service Orthodoxe de Presse* 45 (1980), pp. 9–11; "In Memoriam: Annie Jaubert (1912–1980)," *Contacts* 33, no. 2 (1981), p. 164, about a Roman Catholic exegete; "Rencontre Oecuménique de Chantilly (6–8 juin 1981)," *Contacts* 33, no. 3 (1981), pp. 235–36; "Colloque de Chevetogne. 23–27 août 1982," *Contacts* 33, no. 4 (1981), pp. 343–46; "L'Athos et le Dialogue avec Rome," *Service Orthodoxe de Presse* 66 (1982), pp. 12–14; "In Memoriam: Dom Olivier Rousseau, 1898–1984," *Contacts* 36, no. 4 (1984), pp. 377–78, about a Roman Catholic monk and friend of Lev Gillet; "Le Schisme de 1054: Origines, Conséquences et Perspectives," *Supplément Service Orthodoxe de Presse* 86-A (1984), pp. 1–16; "Les Lendemains du BEM," *Supplément Service Orthodoxe de Presse* 102-B (1985), pp. 1–4; "Semaine de l'Unité: Faire l'Effort d'Aller vers l'Autre," *Service Orthodoxe de Presse* 104 (1986), pp. 12–13; "Orthodoxie et Catholicisme (Quelques Points de Divergence Doctrinale)," *Courrier de l'ACAT* 109 (1990), pp. 22–23; "VIIᵉ Assemblée du Conseil Oecuménique des Eglises," *Bulletin de la Crypte* 190 (1991), p. 24; "Le 30ᵉ Anniversaire de la Rencontre Paul VI-Athénagoras," *Bulletin de la Crypte* 220 (1994), p. 24; "La Fraternité Saint-Elie," *Bulletin de la Crypte* 227 (1994), p. 22; "Au Tournant de l'Histoire, Chrétiens et Chrétiennes Vivent de Nouvelles Alliances. Lyon 7–8 mars 1997," *Oecuménisme Information* 274 (1997), p. 7; "La Place des Orthodoxes dans le Mouvement Oecuménique," *Oecuménisme Information* 287 (1998), pp. 20–21; "Dixième Anniversaire de la Fraternité Saint-Elie," *Oecuménisme Information* 320 (2001), pp. 5–6; "Un Anniversaire," *Bulletin de la Crypte* 299 (2002), pp. 19–20, namely of the monastery of Chevetogne; "Le 75ᵉ Anniversaire de Chevetogne," *Service Orthodoxe de Presse* 265 (2002), pp. 27–29; "Célébration Oecuménique de la Fête du Prophète Elie," *Mikhtav* 34 (2002), pp. 3–4. And all this is to say nothing of her many book reviews by non-Orthodox theologians or on non-Orthodox topics.

marriage. The resemblance to Martin Luther is obvious enough, and it wasn't lost on the Russian hierarchy of the time, which "slanderously treated [Bukharev] as a Lutheran."[36] "Lutheran" was certainly intended as a pejorative term. According to Behr-Sigel, Bukharev defended himself on the grounds that

> his intention was not at all to abolish "or weaken the tradition and the ecclesiastical rules, but to restore to them their authentic sense." Rather than a reformation—in the western sense of this word—his appeal aimed at a resurrection, a new Pentecost of the Spirit . . . His appeal did not aim either at a reformation or a revolution, but at a creative metanoia of a new life.[37]

Whether this is an apt characterization of the Western reformers is beside the point. What matters is that Behr-Sigel was careful to distinguish Bukharev's work from any identification with Protestantism. It is quite possible, of course, that she had her own reasons for wanting to do so, perhaps to prove herself fully divested of her Protestant past or to make Bukharev a more attractive figure to Orthodox theologians who would flee even a fellow Orthodox if he smelled of Protestantism. In any event, she theologically aligned neither herself nor Bukharev with Western tendencies.

Another such figure she studied was St. Tikhon of Zadonsk. Tikhon, as Behr-Sigel well knew, was a reader of and commentator on the writings of St. Augustine—most unusual for an Eastern Christian. He admired both Anglican bishop Joseph Hall and German Lutheran theologian Johann Arndt.[38] Tikhon even took the title of his most famous book, *On True Christianity*, from Arndt's of the same name, which Tikhon "particularly enjoyed reading and re-reading."[39] The Russian saint emphasized pious and intelligent Scripture reading as an "instrument of spiritual and theological renewal," certainly a typical Protestant theme.[40] "The *lectio divina* is for Tikhon an encounter with God, with the Living God, here and now,"[41] and Behr-Sigel was certainly fond of anything addressing the here and now. She judged that Tikhon's spirituality, though grounded in Orthodox trinitarianism with its emphasis on the indwelling of the Holy Spirit in the human heart, was "essentially christocentric."[42]

If anything, Behr-Sigel makes bold to emphasize the Western, Roman Catholic, and Protestant currents in Tikhon's thought rather than downplaying them in this study for the collection *Christian Spirituality Post-Reformation and Modern*. There is a particular reason she does so. Tikhon had acquired something less than a pristinely Orthodox reputation under the inspection of Georges Florovsky in his massive study *Ways of Russian Theology*. According to Florovsky, Tikhon—though in many ways a

---

[36] Behr-Sigel, "Un Prophète Orthodoxe," p. 105. All quotations are my translation.
[37] Ibid., p. 106.
[38] Behr-Sigel, *The Place of the Heart*, p. 5.
[39] Lewis Shaw, "John Meyendorff and the Heritage of the Russian Theological Tradition," in *New Perspectives on Historical Theology: Essays in Memory of John Meyendorff*, p. 24 (ed. Bradley Nassif; Grand Rapids, MI: Eerdmans, 1996).
[40] Behr-Sigel, *The Place of the Heart*, pp. 11–12.
[41] Behr-Sigel, "Tikhon de Zadonsk," *Contacts* 26, no. 1 (1974), pp. 35–65 (60). All quotations are my translation.
[42] Ibid.

laudable figure in the reawakening of Russian monasticism—was still marked by the "pseudomorphosis" of Orthodoxy into a latinized, Westernized, Thomistic imitation of its former Eastern glory. During Tikhon's time, schools of Orthodox theology and the "manuals" that came out of them looked more scholastic than anything else and therefore were not faithful to Orthodox tradition.[43] Tikhon himself read and taught in Latin.[44]

Behr-Sigel, unabashedly an ecumenical Westerner even while Orthodox, sets out to reinterpret the data.

> For if on the one hand servile imitation and lack of discernment led to a real alienation, above all in the realm of theology as taught in the Orthodox schools and manuals, on the other it must be said that Orthodoxy's encounter with Western spirituality was not without some stimulating effects . . . Those who were strong spiritually, rooted in the bedrock of the tradition of the church, and free (precisely because of this rootedness) from a fear of "the other," were able to transform this encounter into an opportunity for a fruitful integration of traditions.[45]

It was precisely Tikhon's ability to synthesize the true treasures of the church catholic, as preserved in the West, with his own Eastern faith and spirituality that Behr-Sigel praises and even commends as "the historic task of the Orthodox church again today."[46]

So, for instance, if Tikhon's christocentrism led him to pray at the stations of the cross in his own cell and to meditate at length on the passion of Christ, Behr-Sigel not only rejects Florovsky's judgment that this is merely a (presumably negative) Western influence but calls attention to other examples of native Russian spirituality centered on the cross, such as the "passion-bearers" St. Boris and St. Gleb, or the nineteenth-century St. Seraphim of Sarov's similar devotion.[47] Tikhon's use of Arndt—and Behr-Sigel is quick to add that Arndt was admired by Roman Catholic readers too—is a "creative assimilation," not a slavish repetition. Joseph Hall, the Anglican bishop, used Jean Mombaer's *Rosetum*, as did Ignatius of Loyola; and such a cross-fertilization does not disqualify Tikhon's Orthodoxy but "indicates that living spiritual experience transcends confessional borders."[48] Tikhon felt "a very Western intimate need for a personal assurance of salvation," which Behr-Sigel compares to Augustine, and he insisted on the need for a *"living faith,"* like Arndt.[49] He used scholastic concepts, even terms like

---

[43] Behr-Sigel, "Hesychasm and the Western Impact in Russia: St. Tikhon of Zadonsk (1724–1783)," in *Christian Spirituality Post-Reformation and Modern*, pp. 432, 437 (ed. Louis Dupré and Don E. Saliers; World Spirituality: An Encyclopedic History of the Religious Quest, 18; New York: Crossroad, 1989).

[44] See Georges Florovsky, *Ways of Russian Theology: Part One*, pp. 157–59 (ed. Richard S. Haugh; trans. Robert L. Nichols; The Collected Works of Georges Florovsky, 5; Vaduz, Liechtenstein: Büchervertriebsanstalt, 1987).

[45] Behr-Sigel, "Hesychasm and the Western Impact in Russia," p. 432.

[46] Ibid., p. 433.

[47] Ibid., p. 437.

[48] Ibid., p. 441.

[49] Ibid., p. 443. Her italics.

"form" and "matter" when speaking of sacraments, and talked about "satisfaction" as part of soteriology.[50] Behr-Sigel concludes that "[t]he spiritual path of Tikhon is of a sort of Orthodox Augustinianism where sometimes the accents of a Pascal, indeed of a Luther and of a Kierkegaard, but above all of Dostoevsky break through."[51]

Tikhon's distinctively Orthodox qualities are not neglected, though. Whatever the Western influence, "Tikhon instinctively placed himself in the great, central trinitarian tradition, in the tradition of the Orthodox faith represented in the persons of Basil the Great and John Chrysostom (the father whom he preferred above all others)." He emphasized the "sacramental realism" of St. Paul and the church as the mystical body of Christ, seamlessly connecting "asceticism, mysticism, and ethics." "In this," Behr-Sigel declares, "resides his Orthodoxy . . . [T]he 'fear' and the 'trembling' are always surmounted by a confident hope and desire for the ultimate transfiguration of humanity and the entire cosmos, characteristic of Eastern spirituality."[52] In other words, Tikhon did not perceive Western and Eastern spirituality as fundamentally at odds with one another. "His interior liberty and his spiritual tact permitted him to recognize and accept, to the extent he was allowed to encounter them, the authentic values of western Christianity, of Roman Catholicism as well as evangelical Protestantism."[53] Behr-Sigel prized the same liberty and tact.

A few of Behr-Sigel's articles pertain more directly to the relationship between the Protestant and Orthodox churches. In 1962 she reviewed a translation of a book by Karl Barth, *La Proclamation de l'Evangile*. Much of the article describes the patterns of Protestant theology in the last century for an Orthodox audience and Barth's own contribution particularly. She is sympathetic in surprising places, even where Barth asserts the problematic nature of visual depictions of Christ and the cross. She sees in his emphasis on transcendence a laudable concern with the Word descending to the human.[54] He insists on the ecclesial nature of preaching, its rootedness in the doctrine of the church, and the deep connection between preaching and sacraments—all of which Behr-Sigel approves.[55] She does note with rather less approval his careful avoidance of ontological language in speaking of the "new life" of the Christian and the equally careful distinction between justification and sanctification: "But why deny, for reasons that seem to be of a philosophical order and strangers to Revelation, that this life in the light of the Divine Face is truly a new life, a life transformed by the gift of the grace of the Holy Spirit Who is light and fire?"[56] And while she appreciates his ressourcement of Luther, Calvin, and Augustine, she judges (inaccurately, in light of Barth's larger corpus) that he follows the old Latin dictum, *Graecum est, non legitur*.[57] Her final sentence is the most telling: "Such are, succinctly summarized, the principal themes of a work where fidelity to life, 'to the life in Christ' in the Church, permits the most

---

50　Ibid., p. 442.
51　Behr-Sigel, "Tikhon de Zadonsk," p. 61.
52　Behr-Sigel, "Hesychasm and the Western Impact in Russia," p. 442.
53　Behr-Sigel, "Tikhon de Zadonsk," p. 65.
54　Behr-Sigel, review of *Proclamation de l'Evangile*, by K. Barth, *Contacts* 14 (1962), pp. 283–87 (284–85). All quotations are my translation.
55　Ibid., p. 285.
56　Ibid., p. 285, fn. 1, and p. 286.
57　Ibid., p. 287. "If it's Greek, don't read it."

current of Protestant theologians to rejoin, through an inner evolution, the ancient and catholic tradition of the Church."[58] The underlying assumption is that Protestants are not necessarily part of the catholic tradition at all, and it is a good thing when they do in fact become a part of it.[59]

A few years later Behr-Sigel turned her attention to another Protestant and "quelque sorte d'antibarth," Paul Tillich.[60] As with her review of Barth, most of the article summarizes the chief points of Tillich's theology, based both on his own works and a study by George Tavard, *Initiation à Paul Tillich*. She generously, perhaps too generously, finds points of contact between Tillich's themes and those of Orthodox theologians, citing Gregory of Palamas, Simeon the New Theologian, Vladimir Lossky, and the Alexandrian school specifically for its interest in the *logoi spermatikoi*, an interest Behr-Sigel perceives Tillich to share.[61] She certainly has plenty of reservations, though: the "subjectivity" of faith that she connects to Luther and Augustine, the dissociation of Jesus from Christ, a break with the dogmas formulated by the early church.[62] A comparison to Origen is just, she concludes, in that Tillich, like his predecessor, tries to "express the Christian kerygma in the language of the culture and, in particular, of the contemporary existential philosophy." (Interestingly, Sergius Bulgakov was also called a "modern Origen.") In so doing, of course, both run the risk of losing the wisdom of God in the wisdom of the world. Behr-Sigel is forgiving: "Doesn't all free thought on the faith, to which the theologian is called, include this risk? Doesn't it belong to a Christian thinker to assume the task with audacity and humility at the same time?"[63] If Tillich lacks in substance, Behr-Sigel admires his style all the same. Still, some years later she expresses the same concerns about Tillich: "Doesn't he tend to drain the Christian faith of all historical content, to disqualify history as the place of divine revelation? Are the incarnation and the humano-divinity of the Son of God not dissolved in an atemporal myth . . .?"[64] It is a difficult balance to maintain.

In another kind of article, Behr-Sigel responds to a Protestant distressed by the Orthodox priest Cyrille Argenti's uncertainty as to whether or not the Reformed church belongs to the body of Christ. Behr-Sigel expresses her commitment to ecumenical rapprochement but clearly speaks as an Orthodox to a Protestant, in no way identifying herself with the latter. She emphasizes the Orthodox ecclesiology of communion and the importance of the Theotokos—an *evangelical* importance, at that.[65]

---

[58] Ibid.

[59] A similar critique appears as a side note in a discussion of Vladimir Lossky, where she anticipates concern from heirs of the Reformation over the Orthodox notions of "contemplation" and "union" with God, but she counters that their concern is in turn an impoverishment of the Word of God, since 2 Pet. 1.4 calls us to "enter into communion with the divine nature." Behr-Sigel, "Théologie et Contemplation: Introduction à Quelques Textes de Vladimir Lossky," *Hokhma* 20 (1982), pp. 17–22 (19).

[60] Behr-Sigel, "Un Origène Moderne. A Propos d'une Initiation à Paul Tillich," *Contacts* 21 (1969), pp. 70–85. All quotations are my translation.

[61] Ibid., pp. 72, 73, 78, 75 respectively.

[62] Ibid., pp. 72, 77, 78 respectively.

[63] Ibid., p. 84.

[64] Review of *Paul Tillich et le Symbole Religieux*, by J. Dunphy, *Contacts* 30 (1978), pp. 80–82. My translation.

[65] Behr-Sigel, "Questions aux Orthodoxes," *Réforme* (May 8, 1976): n.p.

Starting in 1981, an annual conference in France brought together Orthodox and Protestants, with the blessing of both the exarch of the ecumenical patriarchate and the president of the Protestant Federation of France. Behr-Sigel attended on a number of occasions and reported on them as well.[66] The 1992 gathering heard two talks on the meaning of salvation. The Orthodox speaker, the aforementioned Cyrille Argenti, spoke on the classic Eastern doctrine of salvation, while the Protestant speaker discussed ways to make the alien term "salvation" more meaningful to contemporary people. Typically, Behr-Sigel finds value in both: the first for expressing the church's Tradition, the second for sharing a concern of the apostles themselves, namely, to speak in a way that the people could understand—exactly what she praised in Tillich. She also reports on a discussion as to whether there could be an exchange of preachers during the Week of Prayer for Christian Unity, as certain Protestant and Roman Catholic parishes had done. Behr-Sigel clearly favors the idea, but a postscript is attached from "Père Boris" explaining the impossibility of allowing non-Orthodox preachers during the divine liturgy.[67] Eleven years later at another such gathering, the subject was prayer, and Behr-Sigel again finds mutual enrichment: while Orthodoxy's liturgical prayer is rich in Tradition, it runs the risk of ritualism, while Protestantism's more spontaneous and individual prayer runs its own risk of impoverishment. She sees no need to oppose ecclesial and private prayer: they need one another.[68]

A few other comments in passing merit notice. Her very early study (1939) on Bulgakov betrays some Protestant sympathy, though the fact that it comes so early in her career, and therefore relatively soon after her conversion to Orthodoxy, may have something to do with that. She writes, "What strikes one in the first place, particularly a theologian of Protestant education, in the Bulgakovian sophiology, is the weakness of its scriptural basis, in particular in the New Testament. Outside of passages in Matt. 11:13 and Luke 7:35, of which the sophiological interpretation is contestable, Fr. Bulgakov can hardly cite evangelical texts favorable to his theses."[69] Behr-Sigel's general critique of church practice regarding women always was based on the same criteria: the failure to have an adequate scriptural basis.[70] Elsewhere she favorably mentions the Protestant Jürgen Moltmann's work on eschatological hope.[71]

On the other side, Behr-Sigel defends Simeon the New Theologian from the Roman Catholic charge of Protestantism (because of Simeon's teaching on the direct inspiration of the Spirit), countering that he was "far from denying the objective reality of sacramental grace."[72] This comment along with one about the "dark doctrine" of

---

[66] Behr-Sigel, "'Rencontre Orthodoxes-Protestantes,'" *Bulletin de la Crypte* 207 (1992), p. 23. "Rencontres Orthodoxes-Protestants en Région Parisienne," *Bulletin de la Crypte* 309 (2003), pp. 20–21.

[67] "Rencontre Orthodoxes-Protestants," pp. 23–24. The additional note is probably from Boris Bobrinskoy, the priest at Behr-Sigel's parish.

[68] Behr-Sigel, "Rencontres Orthodoxes-Protestants en Région Parisienne," pp. 20–21.

[69] Behr-Sigel, "La Sophiologie du Père Boulgakoff," p. 46. My translation.

[70] Olga Lossky suggests that, "[i]n accordance with the Lutheran rigor of her biblical education, Elisabeth was very careful to anchor her reflection in an analysis of the Scriptures." *Toward the Endless Day*, p. 203.

[71] Behr-Sigel, *The Place of the Heart*, p. 24.

[72] Ibid., p. 94.

predestination in Calvin[73] and a few others indicate that Behr-Sigel was not particularly careful about what qualifies as Protestant or a particular kind of Protestant—hardly the kind of mistakes a closet sympathizer would make.

A more personal reflection on the subject appeared in the WCC magazine *One World*. Behr-Sigel's conversation with Anna-Karin Hammar, the director of the WCC sub-unit on Women in Church and Society, was given the notable title, "A 'Protestant Orthodox.'"[74] Properly speaking, Behr-Sigel's religious roots were Jewish—her mother was a Czech Jew. Other than occasionally reporting this fact, it seems to have made little impact on Behr-Sigel, though she did have to quit her job as a teacher during the Second World War because of background checks on all employees that would have exposed her Jewish "blood."[75] Behr-Sigel was also a very distant relative of Sigmund Freud; her maternal grandmother was a Freud and came from the same village as the famous psychoanalyst.[76]

Religiously, however, she was always a Christian. In the *One World* article she says, "I was baptized in the Lutheran tradition, and my religious education—of which I have very fond memories—was also Lutheran."[77] Her first "conversion" was through participation in the World Student Christian Federation, a Protestant youth organization, where after a crisis of faith she accepted "Christ as master of my life and giver of the true life which is 'love as strong as death.'"[78] Her university education, however, was "weak," with "nothing specifically Protestant," though she made the intriguing comment that "Karl Barth was already well known in Germany then, but not yet in France," suggesting that knowledge of Barth might have made some difference to her.[79]

But her heart was captivated by Orthodoxy, especially by the Easter celebration as a foretaste of the heavenly kingdom. With the encouragement of Lev Gillet (himself a recent convert from Roman Catholicism) she moved toward joining the Orthodox church. Only in this interview with Hammar does Behr-Sigel ever mention having had any feelings of uncertainty about her conversion. "I hesitated before making my decision. Finally, I decided that I wasn't giving up any of the positive aspects of Protestantism that I prized—like respect for one's freedom of conscience—but would gain roots in an extremely rich tradition, that of *una sancta catholica apostolica*, one holy catholic church." She added that she still retained that conviction, though she had become much more aware of the "historical limitations" in Orthodoxy. However, "[y]ou won't see me returning to Protestantism," though she did occasionally participate in Protestant worship services, even taking communion on rare occasions.[80]

---

[73] Ibid., p. 4.
[74] Behr-Sigel, "A 'Protestant Orthodox,'" *One World* 156 (1990), pp. 14–15.
[75] Interview with Elisabeth Behr-Sigel, 2003.
[76] Behr-Sigel, "My Journey to the Orthodox Church," in *Discerning the Signs of the Times*, p. 5.
[77] Behr-Sigel, "A 'Protestant Orthodox,'" p. 14.
[78] Behr-Sigel, "Introduction," in *The Ministry of Women in the Church*, p. 5.
[79] Behr-Sigel, "A 'Protestant Orthodox,'" p. 14.
[80] Ibid., p. 15.

Interestingly, although according to Behr-Sigel her parents were never active practitioners of their respective faiths, she says:

> When I left Protestantism, my father was very sad, perhaps because he hadn't been a practicing Christian and, because of me, had come back to the faith. The Reformed pastor and ecumenical pioneer Marc Boegner, whom I knew very well, also asked how I could have done what I did. But I wasn't actually excommunicated, and I've always kept very close ties with my Protestant friends. I always say I'm an orthodox Protestant, or a protestant Orthodox. It's a bit complicated . . .[81]

Olga Lossky mentions that Elisabeth's father's disappointment at her conversion had another aspect: it meant "she would never become the pastor that he dreamed she would be."[82] A letter of Behr-Sigel's from early in her marriage also mentions meeting a Russian priest named Ioan Schakhovskoï who "understands very well my situation as a Protestant Orthodox."[83]

It is worth noting that the chief thing Behr-Sigel identifies as a Protestant value is "respect for one's freedom of conscience," though this is likely not what either Luther or Calvin would have claimed as their principal legacy to the Protestant churches stemming from their reforming work. All mentions of Protestantism in her biography of Lev Gillet refer either to freedom or conscience but otherwise have no dogmatic substance. In a personal letter to Eliane Poirot she once wrote: "It is often good to obey. But sometimes it is also necessary to know in one's conscience how to disobey. I remain on this point a Protestant!"[84] As much as anything, this perception of Protestantism was due to the kind of theological education she received during her time in Strasbourg. The faculty in the 1920s and 1930s was predominantly Reformed of the liberal Protestant variety, with as yet no challenge from Karl Barth's dialectical theology or Pietist influence among the faculty.[85]

Elsewhere Behr-Sigel quotes approvingly the Reformation slogan *ecclesia semper reformanda*, comparing it to Vladimir Lossky's dictum that Tradition is the "critical spirit of the Church,"[86] and also "*semper justus, semper peccator,*" which she judges to be "a saying that the Orthodox ascetics and saints would not reject."[87] Much of Behr-Sigel's critique of practices within the Orthodox church revolves around their failure to reflect the gospel, or their actively impeding the gospel, denying the fundamental freedom accorded to believers by the gospel.

---

[81] Ibid.
[82] Olga Lossky, *Toward the Endless Day*, p. 29.
[83] Ibid., p. 45.
[84] Poirot, "Elisabeth Behr-Sigel et le Carmel Saint-Elie," p. 464. My translation.
[85] See Marc Lienhard (ed.), *La Faculté de Théologie Protestante de Strasbourg Hier & Aujourd'hui, 1538–1988*, pp. 60–66 (Strasbourg: Oberlin, 1988).
[86] Behr-Sigel, "Introduction," in *The Ministry of Women in the Church*, p. 9, and "The Place of Women in the Church," in *The Ministry of Women in the Church*, p. 156.
[87] Behr-Sigel, "Toward a New Community," in *The Ministry of Women in the Church*, p. 96. She mentions Luther by name, too, though she didn't get the slogan quite right—it should read *simul justus et peccator*.

The clearest statement of her fundamental orientation appears in the two-part article published in 2000, "Regards Orthodoxes sur le Protestantisme."[88] The first half simply summarizes the Reformation, the Orthodox diaspora, and the twentieth-century ecumenical movement, with specific comments on the basically friendly Orthodox-Protestant relations in France. The second half, however, delves into actual theological critique. She describes Luther's search for a merciful God (drawn heavily, it appears, from the work of Laurent Gagnebin, *Le Protestantisme*). She identifies as stemming from Luther's experience a "triptych of Protestant spirituality": justification by faith or grace, the Holy Scriptures recognized as the only rule of faith, and the obligation to obey one's personal conscience insofar as it has been enlightened by the word of God.[89] To each of these points she poses an Orthodox challenge. Justification understood as sheer amnesty from the penalty of sin neglects the healing aspect of salvation, causing Good Friday to intrude upon Easter Sunday; the focus on the Scriptures leads to fundamentalism; and the insistence on the sovereign conscience is destructive or at least neglectful of the ecclesial community.[90] Though she is in many ways appreciative of Luther specifically and Protestantism generally, her sympathies and critiques land her on the Orthodox side of the fence.

Altogether it becomes clear that Behr-Sigel's desire was not to criticize the *doctrine* of the Orthodox church, either from a "Protestant" perspective on justification by faith (for instance) or from a more contemporary point of view. The meat of her critique lay chiefly if not solely in the inconsistency between Orthodox teaching and Orthodox practice. She did not require resources outside the Orthodox tradition to make her case about theological anthropology. If anything, it was a maturation in her understanding of the church fathers and more recent Orthodox theologians like Vladimir Lossky that led to her newfound convictions about the basic human identity of men and women sharing common personhood alongside each individual's uniqueness. Likewise, it was the *sobornost*, conciliarity or symphonicity, of Orthodox ecclesiology—which she explicitly claimed as a way out of the Western Christian conflict between the "judicial and authoritarian unity of the Roman Catholic church" and "Protestant libertarian individualism"[91]—that shaped her convictions about the ultimate harmony and mutual service of the clerical and lay priesthoods. And though with Evdokimov she shared a passion for the royal priesthood of all believers, she did not reject the Orthodox conception of the clerical priesthood. She found it inaccurate and even inadequate to align priesthood with masculinity, but she did not, as a Protestant normally would, reject the concept of priesthood altogether; quite the contrary.

If anything, the difficulty in asking how Protestant Behr-Sigel was has to do with defining the strict line of demarcation between what is "properly" Protestant and "properly" Orthodox. One would hardly want to say that close attention to scriptural evidence is a Protestant concern but not especially Orthodox, nor that the

---

[88] Behr-Sigel, "Regards Orthodoxes sur le Protestantisme," *Oecuménisme Information* 301 (2000), pp. 12–16, and "Regards Orthodoxes sur le Protestantisme II," *Oecuménisme Information* 302 (2000), pp. 13–16.

[89] Behr-Sigel, "Regards Orthodoxes sur le Protestantisme II," p. 14.

[90] Ibid., p. 15.

[91] Behr-Sigel, "My Journey to the Orthodox Church," in *Discerning the Signs of the Times*, p. 6.

Orthodox alone are concerned with the conciliar Tradition of the church. Following Behr-Sigel's own clues, one could perhaps says that she was Protestant in style—valuing freedom of conscience and expression, judging traditions by the Scriptures, allowing for creative interpretation and renewal—but Orthodox in substance. Yet even that is misleading because it assumes that there is only one Orthodox "style" of theology that holds little or nothing in common with the Protestant stylistic features suggested here (or that there is only one kind of Protestant "substance"). In point of fact, there is more than one way to be a modern Orthodox theologian. The school of Orthodox theology to which Behr-Sigel belonged accounts better for her apparently "Protestant" features, so to that question we will now turn.

Which school of Orthodox theology?

It is generally recognized that there are two distinct streams in Orthodox theology of the past two centuries, originating in Russia and traveling with the "diaspora" to France and the United States. The difficulty is in identifying just what absolutely distinguishes the one from the other. The lines are blurry and, as is often the case with typologies, nobody fits quite perfectly within his own type. Recognizing the limits of the tool, it will still be useful to discuss generally what composes these two schools and then examine how well Behr-Sigel fits in either.

Georges Florovksy started the business of distinguishing types of Orthodox theology. He began his career in Russia, moved on to Prague and then to Paris, and finished his life in the United States, at St. Vladimir's Seminary where he was dean, at Harvard Divinity School, and finally as a professor at Princeton University. He wrote the first history of Russian theological thought in the nineteenth and twentieth centuries, *Ways of Russian Theology*. His express purpose was to promote one way of Russian theology and to disparage the other. As his preface explicitly states:

> Studying the Russian past has led me to the conviction and has strengthened me in it that in our day the Orthodox theologian can only find for himself the true measure and living source of creative inspiration in patristic tradition. I am convinced the intellectual break from patristics and Byzantinism was the chief cause for all the interruptions and failures in Russia's development. All the genuine achievements of Russian theology were always linked with a creative return to the patristic sources.[92]

Florovsky's book details the "interruptions and failures" in Russian theology, starting with the sixteenth century when patristic theology was abandoned under Tsar Peter the Great's Westernizing project.[93] Eastern theology absorbed Western categories, even being taught in Latin at times, under Polish Roman Catholic influence.

---

[92] Georges Florovsky, *Ways of Russian Theology: Part Two*, p. x. (ed. Richard S. Haugh; trans. Robert L. Nichols; The Collected Works of Georges Florovsky, 6; Vaduz, Liechtenstein: Büchervertriebsanstalt, 1987).

[93] Ibid., p. 294.

In an otherwise laudatory review of Florovsky's intellectual contributions, Mark Raeff notes that this Russian thinker never had much interest in social questions; rather, "his concern was always exclusively for philosophy, culture, theology, and scholarship."[94] Florovsky's own occasional comments confirm this fact. He says the Russian soul needs asceticism, not social work, to be healed[95]; and at the very end of his book Florovsky strongly denounces the temptation to build "the New City" through "social work" instead of contemplation and theology.[96] But this predilection does not arise in a vacuum. Florovsky was reacting to the idealistic, even utopian visions of Russia's planetary destiny, of which Vladimir Soloviev was a chief proponent. After the Revolution, living in exile, Florovsky had become disenchanted with the Russian enchantment.

The preference for the church fathers and the Byzantine synthesis was, for Florovsky, as much a progression away from Russian absolutism as it was a conservative return to the roots. His "patristic 'fundamentalism,'" as Raeff puts it,[97] was a strategic as well as a substantive move. If Russia's intellectual trouble, culminating in the catastrophe of Revolution, stems from selling out to German idealism or any other contemporary continental philosophy, the clear antidote is "Christian Hellenism," an ancient philosophy fully transfigured by Scripture.[98] This Hellenism has the further advantage of being the common starting-point of the whole Christian church and thus the best ecumenical hope, even though it has only been preserved to date by the Orthodox church. As Florovsky himself explains, "Hellenism in the Church has been, so to speak, immortalized, having been incorporated into the very fabric of the reality of the Church as an eternal category of Christian existence . . . Theology can be catholic only in Hellenism."[99]

Florovsky's consequent dislike is not even so much for Western philosophers as for the Slavophiles—those Russians who envisioned a special destiny for Russia, as mentioned above—whose desire was to rewrite theology in a "Slavic key, to fit the 'Slavic soul' newly acquired for Christ."[100] He criticizes the Slavophile M. M. Tareev for suggesting that "Greek oppression" and a "Byzantine yoke" prevented the full development of Russia's intellectual life. Quite the contrary, Florovsky argues, the problem was not in keeping Hellenism but in breaking from it. "This falling out from tradition long left the Russian soul spellbound and barren, for creativity is impossible

---

[94] Mark Raeff, "Enticements and Rifts: Georges Florovsky as Russian Intellectual Historian," in *Georges Florovsky: Russian Intellectual and Orthodox Churchman*, p. 244 (ed. Andrew Blane; Crestwood, NY: St. Vladimir's Seminary Press, 1993).

[95] Florovsky, *Ways of Russian Theology: Part Two*, p. 289.

[96] Ibid., p. 305.

[97] Raeff, "Enticements and Rifts," p. 258.

[98] See George H. Williams, "The Neo-Patristic Synthesis of Georges Florovsky," in *Georges Florovsky: Russian Intellectual and Orthodox Churchman*, p. 292.

[99] Florovsky, *Ways of Russian Theology: Part Two*, p. 297. See the critical comparison of Florovsky with Harnack in Paul L. Gavrilyuk, "Harnack's Hellenized Christianity or Florovsky's 'Sacred Hellenism': Questioning Two Metanarratives of Early Christian Engagement with Late Antique Culture," *St. Vladimir's Theological Quarterly* 54, nos 3–4 (2010), pp. 323–44.

[100] Florovsky, *Ways of Russian Theology: Part Two*, p. 299.

outside of living traditions. Any rejection of the 'Greek inheritance' now can only mean the Church's suicide."[101]

From Florovsky's comments a basic sense of the two trends in Orthodox theology emerges. The older one, stemming directly from the prerevolutionary Russian intellectual milieu, posits a distinct Russian destiny, yet strives to express Russian faith and aspirations in the language of modern continental philosophy. Florovsky, in reaction, declares the need to express the Orthodox faith—but not necessarily the Russian faith per se—in patristic terms alone.

Alexander Schmemann was the first to identify explicitly the two streams emerging from these contrasting approaches. In an article honoring Florovsky on his sixtieth birthday, Schmemann indulges in some "meditation on the destiny of Orthodox theology in the past decades."[102] He speaks of a "Parisian school," which itself has been identified with Florovsky's neopatristic project, but Schmemann argues that it was never "a unified school of thought" and in fact represented "two different types of theological approach."[103] The first, which he calls the "Russian school," continued the pattern of Russian religious and philosophical speculation and is best represented by figures such as Khomiakov, Soloviev, Dostoesvky, Khrapovitzky, Nesmelov, and Florensky.

Florovsky is the source, so to speak, of the second stream of thought, one that chooses as the "cornerstone of the Orthodox theological revival not any modern traditions of the [Russian] school, but the sacred Tradition of the Church"—in short, "sacred Hellenism."[104] Hellenism ought to judge modern Russian experience, not the other way around. The resulting "neopatristic" historical and theological studies do not, in Schmemann's judgment, result in antiquarianism but make modern people into "contemporaries of the Fathers" who recognize the "eternal life" and "unpassing relevance" of the latter's theological achievement.[105] Schmemann witnesses to the impact of Florovsky's work:

[F]or me, personally, and for many people of my generation this book had a liberating effect. In the atmosphere of exultant religious nationalism in the circles of Russian emigration we received the book as a lesson of a sane and honest love to our own past—a lesson of love which does not extol the past because it was one's own, but judges everything by the higher measure of Truth. Severe and even merciless in its judgment on certain aspects of the Russian spiritual culture, the

---

[101] Ibid., p. 300. See the incisive, even devastating evaluation of Florovsky in Brandon Gallaher, "'Waiting for the Barbarians': Identity and Polemicism in the Neo-Patristic Synthesis of Georges Florovky," *Modern Theology* 27, no. 4 (2011), pp. 659–91. A more positive reading of the history, from a contemporary of Florovsky's, can be found in V. V. Zenkovsky's two-volume work, *A History of Russian Philosophy* (trans. George L. Kline; London: Routledge and Kegan Paul, 1953), especially pp. 1–15 in vol. 1 and pp. 920–24 in vol. 2. Behr-Sigel knew Zenkovsky. See "A la Memoire du Père Basile Zenkovsky," *Contacts* 15 (1963), pp. 65–66.

[102] Alexander Schmemann, "Roll of Honour," *St. Vladimir's Seminary Quarterly* (old series) 2, no. 1 (1952), pp. 5–11 (5).

[103] Ibid., p. 6.

[104] Ibid.

[105] Ibid., p. 7.

book is a valuable contribution to that culture, in which all real achievements were always marked by a severe self-judgment and humility before the Truth.[106]

To the Russian émigrés, criticism of Russia was nothing short of liberation. The way forward was the way backward, to the fathers of the church.

Thirty years later, Schmemann offered a further assessment of contemporary Orthodox theology in the West, following much the same pattern as his previous article. He still takes the same view as Florovsky, namely, that since the sixteenth century Orthodox theology's task has been to overcome the "alienation" caused by the adoption of Western modes of thought. What actually happened in Russian history was a tragic accident that requires recovery and return to the Greek and Byzantine patristic synthesis.[107] The difficulty is seen most clearly in dogmatic theology, where one sees "two main trends or orientations whose correlation and mutual opposition constitute the main theme of modern Russian theology." He rejects labeling one as liberal and the other conservative and notes their common criticism of the "Western captivity" of Orthodox theology through deeper engagement with the traditional sources. Despite the commonality, though,

> a sharp divergence is expressed in two basic attitudes. For one group, the critique of the theological past includes, although on a level different from that of western theology, the patristic period itself. Orthodox theology must keep its patristic foundation, but it must also go "beyond" the Fathers if it is to respond to a new situation created by centuries of philosophical development. And in this new synthesis or reconstruction, the western philosophical tradition (source and mother of the Russian "religious philosophy" of the nineteenth and twentieth centuries) rather than the Hellenic, must supply theology with its conceptual framework. An attempt is thus made to "transpose" theology into a new "key," and this transposition is considered as the specific task and vocation of Russian theology. This attitude is opposed by another in which the main emphasis is laid on the "return to the Fathers." The tragedy of Orthodox theological development is viewed here precisely as a drifting away of the theological mind from the very spirit and method of the Fathers, and no reconstruction or new synthesis are thought possible outside a creative recovery of that spirit . . . The divergence thus concerns the basic question of theological orientation itself, of the very spirit and task of modern Russian theology. One must add, however, that neither of these two trends was organized into a disciplined "school" and that a great variety of emphases existed within each one of them.[108]

Bulgakov is identified as the chief postrevolutionary proponent of the first school, Florovsky and Vladimir Lossky of the second.

Since Schmemann, other attempts to schematize recent Orthodox theology have been made. Lewis Shaw develops his own distinctions in an attempt to situate John

---

[106] Ibid., p. 8.

[107] Alexander Schmemann, "Russian Theology: 1920–1972, An Introductory Survey," *St. Vladimir's Theological Quarterly* 16, no. 4 (1972), pp. 172–94 (173).

[108] Ibid., pp. 178–79.

Meyendorff in twentieth-century Orthodoxy.[109] He too argues that the so-called Paris school actually contains two streams of Orthodox theology, the one following Bulgakov and preferring "speculative dogmatics" over against the Florovsky and Lossky stream that Shaw labels "traditionalist."[110] Shaw finds the critical difference to lie in their respective attitudes to the most famous of Russian religious philosophers, Vladimir Soloviev.

Soloviev was most notorious for his sophiology, the chief import of which was the need to engage modernity. The neopatristic stream acknowledged this need as well but, as Shaw puts it, "Solovievan speculation was so repugnant to Florovsky, Lossky, Afanasiev, Schmemann, Meyendorff, et al. that they felt an urgency to get their own ideas into print as an antidote to that which they regarded as poisonous and seductive. In a sense, the 'neo-patristic synthesis' . . . can be read as a 'confessionalist' response to Solovievan Sophiology."[111] It was again a reaction against the notion of a uniquely Russian destiny, explored in modern philosophical terms, which diminished or even betrayed "the patristic tradition that gave a distinctive and universal grammar of philosophical-theological discourse to Orthodoxy." Shaw adds that the sophiologists were interested in "the nature of God and the Trinity," while neopatrologues sought the "underlying principle of history."[112]

Florovsky, Schmemann, and Shaw all developed their typologies to express favor for one stream of modern Orthodox theology over the other, specifically the neopatristic type over against the Russian speculative and sophiological type. Paul Valliere accepts the distinction—with some nuances of his own—but to favor the latter over the former.[113] Calling the two streams the "Russian school" and the "Neopatristic school," Valliere explains the fate of each as the twentieth century unfolded:

> The Neopatristic school, as the new approach came to be called, effectively sidelined the Russian school by the late 1940s, partly because of its own dynamism, partly

---

[109] Shaw, "John Meyendorff and the Heritage of the Russian Theological Tradition." Shaw acknowledges his debt to Aidan Nichols, O. P., and the work he did for Nichols's book, *Theology in the Russian Diaspora: Church, Fathers, Eucharist in Nikolai Afanas'ev (1893–1966)* (Cambridge: Cambridge University Press, 1989), especially ch. 1. Nichols suggests three streams leading to twentieth-century theology, one from Russian scholasticism, a second from the Slavophiles, and a third from the "*fin-de-siècle* revival" to which Soloviev belongs. However, since his main subject is the ecclesiology of Afanasiev, his categorization is based on ecclesiology too, and in any event the schematization does not refer directly to the "Paris school" or the broader swaths of Orthodox theology in the twentieth century.

[110] Shaw, "John Meyendorff and the Heritage of the Russian Theological Tradition," p. 11. Interestingly, Shaw identifies Paul Evdokimov as a traditionalist. Based on the evidence provided below, this must be considered an error. Shaw himself notes a difference between Evdokimov and the other neopatrologues in the realm of eschatology, p. 22.

[111] Ibid., p. 20.

[112] Ibid., p. 28. Meerson argues approvingly that Soloviev's sophiology represents a turn to anthropocentrism, in response to Kant's destruction of religious knowledge. Sophiology, Meerson claims, won back the doctrine of the Trinity, understood as a communion of persons in a fellowship of love. See *The Trinity of Love in Modern Russian Theology*, pp. xiii–xvi. In this light, concern with "the nature of God and the Trinity" was a timely response to philosophical threats rather than speculation for its own sake.

[113] Paul Valliere makes his case at length in *Modern Russian Theology, Bukharev, Soloviev, Bulgakov: Orthodox Theology in a New Key* (Edinburgh: T&T Clark, 2000). Two articles by Valliere detail different angles of the same subject, though I will draw on his book here. "The Liberal Tradition in

because of the natural attrition of Russian-school thinkers. The Russian school found it difficult to reproduce itself in emigration because of its connection with a Russian civilization which had been either destroyed by the Russian Revolution or isolated behind the insuperable barriers erected by the Soviet state. The Neopatristic initiative, by contrast, found an audience among the younger generation of diaspora Russians who recognized their future lay in the West. It was helped along also by western converts to Orthodoxy who shared its passion for the liturgical, ascetical and mystical traditions of the fathers. By the middle of the twentieth century the ascendancy of the Neopatristic school was secure. Almost no one in the Orthodox world talked any longer about going "beyond the fathers."[114]

Furthermore, Valliere notes, what the new generation learned of the Russian school was filtered through Florovsky's lens in his critical *Ways of Russian Theology*.

For himself, Valliere is not entirely pleased with the situation. The substance of his book is to validate the project of the Russian school thinkers, chief among them the little-known Bukharev (about whom Behr-Sigel wrote her dissertation), the infamous Soloviev, and the usually loved but not well understood Bulgakov. Valliere gives the neopatristic school its due. He notes that the concern with patristics put it in good ecumenical stead, while still thinking about the destiny of "Holy Russia" would have all but cut it off.[115] All the same, he doubts that the "unchallenged hegemony" of the neopatristic school is a good thing, especially since the parallel classicists in Roman Catholic and Protestant circles are always engaging with critics who hold them to account. "The existence of principled alternatives in Orthodox theology," Valliere comments, "is rarely suspected."[116] The chief guidance the Russian school could offer, Valliere suggests, is in tackling problems unique to modernity about which the patristic sources offer little or no comment: "free markets, new republics, constitution-making, ethnic relations, religious pluralism, gender roles, poverty, crime."[117]

To crystallize the difference between the two, Valliere makes this instructive suggestion: "The issue concerns that which is added to the [patristic] foundation. Does it involve substantive additions and new discoveries, or does it simply entail new ways of expressing, articulating, or defining that which the church has always known and

---

Russian Orthodox Theology," in *The Legacy of St. Vladimir: Byzantium, Russia, America*, pp. 93–106 (ed. John Breck, John Meyendorff, and Eleana Silk; Crestwood, NY: St. Vladimir's Seminary Press, 1990), and "Sophiology as the Dialogue of Orthodoxy with Modern Civilization," in *Russian Religious Thought*, pp. 176–92 (ed. Judith Deutsch Kornblatt and Richard F. Gustafson; Madison, WI: University of Wisconsin Press, 1996). It is interesting to note that the three Russian Orthodox thinkers Behr-Sigel thought to compare to Tillich in her 1969 essay were, in fact, Bukharev, Soloviev, and Bulgakov, particularly their "theandric and sophianic" elements. "Un Origène Moderne," p. 80.

114 Valliere, *Modern Russian Theology, Bukharev, Soloviev, Bulgakov*, pp. 4–5.

115 Ibid., p. 375.

116 Ibid., p. 6. A similarly critical voice against neopatristic domination of Orthodoxy is Pantelis Kalaitzidis; see his "Challenges of Renewal and Reformation Facing the Orthodox Church," *Ecumenical Review* 61, no. 2 (2009), pp. 136–64, and "From the 'Return to the Fathers' to the Need for a Modern Orthodox Theology," *St. Vladimir's Theology Quarterly* 54, no. 1 (2010), pp. 5–36.

117 Valliere, *Modern Russian Theology, Bukharev, Soloviev, Bulgakov*, pp. 6–7.

preached?"[118] The former is the Russian school's stance, the latter the neopatristic's. Meyendorff and Hopko express their neopatristic commitments in speaking of the unchanging Tradition of the church, which in the former's view *is* the church and in the latter's view does not change or develop substantially but only in its form of address to the contemporary situation.[119] They certainly recognize the difference between Tradition and traditions—a distinction of which Behr-Sigel herself was extremely appreciative—but Tradition *is* the body and substance of all truth for the church, adequately and comprehensively provided for the church by the fathers. The Russian school, by contrast, thought there was a limit even to Tradition; new things need to be said, and new thoughts can come into the church, even via secular sources.[120] Sergius Bulgakov went so far as to suggest that "the Patristic sources, however basic they may be for the Eastern Orthodox tradition, are nonetheless not inexhaustible; indeed they are already exhausted."[121]

The Russian school's take on theology is perhaps best expressed in Bulgakov's short essay "Dogma and Dogmatic Theology," which first appeared in the controversial 1937 anthology *Living Tradition*, a charter of sorts for Orthodox engagement with the modern world issued by the exiles of the Russian Revolution.[122] In this essay, Bulgakov argues repeatedly, with varying nuances, for balancing the deposit of truth in the seven ecumenical councils (dogmas) with creative explorations in dialogue with contemporary philosophy and concerns (dogmatic theology). The church fathers are not infallible nor in perfect accord; their historical situation must be taken into account; their works do not form a completed canon; and as often as not they simply didn't consider questions that need answers now. The church is obligated to continue their thought creatively. "It is therefore necessary," Bulgakov writes, "to cast aside the preconception that what is new is not of the church," because "Orthodoxy is alive and, therefore, a growing and developing tradition, just as it was during the flourishing period of the history of dogma."[123] A living tradition engages with the world around it. So Bulgakov does not shrink from calling for a theological use of philosophy, even a "religious philosophy" proper, which was Soloviev's self-appointed task.[124] Bulgakov's overriding point is that dogmatic theology must be tolerated, and more than that *encouraged*, for it is only through the creative risk of research—the possibility of *not*

<hr>

[118] Ibid., p. 376. See also Ware's discussion in "Orthodox Theology Today: Trends and Tasks," *International Journal for the Study of the Christian Church* 12, no. 2 (2012), pp. 105–21, especially pp. 109–15, where he accepts the basic distinctions between the schools but also points out the significant amount of overlap between them.

[119] Valliere, *Modern Russian Theology, Bukharev, Soloviev, Bulgakov*, p. 377. Valliere cites comments from both Meyendorff and Hopko to this effect.

[120] See Valliere's discussion starting on p. 379.

[121] Meerson, *The Trinity of Love in Modern Russian Theology*, p. xix.

[122] Bouteneff's English translation of the essay can be found in *Tradition Alive: On the Church and the Christian Life in Our Time: Readings from the Eastern Church*, pp. 67–80 (ed. Michael Plekon; Lanham, MD: Sheed and Ward, 2003). Valliere points out, however, a critical mistranslation in Bouteneff, which omits the word "new" before "doctrines" when Bulgakov is trying to argue for the legitimacy of the dogmatic theological project opening up new terrain altogether. See this point and related discussion in Valliere's unpublished (in English) essay, "The 'Paris School' of Theology: Unity or Multiplicity?"

[123] Bulgakov, "Dogma and Dogmatic Theology," in *Tradition Alive*, p. 75.

[124] Ibid., pp. 78–79.

finding as well as of finding an answer—that genuine dogmatic development can take place.

For the purposes of the discussion here, it will be useful now to narrow down to a pair of names for the two schools and a precise definition of their respective qualities, however imprecise the business of typology may be. Without a doubt it makes sense to call the school of thought issuing from Florovsky "neopatristic," the name he himself favored and his intellectual followers gladly claimed. The other is a bit trickier— "Russian school," "sophiologists," "Slavophiles" have all been applied—but here I will coin the term "suprapatristic," taking the chief characteristic of this school to be the movement *beyond* the patristic foundation, as Valliere suggests, and taking creative risks in theological development, as Bulgakov proposes. The interest in Russia's destiny is therefore seen as contiguous with the larger project of the suprapatristic school, but not definitive of the movement in and of itself. This term will be especially useful in identifying later twentieth-century members of the school who were not immediately connected to Russia.

While dogmatic speculation is the chief interest for this school, there is another vital component: the application of dogmatic theology to social problems. This too has its roots in Soloviev and Bukharev. Their principal dogmatic key was the Russian term *bogochelovechestvo*, often translated literally "Godmanhood," though Valliere favors the phrase "the humanity of God" instead.[125] The term emphasizes the depth of involvement, even the identification, of God with all things human, at its apex in the incarnation but including artistic expression and concern for social issues. *Bogochelovechestvo* insists on the eternal connectedness of the divine and human, as opposed to the absolute distinction of the transcendent God from the creaturely and human.

With these definitions in place, we can assess where Elisabeth Behr-Sigel, and alongside her Paul Evdokimov, fit in the modern Orthodox line-up. There should be no doubt that Evdokimov belongs primarily to the suprapatristic school. He had intense interest in social welfare issues, spending the first half of his working life in a kind of diaconal service. Theologically, he lies directly in the stream of Bukharev, Soloviev, and Bulgakov, sharing their common passion for *bogochelovechestvo*. This being the case, in Evdokimov's view, theology must of necessity engage human culture and social issues, even be shaped by them, instead of claiming to be a static deposit of truth from on high.

Evdokimov demonstrates his loyalty to the suprapatristic school on the very first page of his *Woman and the Salvation of the World*, where he says: "A theological reflection strongly rooted in dogma, but flexible and open to the human, demands that we overcome the hardening of premises, the great poverty of any theological construct that is 'cut off' from human life."[126] Later he writes, "The creative assimilation of the thought of the Fathers, the restructuring of elements of the Christian tradition and of various branches of learning into a strong synthesis, will probably be the major work

---

[125] See Valliere's discussion of the term, "Note on Translation: 'The Humanity of God,'" in *Modern Russian Theology, Bukharev, Soloviev, Bulgakov*, pp. 11–15.
[126] Evdokimov, *Woman and the Salvation of the World*, p. 9.

of the twentieth century"[127]—an endorsement of Bulgakovian suprapatristic theology if ever there was one. Throughout his developing theological anthropology in the pages that follow, Evdokimov sounds the note of "the humanity of God" again and again, most powerfully when he writes that "man is the human face of God. The image (*imago*) is the third term of affinity, conformity, and correspondence which reveals the human in the divine, and God in the human . . . God and man glance toward one another as in a mirror, and ultimately recognize each other."[128] Evdokimov also deploys the concept of Sophia à la Soloviev and Bulgakov[129]: "Sophiology [is] the glory of present-day Orthodox theology."[130] Evdokimov was also such a fan of Bukharev that he encouraged Behr-Sigel to write her dissertation on him; and Bukharev is, as Valliere demonstrates at length, *the* source of the suprapatristic school in modern Orthodoxy.[131] Above all, Evdokimov's writings on women and marriage—fascinating if bizarre blends as they are of patristic Orthodoxy with Jungian psychology, existentialists like Kierkegaard, Camus, and Heidegger, and secular thinkers like Simone de Beauvoir and J. J. Bachofen—are beyond any doubt creatively risky interplays of Christian dogma and contemporary thought. The church fathers said very little about women, certainly very little that was positive, and Evdokimov set out deliberately to remedy the situation.

Final confirmation of Evdokimov's placement in modern Orthodoxy comes from Olivier Clément's study *Orient-Occident–Deux Passeurs: Vladimir Lossky, Paul Evdokimov*, in which Clément pays tribute to these two beloved friends and teachers. Lossky epitomized the neopatristic approach: historical, doctrinal, and traditional, though in the sense of living Tradition. Evdokimov appropriated the patristic heritage, too, but was compelled to engage with the world and make sense of the horrors of the Second World War, the mysteries of marital love, and the nihilism of secular culture.[132]

What about Behr-Sigel? Already in 1939, she published an essay on "La Sophiologie du Père S. Boulgakoff," an article in the main sympathetic to the theologian and his subject alike. Just *how* she is sympathetic to Bulgakov is instructive. She wants to introduce him to a Western audience, though she is quick to say that his sophiology is a "personal theological opinion" and nothing more official than that. And she is certainly not uncritical of him. She notes that the scriptural foundation for his sophiology is weak.[133] Nor does progressive deification as Bulgakov depicts it do justice to the "catastrophic eschatology" of the New Testament.[134] She also perceives a "certain rupture of equilibrium between the evangelical element and the speculative element, to the benefit of the latter," a habit of mind she compares to Clement of Alexandria and

---

[127] Ibid., p. 31.

[128] Ibid., p. 57. See also, for instance, ibid., pp. 10–11, and "We must start from anthropology," p. 17.

[129] Ibid., p. 11. He even follows Soloviev's theology of history in his chapter "The Church in the World and the Last Things." The "theocratic mission" of the church is an unmistakably Solovievan term.

[130] Ibid., p. 66.

[131] See Part I of Valliere, *Modern Russian Theology, Bukharev, Soloviev, Bulgakov*, on "Bukharev: Orthodoxy and the Modern World," pp. 19–106.

[132] See Clément's comments on the bottom of the page, *Orient-Occident—Deux Passeurs*, p. 14.

[133] Behr-Sigel, "La Sophiologie du Père Serge Boulgakoff," p. 46. All quotations are my translation.

[134] Ibid., p. 48.

Origen, of whom Bulgakov was "without doubt a modern disciple." She worries that Sophia displaces Christ in his system, that the incarnation itself loses some of its punch; instead of being the drama played out between God and man, between the heavenly Father and His lost child, it becomes "only a quasi-normal stage in the deification of human nature and of the whole creation." She concedes that she may have been pushing Bulgakov's thought too far but maintains that he skirts a genuine danger of "drowning the evangelical image of the Son of Man in cosmological speculations."[135]

Yet for all that, Behr-Sigel does not object to the larger project Bulgakov pursued in his sophiology. She believes that, however much he spoke out of the hopes and concerns of nineteenth-century Russia, he tapped into a "tradition purely Christian and ecclesial."[136] She outlines the type much the same way Schmemann and Valliere would years later.

> One of the characteristics of Russian thought in the 19th century is an extreme preoccupation with the human [*l'homme*], in the sense of his earthly destiny and his creative action in the world. The young Russian intelligentsia attempted to oppose the ideal of flight from the world, inherited from Byzantium and predominant in traditional Russian monastic spirituality, to a humanity faithful to its vocation and its earthly tasks.[137]

Such "metaphysical poetry" as expressed by Bulgakov and others like him holds for Behr-Sigel an "indisputable aesthetic attraction,"[138] especially the effort to understand and validate, from a Christian point of view, "the efforts of man, not only of the spiritual order, but also of the social, scientific, and artistic order."[139] For Bulgakov, this was certainly intended to be an alternative to the neopatristic program, as he wrote in a private letter to Behr-Sigel: "Someday I'll be able to loan you Florovsky's book. He's an exceptional scholar but on the level of intuitions and intentions we totally disagree with him . . . he sees heresies everywhere and thinks he has to refute them."[140] Behr-Sigel concludes her essay on Bulgakov with a kind of rallying cry of the suprapatristic school against neopatristic contentment. Bulgakov, she says, "shakes us from our intellectual torpor, forcing us to reconsider certain problems that we had definitively classed among the questions of above all historical and retrospective interest. His living ontology makes us leave the ruts of scholastic aristotelianism where we often remain bogged down in that which concerns our trinitarian theology."[141] The reference to "scholastic aristotelianism" demonstrates the mutual dislike of the suprapatristic school and the neopatristic school for the "manual theology" of early modern Orthodoxy, though the latter is generally harsher in its judgments than the former. As Valliere notes, it is common enough for members of the suprapatristic

---

[135] Ibid., p. 47.
[136] Ibid., p. 22.
[137] Ibid., p. 24.
[138] Ibid., p. 46.
[139] Ibid., p. 48.
[140] Olga Lossky, *Toward the Endless Day*, p. 81.
[141] Ibid.

school to disagree with each other in detail and substance, but they share common convictions about what theology ought to be doing. That describes exactly the relationship between Bulgakov and Behr-Sigel.

A more recent example of Behr-Sigel's use of Bulgakov can be found in her proposal for "disciplinary pluralism" on the practice of ordaining women. If it is simply wrong to ordain women, as her English translator Steven Bigham observes, then it would seem that there could be no tolerance of the practice; and if it is right to ordain them, then the Orthodox church needs to get on board and make the change *now*. Given these two sole options, Bingham finds Behr-Sigel's "disciplinary pluralism" incoherent, despite his admiration for her otherwise.[142] But her proposal *does* make sense in the light of Bulgakov's dogma-versus-dogmatic theology distinction. The ordination or not of women does not have the status of dogma, but the question *is* being explored deeply and conscientiously in dogmatic theology. It benefits no one to suppress the latter as long as it is not securely part of the former; thus, following the rule *in necessariis unitas, in dubiis libertas* (in fact an originally Protestant principle, which Bulgakov cited!) disciplinary pluralism is a coherent and appropriate response.[143]

Bulgakov was not the only suprapatristic influence on Behr-Sigel. Equally important was the priest-monk Lev Gillet, her lifelong friend and spiritual mentor. Behr-Sigel's biography *Lev Gillet, "Un Moine de l'Eglise d'Orient,"* discusses his attraction to Soloviev and Bulgakov and their sophiology alongside his critical distance from them. Gillet had an enormous impact on Behr-Sigel's own development into an Orthodox Christian and theologian—she gained from him her interests in ecumenism, sophiology, Russian hagiography, attention to the "signs of the times," overcoming dead traditions with Tradition, and the desire to embody a truly Western form of Orthodoxy. Her sympathy to the suprapatristic school was in large part a result of her formation by Gillet.

The fact that Behr-Sigel made occasional positive remarks about neopatristic theologians should cast no doubt on her ultimate loyalties.[144] The suprapatristic school is generally more appreciative of the neopatristic school than vice versa. The suprapatristic school does not intend to reject the patristic heritage in any sense; the difference lies in what they want to do with it. Behr-Sigel makes a pledge of suprapatristic school allegiance when she writes: "[The] conciliar definitions have become normative for all thinking about the faith that defines itself as ecclesial. They do not, however, exempt Orthodox theologians from the obligation of thinking in a creative, living, but rigorous way. Such thought must also be open to the questions and inspirations of the world *here and now*."[145] She goes on to list the great Russian religious thinkers (whom she aligned with early church Alexandrians): Skovoroda, Bukharev, Berdiaev, Soloviev,

---

[142] He did, after all, translate her *Le Ministère de la Femme dans l'Eglise* into English. See his reflections in "*The Ministry of Women in the Church:* Comments by Fr. Steven Bigham," *MaryMartha* 1, no. 3 (1991), pp. 16–18.

[143] Bulgakov, "Dogma and Dogmatic Theology," in *Tradition Alive*, p. 75.

[144] For instance, on Florovsky, in Behr-Sigel, *The Place of the Heart*, p. 36.

[145] Ibid., pp. 43–44. "Here and now" is Behr-Sigel's favorite phrase, which certainly characterizes a suprapatristic school thinker.

Florensky, Bulgakov, Evdokimov, and Vladimir Lossky. All but the last of these are habitually identified as Russian school (hence, for our purposes, suprapatristic school) theologians.

Vladimir Lossky is a difficult case to assess. Behr-Sigel and Evdokimov repeatedly referred to Lossky's *Mystical Theology of the Eastern Church*. Lossky repaid the favor by calling Evdokimov "Orthodoxy's Protestant"—certainly not meant as a compliment.[146] Behr-Sigel makes her own judgment on the two theologians and their relative loyalties. Lossky's ideas today appear to be "somewhat 'up in the air' in a western society secularized to its foundations." Lossky opposed Bulgakov's excessive theological creativity, "betraying" him to the Russian ecclesial authorities in an act of "patricide." "But," Behr-Sigel asks, has not Lossky "in turn today been betrayed by those who have made a rigid scholastic structure of what was once molten lava—a creative reassimilation of the thinking of the great theologians of the undivided church and their Byzantine successors?" Paul Evdokimov, on the other hand, for all his "tentative, groping search" that causes him "occasionally [to] lose his way," still points in another direction: "He could be the inspiration of the Orthodox theologians whose task it is to express the eternal message in a language accessible to men and women of today," doing theology "which is both *in the tradition* and attentive to the creation today groaning in travail as it waits for the adoption of the children of God." Behr-Sigel wrote these words in 1988 after she'd already rejected Evdokimov's ideas about women, but his basic approach to theology still merited her praise.[147]

Behr-Sigel was not ignorant of the Russian school's dangers—she herself recognized that it came "dangerously close to heresy at times"—yet lauded it for the "renewed awareness of the human-divine Mystery" that it brought back to the church's attention in modern times, namely, the theme of *bogochelovechestvo*. Her frequent use of the term "divino-human" is further evidence of the inheritance she received for Soloviev.[148]

Certainly engagement with modernity was Behr-Sigel's constant battle-cry. Answering questions about women in the life of the church was a necessity imposed by the wide world, even if it originated ultimately in the Christian faith: it was a "sign of the times." Agapia's quest was to "rediscover, under the deposits of the past, the authentic ecclesial Tradition about women, as it sprang forth from the liberating Gospel of Christ," but even more, to take and "apply that Tradition creatively to new situations."[149] Behr-Sigel was, furthermore, keenly interested in the cultivation of a *French* Orthodoxy—hence her resistance to jurisdiction under the Moscow instead of

---

[146] Clément, *Orient-Occident—Deux Passeurs*, p. 12.

[147] "Developments in Orthodox Theology in Western Europe," pp. 81–82.

[148] Behr-Sigel, *The Place of the Heart*, p. 45. The phrase "divino-human mystery" appears all over Behr-Sigel's work; here are three examples. "Orthodox anthropological research could help the Universal Church to speak the catholic word—that is to say, oriented to the plenitude of the divine-human mystery—this word to the community of men and women which is waiting so much for it today." In "Oecuménisme au Féminin," pp. 339–40. Behr-Sigel equates the "total feminism" of France Quéré with "total humanism" or even "total divino-humanism." In her review of F. Quéré, p. 350. In her article on Tillich, she lifts up his discussion of "the divino-human essence," though not without some challenge to his interpretation. In "Un Origène Moderne," p. 79.

[149] Behr-Sigel, "Introduction," in *The Ministry of Women in the Church*, p. 11.

the ecumenical patriarchate—but this itself can be seen as the same species of interest as Soloviev and others had in the destiny of Orthodox Russia, transposed onto new soil. Similarly, in her biography of him she discusses sympathetically Lev Gillet's efforts to bring a Western-rite parish into the French Orthodox church with the hopes of making Orthodoxy even more universal in its scope (though in the end the project failed).[150] She was active in social causes, chief among them as lay president of the Orthodox branch of l'ACAT.

Besides affirming again and again the themes of the suprapatristic school, Behr-Sigel did on occasion express outright criticism of the neopatristic. A conference in 1976 on the diaconate was long overdue, Behr-Sigel judged, and she doesn't hesitate to lay some blame for the delay at the door of the neopatristic contingent who, she says, are "little interested in the problems of social ethics and action in the world *here and now*."[151] Poor attendance from her own church at the Sheffield conference in 1981 signifies "a lack of interest, evident among many of the Orthodox—but not at all conforming to the authentic ecclesial Tradition—in the existential implications of the great doxological affirmations of the creed of faith and for the ethical problems of a planetary scope,"[152] a judgment against Orthodox who care little for the world as it is now. Her address at Sheffield speaks to Orthodox enchantment with a vision of heaven that sometimes serves as "an excuse for laziness, a justification for rigid conservatism claiming not to know about the questions that modern non-believers are asking."[153] Her review of *Women and the Priesthood* mentions Hopko's reclamation of Lossky over Bulgakov "in the triumphant neopatristic climate" of the past several decades.[154] Last but not least we have Behr-Sigel's unusually strong words after the Rhodes Consultation of 1988 expressing relief that Orthodoxy was finally emerging from its "straitjacket of neopatristic scholasticism."[155] In the context of the article, her point was that Orthodoxy had been refusing to deal with questions about women altogether. Afterwards, even if Behr-Sigel wasn't particularly thrilled with Rhodes's results, the very fact that the matter was being addressed at all represented a huge improvement.[156]

At the end of her life, despite her complete rejection of any notion of "feminine" and "masculine" charisms, Behr-Sigel was still sympathetic to Evdokimov's larger project

[150] See also her article "A Propos de 'La Queste d'Irénée Winnaert,'" *Contacts* 18 (1966), pp. 315–19. A similar situation is briefly discussed by Behr-Sigel in her evaluation of "Débat sur un Rite Orthodoxe Occidental," *Contacts* 22, no. 1 (1970), pp. 54–60.

[151] Behr-Sigel, "Après le Colloque de Crète sur la Diaconie," *Service Orthodoxe de Presse* 34 (1979), pp. 7–11 (7). My translation.

[152] Behr-Sigel, "Vers une 'Communauté Nouvelle,'" p. 239. My translation.

[153] Behr-Sigel, "Towards a New Community," in *The Ministry of Women in the Church*, p. 102.

[154] Behr-Sigel, review of *Women and the Priesthood*, 1st edn, p. 210.

[155] Behr-Sigel, "La Consultation Interorthodoxe de Rhodes," p. 91. My translation.

[156] It would take too long to review each instance in detail, but further examples of Behr-Sigel's allegiance can be found in the following articles. "Perspectives de l'Orthodoxie en France," *Contacts* 16, no. 1 (1964), pp. 42–43 (48). "Quelques Aspects de la Théologie et de l'Expérience de l'Esprit Saint dans l'Eglise Orthodoxe Aujourd'hui," 267–71. Review of *Berdiaev. Un Philosophe Russe en France*, by O. Clément, *Contacts* 44 (1992), pp. 68–70. Review of *L'Eglise Orthodoxe Hier et Aujourd'hui*, by J. Meyendorff, *Contacts* 48 (1996), pp. 62–63. Review of *Augustine and Russian Orthodoxy: Russian Orthodox Theologians and Augustine of Hippo: A Twentieth-Century Dialogue*, by M. I. Tataryn, *Contacts* 54 (2002), pp. 107–11.

of articulating the place of women in the church, insofar as it represented a genuine attempt to address contemporary questions faithfully. She was sympathetic because she shared with him a common grounding in the suprapatristic school of Orthodox theology. Like Bulgakov, Behr-Sigel and Evdokimov could risk and tolerate errors in dogmatic theology en route to the truth. They even *relied* on dogmatic errors to get them there. Secure in her Orthodox serenity, Behr-Sigel was grateful to Evdokimov, Hopko, and the Rhodes Consultation for all of their dogmatic errors: they were essential in getting her to the truth.

8

Tradition, Priesthood, Gender and Personhood

In the 1950s, when Paul Evdokimov suggested that "woman" could not become a priest without betraying her ontological alignment with the Holy Spirit, no one in the Orthodox church was actually entertaining the possibility of female priests.[1] He answered the question in passing, a small part of his larger project to illuminate the spiritual dimension of femininity against the traditional tendency to demean women. Likewise, Orthodox theologians Nicolae Chitescu and George Khodre could answer a simple "no" to the hypothetical question of women in the priesthood at a Faith and Order conference in 1963; the idea was not worth a second thought.[2] At the first-ever international gathering of Orthodox women at the Agapia convent in Romania in 1976, the ordination of women was not on the agenda for discussion. Only one woman brought it up at all, in her keynote address. Even her answer was a provisional no—but also a charge to engage in better and deeper reflection on the issue. She called upon the Orthodox church to "internalize" the question.[3]

Since the 1970s, Orthodox churches have indeed internalized it, at least the Orthodox churches in Western countries. There is a growing body of literature on the subject,[4] nowhere near the amount in Protestant and Roman Catholic circles but enough to prove that it has become a live issue, live and contested enough to have strangled all recommendations to reinstate the female diaconate. There is still no consensus on whether deaconesses should be ordained to their office, and given the interrelationship among the ordained offices, the diaconate may well appear to be a "slippery slope" toward the ordination of women to the priesthood as well.[5]

So far, no one from within has outright petitioned the Orthodox church to ordain women to the priesthood, though many have suggested the possibility in

---

[1] Evdokimov, *Woman and the Salvation of the World*, p. 216.
[2] See their essays in *Concerning the Ordination of Women*.
[3] Behr-Sigel, "Keynote," in *Orthodox Women*, pp. 17–29.
[4] See, for example, the review by Pauline Kollontai, "Contemporary Thinking on the Role and Ministry of Women in the Orthodox Church," *Journal of Contemporary Religion* 15, no. 2 (2000), pp. 165–79.
[5] See the informative discussion in Natallia Vasilevich, "The Issue of Female Ordination/Priesthood in the Ecumenical and Inter-Orthodox Discussion," in *Many Women Were Also There . . .*, pp. 139–55.

their scholarship. It is not surprising that Orthodox women are at the front of the debate. Among them are Leonie B. Liveris, editor of the journal *MaryMartha* in the 1990s,[6] and a number of American Orthodox connected to *St. Nina's Quarterly*, including Teva Regule,[7] Maria McDowell,[8] and Valerie Karras.[9] Eva Catafygiotu Topping addresses the topic indirectly through her studies of women saints.[10] Susan Ashbrook Harvey anticipates the ordination of women in the Orthodox church, not soon, but someday, and laments the unanswered calls to ministry of Orthodox women until then.[11] Kalliope Bourdara, professor of law at the University of Athens, expressed her support at an Orthodox-Old Catholic dialogue conference.[12] The most prominent Orthodox woman to speak on the subject, however, was and remains Elisabeth Behr-Sigel.

It is not a little surprising that several male Orthodox theologians have gradually moved toward Behr-Sigel's position. Metropolitan Anthony Bloom's public support of Behr-Sigel left little doubt as to his opinion.[13] Kallistos Ware has admitted that

[6] In addition to her book *Ancient Taboo and Gender Prejudice: Challenges for Orthodox Women and the Church* and her articles for *MaryMartha*, see Liveris's "Ecumenism at a Cost: Women, Ordination, and Sexuality: 'Disagree with the Umpire—Take the Ball, and Go Home,'" *Journal of Ecumenical Studies* 41, no. 1 (2004), pp. 55–73, and "Women, Leadership and the Orthodox Church in Australia: Always Second, Secondary or Seconded," *Studies in World Christianity* 13, no. 1 (2007), pp. 13–32, both of which make reference to Behr-Sigel.

[7] Teva Regule, "The St. Nina Quarterly: Bringing Together a Community of Women," *Ecumenical Review* 53, no. 1 (2000), pp. 101–04, which cites Behr-Sigel's work.

[8] Maria Gwyn McDowell has made the most compelling case for the ordination of women in the Orthodox church since Behr-Sigel. See her dissertation at Boston College, "The Joy of Embodied Virtue: Toward the Ordination of Women to the Eastern Orthodox Priesthood" (2010), and her articles "Newness of the Spirit: The Ordination of Men and Women," *Word* 48, no. 5 (2004), pp. 9–11, and "The Hands of a Woman," in "*A Communion Lived in Faith and Love.*"

[9] Valerie Karras's works pertinent to this topic include: "Patristic Views on the Ontology of Gender," in *Personhood: Orthodox Christianity and the Connection between Body, Mind, and Soul*, pp. 113–19 (ed. John T. Chirban; Westport, CT: Bergin and Garvey, 1996); "Women in the Eastern Church: Past, Present, and Future," *St. Nina Quarterly* 1, no. 1 (1997), pp. 1, 11–13; "Sermon: The Significance of the Maleness of Jesus Christ?" *St. Nina Quarterly* 1, no. 2 (1997), p. 12; "The Theotokos: Icon for Humanity," *St. Nina Quarterly* 1, no. 3 (1997), pp. 1, 7–8; "Flesh of My Flesh—Greek Patristic Exegeses of the Creation of Eve," *St. Nina Quarterly* 2, no. 1 (1998), pp. 1, 9–10, 12, 19; "The Mystery of the Trinity Revealed and Experienced: Language, Metaphor and Personhood," *St. Nina Quarterly* 2, no. 3 (1998), pp. 12–14.

[10] "Orthodoxy's women saints pose a question that demands an honest answer. By what prejudices are Orthodox women in 1985 [the year the talk was delivered] denied equal dignity and full participation in the life of the Church?" Eva Catafygiotu Topping, "Heroines and Haloes," *Greek Orthodox Theological Review* 32 (1987), pp. 131–42 (142). See also the chapter "Reflections of an Orthodox Feminist," in her *Holy Mothers of Orthodoxy: Women and the Church*, pp. 3–11 (Minneapolis: Light and Life, 1987), and "Orthodox Women and Our Church," in *Project for Orthodox Renewal: Seven Studies of Key Issues Facing Orthodox Christians in America*, pp. 63–89 (ed. Stephen J. Sfekas and George E. Matsoukas; Chicago: Orthodox Christian Laity, 1993).

[11] Teva Regule, "An Interview with Susan Ashbrook Harvey," *St. Nina Quarterly* 1, no. 4 (1997), pp. 5–8. See also Harvey's review of Behr-Sigel's *Ministry of Women in the Church* in *St. Vladimir's Theological Quarterly* 37, no. 1 (1993), pp. 101–03.

[12] Kalliope A. Bourdara, "The Ordination of Women in the Eyes of an Orthodox Woman," *Anglican Theological Review* 84, no. 3 (2002), pp. 681–89.

[13] Bloom gave an address at the London School of Economics in 1989 in which he expressed his hopes that women would someday be permitted to become not only priests but even bishops in the Orthodox church. See also his "Introduction" to *The Ministry of Women in the Church*, which he hails as the "first swallow that announces the coming of spring," p. xiii.

the proffered reasons against women in the priesthood do not persuade him anymore,[14] and Olivier Clément could see no compelling reason not to ordain women.[15] Already in 1968, John Zizioulas commented that, "[o]n the ordination of women, Orthodox theologians could find no theological reasons against such an ordination"![16]

There are still plenty of Orthodox opponents of the ordination of women, likely the majority within the churches and certainly a vocal contingent in publication. The articles range from popular diatribes to serious theological scholarship. What is chiefly striking about them, though, is how much the substance of the opposition has changed.

In the 1960s, it was still possible for the Orthodox in Western countries to talk about women's spiritual and physical weakness, menstrual cycles, incompetence, lack of intelligence, or general inferiority, all without a qualm.[17] That is no longer the case. Among the opponents of women's ordination there is a nearly unanimous desire to disprove charges of misogyny and to affirm the goodness of women as created in God's image. The Interorthodox Rhodes Consultation of 1988, convoked especially to discuss the ordination of women, stated as much, identifying sexism as a sin.[18] There is no suggestion anymore that women are *functionally* incompetent to perform such tasks as preaching, teaching, and pastoral care.

In reality, the discussion is no longer about women's capacities at all. Not actions but *natures* are under dispute. Thus the current arguments about the ordination of women in the Orthodox church revolve around three interconnected points: the nature of tradition, the nature of the priesthood, and the nature of gender and personhood. In what follows, we will consider each point in turn, the current state of the discussion within the Orthodox church, and Behr-Sigel's contribution.

---

[14] "I am far from convinced by many of the current arguments advanced in favour of women priests; but at the same time a number of the arguments urged on the other side now appear to me a great deal less conclusive than they did twenty years ago." Ware, "Man, Woman and the Priesthood of Christ," in *The Ordination of Women in the Orthodox Church*, p. 50.

[15] "My opinion—I know that very few Orthodox theologians share it—is that there are no strictly theological reasons to bar women from the priesthood." See Clément, "Orthodoxy, Olivier Clément and the Ordination of Women," *MaryMartha* 3, no. 1 (1993), pp. 27–29.

[16] John Zizioulas, "By John Zizioulas (Greek Orthodox Church), Faith and Order Secretariat," *Study Encounter* 4, no. 4 (1968), pp. 191–93. He admits, however, that "the entire matter is so deeply tied up with their tradition that they would find it difficult in their majority to endorse without reservations the rather enthusiastic statements" made in its favor in the paper to which Zizioulas is responding. An Archimandrite Ephrem also reports that Zizioulas confessed to having seen no good theological arguments about the ordination of women, either for *or* against. See his review of *Le Ministère de la Femme dans l'Eglise* by Behr-Sigel, *Sourozh* 57 (1994), pp. 46–49 (48).

[17] Chitescu: "Then there is the period when women are 'impure' . . ." *Concerning the Ordination of Women*, p. 57. Khodre: "[I]s the feminist movement well-founded? Does it not express the dissatisfaction of those women who suffer from the Diana-complex? . . . [T]he biological rhythms fluctuate more in women than in men and their moods are affected by these rhythms." *Concerning the Ordination of Women*, p. 61. Michael Azkoul seems to support the maintaining of purity taboos in *Order of Creation, Order of Redemption: The Ordination of Women in the Orthodox Church* (Rollinsford, NH: Orthodox Research Institute, 2007).

[18] See "Conclusions of the Consultation," B.VI.22, in *The Place of the Woman in the Orthodox Church and the Question of the Ordination of Women*.

Tradition

For many Orthodox, the ordination of women is a nonissue, plain and simple, because it diverges from past practice.[19] The near-complete lack of discussion on the issue within the 2,000 years of tradition makes no difference and suggests no need to consider the possibility now.[20] If it *ever* was right to ordain women, the reasoning goes, the church would have done so. This is not fear of the new per se, at least not on the theological level. (Certainly fear of the new is a common enough psychological phenomenon in church bodies, and not only in Orthodox ones.) The tradition question turns out to be a *theodicy* question.

The point is simply this: could the one, holy, catholic, and apostolic church really have failed so dreadfully? If God calls women to the priesthood, then, it seems, one must infer that the church has uniformly blocked and rejected God's calls to women for two straight millennia. The church then appears to be an eminently untrustworthy body—not a fellowship of faith and love, but a hierarchical, patriarchal, Spirit-less institution. If it is wrong on this point, on how many other points is it wrong too? How faithlessly has it proclaimed the gospel? The implications are staggering.

This concern appears repeatedly in articles rejecting women's ordination. George Morelli, for instance, argues that the traditions of the church are as unchanging as its doctrine. Proposals for ecclesial change now are simply the inroads of secularism.[21] Hopko wonders the same thing: could the church have been so dramatically in error all along? Surely not. Perhaps the tradition did not know exactly why it was impermissible to ordain women, but that only means that the Orthodox today are called to articulate the deeply seated reasons for their wisely unchanging practice.[22] Michael Azkoul reasons that if a "male-dominated Church has presumed deliberately to deny competent and pious women a place in the sacerdotal ministry in contradiction to the express command of the Lord and the Apostles, then nothing her Fathers, Councils, and hierarchy [say] in general is worthy of trust."[23] It isn't only men arguing this way, either. Katerina Karkala-Zorba, who cites Behr-Sigel in her article, argues that the tradition has not failed the faithful and thus the refusal to ordain women can be trusted.[24] For

---

19 The papal encyclical *Inter Insigniores* from 1976 begins with the same point: "The Catholic Church has never felt that priestly or episcopal ordination can be validly conferred on women." *From "Inter Insigniores" to "Ordinatio Sacerdotalis": Documents and Commentaries,* p. 25 (Washington, DC: United States Catholic Conference, 1988).

20 As Hopko acknowledges: "There are no specific sources dealing with it in church tradition, where the question is not treated even in the most rudimentary form." "On the Male Character of the Christian Priesthood," in *Women and the Priesthood*, 1st edn, p. 97.

21 George Morelli, "Whose Church Do I Belong To: My Church or the Orthodox Church of Christ?" *OrthodoxyToday.org,* <www.orthodoxytoday.org/articles6/MorelliSecularism.php> [accessed December 10, 2012].

22 Thomas Hopko, "Presbyter/Bishop: A Masculine Ministry," in *Women and the Priesthood*, rev. edn, p. 140.

23 Azkoul, *Order of Creation, Order of Redemption*, p. 40.

24 Katerina Karkala-Zorba, "The Role of Women in the Orthodox Church Today," *MaryMartha* 5, no. 1 (1996), pp. 3–8. There is reason to think she later changed her mind; see her contribution, "The Ordination of Women from an Orthodox Perspective," in *Women and Ordination in the Christian Churches: International Perspectives*, pp. 54–63 (ed. Ian Jones, Kirsty Thorpe, and Janet Wootton; London: T&T Clark, 2008).

Maximos Aghiorgoussis it is a matter of "the preservation of the revealed truth"[25] and for Alister Anderson a matter of "worshipping in the same way Jesus Christ told our ancestors to worship God for our salvation."[26] "Ultimately," writes Andrew Philips, "we would even be led to the thought that God must hate women, that therefore He is not the God of Love, since He allowed His Church to err for 2,000 years."[27]

Another feature of the perception of tradition among opponents of women's ordination is the great number of arguments from silence. It is suggested that if Jesus wanted women priests, he would have chosen women disciples; if any woman were to be a priest, it should have been Mary, and yet she was not[28]; and the tradition itself would have spoken up sooner if ordaining women were a good thing. The silence of the tradition is not taken at face value, as silence.

While the tradition is silent about women priests, it is not silent about women. And yet the actual *content* of the tradition—particularly the patristic tradition—is disputed. Some scholars claim that all the fathers agree that gender is secondary to the first creation of *anthropos*.[29] Others claim there is a difference of opinion among the fathers, or that some of them changed their mind on the issue one way or another.[30] Still others simply reject any such patristic notion wherever it may appear, crying foul against

[25] Maximos Aghiorgoussis, *Women Priests?*, p. 1 (Brookline, MA: Holy Cross Orthodox Press, 1976).

[26] Alister Anderson, "The Orthodox Priest: An Icon of Christ," <www.antiochian.org/midwest/Articles/The_Orthodox_Priest_An_Ikon_Of_Christ.htm> [accessed December 10, 2012].

[27] Andrew Philips, "Some Reasons Why the Orthodox Church Does Not Admit Women to the Priesthood," *Orthodox Life* 43, no. 2 (1993), pp. 43–47 (46). See also the tirade against feminism and "feminized" religion by John Morris, "Thoughts on Women's Ordination," *The Word* 48, no. 3 (2004), who among other things argues that "it would be the height of arrogance for some in the twenty-first century to claim they are qualified to declare that the Church has been wrong for almost 2,000 years." Matthew J. Streett, in "Deacons, Apostles and the Place of Women in the Orthodox Church," *The Word* 48, no. 3 (2004), pp. 12–13, gently rebukes Morris for assuming all feminisms to be equal, overlooking the legitimate ordination of women to the diaconate, and forgetting about the apostle Junia; at the same time, he repeatedly comments that the ordination of women to the priesthood is "an innovation" and excluded because it is "not part of our tradition."

[28] FitzGerald takes issue with this particular argument from silence, endorsed by the Rhodes Consultation, in her incisive article, "The Eve-Mary Typology and Women in the Orthodox Church: Reconsidering Rhodes."

[29] "Beyond physical sex, gender itself is seen by all of the Fathers as an element added to humanity only because of God's foreknowledge of man's fall. Several modern theologians mistakenly believe this view to be limited to two of the most speculative Greek Fathers—Gregory of Nyssa and Maximos the Confessor." Karras, "Patristic Views on the Ontology of Gender," p. 116.

[30] "[W]e can identify a difference of opinion among the patristic writers. John of Damascus, when he speaks of the creation of humanity, claims that the first human being was male. But later he moves to another line of thought." Constantine Yokarinis, "A Patristic Basis for a Theological Anthropology of Women in Their Distinctive Humanity," *Anglican Theological Review* 84, no. 3 (2002), pp. 585–609 (590). His is one of the many papers presented during the Old Catholic-Orthodox dialogue on the ordination of women, all published in this issue of *Anglican Theological Review*. Behr-Sigel wrote an (unsurprisingly) favorable review of the collected papers that were published in the German journal *Internationale Kirchliche Zeitschrift* for *Contacts* 53 (1999), pp. 179–81. Belonick admits that "patristic exegetes had varied opinions even when interpreting Genesis"; see "Women in the Church," in *Orthodox Perspectives on Pastoral Practice: Papers of the Intra-Orthodox Conference on Pastoral Praxis (24–25 September 1986) Celebrating the 50th Anniversary of Holy Cross Greek Orthodox School of Theology (1937–1987)*, p. 84 (ed. Theodore Stylianopoulos; Brookline, MA: Holy Cross Orthodox Press, 1988). But she eventually takes sides: "If God willed gender distinction for the sole purpose of procreation, then differences in women and men are reduced to bodily function," which is unacceptable to her, p. 85.

the supposed Platonism that made the fathers denigrate sexuality and alienated them from the Christian truth.[31] The point here is not to adjudicate between the competing claims, only to demonstrate that what the fathers say about gender within the realm of theological anthropology and the divine intention remains disputed.

And if the content of the tradition is not clear, the implications of patristic anthropology are even less so. Yet often patristic anthropology is perceived to be both uniform and decisive. Evdokimov grounds his alliance of women with the Spirit in the use of the feminine pronoun for the Holy Spirit in Syriac liturgies and other apparent similarities between femininity and the action of the Spirit.[32] Yet Verna Harrison argues from the same fathers that the apophatic principle prohibits any imaging of the divine in sexual terms.[33] Kenneth Paul Wesche argues that Scripture and fathers alike plainly witness to the ontological primacy of the male.[34] But Valerie Karras demonstrates how many *homo-* words were used or invented by the fathers to describe the parity between men and women: *homogenis* (same race), *homotimos* (same honor), and even *homoousios*.[35] Constantine Yokarinis suggests that patristic anthropology assumes fundamental equality between men and women such that any gender differentiation within the service of the church is an error, and yet the same fathers did not see fit to ordain women to the priesthood.

What emerges here is how much the opponents and proponents of the ordination of women have in common *methodologically*. Both assume that the Tradition has been correct from the start; both attempt to read the Tradition's silence in their own favor; both invoke the church fathers in an attempt to settle the dispute. In short, both assume that an answer is already conclusively to be found in the Tradition of the church. Neither seriously entertains the idea that the silence of the church is, in fact, *silence*. More to the point, both share a static understanding of the Tradition. Neither imagines a Tradition that develops and changes in continuity with what has come before or the genuine possibility of something new that was not always required.[36]

---

[31] Karras notices this, too. "[S]everal modern Orthodox theologians . . . assume that Fathers such as Gregory of Nyssa must be overly influenced by androgynous and dualistic Platonic thought because these Fathers believe that humanity's gender differentiation is purely physical." In "Patristic Views on the Ontology of Gender," p. 115. For example, Hopko says, "Is there a *consensus patrem* on the subject [of gender in the life to come], or are these views, clearly influenced by hellenistic sources and teachings, upheld by only some strands of patristic teaching . . . ?" "The Debate Continues—1998," in *Women and the Priesthood*, rev. edn, p. 254. See also Wesche: when Gregory of Nyssa "turns to the mystery of gender, he forgets and, falling back into the androgyny of Greek philosophy, attributes gender to the Fall." "Man and Woman in the Orthodox Tradition," p. 242.

[32] Harvey also discusses the usage, though she draws different conclusions from it, in her study, "Feminine Imagery for the Divine: The Holy Spirit, the Odes of Solomon, and Early Syriac Tradition," *St. Vladimir's Theological Quarterly* 37, nos 2–3 (1993), pp. 111–39.

[33] Verna F. Harrison, "The Fatherhood of God in Orthodox Theology," *St. Vladimir's Theological Quarterly* 37, nos 2–3 (1993), pp. 185–212.

[34] Such is the thrust of his article, "Man and Woman in Orthodox Tradition."

[35] Karras, "Flesh of My Flesh."

[36] A curious corroborating example comes from post-Christian feminist Daphne Hampson. She, too, raises the theodicy question: "How can God be seen to be good when one considers what history has been, and what it has meant for women that God has been conceived in primarily male terms?. . . . [W]hy, if God be good, has any harm come to women?" In *Theology and Feminism* (Oxford: Basil Blackwell, 1990), p. 11. She similarly rejects any notion of developing Tradition

The concept of the development of doctrine remains a disputed point within Orthodoxy. Some Orthodox theologians repudiate the very idea.[37] It is a common judgment that Orthodoxy has spent most of the modern era in "captivity" to "manual theology," namely Western theology of the scholastic stripe, imposed from the outside on the Orthodox faith, resulting in a "pseudomorphosis" of Eastern theology.[38] The project of the neopatristic school following Georges Florovsky has been to shake off the outsiders and teach Orthodoxy to speak in its own voice. Consequently, the notion of a developing and changing Tradition is unattractive to those who are struggling for the very existence of their own tradition against outside forces imposing alien development and change. Perhaps the closest Orthodoxy has come to the concept of development is in Bulgakov's essay on "Dogma and Dogmatic Theology." But Bulgakov and especially his sophiology were suppressed by the neopatristic contingent and have never subsequently gained a wide hearing in the East.[39] The developing Tradition remains largely a foreign idea.

Here is precisely where Behr-Sigel makes her first insightful contribution. It was perhaps her Protestant past that ingrained in her the idea of doctrinal development; her friendship with Sergius Bulgakov undoubtedly impacted her as well. Throughout her career she insisted on the role of Scripture in judging tradition(s), though she

permitting the ordination of women at a later point in Christian history—the "kairos" position, as she calls it. Such a position only absolves the church of its sexism and whitewashes the past. Ibid., pp. 22–24. In Hampson we see the same underlying assumption of a static, ahistorical Tradition as defended by the various Orthodox thinkers discussed above.

[37] Hopko writes, "The Orthodox Church does not have a teaching of 'dogmatic development.' Orthodox believe that expressions of Christian faith and life can change and indeed must change as the Church moves through history. But the Orthodox interpret these changes as being merely formal and not in any sense substantial. They would never agree that there can be anything in the Church of Christ today that was not essentially present at any moment of the Church's life and history." "Women and the Priesthood: Reflections on the Debate," in *Women and the Priesthood*, 1st edn, p. 177. Likewise Azkoul, quoting Ware's statement that "Holy Tradition, rightly understood, is dynamic, not static and inert," concludes: "With just these few words, the entire ecclesial and social legacy of the Orthodox faith is thrown into doubt." *Order of Creation, Order of Redemption*, p. x. The chief point of Azkoul's book is that any change or criticism of the Tradition where women are concerned renders the entire Christian faith void. Vladimir Lossky is skeptical of a progressivist understanding of developing doctrine, in the sense that the church started in some kind of "immaturity" and is presently approaching full wisdom. He particularly takes issue with the use of Gregory of Nazianzus's ideas about the Father's full revelation in Old Testament, the Son's in the New, and the Spirit's in the church. But the form of "developing doctrine" that he *can* accept is this: "[T]he Church extends the rule of faith while remaining, in her new definitions, in conformity with the dogmas already received by all." Behr-Sigel would surely agree with Lossky here. See "Tradition and Traditions," in *In the Image and Likeness of God*, p. 164 (ed. John H. Erickson and Thomas E. Bird; Crestwood, NY: St. Vladimir's Seminary Press, 1974). See also the very valuable discussion in Daniel J. Lattier, "The Orthodox Rejection of Doctrinal Development," *Pro Ecclesia* 20, no. 4 (2011), pp. 389–410, where he cites further instances of this but also demonstrates important convergences of such Orthodox theologians as Georges Florovsky and Dumitru Staniloae with John Henry Newman's seminal work on the subject.

[38] This judgment stems from Florovsky's *Ways of Russian Theology*. See also the discussion in Dorothea Wendebourg, "'Pseudomorphosis': A Theological Judgement as an Axiom for Research in the History of Church and Theology," *Greek Orthodox Theological Review* 42, nos 3–4 (1997), pp. 321–42.

[39] Westerners, however, have tended to be very appreciative: for instance, Hans Urs von Balthasar, Rowan Williams, and John Millbank.

didn't posit a fundamental opposition between Scripture and Tradition, which is more common in Protestant thought.

Her proposal to this conversation within Orthodoxy is the idea that the gospel itself takes time to do its work. Even while she described herself as "patiently impatient,"[40] she did not assume that the gospel would have fully transformed society within a century of Christ's resurrection, setting the parameters of possibility forever after. Again and again she used the metaphor of the gospel "leaven," slowly raising and enlightening ancient pagan societies. In her judgment, it has taken 20 centuries for the gospel's leaven to permeate relationships between men and women. The secular women's movement is the long-time-in-process outcome of Gal. 3.28.[41]

Therefore, one need not infer either that the church has faithlessly suppressed women's calls or that God has neglected the cries of women all along. The gospel works in and through history. It takes time. It does not (and perhaps cannot) change everything all at once. This approach to the church is more historical and less Platonic— a change in understanding that Behr-Sigel called for[42]—as well as more ecclesial and less individualistic. In short, God may indeed not have called women to the priesthood before; yet God may indeed be doing so now, for the good of the whole body of the church, and through the slow and steady transformations of the gospel leaven.

Of course, this perspective assumes a disturbing truth: that it is possible for there to be a genuine difference of opinion, or at least a lack of resolution, within the Scriptures, the Tradition, and the church fathers. Chiefly the opponents but occasionally also the proponents of women's ordination seek and find universal consensus, however implicit the consensus might be.[43]

Behr-Sigel disagrees. There *is* a difference of opinion, she asserts, and therefore there *is* a lack of resolution on the issue. Behr-Sigel posits that there are in fact two trends of thinking about women that have persisted throughout the whole life of the church.[44] One anthropology has happily baptized and chrismated women, recognized them as saints, martyrs, evangelists, and even apostles, proclaimed their soteriological unity with men, and anticipated a heavenly kingdom where sexuality will be outmoded. At

---

[40] Behr-Sigel, "The Ordination of Women: Also a Question for the Orthodox Churches," in *The Ordination of Women in the Orthodox Church*, p. 55.

[41] Moberly suggests much the same in her review of *Women and the Priesthood*. Silence may not mean that the ordination of women is *contrary* to the Tradition but rather *latent* in it, "a possibility to be actualised in the fullness of time," p. 86. Like many others, she invokes slavery as an example of the church's changing its mind over time. "Whether this happens speedily or slowly is another matter," p. 87.

[42] Behr-Sigel, "La Consultation Interorthodoxe de Rhodes," p. 103.

[43] Hopko writes, "According to Orthodox tradition, there can be no contradictions between any teachings presented as divine revelation in any of the writings accepted by the Church as witnessing to its life and teaching . . . And so there can also be no contradictions between anything taught from God in the authorized scriptures and the Church's official teaching, worship and spiritual practice in history." See "Galatians 3:28: An Orthodox Interpretation," *St. Vladimir's Theological Quarterly* 35, nos 2–3 (1991), pp. 169–86 (179). On the next page he says: "There are those who see real contradiction in the scriptures and subsequent church teaching and practices, as well as perversions in the canonically-received scriptures because of (among other things) male wickedness," p. 180, fn. 12. A whole host of offending feminists is then listed, including the Orthodox Eva Catafygiotu Topping.

[44] Of course, there is a mixed report on men, too, but somehow that question never gets asked.

the same time, another anthropology has excluded women from roles of leadership, denigrated their abilities and bodies, blamed them for causing men to sin, and subordinated them to men.

There is an inability to reach a consensus today rooted solely in the Tradition and church fathers because no such consensus exists. "The tension between these two anthropologies runs through the Bible and the whole of the Church's history," Behr-Sigel writes.[45] Where before, the conflict between the two was unnoticed or perhaps just endured, now the "signs of the times" require of the church a decision, a discernment, a separation of the one from the other that was not required before. To refuse to decide and act is finally to decide and act anyway.

An analogy can be drawn to previous matters of grave dispute in the church. In the first three centuries, there were ways of talking about Jesus Christ in relation to God that were permissible, if not strictly accurate in later perspective; but once the conciliar decision had been made, there was no turning back. For Behr-Sigel, the burning questions today about men and women require the same kind of decision—in continuity with the past but also discerning of the past and perhaps stepping forward into new territory.

Priesthood

Just because a new thing is proposed, though, doesn't mean that the new thing is good. It can in fact be very bad; for proof one need only think of the various ideologies that the churches latched onto during the twentieth century. Acknowledging the fact of developing Tradition permits one to talk about the possibility of women priests, but it does not decide automatically in its favor.

The problem is that the very question of women in the priesthood alters the results of any study of the clerical office. As the assumption of the functional inability of women to perform priestly tasks withered away, new arguments had to come forward if the practice of ordaining men alone was to be maintained. The central criterion for Orthodox priesthood became "iconic resemblance" (or "natural resemblance" in Roman Catholic parlance). This criterion, however, is entirely new, not a long-standing component of the tradition at all.

Four brief examples suffice to illustrate the point. The patristic classic on the office of ministry is John Chrysostom's *Six Books on the Priesthood*. It is, if anything, a heartfelt warning against becoming a priest, given the vast number of gifts required and the oppressive number of duties involved. But there is not the

---

[45] Behr-Sigel, "The Bible, Tradition, the Sacraments," in *Discerning the Signs of the Times*, p. 89. Yokarinis makes a similar point. "[T]he fathers tried very hard to overcome the dominant ideology of a society deeply influenced by the idol of masculinity. At times when they attempt to enter into the mystery of humanity's creation, the fathers appear to contradict themselves. This happens because, while they try to free Christians from a sinful world, the world of division and conflict, and to show them the new world of the reign of God, they find themselves trapped in the conditions of the fall." "A Patristic Basis," p. 590. Ioannis Petrou puts it more starkly: "The appeal to tradition cannot establish anything." In "The Question of Women in Church Tradition," *Anglican Theological Review* 84, no. 3 (2002), pp. 645–61 (659).

slightest mention of the priest's resemblance to Christ or standing in Christ's place. Topping explains:

> The priest as the "iconic image" of Christ does not appear in patristic discussions of the priesthood . . . Chrysostom, to be sure, categorically excludes women from the priesthood. He does so not because women cannot physically image Christ. He excluded all women because he believed, as did all the Fathers, in the innately inferior and flawed sinful nature of the female sex.[46]

The "Orthodox-Roman Catholic Consultation on Bishops and Presbyters" in 1976 serves as another example.[47] This brief statement of the North American dialogue—the longest-running between the Roman Catholic and Orthodox churches—only once mentions any iconic or natural resemblance of the priest to Christ. Instead, the chief concern is the Roman Catholic "weakness" in its historical practice of "absolute ordination" (ordaining to the priesthood without the priest being assigned to an actual congregation), because it denies the *pastoral* character of the priesthood (§I). "Pastoral character" is indeed the focus of the statement overall. Presidency at the eucharist is a supremely pastoral act (§II.2). Further, "[b]ishops and presbyters can only represent Christ as bishops and presbyters when they exercise the pastoral office of the church. Therefore, the church can recognize only an ordination which involves a bishop with a pastoral office and a candidate with a concrete title of service" (§II.7). It is striking here how the representation of Christ is linked to the *pastoral* work of the priest. Further, the chief similarity is found not between Christ and priests but between the apostles and priests. An ordination in apostolic succession "proclaims that pastoral office is founded on Christ and the Spirit who give the grace to accomplish the task of exercising the ministry of the apostles" (§II.5)—note that *both* Christ *and* the Spirit are necessary.

The document also notes that some Roman Catholic theologians are "challenging the traditional presentation of the pastoral office as the direct representation of Christ," suggesting instead it should be one of "directly representing the faith of the church and, consequently, Christ who is the living source of the faith" (§III.1). This, notably, is *not* linked to the challenge of women priests. In other words, there is a substantial theological objection to depicting priests as uniquely bearing Christ's image when the matter is considered in and of itself. However, when the subject of women in the priesthood does come up, toward the end of the document, the "iconic representation" of Christ (on the basis of sex) is offered as grounds for refusal, especially by the Orthodox. But "iconic representation" is by no means the substance of the rest of the document's theological proposal about the meaning of the priesthood (§III.2).

Two years later, another joint statement was released: "Orthodox-Roman Catholic Reflections on Ministries." Here again, while the bishop (in particular) is called upon to be an image of Christ, he is also linked closely to the ministry of the apostles through

---

[46] Topping, *Holy Mothers of Orthodoxy*, p. 125.
[47] The statement was published in *Diakonia* 11, no. 3 (1976), pp. 293–95.

his ordination in apostolic succession. No mention of natural or iconic resemblance is made at all.[48]

In this same year, 1978, the Anglican-Orthodox Joint Doctrinal Commission met in Athens and released a statement on the ordination of women. The Orthodox position made no mention of iconic representation whatsoever. It was, in fact, the *Anglicans* opposed to the ordination of women who advanced that argument! The Orthodox position was based solely on tradition, employing the same themes discussed in the previous section of this chapter.[49]

By the time of the Rhodes Consultation ten years later, however, iconic representation was the chief cornerstone of official Orthodox pronouncements against the ordination of women.[50] There is some suggestion of it in Khodre and Chitescu in the 1960s, though there it appears simply as one argument among others. Kallistos Ware, who also highlights the argument's recent provenance, traces it more specifically to "A Letter to an Episcopal Friend," which Alexander Schmemann published in *St. Vladimir's Theological Quarterly* in 1973.[51]

In this "letter," Schmemann charges that the prospective ordination of women by the Anglican communion—a church body to which the Orthodox in France and England had warmed considerably over the course of the twentieth century—would amount to "a radical and irreparable mutilation of the entire faith, the rejection of the whole Scripture—and, needless to say, the end of all 'dialogues.'"[52] A few pages later he explains why. First and foremost, the priesthood belongs to Christ, not to anyone else, and no one has a "right" to it. In fact, a priest in the church is not "another" priest beside Christ offering any distinct sacrifice from Christ's own. Christ is the one present doing all the priestly work. Then comes Schmemann's crowning point.

> [T]hus the "institutional" priesthood in the church has no "ontology" of its own. It exists only to make Christ Himself present, to make His unique Priesthood and His unique Sacrifice the source of the Church's life and the "acquisition" by men of the Holy Spirit. And if the bearer, the icon, and the fulfiller of that unique priesthood is *man* and not woman, it is because Christ is *man* and not woman . . .[53]

[48] "Orthodox-Roman Catholic Reflections on Ministries," *Origins* 7, no. 44 (1978), pp. 702–04.

[49] "Appendix 2: The Athens Report 1978," in *Anglican-Orthodox Dialogue: The Dublin Agreed Statement 1984*, pp. 58–63 (Crestwood, NY: St. Vladimir's Seminary Press, 1985). For example: "The ordination of women to the priesthood is an innovation, lacking any basis whatever in Holy Tradition. . . . In this constant and unvarying practice [of ordaining only men] we see revealed the will of God and the testimony of the Holy Spirit, and we know that the Holy Spirit does not contradict himself. . . . Holy Tradition is not static, but living and creative"! Ibid., §III.3 and §III.4.

[50] There are already signs of it developing in the 1980 *Women and Men in the Church: A Study of the Community of Women and Men in the Church*, a product of the ecumenical task force of the Orthodox Church in America. No names are appended but it sounds greatly influenced by Hopko: God is in no way sexual and yet there is an analogy between the Son and men, and the Spirit and women; Jesus is the model for men, Mary for women; only men can image Christ in the priesthood.

[51] Ware, "Man, Woman and the Priesthood of Christ," in *The Ordination of Women in the Orthodox Church*, p. 78.

[52] Schmemann, "Concerning Women's Ordination: A Letter to an Episcopal Friend," *St. Vladimir's Theological Quarterly* 17, no. 3 (1973), pp. 239–43 (239).

[53] Ibid., p. 242.

And this itself is necessary because the relationship between Christ and the church is a "mystical marriage," in which the latter is a bride and the former is a bridegroom. Presumably, to alter the sex of the priest is to void the symbolism of its meaning.[54]

The iconic representation argument is now the decisive one in Orthodox opposition to the ordination of women.[55] Thomas Hopko has argued it most consistently. He has, to his credit, tried to prevent it from being isolated from all other aspects of the priesthood. He wants it to be one criterion among many, including spiritual gifts, moral character, public witness, and so forth. Generally speaking, he is correct: a priest must indeed have spiritual gifts, exemplary moral behavior, a believing family, and so forth. The problem is simply that women can have all these things too. The only trait that disqualifies them is their femaleness, which forces the maleness of the priest once again to be the decisive factor.[56]

The iconic argument has not won universal approval, however. Kallistos Ware admits to the argument losing its force for him.[57] The participants at the bilateral dialogue between the Orthodox and Old Catholic churches collectively rejected the iconic argument, too.[58] One paper in particular was devoted to demonstrating how the theology of icons does not permit the conclusion that women cannot be icons of Christ in the priesthood.[59] John Erickson, who was present at Rhodes, goes so far as to suggest that very term "priesthood" misleads contemporary people as to the patristic understanding of the clerical office. There was far more to it than cultic action in the eucharist, and in any event "natural resemblance" to Christ is a spiritual, not physical, quality.[60]

---

[54] As far as I can tell, no one among the Orthodox has yet called into question the other implications of taking the nuptial imagery as a literal requirement for the sexuality of the clergy and laity. To raise just one question among many, what of lay *men*? Do they culpably fail to develop their "christic" virtues in not becoming priests, yet because they are not women, either, do they lack "pneumatic" virtues as well? Or do they themselves become "female" or "feminine" as part of the body of the church? If they do not become female, are they in a homosexual relationship to the priest and to Christ? One must assume that all of these implications would be offensive to Orthodox Tradition as well. The issues have been explored by Western theologians, however, in particular Sara Coakley and Tina Beattie in response to the work of Hans Urs von Balthasar.

[55] Aghiorgoussis uniquely claims that it is not only Christ but the Father as well that the priest symbolically presents, in *Women Priests?*, p. 3. Most other Orthodox theologians steer clear of this argument, since it ends up positing some kind of sexuality in the Father that human males must represent. In general, the maleness of the incarnate Christ is considered sufficient reason to restrict the priesthood to men.

[56] See Hopko's essays "On the Male Character of the Christian Priesthood," in the first edition of *Women and the Priesthood*, and "Presbyter/Bishop: A Masculine Ministry," in the revised edition.

[57] See the section entitled "'An Icon of Christ': But in What Sense?" in Ware's "Man, Woman, and the Priesthood of Christ," in *The Ordination of Women in the Orthodox Church*, pp. 78–90.

[58] "We have reached the common conclusion that there are no compelling dogmatic-theological reasons for not ordaining women to the priesthood." See Urs von Arx and Anastasios Kallis, "Common Considerations: The Orthodox-Old Catholic Consultation on the Role of Women in the Church and the Ordination of Women as an Ecumenical Issue: Preliminary Remarks," *Anglican Theological Review* 84, no. 3 (2002), pp. 501–07 (505).

[59] See Anastasios Kallis, "Presidency at the Eucharist in the Context of the Theology of Icons: Questions about the Ecclesial Representation of Christ by the Priesthood," *Anglican Theological Review* 84, no. 3 (2002), pp. 713–30.

[60] John H. Erickson, "The Priesthood in Patristic Teaching," in *The Place of the Woman in the Orthodox Church*, pp. 103–15.

To summarize, then, the majority of Orthodox opponents to the ordination of women reason this way. The bedrock, irreplaceable, and unique role of the priest is to present Christ iconically at the eucharist; to be an icon of Christ, one must be male; therefore, only males can be priests.[61] Behr-Sigel took issue with both premises of the syllogism.

First, the very approach of reducing the priesthood to one indispensable element is foreign to the whole tradition of Orthodox theology. If anything, it sounds more like the scholastic "manual" theology imported from the West. Eucharistic presidency is not to be isolated from other aspects of the priesthood. If anything is to characterize the priest, Behr-Sigel reasons, it should be love—"maternal love," as Evdokimov put it—gathering and leading the whole flock in worship and holiness of life. The exclusive focus on eucharistic presidency in fact impoverishes the priesthood.

The same is the case in focusing on the maleness of the priest. For Behr-Sigel, it is a misunderstanding of the eucharistic liturgy itself. The priest does not represent only Christ. He certainly does so during portions of the liturgy. But he also represents the church, speaking for and with the whole assembled body. The apex of Orthodox eucharistic liturgy is the epiclesis, the invocation of the Holy Spirit. At that point, the priest ceases to speak on behalf of Christ and begins to speak on behalf of the congregation, using the pronoun "we" and calling upon the Holy Spirit. There the priest identifies with the apparently "feminine" church, the bride awaiting the arrival of the bridegroom. It is thus not accurate to emphasize only the "masculine" aspects of priesthood iconically presenting Christ. A female priest would in fact redress an imbalance in the symbolism by her presentation of the bridal church.

This line of thought, of course, still assumes a distinct symbolism of male and female, aligning the masculine with Christ and the feminine with the church. Behr-Sigel herself rejects this symbolic usage. If one were to insist on the symbolism, she contends, there is still no reason not to ordain women and thus permit them eucharistic leadership. But far better, in her judgment, is the abandonment of the distinction between masculine and feminine roles in the liturgy, and thus in the priesthood, altogether.

Behr-Sigel emphasizes one other aspect in the Orthodox understanding of the priest's role in the liturgy. It is truly not the priest who acts. He does not stand in for an absent Christ (as Schmemann insisted!). He is rather a vessel by which the entire Holy Trinity acts. He "lends his tongue and hands" to God, as John Chrysostom said and Behr-Sigel so frequently quoted. Why then, Behr-Sigel proposes, could a woman not lend her tongue and hands to God? And why should God not make use of them?

This in turn has implications for the iconic understanding of the priesthood. It is not maleness that makes for an image of Christ. As Orthodox soteriology demands, Christ is full and entire humanity, *anthropos*, assuming the flesh of men and women alike in order to restore it. Both men and women must be icons of Christ because the humanity of both has been assumed by Christ, as in Gregory of Nazianzus's famous dictum, "That which is not assumed is not healed." All matters of symbolism aside, the

---

[61] This is the substance of the argument in Anderson, "The Orthodox Priest: An Icon of Christ." Significantly, his focus is not on the humanity of Christ, as one finds in the Cappadocians, but repeatedly that Christ was a "perfect man."

very christology of the church demands the recognition of women as images of Christ. Given the polyvalence of symbols, as Behr-Sigel observes, the refusal to ordain women now suggests the very opposite—that women are not adequate icons of Christ. The result is to leave both their humanity and their salvation in doubt.

The thing of it is, even the most stringent opponents of the ordination of women in the Orthodox church do not deny the full humanity assumed by Christ. They agree that women's humanity is assumed by Christ too and, with Basil of Caesarea, deny that the salvation of women should be doubted in the slightest. What then is the difficulty?

Following the reasoning to its logical end, the final matter at stake is the meaning of the incarnate Word's becoming a human male rather than a human female. For the opponents of women in the priesthood, the maleness of Christ is intrinsic to his "being," or mission, or imaging of God the Father. It is proof of the reality of the incarnation: humans only appear (with a tiny minority of exceptions) as males or females; the Word became male; therefore his maleness is inseparable from his meaning. To say otherwise is to engage in any number of heresies: docetism, perhaps, for denying the reality of Christ's body, or trinitarian modalism, for confusing the work of the Son and the Spirit—this especially is the charge leveled by Evdokimov, Hopko, and their followers. The maleness of Christ is so important that any image of Christ must also be male.

The objection is, once again, that being male itself becomes the chief criterion.[62] The love and grace that Christ offered are curiously demoted. And this emphasis in turn produces heresies of its own: a Nestorian tendency to award the male body of Christ its own kind of independent existence,[63] or a fundamental rejection of the soteriological unity of men and women in Christ,[64] or a violation of the apophatic denial of sexuality being in any way proper to God's own essence.[65] Once again, the church fathers offer very little help in this matter.[66]

---

[62]   As Yokarinis comments, "The differentiation within humanity is at the heart of the problem. The issue is the fact that a human being, who happens to be female, must because of her gender be excluded from the priesthood. Maleness, a form of division connected with the fall and sin, has unfortunately here become a divine characteristic!" "A Patristic Basis," p. 603.

[63]   Behr-Sigel, "Les Eglises Orthodoxes s'Interrogent," p. 527.

[64]   "If by baptism the Christian has 'put on Christ,' is not every Christian in some sense an icon of Christ? And therefore can a woman not equally be an icon of Christ?" Archimandrite Ephrem, review of *Le Ministère de la Femme dans l'Eglise*, p. 49. Behr-Sigel reports Iouriev's suggestion that this is the theological-anthropology version of the Arian heresy: as Arius denied the unity of divine and human in Christ, this argument denies the unity of male and female in humanity. Review of *L'Eglise et les Femmes*, pp. 136–41.

[65]   This is a recurring theme in the work of Verna Harrison.

[66]   Some Orthodox studies that have analyzed patristic views on the maleness of Christ are as follows. Valerie Karras, "The Incarnational and Hypostatic Significance of the Maleness of Jesus Christ according to Theodore of Stoudios," in *Studia Patristica*, pp. 320–24 (ed. Elizabeth A. Livingstone; vol. XXXII; Louvain: Peeters, 1997), and "Sermon: The Significance of the Maleness of Jesus Christ." Verna F. Harrison, in "The Maleness of Christ," *St. Vladimir's Theological Quarterly* 42 (1998), pp. 111–51, discusses a number of patristic writers. Yokarinis, in "A Patristic Basis," quotes John of Damascus: "[T]he Son of God became 'son of man' in order that his individuality might endure. For since he was the Son of God, he became 'son of man,' being made flesh of the holy virgin and not losing the individuality of his sonship," p. 604, fn. 66. Yokarinis also points out that if we think of gender in complementary terms, the one completing the other, then the

Behr-Sigel herself never pursued the meaning of Christ's maleness. This is likely because, once she had abandoned Evdokimov's theory about "christic" males and "pneumatic" females, she also abandoned the attempt to concoct any gender theory of her own. She followed the lead of Scripture and Tradition in having very little interest in the question at all. This is a strength in that she most accurately reflected the wisdom of the church catholic before her. She was also not entangled in any set of theories that failed to do justice to the scriptural and patristic witness. Evdokimov's debt to Jungian theory, which he did not always use accurately, is warning enough.

At the same time, Behr-Sigel's lack of an answer to the pressing question about Christ's maleness is a weakness. When accusations of trinitarian, christological, soteriological, and anthropological heresies fly in both directions, there is no choice but to press on. I submit that none of the questions about men and women in the church are going to be resolved until the church reaches some kind of consensus about the ontological implications of the incarnate Word's male human body.[67]

Gender and personhood

The basic dispute among contemporary Orthodox theologians regarding gender is whether it has any spiritual significance at all, and if so, what kind.[68] The question seems innocuous enough, but the answer is the foundation for any subsequent decision about the priesthood of women. Gender matters so much in the debate on the ordination of women because it is the lynchpin of the iconic argument. The icon expresses a typological relationship, such that the male priest is a type of Christ, just as Christ was a type of Adam (or vice versa), while a woman is a type of Mary, or Eve, or perhaps the Holy Spirit. The connecting link between the types, in all these cases, is gender. If gender is not somehow constitutive and essential, then the typology itself falls apart or at least becomes strictly limited in its scope.[69]

Son's humanity was imperfect since he only took on one of the two complementary genders; this, however, is at odds with Chalcedonian christology, which insists on the perfection and completeness of Christ's humanity. Outside the Orthodox fold, Richard A. Norris, Jr, discusses the topic with many themes in common to those already treated here in "The Ordination of Women and the 'Maleness' of Christ," *Anglican Theological Review* 6 (1976), pp. 69–80.

[67] Some attempts have been made by the Orthodox already. Harrison argues that we cannot really know, for God only reveals what He has done, not what He *could* have done. One possibility, though, is that being born of a woman in the flesh of a male sanctifies both sexes. See "The Fatherhood of God in Orthodox Theology," pp. 209–10. According to Wesche, it is the ontological headship of Adam the male over Eve the female that requires a male Jesus to include all of humanity in salvation. "Man and Woman in Orthodox Tradition," p. 242. Perhaps the most famous attempt to answer this question in the West is Rosemary Radford Ruether's chapter, "Can a Male Savior Save Women?," in her book *Sexism and God-Talk: Toward a Feminist Theology*, pp. 116–38 (Boston: Beacon Press, 1983).

[68] See John Behr's discussion of the dispute over the meaning of the patristic sources in "A Note on the 'Ontology of Gender,'" *St. Vladimir's Theological Quarterly* 42, nos 3–4 (1998), pp. 363–72.

[69] Petrou takes the opinion that "this question can no longer be interpreted through typology. Typologies, like images, are no more than symbols. But symbols are filled with significance by human beings—they can encompass whatever people want them to, depending on their wishes and ideas." "The Question of Women in Church Tradition," p. 658. One might add that the most profound problem in the typology proposed by Rhodes is that it aligns males with a person of

If, as with Evdokimov, the spiritual calling of the "woman" is thoroughly defined by her gender, then she cannot become a priest without betraying her very nature. Wesche attempted to demonstrate that a female priest is an "ontic impossibility—i.e., it is contrary to nature."[70] Deborah Belonick spoke of the "ontology of woman" wherein "anatomical image is related to the soul."[71] Ware, though skeptical of such conclusions, still holds to the spiritual significance of gender.[72] Hopko has given the most sustained attention to the matter over the years. In an early article he explained his own project simply: "[I]f human sexuality is *spiritually* necessary to proper human being and life beyond the need for the biological reproduction of the species, then its reason and purpose must be discovered and disclosed."[73]

The surprising fact here is that all these Orthodox strongly resemble a particular stripe of theological feminism preoccupied with a supposed distinctive female essence.[74] The irony is rich since these conservative Orthodox are at such pains to prove that feminism—depicted as a monolithic entity—is completely and utterly at odds with the Christian faith. Wesche says, for instance, that arguments for the ordination of women always require starting with feminist rather than Christian foundational principles.[75] Here he is operating from the same set of assumptions as feminists like

God—the incarnate Son—and females with another human, not God at all—the Theotokos. Wesche redresses the balance by suggesting parallel soteriological acts on the part of the Son and his mother, an ambiguous solution at best. See "Man and Woman in Orthodox Tradition," p. 242.

70   Wesche, "Man and Woman in Orthodox Tradition," p. 214.

71   Belonick, "Women in the Church," in *Orthodox Perspectives on Pastoral Praxis*, p. 84.

72   "For myself, I believe most strongly that maleness and femaleness, as gifts from God, have dimensions that are not only biological but spiritual." Ware, "Man, Woman and the Priesthood of Christ," in *The Ordination of Women in the Orthodox Church*, p. 77. Ian Graham has an excellent review of Ware's essay (and Behr-Sigel's too) in *Sourozh* 83 (2001), pp. 49–55.

73   Hopko, "The Masculine Character of the Priesthood," in *Women and the Priesthood*, 1st edn, p. 103. His various works on the subject are, in chronological order: the chapter entitled "The Spirit in the Sacraments," in *The Spirit of God* (Wilton, CT: Morehouse-Barlow, 1976); "The Lima Statement and the Orthodox," *Journal of Ecumenical Studies* 21, no. 1 (1984), pp. 55–63; "On the Male Character of the Christian Priesthood," in *Women and the Priesthood*, 1st edn; "Women and the Priesthood: Reflections on the Debate," in *Women and the Priesthood*, 1st edn; "Apophatic Theology and the Naming of God in Eastern Orthodox Tradition," in *Speaking the Christian God*; "Galatians 3:28: An Orthodox Interpretation"; "God and Gender: Articulating the Orthodox View"; "Presbyter/Bishop: A Masculine Ministry," in *Women and the Priesthood*, rev. edn; "The Debate Continues—1998," in *Women and the Priesthood*, rev. edn; "A Response from Fr. Hopko," *St. Nina Quarterly* 3, no. 3 (1999), pp. 22–23.

74   To cite a number of examples: Valerie Saiving, "The Human Situation: A Feminine View," in *Womanspirit Rising: A Feminist Reader in Religion*, pp. 25–42 (ed. Carol P. Christ and Judith Plaskow; San Francisco: Harper and Row, 1979), argues that men and women sin in essentially different ways, so the church's teaching about sin has missed the mark with women and in fact reinforced their sin rather than quenching it. Judith Plaskow picked up this theme and further essentialized men and women in *Sex, Sin, and Grace: Women's Experience and the Theologies of Reinhold Niebuhr and Paul Tillich* (Washington, DC: University Press of America, 1980). Mary Daly is perhaps the best known of essentializing feminists; see in particular her *Beyond God the Father: Toward a Philosophy of Women's Liberation* (Boston: Beacon Press, 1973). Essentialism remains a disputed point across the various kinds of feminist theology. Any supposed common quality shared by all women is the very axis of misogyny, but it is also the engine of communal feminist efforts at social and theological reform. The salient point here is that positing something in common among all women can equally serve the causes of conservative Orthodox Christians and radical feminist Christians and post-Christians.

75   Wesche, "Man and Woman in the Orthodox Tradition," p. 216.

Elisabeth Schüssler-Fiorenza and Rosemary Radford Ruether, who would reconceive Christian thought and practice along feminist lines, rather than those of his fellow Orthodox theologian Elisabeth Behr-Sigel, whose arguments derive from within the Christian faith itself. Belonick, too, posits an absolute distinction between Orthodoxy and feminism, and yet, curiously, finds a possible point of commonality between them in their identifying females with the Holy Spirit.[76] In neither case do the Orthodox theologians' unexpected feminist allies give rise to any uneasiness about their position!

On the other hand, along with Behr-Sigel, Karras and Harrison—both patristic scholars—have been most consistently critical of this essentialist approach to gender. Karras argues outright that "there is no spiritual dimension, no ontological significance, to gender."[77] If there were, then people would be "determined" by their gender to the detriment of their personal freedom.[78] While Harrison doesn't go that far, she certainly advises extreme caution in attributing anything sexual or gendered to God and finds that the church fathers took very little interest in the subject at all.[79] Gender-based spirituality is almost entirely without grounding in the Tradition.

But even if everyone did agree that gender means *something* spiritual, how would the church determine *what* exactly it means? Neither the Scriptures nor the church fathers offer any clear resolution. The essence of the Holy Trinity is apophatically unknowable, yet the first and second persons of the Trinity are called Father and Son; they are called Father and Son, and yet it is forbidden to draw any analogy to creaturely ways of begetting and being begotten.[80] All contenders in this debate are agreed that gender is not in God's essence, but some suggest that God's "energies" take on distinct gendered qualities. Humanity is gendered, but there are two creation stories, and furthermore there are three human states: one before the fall, one after the fall but before the eschaton, and one to come about in the eschatological resurrection.

The dispute is ultimately over how to define the "difference" between men and women. It is obvious enough that men and women are different, but what is the nature of the difference? As we have noted before, the content of the dispute itself has changed. The patristic question, set in the context of monastic celibacy, was whether sexual differentiation is intrinsic to creation or a secondary provision for the inevitable state of sin. The modern question, set in the context of social movements toward equality, asks whether sexual differences are biological and psychological or ontological and transcendental. Most contemporary theologians opt for the intrinsic-to-creation side of the patristic discussion, fearing a gnostic contempt of the body. But that does little

---

[76] Deborah Belonick, "The Spirit of the Female Priesthood," in *Women and the Priesthood*, 1st edn, p. 165. For instance, Alwyn Marriage, *Life-Giving Spirit: Responding to the Feminine in God* (London: SPCK, 1989); Rachel Conrad Wahlburg, "The Women's Creed," in her *Jesus and the Freed Woman*, pp. 155–57 (New York: Paulist Press, 1978); Alla Bozarth-Campbell, *Womanpriest: A Personal Odyssey* (New York: Paulist Press, 1978).

[77] Karras, "Patristic Views on the Ontology of Gender," p. 117.

[78] Ibid., p. 118.

[79] Harrison, "The Fatherhood of God in Orthodox Theology," pp. 189–90.

[80] Verna F. Harrison, "Male and Female in Cappadocian Theology," *Journal of Theological Studies* 41, no. 2 (1990), pp. 441–71.

to resolve the modern question. How much does gender determine, limit, or form who one is and what one can do?[81]

For Behr-Sigel, the common flaw in all of these approaches is to treat the sexual component of each human being as a quantifiable thing. Such a move is not in keeping with the broader tradition of Orthodox theology that regards human being itself as a mystery in the spiritual sense. It is in Vladimir Lossky's personalism that Behr-Sigel found the outline of a resolution to the mysterious, Trinity-imaging combination of person and nature in humanity.[82] She didn't spend much time herself developing a theological conception of personhood, though she regularly alluded to Lossky's work as the foundation for her ultimate convictions about men and women in the church, and her mentions of his name in her writings are far too numerous to list. It will be useful here first to sketch Lossky's own vision, then to indicate what Behr-Sigel probably found attractive in it, and finally to suggest how their combined insights might suggest an answer to the questions posed by the possibility of women in the priesthood.

In his first study, Lossky admits that there is no "elaborated doctrine of the human person in patristic theology, alongside its very precise teaching on divine persons

---

[81] An excellent study on this question from an Orthodox theologian is David J. Dunn's "'Her That Is No Bride': St. Thecla and the Relationship between Sex, Gender, and Office," *St. Vladimir's Theological Quarterly* 53, no. 4 (2010), pp. 37–68. Dunn exegetes the Acts of Paul and Thecla to demonstrate how Thecla's progressive conversion to Christ entailed leaving behind her "femininity" as it was defined for her by her culture, such as being a cloistered fiancée, a bride, an eventual mother, and a potential object of rape. The deeper her commitment to Christ, the more "masculine" she became in quality, eventually becoming an itinerant apostle analogous to and approved by Paul. Dunn concludes then that if, as Hopko argues, the priesthood is a "masculine" ministry, Thecla's case shows that women can successfully undertake it themselves; but the fact that women can indeed succesfully embody "masculine" qualities calls into question the alignment of "masculine" qualities with biological males and "feminine" qualities with biological females.

[82] Behr-Sigel had read *The Mystical Theology of the Eastern Church* and frequently cited Lossky's dictum "Tradition represents the critical spirit of the Church," which comes from the essay "Tradition and Traditions." That her thinking on the Trinity and personhood was already being shaped by Vladimir Lossky in the 1960s is evident in an article she wrote on Gregory Palamas, where she comments: "[P]alamism puts the accent on the revelation of a personal God, absolutely transcendent but who, according to the expression of V. Lossky, 'crosses the wall of transcendence to make himself totally participable.'" Behr-Sigel, "Réflexions sur la Doctrine de Grégoire Palamas," *Contacts* 12, no. 2 (1960), pp. 118–24 (122). My translation. She wrote one article about how Lossky's work connected theology and mysticism, "Théologie et Contemplation: Introduction à Quelques Textes de Vladimir Lossky," but she makes no mention of "personalism" here at all. Though she regularly referred to Lossky's personalism, only once did she indicate where she found it, in fn. 25 of her article "L'Ordination des Femmes: Un Problème Oecuménique," where she points the reader to his essay "La Notion Théologique de la Personne Humaine," which appeared in the posthumous collection of Lossky's works, *A l'Image et à la Ressemblance de Dieu* (Paris: Aubier-Montaigne, 1967), a work also noted in the footnotes of her aforementioned study "Théologie et Contemplation." This same collection was subsequently translated into English as *In the Image and Likeness of God* (ed. John H. Erickson and Thomas E. Bird; Crestwood, NY: St. Vladimir's Seminary Press, 1974). In this collection are two other essays on theological anthropology, "The Theology of the Image," pp. 125–39, and "Catholic Consciousness: Anthropological Implications of the Dogma of the Church," pp. 183–94, which express the same basic ideas as "The Theological Notion of the Human Person," pp. 111–24. Because of their common themes, and the likelihood that Behr-Sigel read them, too, these other two essays will also be used here to develop a description of Lossky's personalism. Quotations are from the English translation.

or hypostases."[83] Later he makes the point more strongly: "In general Christian anthropology has not received sufficient theological elaboration."[84] What little attention the topic got was usually wrapped up in philosophical packages not necessarily conformed to Christian teaching. For Lossky, a proper theological anthropology must flow from the top down, from God to humanity, quite aside from sociological data.[85]

For this reason, Lossky assumes that both the Trinity and the incarnate Christ will illuminate human being. This is not a unique move; the twentieth century was awash with attempts to explain individuality and community, likeness and otherness, unity and diversity on the basis of the Trinity. But where Evdokimov and others like him find in the Trinity and the person of Christ alike an archetype or pattern setting the bounds for human beings, Lossky moves in quite a different direction.

In the triune God, Lossky explains at length, the hypostasis is the same as the ousia, and yet the hypostasis cannot be reduced to the ousia. Because of the personal nature of the triune God, the term hypostasis is more like a placeholder than a delimitable concept. As Lossky puts it, the hypostasis "is no longer a conceptual expression but a sign which is introduced into the domain of the non-generalizable, pointing out the radically personal character of the God of Christian revelation."[86]

Such is the case with God. Does the ousia-hypostasis distinction apply to human beings as well? Is the human hypostasis equally irreducible to the human ousia? To Lossky, these questions are the same as asking "whether Trinitarian anthropology has had any repercussion on Christian anthropology—whether it has opened up a new dimension of the 'personal' by discovering a notion of the human hypostasis not reducible to the level of natures or individual substances, which fall under the hold of concepts."[87] After reviewing and rejecting a number of ways of formulating such terms as hypostasis, person, and individual, Lossky arrives at his conclusion.

> [I]t will be impossible for us to form a concept of the human person, and we will have to content ourselves with saying: "person" signifies the irreducibility of man to

---

83 Vladimir Lossky, "The Theological Notion of the Human Person," in *In the Image and Likeness of God*, p. 112.

84 Vladimir Lossky, "Catholic Consciousness," in *In the Image and Likeness of God*, p. 185. In light of these remarks, one must wonder whether Lossky was really as purely neopatristic as he claimed to be. His remarks here strongly suggest the need to go "beyond the fathers" to give an account of theological anthropology that they lack, in continuity with them but saying more than they ever did.

85 "Theological anthropology must be constructed from the top down, beginning from Trinitarian and Christological dogma, in order to discover in human reality the unity of nature and the multiplicity of created hypostases, the will which is a function of the common nature, the possession of divine grace by created persons, *etc.*" Ibid.

86 Vladimir Lossky, "The Theological Notion of the Human Person," in *In the Image and Likeness of God*, p. 113.

87 Ibid., p. 115. As we have seen, other Orthodox theologians have tried to derive an anthropology from the doctrine of the Trinity, but they have made gender an integral part of it in a way that Lossky did not. For instance, Kyriaki Karidoyanes FitzGerald writes, "The relationship between men and women reflects, in a certain sense, the relationship which exists between the Persons of the Trinity. Women and men share totally and equally in their common humanity, as do the Persons in the Trinity share in the common Divinity. However, just as there is genuine distinction between the persons of the Trinity, so also is there a genuine distinction between male and female human

his nature—"irreducibility" and not "something irreducible" or "something which makes man irreducible to his nature" precisely because it cannot be a question here of "something" distinct from "another nature" but of *someone* who is distinct from his own nature, of someone who goes beyond his nature while still containing it, who makes it exist as human nature by this overstepping and yet does not exist in himself beyond the nature which he "enhypostasizes" and which he constantly exceeds.[88]

Behr-Sigel offers a very similar description of the image of God—thus one very likely drawn right from Lossky.

The image of God is not a *thing* or a part of man. It relates to the dynamic and global orientation of an existing being who is endlessly called upon to go beyond himself and to transcend his nature. As such, the image of God is both a gift and a task: the task of *becoming* "the likeness of God."[89]

One of the tasks of deified humanity, then, is to go "in grace beyond the individual limits which divide nature and tend to reduce persons to the level of the closed being of particular substances," as Lossky explains.[90] The hypostases of God demonstrate that God Himself is not enclosed in His own nature. That is what it means for God—and therefore for the human—to be a person. So the common feature between God and humans that makes both of them "personal" is not a certain set of characteristics, not even *nous* or mind as Gregory of Nyssa was tempted to suggest.[91] It is the common self-transcendence of their own nature: in short, their personhood.

The same ideas apply when considering humanity from the point of view of "the image and likeness of God" in Gen. 1.28. Lossky writes:

[A]s in Trinitarian theology, the term "image"—or rather, "in the image"—applied to man must be given a new meaning along the same line of thought which made us distinguish in God the personal or hypostatic from the essential or natural. Man is

---

persons." "The Ministry of Women in the Orthodox Church: Some Theological Presuppositions," *Journal of Ecumenical Studies* 20, no. 4 (1983), pp. 558–75 (562). Hopko, as we have seen, draws still more extensive parallels between male and female human persons and the various persons of God. Andrew Walker critiques Hopko's views at length. He detects in them an "ominous lopsidedness. The Spirit, as person, is hemmed in, cramped, and fleeting like an eternal Cinderella. Functionally, though not ontologically, the Spirit begins to fade into the background, like a good servant girl, which is precisely what the filioque achieved for the western tradition." "Resexing the Trinity: The Spirit as Feminine," *King's Theological Review* 13 (1990), pp. 41–44 (43).

[88] Vladimir Lossky, "The Theological Notion of the Human Person," in *In the Image and Likeness of God*, p. 120.

[89] Behr-Sigel, "Woman Is Also Made in the Image of God," in *The Ministry of Women in the Church*, p. 84. See also the discussion of "apophatic anthropology" in Kallistos Ware, *Orthodox Theology in the Twenty-First Century* (Doxa and Praxis: WCC Publications, 2012). If one were to follow Ware's insights, which here share much in common with both Vladimir Lossky and Behr-Sigel, it would be simply impossible to give a definition of "woman" and positively wrongheaded to try.

[90] Vladimir Lossky, "The Theological Notion of the Human Person," in *In the Image and Likeness of God*, p. 122.

[91] Vladimir Lossky, "The Theology of the Image," in *In the Image and Likeness of God*, pp. 138–39.

not merely an individual of a particular nature, included in the generic relationship of human nature to God the Creator of the whole cosmos, but he is also—he is chiefly—a person, not reducible to the common (or even individualized) attributes of the nature which he shares with other human individuals. Personhood belongs to every human being by virtue of a singular and unique relation to God who created him "in His image." This personal element in anthropology, discovered by Christian thought, does not indicate, in itself, a relationship of participation, much less a "kinship" with God, but rather an analogy: like the personal God, in whose image he is created, man is not only "nature." This bestows on him liberty in regard to himself, taken as an individual of a particular nature.[92]

While the image of God in all human persons is "inalienable," it will manifest God to a greater or lesser degree depending on the deification or sin of the person.[93]

Human uniqueness, then, does not lie in any set of individual qualities, nor is it threatened by qualities shared with others. Human uniqueness lies in the analogous-to-God non-reducibility to one's own nature.[94] Thus "[n]o differences of created nature—sex, race, social class, language, or culture—can affect the unity of the Church . . . There is no Church of the Jews or of the Greeks, of the Barbarians or of the Scythians, just as there is no Church of slaves or of free men, of men or of women."[95]

The appeal of Lossky's personalism to a thinker like Behr-Sigel is clear enough. Instead of focusing on natures, which so often turns into stereotypes and essentialism, Lossky focuses on the person. The person is not cut off from his or her own nature nor from other persons. But the person is not defined, pinned down, or limited, either. The very quality that makes a person a person is self-transcendence, which includes among other things the possibility of love. And the anchoring in trinitarian doctrine is not lost. This understanding of personhood derives directly from the Christian "discovery" of the ousia of God in three hypostases, indissolubly united and yet utterly unique.

What, then, of sexual differences? Lossky pays little attention to the question, only to lump them together with ethnic, social, and economic differences as irrelevant in the church. They are certainly not identified as part of God's own nature, nor is an extra stratum accounting for gender added to human nature. Lossky died before gender questions were raised *en masse* in the church. Is this an oversight that needs correcting?

Not at all. In Lossky's way of thinking, it would not matter at all if gender were inserted as another level of human "nature."[96] A male person and a female person will always exceed and transcend his nature and her nature, however distinct those natures may be from one another. What makes him and her the same, in the end, is their common ability to transcend themselves; that neither is reduced to their respective natures.

---

[92] Ibid., pp. 137–38.
[93] Ibid., p. 139.
[94] Vladimir Lossky, "Catholic Consciousness," in *In the Image and Likeness of God*, p. 186.
[95] Ibid., p. 184.
[96] John Behr suggests this solution, though without Lossky's distinctions in mind, in "A Note on the 'Ontology of Gender,'" p. 368.

The ramifications of such personalism shaped Behr-Sigel's mature position on the place of women in the church. The nature of any given woman is not a limiting factor in her capacity to serve the church. It is not alien to who she is, but it does not contain her, either. She is like to God (the Trinity as a whole or the Holy Spirit in particular) *not* in any particular set of feminine qualities resulting from her nature. She is like to God, she is in God's image, in her self-transcendence as a person, in her non-reducibility to her human (and indeed, if there is such a thing, her female) nature. Therefore, Behr-Sigel's growing intuition that "women's charisms" represent a false trail recognizes that the very attempt to elevate women in their distinctive femininity is precisely to deny them both their unique personhood and their participation in common humanity. Women are not a set of feminine charisms. They are persons with a variety of charisms who, again, transcend the nature of which they are an instance, the ousia of which they are a hypostasis.

In this light, then, we can see that the anthropologies of Evdokimov, Hopko, and their followers make the error of identifying the hypostasis of humanity not with the person but with the gender. "Woman"—always rendered in the singular—occupies the category of the hypostasis, not, for example, the individual "Elisabeth." The same error appears in treating "Eve" as equivalent to "woman" and "Adam" as equivalent to "man." They are no longer persons but genders. Awarding gender the status of the hypostasis of humanity, and then tying it to the trinitarian hypostases, forces the identification of the Son with men (or "man") and the Spirit with women (or "woman"). In both cases, the trinitarian hypostasis is aligned with an entire gender. But every individual male person is lost this way, subsumed in his gender and reduced to his nature, in supposed hypostatic analogy to the Son; the same for women and the Spirit. While Evdokimov and Hopko correctly avoided identifying a particular gender with the human ousia— which would indisputably have called into question the soteriological unity of men and women—they failed to recognize that putting gender in the place of the hypostasis would lead to a radical division of the Son from the Spirit and both from the Father. And it would certainly destroy unique personhood if gender occupied the place of the hypostasis. All then would be nature, and personhood would be lost. Ironically, Evdokimov and Hopko committed a classically *Western* trinitarian error, subsuming the person under the nature!

Gender does not exist as such, but gendered humans do. They are hypostases of the shared human ousia, whether they are male or female. Inserting gender as such into the ontological scheme (whether in the place of the ousia *or* the hypostasis) obscures actual persons, concealing them within their gender. In short, the hypostasis must be the person, not the person's gender. That is the proper trinitarian analogy. The person is not accordingly alienated from his or her own gender. But neither is he or she contained by it.

It matters little whether the attempt is to introduce "feminine" language for God and defend "feminine" ways of being in the church, or to preserve "masculine" names for God on the assumption that God has distinctly "masculine" traits. Each attempt comes to a different conclusion, but they are *methodologically* indistinguishable. Both start "from below" with assumptions about what qualifies as masculine or feminine. Both emphasize gender to such an extent that personhood is lost. The whole sweep of Behr-Sigel's thought moves to the conclusion that this approach is a dead-end for traditionalists and revisionists alike. Any attempt to invoke the "feminine" (or the "masculine") always ends up reducing women (and men) to mere replications of their natures, rather than allowing them to be self-transcending persons in God's own image. In truth, women are persons and men are persons, because the Father, the Son, and the Holy Spirit are Persons, too.

Published Works of Elisabeth Behr-Sigel

"La Vie Estudiantine à Berlin—Impressions d'Allemagne," *Les Dernières Nouvelles* (December 2, 1931). Reprinted in *Le Petit Marseillais*.

"Notes sur l'Idée Russe de la Sainteté d'après les Saints Canonisés de l'Eglise Russe," *Revue d'Histoire et de Philosophie Religieuses* (November–December 1933), pp. 537–54.

"Le Temps Pascal dans l'Eglise Orthodoxe d'Orient," *La Quinzaine Protestante* 16 (May 1935).

"Vie et Pensée de la Jeunesse Protestante," *La Vie Intellectuelle* 38 (October 10, 1935).

"Etudes d'Hagiographie Russe," *Irénikon* 12 (1935), pp. 242–54, 581–98.

"Etudes d'Hagiographie Russe," *Irénikon* 13 (1936), pp. 25–37.

"Etudes d'Hagiographie Russe," *Irénikon* 14 (1937), pp. 363–77.

"La Sophiologie du Père Serge Boulgakoff," *Revue d'Histoire et de Philosophie Religieuses* 2 (1939), pp. 130–58. Reprinted in *Le Messager Orthodox* 57 (1972), pp. 21–48.

"Les Fous pour le Christ et la Sainteté Laïque dans l'Ancienne Russie," *Irénikon* 15 (1939), pp. 554–65.

"La Prière de Jésus ou le Mystère de la Spiritualité Monastique Orthodoxe," *Dieu Vivant* 8 (1947), pp. 69–94. "Prayer to Jesus or the Essence of Orthodox Monastic Spirituality," *Eastern Churches Quarterly* 7 (1947), pp. 132–50. Reprinted in *Pages de Spiritualité Orthodoxe* (1957), pp. 27–39. Reprinted in *Contacts* 9 (1957), pp. 1–13. Reprinted with additional material in *La Douloureuse Joie*, pp. 81–129 (Spiritualité Orientale, 14; Bégrolles: Abbaye de la Bellefontaine, 1974). Reedited and reprinted in *La Douloureuse Joie: Aperçus sur la Prière Personnelle de l'Orient Chrétien* (ed. Olivier Clément; Bégrolles: Abbaye de la Bellefontaine, 1999). Translated into Romanian in *Fericita Întristare*, pp. 83–129 (1997).

Prière et Sainteté dans l'Eglise Russe; Essai sur le Rôle du Monachisme dans la Vie Spirituelle du Peuple Russe (Paris: Cerf, 1950). Republished as *Prière et Sainteté dans l'Eglise Russe* (Spiritualité Orientale, 33; Bégrolles: Abbaye de Bellefontaine, rev. edn, 1982). Translated into Portuguese as *Oraçào e Santidade na Igreja Russa* (São Paulo: Paulinas, 1993).

Review of *Mes Missions en Sibérie*, by Arch. Spiridon, *Dieu Vivant* 19 (1951), n.p.

Review of *Saint Tikhon de Zadonsk*, by N. Gorodetsky, *Dieu Vivant* 22 (1952), n.p.

"Monachisme et Contemplation dans l'Eglise Orthodoxe," *Bulletin du Cercle Saint-Jean-Baptiste* (1953), n.p.

"L'Orthodoxie Universelle et la Vocation Spirituelle de la Russie," *Le Messager Ecclésial* (May–December 1957), pp. 25–28.

"'Orthodoxie Occidentale.' Réflexions sur la Brochure de L. Zander," *Le Messager Orthodoxe* (1958), pp. 12–17.

Review of *Orthodox Spirituality*, by A Monk of the Eastern Church, *Contacts* 11, no. 1 (1959), pp. 47–54.

"Vers l'Unité Chrétienne," *Contacts* 11, no. 2 (1959), pp. 121–26.

"Du Phanar au Vatican," *Contacts* 11, no. 4 (1959), pp. 257–59.

"Le Message Spirituel de Gogol," *Contacts* 11, no. 4 (1959), pp. 233–56, and 12, no. 1 (1960), pp. 22–37.

"Réflexions sur la Doctrine de Grégoire Palamas," *Contacts* 12, no. 2 (1960), pp. 118–24.

Review of *Simples Regards sur le Sauveur*, by A Monk of the Eastern Church, *Contacts* 12 (1960), p. 145.

Review of *Der Rebell von Kamtchatke*, by D. H. Teuffen, *Contacts* 12 (1960), pp. 151–52.

Review of *Um die Wiedervereinungen im Glauben*, by H. Schütte, *Contacts* 12 (1960), p. 222.

"Réflexions sur l'Iconostase," *Contacts* 12, no. 4 (1960), pp. 309–12. Reprinted in *Lumière du Thabor* 28 (2006), pp. 29–31.

"De Fil en Aiguille: Un Philosophe en Quête de l'Eglise," *Contacts* 13, no. 1 (1961), pp. 15–27.

Review of *Commonitorium*, by Vincent of Lérins, *Contacts* 13 (1961), pp. 76–80.

Review of *Introduction à la Vie Spirituelle*, by L. Bouyer, *Contacts* 13 (1961), pp. 150–52.

"La Vie Religieuse en U.R.S.S.," *Contacts* 14 (1962), pp. 62–65.

Review of *N. B. Gogol* (in Russian), by V. Zenkovsky, *Contacts* 14 (1962), pp. 68–69.

"Introduction à la 'Tribune Libre,'" *Contacts* 14 (1962), pp. 265–68.

Review of *La Proclamation de l'Evangile*, by K. Barth, *Contacts* 14 (1962), pp. 283–87.

"Aspects Majeurs de la Spiritualité Russe du 14ᵉ au 16ᵉ Siècles," *Contacts* 15, no. 1 (1963), pp. 34–40.

"A la Memoire du Père Basile Zenkovsky," *Contacts* 15 (1963), pp. 65–66.

Review of *Sois Mon Prêtre*, by A Monk of the Eastern Church, *Contacts* 15 (1963), pp. 69–71.

Review of *Die ostliche Welt*, by D. H. Teuffen, *Contacts* 15 (1963), pp. 71–72.

"Un Mot de Madame Behr-Sigel," *Contacts* 15 (1963), pp. 127–29.

"Les Orthodoxes et le Pèlerinage de Paul VI," *Le Messager Orthodoxe* 24–25 (1963–64), pp. 31–33.

"Perspectives de l'Orthodoxie en France," *Contacts* 16, no. 1 (1964), pp. 42–55.

"Rencontre avec la Grèce Chrétienne," *Contacts* 16 (1964), pp. 56–62.

Review of *Dictionnaire Théologique*, by L. Bouyer, *Contacts* 16 (1964), pp. 150–55.

"'Le Messager Orthodoxe,' no. 24–25, 1963–1964," *Contacts* 16 (1964), pp. 237–40.

"Repenser la Théologie du Mariage?" *Contacts* 16, no. 4 (1964), pp. 291–301.

"A Propos de la Présence Orthodoxe en France," *Contacts* 16 (1964), pp. 311–12.

Review of *La Piété Russe*, by N. Arseniew, *Revue d'Histoire et de Philosophie Religieuses* 44 (1964), pp. 165–66.

"Les Conférences de Rhodes. Bilan et Voeux," *Le Messager Orthodox* 29–30 (1965), pp. 18–23.

"Inauguration d'un Centre d'Etudes Oecuméniques (Strasbourg, 31 Janvier et 1er Fevrier 1965)," *Contacts* 17 (1965), pp. 73–76.

"Réponse à Panayiotis Nellas," *Contacts* 17 (1965), pp. 80–82.

"Pour le Vingtième Anniversaire de la Mort de Mère Marie Skobtzoff," *Contacts* 17 (1965), pp. 178–93.

Review of *Pearl of Great Price: The Life of Mother Maria Skobtsova*, by S. Hackel, *Contacts* 17 (1965), pp. 260–61.

"Pèlerinage de la Jeunesse Orthodoxe à Jérusalem et Conférence de 'Syndesmos' à Broumana," *Contacts* 17 (1965), pp. 327–34.

"La Fraternité Orthodoxe en Europe Occidentale," *Contacts* 18 (1966), pp. 198–203.

"A Propos de 'La Queste d'Irénée Winnaert,'" *Contacts* 18 (1966), pp. 315–19.

Review of *Le Visage de Lumière*, by A Monk of the Eastern Church, with G. R. A., *Contacts* 19 (1967), p. 93.

Review of *La Spiritualité Orthodoxe et la Spiritualité Protestante et Anglicane*, by L. Bouyer, *Contacts* 19 (1967), pp. 93–96.

"Un Essai de Spiritualité Contemporaine: Le Combat de Jacob," *Contacts* 19, no. 3 (1967), pp. 167–75.

Review of *Les Sources de la Foi*, by J. Hermel, *Contacts* 19 (1967), p. 184.

Review of *Renouveau Communautaire et Unité Chrétienne*, by A. Perchenet, *Contacts* 19 (1967), pp. 330–33.

"Le Christ Kénotique dans la Spiritualité Russe," *La Table Ronde* 250 (1968), pp. 204–17. Reedited for *Cahiers Saint-Dominique* 170 (1977). Reprinted in Elisabeth Behr-Sigel, *Prière et Sainteté dans l'Eglise Russe*, pp. 219–36 (Spiritualite Orientale, 33; Bégrolles: Abbaye de la Bellefontaine, rev. edn, 1982).

"Les Startsy Russes," *Concilium: Revue Internationale de Théologie* 37 (1968), pp. 55–69. "The Russian Startsy: The Monks of 'Holy Russia,'" *Concilium: International Journal for Theology* 7 (1968), pp. 30–40. Reprinted in *Prophets in the Church*, pp. 57–77 (ed. Roger Aubert; New York: Paulist Press, 1968).

"Un Origène Moderne. À Propos d'une Initiation à Paul Tillich," *Contacts* 21 (1969), pp. 70–85.

Review of *Comme le Feu Mêlé d'Aromates*, by G. Matzneff, *Contacts* 21 (1969), pp. 342–44.

"A Propos du Débat sur le Célibat Sacerdotal dans l'Eglise Latine," *Contacts* 22, no. 1 (1970), pp. 54–60.

Review of *Le Diaconat*, by S. Charalambidis et al. and *Le Peuple de Dieu*, by Elie Mélia et al., *Contacts* 22 (1970), pp. 165–67.

"Impressions du Congrès de la Jeunesse Orthodoxe. Annecy 1971," *Bulletin de la Crypte* 2 (1971), pp. 5–6. Reprinted in *Vers l'Unité Chrétienne* (1972), pp. 30–32.

"Témoignage sur Paul Evdokimov," *Contacts* 23 (1971), pp. 237–40.

"La Prière de Jésus," *Unité des Chrétiens* 3 (1971), pp. 17–19.

Review of *The Burning Bush*, by L. Gillet, *Contacts* 24 (1972), pp. 73–75.

"Charles Westphal (1896–1972)," *Contacts* 24 (1972), p. 214.

Review of *God and Man*, by A. Bloom, *Contacts* 24 (1972), pp. 233–35.

Review of *Amour sans Limites*, by A Monk of the Eastern Church, *Contacts* 24 (1972), pp. 316–19.

Review of *Recherches et Réflexions à Propos de l'Habit Monastique*, by Frère Marie-Félix, *Contacts* 25 (1973), p. 64.

Review of *Christianisme Social et Socialisme Scientifique*, by N. Psaroudakis, *Contacts* 25 (1973), pp. 68–70.

"Un Prophète Orthodoxe: Alexandre Boukharev," *Contacts* 25, no. 2 (1973), pp. 93–111.

Review of *Concert Spirituel*, by A. Lequeux, *Contacts* 25 (1973), pp. 254–55.

"Questions à Propos d'une Célébration Oecuménique," *Bulletin de la Crypte* 13 (1973), p. 8.

"Dimanche de l'Orthodoxie," *Bulletin de la Crypte* 15 (1973), p. 14.

Review of *La Prière de Jésus*, by A Monk of the Eastern Church, *Bulletin de la Crypte* 29 (1974), pp. 15–16. Reprinted in *Contacts* 26 (1974), pp. 368–70.

"Tikhon de Zadonsk," *Contacts* 26, no. 1 (1974), pp. 35–65.

"Situation du 'Christianisme Social,'" *Contacts* 26 (1974), pp. 92–93.

Review of *L'An de Grâce du Seigneur*, by A Monk of the Eastern Church, *Contacts* 26 (1974), p. 96.

Review of *Ages Qui Passent et Demeurent*, by P. Fidler [Reldif-Fidlerski], *Contacts* 26 (1974), p. 192.

Review of *Voyage Spirituel*, by A. Bloom, *Contacts* 26 (1974), p. 373.

"Retraite de la Fraternité Orthodoxe de la Région Parisienne les 12 et 13 octobre, au Moulin de Senlis à Montgeron," *Bulletin de la Crypte* 29 (1974), pp. 14–15.

"Deuxième Congrès de la Jeunesse Orthodoxe—Dijon 1–3 Novembre 1974," *Bulletin de la Crypte* 30 (1974), pp. 5–7.

"Editorial [Semaine de Prières pour l'Unité]," *Bulletin de la Crypte* 32 (1975), pp. 1–2.

"Des Orthodoxes Oeuvrent au Sein de la Cimade," *Contacts* 27 (1975), pp. 209–11. Reprinted in *Bulletin de la Crypte* 34 (1975), pp. 25–26.

Review of *Ils Regarderont vers Lui*, by A Monk of the Eastern Church, *Contacts* 27 (1975), p. 248. Reprinted in *Bulletin de la Crypte* 36 (1975), p. 19.

Review of *La Colonne et le Fondement de la Vérité*, by P. Florensky, *Bulletin de la Crypte* 36 (1975), p. 19.

"Rassemblement Panorthodoxe du 9 Mars 1975," *Bulletin de la Crypte* 34 (1975), pp. 24–25.

"Fraternité Orthodoxe en Europe Occidentale," *Bulletin de la Crypte* 36 (1975), p. 17. Reprinted in *Contacts* 27 (1975), pp. 228–30.

"Orthodoxie Occidentale: A la Recherche de son Unité," *Réforme* (December 14, 1974), p. 27. Reprinted in English as "Western Orthodox Seeking for Unity," *Sobornost* Series 7, no. 1 (1975), pp. 49–52.

"Des Voix sous les Décombres," *Contacts* 28 (1976), pp. 60–69.

"Un Colloque Vladimir Soloviev à Paris," *Contacts* 28 (1976), pp. 70–72.

"Editorial [Le Carême]," *Bulletin de la Crypte* 42 (1976), pp. 1–2.

Review of *L'Autre Soleil*, by O. Clément, *Contacts* 28 (1976), pp. 168–71.

Review of *La Prière des Heures*, *Contacts* 28 (1976), p. 171.

Review of *J'étais Pasteur en Algérie*, by E. Schmidt, *Contacts* 28 (1976), p. 172.

Review of *L'Eglise du Saint-Esprit*, by N. Afanasieff, *Contacts* 28 (1976), pp. 263–68.

Review of *Orthodox Spirituality*, by A Monk of the Eastern Church, *Contacts* 28 (1976), pp. 351–52.

"Fraternité Orthodoxe de la Région Parisienne," *Bulletin de la Crypte* 45 (1976), pp. 13–14.

"Consultation des Femmes Orthodoxes à Agapia (Roumanie) 11–17 septembre 1976," *Bulletin de la Crypte* 47 (1976), pp. 11–13.

"Femmes et Hommes dans l'Eglise," *Service Orthodoxe de Presse* 12 (1976), pp. 8–11. Reprinted and augmented in *Unité Chrètienne* 46 (1977), pp. 40–45. Reprinted in *Supplément au Service Orthodoxe de Presse* 64 (1982), pp. 8–11.

"Le Moine dans la Ville: Alexandre Boukharev (1822–1871)," *Revue d'Histoire de la Spiritualité* 52 (1976), pp. 49–88. "A Monk in the City: Alexander Bukharev, 1822–1871," trans. Lyn Breck, in Elisabeth Behr-Sigel, *Discerning the Signs of the Times*, pp. 55–79 (ed. Michael Plekon and Sarah E. Hinlicky; Crestwood, NY: St. Vladimir's Seminary Press, 2001). Original French reprinted in Elisabeth Behr-Sigel, *Discerner les Signes du Temps*, pp. 65–97 (Paris: Cerf, 2002).

"Chrétiens Face au Drame Libanais et au Destin de Jérusalem," *Service Orthodoxe de Presse* 6 (1976), pp. 7–11.

"Questions aux Orthodoxes," *Réforme* (May 8, 1976), n.p. Extracts reprinted in *Service Orthodoxe de Presse* 9 (1976), pp. 8–9.

"A Propos de 'L'Eglise du Saint-Esprit,'" *Istina* 21 (1976), pp. 430–34.

"Keynote: The Meaning of the Participation of Women in the Life of the Church," in *Orthodox Women: Their Role and Participation in the Orthodox Church*, pp. 17–29 (ed. Constance J. Tarasar and Irina Kirillova; Geneva: WCC, 1977). Reprinted as "The Participation of Women in the Life of the Church," *Sobornost Series* 7, no. 6 (1978), pp. 480–92. Excerpts reprinted in *Classic Texts in Mission and World Christianity*, pp. 254–55 (ed. Norman E. Thomas; American Society of Missiology Series, 20; Maryknoll, NY: Orbis Books, 1995). Excerpts reprinted as "The Participation of Women in the Life of the Church," in *Martyria/Mission: The Witness of the Orthodox Churches Today*, pp. 52–59 (ed. Ion Bria; Geneva: WCC, 1980).

Alexandre Boukharev, un Théologien de l'Eglise Orthodoxe Russe en Dialogue avec le Monde Moderne (Paris: Beauchesne, 1977).

Review of *Le Courage d'Avoir Peur*, by M. D. Molinié, *Contacts* 29 (1977), pp. 87–88.

Review of *L'Espérance Qui Est en Nous: Entretiens de Moscou* and *Les Entretiens du P. Dimitri Doudko*, by D. Doudko, *Contacts* 29 (1977), pp. 160–64.

Review of *La Prière de Jésus Suivant l'Evêque Ignace Briantchaninoff 1807–1867*, by E. Simonod, *Contacts* 29 (1977), pp. 250–51.

"La Femme dans l'Eglise Orthodoxe: Vision Céleste et Histoire," *Contacts* 29, no. 4 (1977), pp. 285–326. Reprinted with a new introductory section in *Unité Chrétienne* 53–54 (1979), pp. 7–43. Reprinted in Elisabeth Behr-Sigel, *Le Ministère de la Femme dans l'Eglise*, pp. 111–55 (Paris: Cerf, 1987). Published in English as "Women in the Orthodox Church: Heavenly Vision and Historical Realities," in Elisabeth Behr-Sigel, *The Ministry of Women in the Church*, pp. 103–47 (trans. Steven Bigham; Redondo Beach, CA: Oakwood Publications, 1991). Reprinted in *Woman in Prism and Focus: Her Profile in Major World Religions and in Christian Tradition*, pp. 81–112 (ed. Prasanna Vazheeparampil, CMC; Rome: Mar Thoma Yogam [The St. Thomas Christian Fellowship], 1996).

Review of *La Femme Avenir*, by F. Quéré, *Contacts* 29 (1977), pp. 348–51.

"Après la Semaine de Prières pour l'Unité des Chrétiens," *Service Orthodoxe de Presse* 15 (1977), p. 7.

"Conférence Jubilaire du Fellowship Saint Alban et Saint Serge," *Bulletin de la Crypte* 57 (1977), pp. 11–12.

"Rencontre Oecuménique Féminine [Kaire]," *Bulletin de la Crypte* 57 (1977), pp. 18–19.

Review of *Paul Tillich et le Symbole Religieux*, by J. Dunphy, *Contacts* 30 (1978), pp. 80–82.

Review of *Mystère et Ministères de la Femme*, by L. Bouyer, *Contacts* 30 (1978), pp. 181–84.

Review of *Un Pape, Un Jour*, by S. Knecht, *Contacts* 30 (1978), pp. 184–87.

"Atelier sur la Place de la Femme dans l'Eglise Orthodoxe," *Contacts* 30 (1978), pp. 391–92.

Review of *Le Visage Intérieur*, by O. Clément, *Contacts* 30 (1978), pp. 410–11.

Review of *La Prière du Coeur*, by J. Serr and O. Clément, *Contacts* 30 (1978), pp. 411–12.

"Roi du Ciel, Consolateur . . . Viens et Fais ta Demeure en Nous," *Bulletin de la Crypte* 64 (1978), p. 1.

"Trinité et Communion," *Bulletin de la Crypte* 64 (1978), pp. 8–12.

"Témoignage sur Irène Tschesnakoff," *Bulletin de la Crypte* 64 (1978), p. 12.

"Après le Colloque de Crète sur la Diaconie," *Service Orthodoxe de Presse* 34 (1979), pp. 7–11.

"Souffrance Innocente et Souffrance Coupable," review of *Suffering, Innocent-Guilty*, by E. Moberly, *Service Orthodoxe de Presse* 36 (1979), p. 10.

"Questions About Men and Women in the People of God," *Service Orthodoxe de Presse* 40 (1979). Reprinted in Elisabeth Behr-Sigel, *Le Ministère de la Femme dans l'Eglise*, pp. 225–34 (Paris: Cerf, 1987). Published in English as "Questions About Men and Women in the People of God," in Elisabeth Behr-Sigel, *The Ministry of Women in the Church*, pp. 217–26 (trans. Steven Bigham; Redondo Beach, CA: Oakwood Publications, 1991).

"In Memoriam. Archevêque Paul 1914–1979," *Bulletin de la Crypte* 70 (1979). Reprinted in *Contacts* 31 (1979), p. 78.

Review of *L'Orthodoxie Hier-Demain*, by M. A. Costa de Beauregard, I. Bria, and T. De Foucauld, *Contacts* 31 (1979), pp. 439–43.

Review of *La Colombe et l'Agneau*, by A Monk of the Eastern Church, *Contacts* 31 (1979), p. 444.

Review of *Au Pays de la Théologie*, by M. Neusch and B. Chenu, *Contacts* 31 (1979), pp. 444–46.

"Consultation de Klingenthal," *Bulletin de la Crypte* 76 (1979), p. 23.

"Dimanche de l'Orthodoxie," *Bulletin de la Crypte* 82 (1980), p. 9.

"In Memoriam: Archimandrite Lev Gillet (1892–1980)," *Bulletin de la Crypte* 83 (1980), pp. 11–16.

"La Cimade Fête Son 40ᵉ Anniversaire," *Bulletin de la Crypte* 87 (1980), p. 12.

"Consultation du C.O.E. à Strasbourg-Klingenthal sur l'Ordination des Femmes," *Contacts* 32 (1980), pp. 68–70.

Review of *La Charité Profanée*, by J. Borella, *Contacts* 32 (1980), pp. 174–75.

Review of *Approches de la Bible*, by J. Goettmann, *Contacts* 32 (1980), p. 179.

"In Memoriam: Archimandrite Lev Gillet (1892–1980)," *Contacts* 32 (1980), pp. 186–87.

"Réponse à l'Enquête du COE sur 'Hommes et femmes dans l'Eglise,'" *Contacts* 32, no. 3 (1980), pp. 246–55.

"Oecuménisme au Féminin: A Propos des Colloques de Bad Segeberg (Juin 1980) et de Niederaltaïch (Septembre 1980)," *Contacts* 32, no. 4 (1980), pp. 337–41.

"In Memoriam: Pasteur Henri Roser, Suzanne de Dietrich," *Contacts* 32, no. 4 (1980), p. 342.

Review of *Foi et Culture dans l'Eglise Aujourd'hui*, by P. Dabosville, *Contacts* 32 (1980), pp. 352–53.

"Les Droits de l'Homme chez les Orthodoxes," *Unité des Chrétiens* 37 (1980), pp. 6–8. Extracts reprinted in *Bulletin de la Crypte* 81 (1980), pp. 5–7.

"Saint Nil Sorsky," in *La Russie: Histoire des Mouvements Spirituels*, cols 356–67 (ed. G. Podskalsky et al.; Dictionnaire de Spiritualité, 14; Paris: Beauchesne, 1980).

"Le Monachisme Russe," in *La Russie: Histoire des Mouvements Spirituels*, cols 1591–603 (ed. G. Podskalsky et al.; Dictionnaire de Spiritualité, 14; Paris: Beauchesne, 1980).

"A Propos de l'Affaire Kung: Une Crise, Mais l'Espérance Est Indéfectible," *Service Orthodoxe de Presse* 45 (1980), pp. 9–11.

"Le Père Lev Gillet (1892–1980)," *Service Orthodoxe de Presse* 48 (1980), pp. 17–20. "In Memoriam: A Monk of the Eastern Church," trans. Brother Stavros, *Saint Vladimir's Theological Quarterly* 24 (1980), pp. 202–8.

"Débat sur un Rite Orthodoxe Occidental (New York)," *Contacts* 33, no. 2 (1981), p. 163.

"In Memoriam: Annie Jaubert (1912–1980)," *Contacts* 33, no. 2 (1981), p. 164.

"Rencontre Oecuménique de Chantilly (6–8 Juin 1981)," *Contacts* 33, no. 3 (1981), pp. 235–36.

"Vers une 'Communauté Nouvelle,' Colloque du Conseil Oecuménique des Eglises, Sheffield 1981," *Contacts* 33, no. 3 (1981), pp. 236–40.

Review of *Le Buisson Ardent*, by P. Evdokimov, *Contacts* 33 (1981), pp. 241–42.

"Jalons pour une Biographie," *Contacts* 33, no. 4 (1981), pp. 263–301.

"Bibliographie du Père Lev Gillet," *Contacts* 33, no. 4 (1981), pp. 359–61.

Review of *The Byzantine Saint*, ed. S. Hackel, *Contacts* 33, no. 4 (1981), pp. 362–63.

"The Concelebrant at Clamart: Lev Gillet in the Years 1927–8," trans. Ignatius Harrison, *Sobornost* 3 (1981), pp. 40–52. "Le Concélébrant de Clamart et la Fondation de la Première Paroisse Orthodoxe Française," *Contacts* 46, no. 1 (1994), pp. 4–21.

"Mort et Transfiguration. L'Expérience Transcendée de l'Amour Humain (Partage de Midi)," *Bulletin de la Société Paul Claudel* 83 (1981), pp. 33–38.

"Offert à Tous, le Triple Sacrement," *Réforme* (June 6, 1981), p. 7. Reprinted in *Bulletin de la Crypte* 87 (1981), pp. 23–24.

"La Femme Aussi Est à l'Image de Dieu," *Supplément au Service Orthodoxe de Presse* 64 (1982), pp. 15–23. "Woman Too in the Likeness of God," *Mid-Stream* 21, no. 3 (1982), pp. 369–75. French reprinted in *Contacts* 35, no. 1 (1983), pp. 62–70. Reprinted in Elisabeth Behr-Sigel, *Le Ministère de la Femme dans l'Eglise*, pp. 87–98 (Paris: Cerf, 1987). "Woman Is Also Made in the Image of God," in Elisabeth Behr-Sigel, *The Ministry of Women in the Church*, pp. 81–92 (trans. Steven Bigham; Redondo Beach, CA: Oakwood Publications, 1991). "Anche la Donna è a Immagine di Dio," in *Maschio e Femmina li Creò*, pp. 19–28 (Spiritualità Ortodossa, 16; Bose, Italy: Qiqajon, 1996).

"Théologie et Contemplation: Introduction à Quelques Textes de Vladimir Lossky," *Hokhma* 20 (1982), pp. 17–22.

"Le Christ, Vie du Monde. Méditation sur I Jn 1,1–4," *Unité des Chrétiens* 48 (1982), pp. 6–7.

"Fête de la Transfiguration," *Bulletin de la Crypte* 105 (1982), pp. 7–8.

Review of *Zéro ou le Point de Départ*, by P. Dumitriu, *Contacts* 34 (1982), pp. 92–93.

Review of *Das Gebet der Orthodoxen Kirche*, *Contacts* 34 (1982), pp. 193–94.

"Vers une Communauté Nouvelle," *Contacts* 34, no. 3 (1982), pp. 270–77. Reprinted in Elisabeth Behr-Sigel, *Le Ministère de la Femme dans l'Eglise*, pp. 99–109 (Paris: Cerf, 1987). Reprinted in Elisabeth Behr-Sigel, *Discerner les Signes du Temps*, pp. 167–74 (Paris: Cerf, 2002). Published in English as "The Energizing Force of Tradition: Orthodox Tradition as a Resource for the Renewal of Women and Men in Community," in *The Community of Women and Men in the Church*, pp. 61–68 (ed. Constance F. Parvey; Philadelphia: Fortress, 1983). Also published in English as "Toward a New Community," in Elisabeth Behr-Sigel, *The Ministry of Women in the Church*, pp. 93–102 (trans. Steven Bigham; Redondo Beach, CA: Oakwood Publications, 1991).

"Colloque de Chevetogne. 23–27 Août 1982," *Contacts* 33, no. 4 (1981), pp. 343–46.

Review of *Les Catholiques et l'Unité Chrétienne du XIXe Siècle*, by E. Fouilloux, *Contacts* 34 (1982), pp. 373–77.

"L'Athos et le Dialogue avec Rome," *Service Orthodoxe de Presse* 66 (1982), pp. 12–14.

"Quelques Aspects de la Théologie et de l'Expérience de l'Esprit Saint dans l'Eglise Orthodoxe Aujourd'hui," *Tantur Yearbook* (1982–3), pp. 129–50. Reprinted in *Contacts* 36, no. 3 (1984), pp. 261–84. Reprinted in *Lumière du Thabor* 28 (2006), pp. 9–12.

"In Memoriam Paul Fidler (1890–1983)," *Contacts* 35, no. 1 (1983), pp. 75–77.

"Eglises et Droits de l'Homme, Le Supplément 141," *Contacts* 35 (1983), pp. 86–88.

Review of *L'Oecuménisme, Où Vont les Eglises?*, by R. Girault, *Contacts* 35 (1983), pp. 94–95.

"In Memoriam Pierre Pascal (1890–1983)," *Contacts* 35, no. 4 (1983), pp. 361–62.

"Chronique Anglo-Russe: Julia de Beausobre, Sunset Years," *Contacts* 35, no. 4 (1983), pp. 363–65.

Review of *Nous, Convertis d'Union Soviétique*, by T. Goritcheva, *Contacts* 35 (1983), pp. 380–81.

"La Place de la Femme dans l'Eglise," *Irénikon* 58, no. 1 (1983), pp. 46–53 and 58, no. 2 (1983), pp. 194–214. Reprinted in Elisabeth Behr-Sigel, *Le Ministère de la Femme dans l'Eglise*, pp. 111–55 (Paris: Cerf, 1987). Published in English as "The Place of Women in the Church," in Elisabeth Behr-Sigel, *The Ministry of Women in the Church*, pp. 149–80 (trans. Steven Bigham; Redondo Beach, CA: Oakwood Publications, 1991).

"De Retour de Jérusalem," *Service Orthodoxe de Presse* 80 (1983), pp. 14–19.

"'Passion du Christ, Passion des Hommes,' Colloque de l'ACAT 1984," *Bulletin de la Crypte* 125 (1984), p. 23.

Review of *Introduction à la Spiritualité Orthodoxe*, by A Monk of the Eastern Church, *Contacts* 36 (1984), pp. 145–47.

Review of *Women and the Priesthood*, ed. T. Hopko, *Contacts* 36 (1984), pp. 207–14.

Review of *Christus in euch: Hoffnung auf Herrlichkeit*, by S. Hausammann and S. Heitz, *Contacts* 36 (1984), p. 227.

"In Memoriam: Dom Olivier Rousseau, 1898–1984," *Contacts* 36, no. 4 (1984), pp. 377–78.

"Le Schisme de 1054: Origines, Conséquences et Perspectives," *Supplément Service Orthodoxe de Presse* 86-A (1984), pp. 1–16. Extracts in *Service Orthodoxe de Presse* 86 (1984), pp. 17–20.

"Passion du Christ, Passions des Hommes," *Supplément Service Orthodoxe de Presse* 89-A (1984), pp. 1–7. Extracts in *Service Orthodoxe de Presse* 89 (1984), pp. 12–16.

"Une Religieuse Russe à Paris: Mère Marie Skobtsov (1891–1945)," *Unité des Chrétiens* 58 (1985), pp. 21–23.

"Passion du Christ et Passion des Hommes," *Le Supplément* 152 (1985), pp. 31–42.

"Que ta Volonté Soit Faite," *Courrier de l'ACAT* 55 (1985), pp. 20–21.

"Les Oubliés de la Visite de Monsieur Gorbatchev," *Service Orthodoxe de Presse* 102 (1985), p. 14.

"Les Lendemains du BEM," *Supplément Service Orthodoxe de Presse* 102-B (1985), pp. 1–4.

Review of *Living in Tension between East and West*, by B. Frost, *Contacts* 37 (1985), p. 73.

Review of *Les Femmes dans l'Eglise*, by M. Hébrard, *Contacts* 37 (1985), pp. 74–76.

"A Propos de la Situation de l'Eglise Orthodoxe dans l'Etat Soviétique," *Contacts* 37, no. 2 (1985), pp. 145–47.

"In Memoriam: Nadejda Gorodetzky (1901–1985)," *Contacts* 37, no. 2 (1985), pp. 147–48. Published in English in *Sourozh* 22 (1985), pp. 7–8.

Review of *Orient-Occident—Deux Passeurs: Vladimir Lossky et Paul Evdokimov*, by O. Clément, *Contacts* 37 (1985), pp. 317–20.

"Marie, Mère de Dieu. Mariologie Traditionelle et Questions Nouvelles," *Irénikon* 58, no. 4 (1985), pp. 451–70 and 59, no. 1 (1986), pp. 20–31. Reprinted in Elisabeth Behr-Sigel, *Le Ministère de la Femme dans l'Eglise*, pp. 189–224 (Paris: Cerf, 1987). Published in English as "Mary, the Mother of God: Traditional Mariology and New Questions," in Elisabeth Behr-Sigel, *The Ministry of Women in the Church*, pp. 181–216 (trans. Steven Bigham; Redondo Beach, CA: Oakwood Publications, 1991).

"L'Altérité Homme-Femme dans le Contexte d'une Civilisation Chrétienne," in *L'Altérité, Vivre Ensemble Différents*, pp. 389–426 (ed. M. Gourgues and G. D. Mailhiot; Paris: Cerf, 1986). Reprinted in Elisabeth Behr-Sigel, *Le Ministère de la Femme dans l'Eglise*, pp. 33–86 (Paris: Cerf, 1987). Published in English as "The Otherness of Men and Women in the Context of a Christian Civilization," in Elisabeth Behr-Sigel,

The Ministry of Women in the Church, pp. 25–79 (trans. Steven Bigham; Redondo Beach, CA: Oakwood Publications, 1991).

"Semaine de l'Unité: Faire l'Effort d'Aller vers l'Autre," *Service Orthodoxe de Presse* 104 (1986), pp. 12–13.

Review of *Essai sur la Fidélité*, by R. Mehl, *Contacts* 38 (1986), pp. 72–75.

Review of *Les Fêtes et la Vie de Jésus. I. L'Incarnation*, *Contacts* 38 (1986), pp. 75–77.

Review of *Vocabulaire Théologique Orthodoxe*, *Contacts* 38 (1986), pp. 77–78.

Review of *La Divine Liturgie de Saint Jean Chrysostom*, *Contacts* 38 (1986), pp. 157–58.

Review of *Sans Tricher ni Trahir sur la Grande Route Oecuménique*, by R. Girault and A. Nicholas, *Contacts* 38 (1986), pp. 161–63.

"L'Eglise d'Orient Est-Elle Patriarcaliste!" *Contacts* 38, no. 3 (1986), pp. 235–37.

"Une Créature Nouvelle, Réconciliée avec Dieu en Jésus-Christ (2 Co 5,17–6,4a)," *Unité des Chrétiens* 64 (1986), pp. 2–3.

"Nil Sorsky, un Hésychaste Lettré," in *Monachisme d'Orient et d'Occident*, pp. 35–54 (Gordes: Les Amis de Sénanque, 1986).

Le Ministère de la Femme dans l'Eglise (Paris: Cerf, 1987). Published in English as *The Ministry of Women in the Church* (trans. Steven Bigham; Redondo Beach, CA: Oakwood Publications, 1991). Published in Greek (Athens: Bonne Presse, n.d.). Published in Russian (Moscow: Institut Saint-André, 2002).

Review of *Das Leben der Heiligen Makrina auf dem Hintergrund der Thekla-Traditionen*, by R. Albrecht, *Contacts* 39 (1987), pp. 77–79.

Review of *Car Toujours Dure Longtemps*, by P. Jérôme, *Contacts* 39 (1987), pp. 79–80.

Review of *Le "Credo" de Nicée-Constantinople*, by C. Aslanoff and P. Minet, *Contacts* 39 (1987), pp. 301–03.

Review of *Saint Séraphin—Sarov et Diveyevo*, by V. Rochcau, *Contacts* 39 (1987), pp. 310–13.

Review of *Des Femmes Diacres. Un Nouveau Chemin pour l'Eglise*, by M.-J. Aubert, *Contacts* 39 (1987), pp. 316–19.

Review of *Die Zukunft der Orthodoxie*, by A. Jensen, *Contacts* 39 (1987), pp. 319–20.

Review of *Une Lecture de l'Evangile de Jean*, by F. Quéré, *Contacts* 39 (1987), p. 321. Reprinted in *Contacts* 40 (1988), p. 134.

"L'Hospitalité Eucharistique," *Courrier de l'ACAT* 75 (1987), pp. 7–8.

"Ordination von Frauen? Ein Versuch des Bedenkens einer aktuallen Frage im Lichte der lebendigen Tradition der orthodoxen Kirche," in *Warum keine Ordination der Frau? Unterschiedliche Einstellungen in den christlichen Kirchen*, pp. 50–72 (ed. Elisabeth Gössman and Dietmar Bader; Munich: Verlag Schnell und Steiner, 1987).

"Assemblée Générale de l'ACAT: Briser sans Cesse les Mécanismes Qui Dégradent l'Homme," *Service Orthodoxe de Presse* 118 (1987), pp. 14–18.

"'Roi du Ciel, Consolateur . . .'" *Service Orthodoxe de Presse* 118 (1987), pp. 21–22.

"Marie, Visage de l'Humanité Nouvelle," *Unité des Chrétiens* 69 (1988), pp. 20–21. Extracts in *Unité des Chrétiens* 95 (1994), p. 37.

"Le Baptême de la Russie," *Courrier de l'ACAT* 84 (1988), pp. 7–8. Reprinted in *Bulletin de la Crypte* 164 (1988), pp. 16–18.

"Les Eglises Orthodoxes s'Interrogent sur la Place de la Femme dans l'Eglise," *Irénikon* 61, no. 4 (1988), pp. 523–29.

Review of *Naissance de la Chrétienté Russe*, by V. Vodoff, *Contacts* 40 (1988), pp. 136–39.

Review of *L'Unité par la Diversité*, by O. Cullmann, *Contacts* 40 (1988), pp. 139–43.

"Présence de l'Orthodoxie Russe en Occident," *Contacts* 40, no. 3 (1988), pp. 226–39.

"Développements de la Théologie Orthodoxe en Europe Occidentale," *Supplément Service Orthodoxe de Presse* 131-C (1988), pp. 1–5. Unpublished English translation,

"Developments in Orthodox Theology in Western Europe," presented at the WCC's
"Doing Theology in Different Contexts: Latin American and Eastern/Central European
Theologians in Dialogue," A Report of a Programme on Theological Education
Consultation in Prague, June 1988.

Le Lieu du Coeur: Initiation à la Spiritualité Orthodoxe (Paris: Cerf, 1989). Published
in English as *The Place of the Heart: An Introduction to Orthodox Spirituality* (trans.
Steven Bigham; Torrance, CA: Oakwood Publications, 1992). *Il Luogo di Cuore:
Iniziazione alle Spiritualità Ortodossa* (Milan: Paoline, 1993).

"Mère Marie Skobtsov," *Le Messager Orthodoxe* 111 (1989), pp. 56–70. Portions reprinted
in *Bulletin de la Crypte* 171 (1989), pp. 14–15 and 224 (1994), pp. 6–11. Integrated into
"Mother Maria Skobtsova, 1891–1945," in Elisabeth Behr-Sigel, *Discerning the Signs of
the Times*, pp. 41–53 (ed. Michael Plekon and Sarah E. Hinlicky; Crestwood, NY: St.
Vladimir's Seminary Press, 2001). Reprinted as "Mère Marie Skobtsov (1891–1945)," in
Elisabeth Behr-Sigel, *Discerner les Signes du Temps*, pp. 51–64 (Paris: Cerf, 2002).

"La Consultation Interorthodoxe de Rhodes: La Femme dans l'Eglise," *Contacts* 41, no. 2
(1989), pp. 81–93.

Review of "Collection 'Catéchèse Orthodoxe,'" *Contacts* 41 (1989), pp. 299–302.

Review of *Rassemblés par l'Esprit: La Grâce Oecuménique du Renouveau*, by P. Hocken,
Contacts 41 (1989), pp. 317–18.

"L'Eglise Orthodoxe et l'ACAT," *Courrier de l'ACAT* 100–01 (1989), pp. 25–27.

"La Folie en Christ dans la Russie Ancienne," in *Mille Ans de Christianisme Russe, 988–
1988: Actes du Colloque International de l'Université Paris X, Nanterre, 20–23 Janvier
1988*, pp. 141–52 (Paris: YMCA-Press, 1989).

"Hesychasm and the Western Impact in Russia: St. Tikhon of Zadonsk (1724–1783)," in
Christian Spirituality Post-Reformation and Modern, pp. 432–66 (ed. Louis Dupré and
Don E. Saliers; World Spirituality: An Encyclopedic History of the Religious Quest, 18;
New York: Crossroad, 1989).

"Orthodoxie et Catholicisme (Quelques Points de Divergence Doctrinale)," *Courrier de
l'ACAT* 109 (1990), pp. 22–23.

"L'Ordination des Femmes, un Problème Oecuménique," *Contacts* 42, no. 2 (1990),
pp. 101–27. Reprinted in *Kirchen im Kontext unterschiedlicher Kulturen: Auf
dem Weg ins dritte Jahrtausend*, pp. 275–94 (ed. Wolfgang Heller; Göttingen:
Vandenhoeck und Ruprecht, 1991). Reprinted as "Femmes et Sacerdoce: Un
Problème Oecuménique, Développements Récents dans la Sphère de l'Eglise
Orthodoxe," in Elisabeth Behr-Sigel, *Discerner les Signes du Temps*, pp. 131–52
(Paris: Cerf, 2002). Published in Italian as "Li Ordinazione delle Donne, un
Problema Ecumenica," in *Donna e Ministero*, pp. 119–49 (ed. Cettina Militello;
Rome: Dehoniane, 1991). Version slightly altered by author and translated into
English as "The Ordination of Women: An Ecumenical Problem," *Sobornost* 13,
no. 1 (1991), pp. 25–40. Abridged version in English published as "The Ordination
of Women, an Ecumenical Problem," *MaryMartha* 2, no. 2 (1992), pp. 9–11. Full
version reprinted in *Theology* 97 (1994), pp. 9–26.

"La Prière d'Intercession dans la Lutte contre la Torture," *Service Orthodoxe de Presse* 152
(1990), pp. 16–21. Reprinted in *Torturés, Tortionnaires, Espérance Chrétienne: Actes de
la Rencontre Internationale de Bâle, 26–28 Octobre 1990*, pp. 73–88 (Paris: Cerf, 1992).
Reprinted in *Le Feu sur la Terre: Mélanges Offerts au Père Boris Bobrinskoy à l'Occasion
de Son 80ᵉ Anniversaire* (Paris: Presses Saint-Serge, 2005). Reprinted in *Lumière du
Thabor* 28 (2006), pp. 12–17.

"A 'Protestant Orthodox,'" *One World* 156 (1990), pp. 14–15.

Review of *Myriam et Israel: Le Mystère de L'Epouse*, by Marie Thérèse Huguet, *Paix* 63, no. 3 (1990), pp. 72–73.

"Orthodoxy and Women in France," with Nicole Maillard, in *Women, Religion and Sexuality: Studies on the Impact of Religious Teachings on Women*, pp. 184–91 (ed. Jeanne Becher; Geneva: WCC, 1990). Published in French as "L'Orthodoxie et Les Femmes en France," trans. Valère de Pryck, *Lumière du Thabor* 28 (2006), pp. 17–21.

"A Propos de l'Ordination des Femmes (Réponse à M. Monsaingeon)," *Contacts* 42, no. 4 (1990), pp. 299–303.

"VIIᵉ Assemblée du Conseil Oecuménique des Eglises," *Bulletin de la Crypte* 190 (1991), p. 24.

Review of *Anachroniques*, by O. Clément, *Contacts* 43 (1991), pp. 69–73.

Review of *La Mystique, La Prière du Coeur*, by J. Beaude, *Contacts* 43 (1991), pp. 73–75.

Review of *Women, Religion and Sexuality*, by J. Becher, *Contacts* 43 (1991), pp. 76–77.

"Ci Si Può Fermare Qui?" in *Le Donne secondo Wojtyla*, pp. 137–59 (ed. M. A. Macciocchi; Milan: Paoline, 1992).

Review of *Berdiaev. Un Philosophe Russe en France*, by O. Clément, *Contacts* 44 (1992), pp. 68–70.

Review of *Les Voies de l'Unité Chrétienne*, by O. Cullmann, *Contacts* 44 (1992), pp. 147–49.

Review of *Nouvelle Petite Philocalie*, *Contacts* 44 (1992), pp. 233–34.

"Le Dieu de l'Espérance," *Courrier de l'ACAT* 123 (1992), p. 7. Reprinted in *Service Orthodoxe de Presse* 166 (1992), pp. 21–23.

"Le Baptême dans l'Esprit chez Syméon le Nouveau Théologien," *Tychique* 97 (1992), pp. 67–75.

"Images Féminines et Spiritualité Orthodoxe: Institut Oecuménique de Bossey: 24 Mai au 3 Juin 1992," *Bulletin de la Crypte* 205 (1992), p. 17. Reprinted as "Institut Oecuménique de Bossey: Seminaire sur 'Images Féminines & Spiritualité Orthodoxe,'" *L'Alliance* (new series) 9 (1992), pp. 24–25.

"'Rencontre Orthodoxes-Protestantes,'" *Bulletin de la Crypte* 207 (1992), p. 23.

"Colloque 'Lev Gillet,' 2–3 Octobre 1993," *Bulletin de la Crypte* 211 (1993), p. 21.

Lev Gillet, "Un Moine de l'Eglise d'Orient" (Paris: Cerf, 1993). Published in English as *Lev Gillet, "A Monk of the Eastern Church"* (trans. Helen Wright; Oxford: Fellowship of St. Alban and St. Sergius, 1999).

"Un Colloque 'Lev Gillet,'" *Contacts* 45, no. 1 (1993), pp. 4–5.

Review of *Gottes Selbstbewusste Tochter: Frauen-Emanzipation im Fruhen Christentum?* by A. Jensen, *Contacts* 45 (1993), pp. 153–56.

"The Ordination of Women: An Ecumenical Problem: A Reply to a Reply," trans. Anthony Greenan, *Sobornost* 15, no. 1 (1993), pp. 20–26.

"Réflexion sur le Ministère et les Ministères dans l'Eglise: Une Voix Orthodoxe," *Trajets* 2 (1993–94), pp. 53–57. Published in English as "The Meaning of Ministry," in *Orthodox Women Speak*, pp. 93–97 (ed. Kyriaki Karidoyanes FitzGerald; Geneva: WCC, 1999). Translated back into French by Valère de Pryck, "La Signification du Ministère," *Lumière du Thabor* 28 (2006), pp. 22–25.

"Le 30ᵉ Anniversaire de la Reconcontre Paul VI-Athénagoras," *Bulletin de la Crypte* 220 (1994), p. 24.

"Célébration Parisienne du Dimanche de l'Orthodoxie," *Bulletin de la Crypte* 222 (1994), p. 26.

Review of *Passé et Présent Religieux en Russie, Revue d'Etudes Comparatives Est-Ouest, Oecuménisme Information* Mai (1994). Extracts reprinted in *Bulletin de la Crypte* 224 (1994), p. 26.

"La Fraternité Saint-Elie," *Bulletin de la Crypte* 227 (1994), p. 22.

Review of *L'Unité Maintenant*, by R. Bichelberger, *Contacts* 46 (1994), pp. 151–53.

"Les Femmes-Prêtres Vues par des Orthodoxes," *Terre des Femmes* 5 (1994), p. 29. French original with English translation published in *MaryMartha* 3, nos 3–4 (1994), pp. 24–25.

"Père Cyrille Argenti," *Courrier de l'ACAT* 151–52 (1995), p. 3.

Review of *Le Mystère de l'Eglise et de l'Eucharistie à la Lumière du Mystère de la Sainte Trinité*, *Bulletin de la Crypte* 231 (1995), p. 23. Reprinted in *Irénikon* 68 (1995), pp. 158–59.

Review of *Le Sacrement du Frère*, by Maria Skobtsova and Hélène Arjakovsky-Klépinine, *Contacts* 47 (1995), pp. 239–40.

"Aux Sources de la Spiritualité Orthodoxe," *Lien des Contemplatives* 120 (1995), pp. 1–18.

"L'Eglise Orthodoxe et la Paix," *Supplément Service Orthodoxe de Presse* 204 (1995), n.p. Published in English as "Orthodoxy and Peace," trans. Rachel Mortimer, *In Communion* 3 (1995), n.p. Reprinted in French as "L'Orthodoxie et la Paix," *Contacts* 48, no. 1 (1996), pp. 5–13. English translation reprinted in Elisabeth Behr-Sigel, *Discerning the Signs of the Times*, pp. 21–27 (ed. Michael Plekon and Sarah E. Hinlicky; Crestwood, NY: St. Vladimir's Seminary Press, 2001). French original reprinted in Elisabeth Behr-Sigel, *Discerner Les Signes du Temps*, pp. 121–27 (Paris: Cerf, 2002).

"L'Ordination des Femmes: Une Question Posée Aussi aux Eglises Orthodoxes," in *Communion et Réunion: Mélanges Jean-Marie Roger Tillard*, pp. 363–87 (ed. Gillian R. Evans and Michel Gourgues; Leuven: Leuven University Press, 1995). Extracts reprinted as "L'Ordination des Femmes: La Consultation de Rhodes," *Unité des Chrétiens* 107 (1997), pp. 12–13. Full article reprinted in Elisabeth Behr-Sigel and Kallistos (Timothy) Ware, *L'Ordination de Femmes dans l'Eglise Orthodoxe*, pp. 17–50 (Paris: Cerf, 1998). Published in Russian in *Strantsi* 4, no. 1 (1999), pp. 24–32 and 4, no. 2 (1999), pp. 190–200. Published in English as "The Ordination of Women: Also a Question for the Orthodox Churches," in Elisabeth Behr-Sigel and Kallistos (Timothy) Ware, *The Ordination of Women in the Orthodox Church*, pp. 11–48 (Geneva: WCC Publications, 2000).

"Conférence Internationale 'Les Femmes Orthodoxes dans une Europe Unie,' Levadia—Grèce," *Terre Des Femmes* 9, no. 1 (1995), pp. 37–40. "International Conference 'The Orthodox Women in a United Europe,' Levadia—Greece 1994," trans. Colin Williams, *MaryMartha* 4, no. 1 (1995), pp. 15–17.

"Women's Decade: Orthodox Participation," *MaryMartha* 4, no. 1 (1995), pp. 23–24.

"Marie Skobtsova 1891–1945," in *Ecumenical Pilgrims: Profiles of Pioneers in Christian Reconciliation*, pp. 216–20 (ed. Ion Bria and Dagmar Heller; Geneva: WCC Publications, 1995). Adapted as "An Orthodox Nun: The Life of Elisabeth Skobtsova," *One World* 208 (1995), pp. 14–15. Reprinted as "The Life of Elisabeth Skobtsova—An Orthodox Nun," *MaryMartha* 4, no. 2 (1996), pp. 16–21.

"Madeleine Barot (1909–1995)," *Courrier de l'ACAT* 163 (1996), pp. 26–27.

Review of *Pont entre l'Orient et l'Occident*, *Bulletin de la Crypte* 242 (1996), p. 28. Reprinted in *Contacts* 48 (1996), pp. 149–50.

"Milan, Bose, Sylvanès . . . Expériences d'Unité Spirituelle," *Bulletin de la Crypte* 245 (1996), pp. 23–24.

Review of *Le Christ dans la Tradition et la Littérature Russe*, by M. Evdokimov, *Bulletin de la Crypte* 246 (1996), pp. 27–28.

"9ᵉ Congrès Orthodoxe en Europe Occidentale," *Bulletin de la Crypte* 248 (1996), pp. 18–19.

"The Community of Women and Men: What Does This Mean for a Prophetic and Sacramental Church?" trans. Maria Rule, *MaryMartha* 4, no. 2 (1996), pp. 22–30.

Review of *L'Eglise Orthodoxe Hier et Aujourd'hui*, by J. Meyendorff, *Contacts* 48 (1996), pp. 60–63.

Review of *L'Incontournable Echange*, by E. J. Lacelle, *Contacts* 48 (1996), pp. 63–65.

"In Memoriam le Père Cyrille Argenti," *Istina* 41 (1996), pp. 30–31.

Review of *Soixante-Dix Ans d'Emigration Russe: 1919–1989*, by N. Struve, *Bulletin de la Crypte* 254 (1997), pp. 22–23. Reprinted in *Contacts* 49 (1997), pp. 196–99.

Review of *Vivre l'Amour de la Trinité*, *Contacts* 49 (1997), pp. 188–90.

Review of *Le Vénérable Georges, Moine de l'Athos (1809–1886). Saint Arsène de Cappadoce (1840–1924)*, by P. Païssos, *Contacts* 49 (1997), pp. 282–84.

"'Un Moine de l'Eglise d'Orient.' Sur Sa Conversion à l'Orthodoxie," *Contacts* 49, no. 4 (1997), pp. 294–99.

Review of *Foi de Prêtre. Père Gabriel (1923–1988)*, *Contacts* 49 (1997), pp. 365–66.

Review of *L'Oeuvre du Sixième Jour. Création de l'Homme*, by D. M. Debuisson, *Contacts* 49 (1997), pp. 366–70.

"Marie et les Femmes," in *Théologie, Histoire et Piété Mariale: Actes du Colloque de la Faculté de Théologie de Lyon, 1–3 Octobre 1996*, pp. 309–24 (ed. Jean Comby; Lyon: Profac, 1997). Published in English as "Mary and Women," in Elisabeth Behr-Sigel, *Discerning the Signs of the Times*, pp. 101–13 (ed. Michael Plekon and Sarah E. Hinlicky; Crestwood, NY: St. Vladimir's Seminar Press, 2001). Reprinted in Elisabeth Behr-Sigel, *Discerner les Signes du Temps*, pp. 21–33 (Paris: Cerf, 2002).

"Au Tournant de l'Histoire, Chrétiens et Chrétiennes Vivent de Nouvelles Alliances. Lyon 7–8 mars 1997," *Oecuménisme Information* 274 (1997), p. 7.

L'Ordination des Femmes dans l'Eglise Orthodoxe, with Kallistos (Timothy) Ware (Paris: Cerf, 1998). Excerpts printed in *Terre des Femmes* 14, no. 1 (1998), pp. 43–47. Published in Russian (Moscow: Institut Saint-André, 1998). Published in English as *The Ordination of Women in the Orthodox Church* (Geneva: WCC Publications, 2000). Published in Bulgarian (Silistra, 2002).

"Les Femmes dans l'Eglise Orthodoxe," in Elisabeth Behr-Sigel and Kallistos (Timothy) Ware, *L'Ordination des Femmes dans l'Eglise Orthodoxe*, pp. 7–16 (Paris: Cerf, 1998). Published in English as "Women in the Orthodox Church," *The St. Nina Quarterly* 2, no. 2 (1998), pp. 1, 8–11. Published again in English in Elisabeth Behr-Sigel and Kallistos (Timothy) Ware, *The Ordination of Women in the Orthodox Church* (Geneva: WCC Publications, 2000).

Review of *Au Coeur de la Fournaise*, by A Monk of the Eastern Church, *Contacts* 50 (1998), pp. 183–84. Reprinted in *Oecuménisme Information* 289 (1998), 20.

Review of *Une Voix chez les Orthodoxes*, by M. Evdokimov, *Contacts* 50 (1998), pp. 184–86.

"La Bible, la Tradition, les Sacrements, Sources de l'Autorité dans l'Eglise," *Contacts* 50, no. 3 (1998), pp. 204–14. Published in English as "The Bible, Tradition, the Sacraments: Sources of Authority in the Church," in Elisabeth Behr-Sigel, *Discerning the Signs of the Times*, pp. 81–94 (ed. Michael Plekon and Sarah E. Hinlicky; Crestwood, NY: St. Vladimir's Seminary Press, 2001). French original reprinted in Elisabeth Behr-Sigel, *Discerner les Signes du Temps*, pp. 111–19 (Paris: Cerf, 2002).

"La Place des Orthodoxes dans le Mouvement Oecuménique," *Oecuménisme Information* 287 (1998), pp. 20–21. Reprinted in *Lumière du Thabor* 28 (2006), pp. 28–29.

"Jesus and Women," *MaryMartha* 6, no. 1 (1998), pp. 35–36. Reprinted as "Women in Jesus' Earthly Life," in *Orthodox Women Speak*, pp. 51–55 (ed. Kyriaki Karidoyanes

FitzGerald; Geneva: WCC, 1999). Reprinted as "Jesus and Women" in Elisabeth Behr-Sigel, *Discerning the Signs of the Times*, pp. 95–99 (ed. Michael Plekon and Sarah E. Hinlicky; Crestwood, NY: St. Vladimir's Seminary Press, 2001). Published in French as "Jésus et les Femmes," in Elisabeth Behr-Sigel, *Discerner les Signes du Temps*, pp. 15–19 (Paris: Cerf, 2002).

"La Création de la Premiére Paroisse Orthodoxe de Langue Française (Fin 1928–Début 1929), Communication à l'Institut Saint-Serge, 28 Février 1999," *Supplément Service Orthodoxe de Presse* 237-B (1999), n.p.

"Ouverture d'une Ecole de Théologie Orthodoxe en Grande-Bretagne," *Contacts* 51, no. 1 (1999), p. 76.

"Les Tâches de la Formation Théologique Orthodoxe au XXIe Siècle," *Contacts* 51, no. 1 (1999), pp. 77–88. Revised and reprinted in *Unité des Chrétiens* 116 (1999), pp. 21–25. Extracts in *Service Orthodoxe de Presse* 235 (1999), pp. 19–28. Published in English as "What are the Tasks of Theological Education for the Twenty-First Century?" trans. Constantin Simon, S. J., *Diakonia* 32, no. 3 (1999), pp. 223–32. Published again in English as "Orthodox Theological Formation in the 21st Century: The Tasks Involved," in Elisabeth Behr-Sigel, *Discerning the Signs of the Times*, pp. 11–19 (ed. Michael Plekon and Sarah E. Hinlicky; Crestwood, NY: St. Vladimir's Seminary Press, 2001). French reprinted in Elisabeth Behr-Sigel, *Discerner les Signes du Temps*, pp. 101–09 (Paris: Cerf, 2002).

Review of *Bild Christi und Geschlecht*, *Internationale Kirchliche Zeitschrift* 88 (1998). Reprinted in *Contacts* 51 (1999), pp. 179–81.

Review of *Pour une Ethique de la Procréation*, by J.-C. Larchet, *Contacts* 51 (1999), pp. 185–87.

"L'Eglise Orthodoxe," *Veillez et Priez, Document ACAT* (1999), pp. 93–105.

"Women," in *The Blackwell Dictionary of Eastern Christianity*, pp. 515–19 (ed. Ken Parry et al.; Oxford: Blackwell, 1999).

Review of *Veillez et Priez*, *Bulletin de la Crypte* 273 (1999), p. 21.

"Pour un Témoignage Chrétien Renouvelé. Communication au 10e Congrès Orthodoxe d'Europe Occidentale," *Supplément Service Orthodoxe de Presse* 243-B (2000), n.p. Reprinted in *Contacts* 52, no. 1 (2000), pp. 35–45. Reprinted in *Lumière du Thabor* 28 (2006), pp. 31–35.

"Regards Orthodoxes sur le Protestantisme," *Oecuménisme Information* 301 (2000), pp. 12–16.

"Regards Orthodoxes sur le Protestantisme II," *Oecuménisme Information* 302 (2000), pp. 13–16.

"20e Anniversaire de la Mort du Père Lev Gillet," *Oecuménisme Information* 306 (2000), p. 12.

"La Place de l'Eglise Orthodoxe dans la Construction Européenne," *Contacts* 52, no. 2 (2000), pp. 157–69. Reprinted in *Oecuménisme Information* 307 (2000), pp. 9–16.

"Vingtième Anniversaire de la Mort du 'Moine de l'Eglise d'Orient,'" *Contacts* 52, no. 3 (1990), pp. 242–43.

Review of *La Compassion du Père*, by B. Bobrinskoy, *Contacts* 52 (2000), pp. 266–68.

Review of *Printemps de la Foi en Russie*, by I. Séménoff-Tian-Chnasky, *Contacts* 52 (2000), pp. 269–71.

"Pour le 20e Anniversaire de la Mort du Père Lev Gillet (1893–1980)," *Bulletin de la Crypte* 281 (2000), pp. 18–19.

Review of *Orthodox Women Speak*, ed. K. K. FitzGerald, *Bulletin de la Crypte* 286 (2000), pp. 21–22. Reprinted in *Contacts* 52 (2000), pp. 271–74.

Review of *Christ Est Ressuscité. Propos sur les Fêtes Chrétiennes*, by O. Clément, *Contacts* 53 (2000), pp. 350–51.

"L'Ordination des Femmes: Un Point Chaud du Dialogue Oecuménique," *Contacts* 53, no. 3 (2001), pp. 236–52. Reprinted in Elisabeth Behr-Sigel, *Discerner les Signes du Temps*, pp. 153–66 (Paris: Cerf, 2002).

Discerning the Signs of the Times: The Vision of Elisabeth Behr-Sigel (ed. Michael Plekon and Sarah E. Hinlicky; Crestwood, NY: St. Vladimir's Seminary Press, 2001). Published in French with some omissions and additions as *Discerner les Signes du Temps* (Paris: Cerf, 2002).

Review of *Mère Marie*, by L. Varaut, *Bulletin de la Crypte* 289 (2001), p. 26.

Review of *Les Chrétiens Orthodoxes*, by M. Evdokimov, *Bulletin de la Crypte* 289 (2001), p. 26. Reprinted in *Oecuménisme Information* 311 (2001), pp. 20–21.

"Vers une Restauration Créative du Diaconat Féminin?" *Contacts* 53, no. 3 (2001), pp. 253–58. "An Orthodox Diaconate for Women?" *Sobornost* 23, no. 1 (2001), pp. 60–63.

"Christianisme et Droits de l'Homme," *Courrier de l'ACAT* 218 (2001), pp. 30–32 and 219 (2001), pp. 32–33. Reprinted in *Oecuménisme Information* 320 (2001), pp. 13–15 and 321 (2002), pp. 10–12.

"Dixième Anniversaire de la Fraternité Saint-Elie," *Oecuménisme Information* 320 (2001), pp. 5–6.

"Un Anniversaire," *Bulletin de la Crypte* 299 (2002), pp. 19–20.

Review of *Augustine and Russian Orthodoxy: Russian Orthodox Theologians and Augustine of Hippo: A Twentieth-Century Dialogue*, by M. I. Tataryn, *Contacts* 54 (2002), pp. 107–11. Reprinted in *Oecuménisme Information* 327 (2002), p. 19.

"Contacts 1949–2002: Retour sur les Origines de la 'Revue Française de l'Orthodoxie,' Un Entretien avec Elisabeth Behr-Sigel," *Contacts* 54, no. 4 (2002), pp. 351–64.

"Porteur de Valeurs," *Réforme* (October 10–16, 2002), p. 11.

"Le 75ᵉ Anniversaire de Chevetogne," *Service Orthodoxe de Presse* 265 (2002), pp. 27–29.

"Célébration Oecuménique de la Fête du Prophète Elie," *Mikhtav* 34 (2002), pp. 3–4. Reprinted in *Bulletin de la Crypte* 306 (2002), p. 21. Reprinted in *Oecuménisme Information* 328 (2002), pp. 11–12.

"Rencontres Orthodoxes-Protestants en Région Parisienne," *Bulletin de la Crypte* 309 (2003), pp. 20–21. Reprinted as "La Rencontre Annuelle Orthodoxes-Protestants," in *Oecuménisme Information* 331 (2003), p. 68.

"L'Oecuménisme au Féminin," *Oecuménisme Information* 334 (2003), pp. 8–9.

Review of *L'Eglise et les Femmes*, by X. Iouriev, *Contacts* 55 (2003), pp. 136–41.

"Au Métropolite Antoine de Souroge, 'Mémoire Eternelle,'" *Contacts* 55 (2003), pp. 456–62.

"The Ordination of Women—A Point of Contention in Ecumenical Dialogue," *St. Vladimir's Theological Quarterly* 48, no. 1 (2004), pp. 49–66.

"Mère Marie Skobtsov et le Père Lev Gillet," *Contacts* 56 (2004), pp. 361–64. Revised version in *Contacts* 57 (2005), pp. 315–18.

Review of *Le Mystère de l'Eglise: Cours de Théologie Dogmatique*, by Boris Bobrinskoy, *Contacts* 56 (2004), pp. 377–82.

"Mère Marie Skobtsov et le Père Lev Gillet," *Bulletin de la Crypte* 322 (2004), pp. 24–25.

"Les Laïcs dans l'Eglise Orthodoxe," ed. Olga Lossky from manuscript notes for Behr-Sigel's course, "The Theology of the Royal Priesthood of the Laity in the Church," at the Institut Supérieur d'Etudes Oecuméniques, *Lumière du Thabor* 28 (2006), pp. 21–22.

"Comment Vivre les Fêtes Religieuses dans une Societé Laique?" ed. Olga Lossky from an
    unpublished manuscript, *Lumière du Thabor* 28 (2006), pp. 26–28.
"Feminine Images and Orthodox Spirituality," *Ecumenical Review* 60, nos 1–2 (2008),
    pp. 7–15. Posthumous publication of 1992 keynote address at Bossey Seminar.

Works Cited and Consulted

Aghiorgoussis, Maximos, *Women Priests?* (Brookline, MA: Holy Cross Orthodox Press, 1976).

Anderson, Alister, "The Orthodox Priest: An Icon of Christ," <www.antiochian.org/ midwest/Articles/The_Orthodox_Priest_An_Ikon_Of_Christ.htm> [accessed December 10, 2012].

"Appendix 2: The Athens Report 1978," in *Anglican-Orthodox Dialogue: The Dublin Agreed Statement 1984*, pp. 58–63 (Crestwood, NY: St. Vladimir's Seminary Press, 1985).

Arnould, Etienne, "'Je Me Souviens,'" *Contacts* 59, no. 4 (2007), pp. 491–97.

Arnould, Nadine, "Elisabeth Behr-Sigel Celebrates Her 90th Birthday," trans. Lyn Breck, *The St. Nina Quarterly* 1, no. 4 (1997), p. 11.

Assaad, Marie, "Introduction," in *Women, Religion and Sexuality: Studies on the Impact of Religious Teachings on Women*, pp. ix–xii (ed. Jeanne Becher; Geneva: WCC Publications, 1990).

Aurenche, Guy, "Quelques Reflets de Sa Présence à l'ACAT," *Contacts* 59, no. 4 (2007), pp. 476–73.

Azkoul, Michael, *Order of Creation, Order of Redemption: The Ordination of Women in the Orthodox Church* (Rollinsford, NH: Orthodox Research Institute, 2007).

Bayne, Jennifer L. and Sarah E. Hinlicky, "Free to Be Creatures Again," *Christianity Today* (October 23, 2000), pp. 38–44.

Becher, Jeanne (ed.), *Women, Religion and Sexuality: Studies on the Impact of Religious Teachings on Women* (Geneva: WCC Publications, 1990).

Behr, John, "A Note on the 'Ontology of Gender,'" *St. Vladimir's Theological Quarterly* 42, nos 3–4 (1998), pp. 363–72.

Belonick, Deborah Malacky, "The Spirit of the Female Priesthood," in *Women and the Priesthood*, pp. 135–68 (ed. Thomas Hopko; Crestwood, NY: St. Vladimir's Seminary Press, 1st edn, 1983).

—"Testing the Spirits," in *Women and the Priesthood*, pp. 189–223 (ed. Thomas Hopko; Crestwood, NY: St. Vladimir's Seminary Press, rev. edn, 1999).

—"Women in the Church," in *Orthodox Perspectives on Pastoral Praxis: Papers of the Intra-Orthodox Conference on Pastoral Praxis (24–25 September 1986) Celebrating the 50th Anniversary of Holy Cross Greek Orthodox School of Theology (1937–1987)*, pp. 81–99 (ed. Theodore Stylianopoulos; Brookline, MA: Holy Cross Orthodox Press, 1988).

"Beyrouth: Rencontre Commémorative à la Mémoire d'Elisabeth Behr-Sigel," *Service Orthodoxe de Presse* 337 (2009), pp. 9–10.

Bigham, Steven, "*The Ministry of Women in the Church*: Comments by Fr. Steven Bigham," *MaryMartha* 1, no. 3 (1991), pp. 16–18.

Billington, James, *The Icon and the Axe: An Interpretive History of Russian Culture* (New York: Knopf, 1966).

Blane, Andrew (ed.), *Georges Florovsky: Russian Intellectual and Orthodox Churchman* (Crestwood, NY: St. Vladimir's Seminary Press, 1993).

Bliss, Kathleen, *The Service and Status of Women in the Churches* (London: SCM Press, 1952).

Bloom, Anthony, "Préface," in Elisabeth Behr-Sigel, *Le Ministère de la Femme dans l'Eglise*, pp. i–ii (Paris: Cerf, 1987). Published in English as "Preface to the French Edition," in Elisabeth Behr-Sigel, *The Ministry of Women in the Church*, pp. xiii–xiv (trans. Steven Bigham; Redondo Beach, CA: Oakwood Publications, 1991).

Bobrinskoy, Boris, "La Place de la Femme dans le Vie de l'Eglise," in *"Toi, Suis-Moi," Mélanges Offerts en Hommage à Elisabeth Behr-Sigel*, pp. 395–406 (Iasi, Romania: Editura Trinitas, 2nd edn, 2003).

—"Le Témoin d'une Orthodoxie Profonde et Libre," *Contacts* 59, no. 4 (2007), pp. 397–402.

Bourdara, Kalliope A., "The Ordination of Women in the Eyes of an Orthodox Woman," *Anglican Theological Review* 84, no. 3 (2002), pp. 681–89.

Bozarth-Campbell, Alla, *Womanpriest: A Personal Odyssey* (New York: Paulist Press, 1978).

Braniste, Ekaterina, "Reflection of a Participant," in *Orthodox Women: Their Role and Participation in the Orthodox Church*, pp. 6–7 (ed. Constance J. Tarasar and Irina Kirillova; Geneva: World Council of Churches, 1977).

Breck, Lyn, "Elisabeth Behr-Sigel—Entretien," *MaryMartha* 5, no. 2 (1997), pp. 13–14.

—"Nearly a Century of Life," in *Discerning the Signs of the Times*, pp. 125–36 (ed. Michael Plekon and Sarah E. Hinlicky; Crestwood, NY: St. Vladimir's Seminary Press, 2001).

Brock, Sebastian, "Deaconesses in the Syriac Tradition," in *Woman in Prism and Focus: Her Profile in Major World Religions and in Christian Tradition*, pp. 205–17 (ed. Prasanna Vazheeparampil, CMC; Rome: Mar Thoma Yogam [The St. Thomas Christian Fellowship], 1996).

Bulgakov, Sergius, "Dogma and Dogmatic Theology," in *Tradition Alive: On the Church and the Christian Life in Our Time: Readings from the Eastern Church*, pp. 67–80 (ed. Michael Plekon; trans. Peter Bouteneff; Lanham, MD: Sheed and Ward, 2003).

Caldecott, Léonie, "Sincere Gift: The Pope's 'New Feminism,'" in *John Paul II and Moral Theology*, pp. 216–34 (ed. Charles E. Curran and Richard A. McCormick, S. J.; Readings in Moral Theology, 10; New York: Paulist Press, 1978).

"Can Women Be Priests?" in *Women Priests: A Catholic Commentary on the Vatican Declaration*, pp. 338–46 (ed. Leonard Swidler and Arlene Swidler; New York: Paulist Press, 1977).

Chitescu, Nicolae, "The Ordination of Women: A Comment on the Attitude of the Church," in *Concerning the Ordination of Women*, pp. 57–60 (Geneva: WCC Publications, 1964).

Chrysostomos of Myra, "Priesthood and Women in Ecclesiological Perspective," in *The Place of the Woman in the Orthodox Church and the Question of the Ordination of Women*, pp. 117–32 (ed. Gennadios Limouris; Katerini, Greece: Tertios Publications, 1992).

Clément, Olivier, "The Eucharist in the Thought of Paul Evdokimov," *Eastern Churches Review* 7, no. 2 (1975), pp. 113–24.

—*Orient-Occident—Deux Passeurs: Vladimir Lossky, Paul Evdokimov* (Perspective Orthodoxe, 6; Geneva: Labor et Fides, 1985).

—"Orthodoxy, Olivier Clément and the Ordination of Women," *MaryMartha* 3, no. 1 (1993), pp. 27–29.

—"Paul Evdokimov 1901–1970," in *Ecumenical Pilgrims: Profiles of Pioneers in Christian Reconciliation*, pp. 86–92 (ed. Ion Bria and Dagmar Heller; Geneva: WCC Publications, 1995).

—"La Vie et l'Oeuvre de Paul Evdokimov," *Contacts* 23 (1971), pp. 88–106.

Concerning the Ordination of Women (Department on Faith and Order and Department on Cooperation of Men and Women in Church, Family, and Society; Geneva: WCC Publications, 1964).

Conclusions of the InterOrthodox Consultation on The Place of the Woman in the Orthodox Church and the Question of the Ordination of Women, Rhodes, Greece, 30 Oct.–7 Nov. 1988 (Minneapolis: Light and Life, 1990).

Crawford, Janet and Michael Kinnamon (eds), *In God's Image: Reflections on Identity, Human Wholeness, and the Authority of Scripture* (Geneva: WCC Publications, 1983).

D'Aloisio, Christopher, "Elisabeth Behr-Sigel, a Father in the Faith," *Syndesmos News* 19, no. 1 (2006), pp. 1, 3–4.

Daly, Mary, *Beyond God the Father: Toward a Philosophy of Women's Liberation* (Boston: Beacon Press, 1973).

Dibo, Amal, "Discerning the Signs of the Times: Women in the Life of the Orthodox Church. WCC Ecumenical Decade of Churches in Solidarity with Women, Damascus, Syria 1996," *MaryMartha* 5, no. 2 (1997), pp. 36–42.

—"Discerning the Signs of the Times: Women in the Life of the Orthodox Church. WCC Ecumenical Decade of Churches in Solidarity with Women, Second Regional Conference, Istanbul, Turkey. May 1997," *MaryMartha* 5, no. 2 (1997), pp. 45–53.

— "Elisabeth Behr-Sigel 'Notre Dame,'" *Contacts* 59, no. 4 (2007), pp. 476–82.

Dunn, David J., "'Her That Is No Bride': St. Thecla and the Relationship Between Sex, Gender, and Office," *St. Vladimir's Theological Quarterly* 53, no. 4 (2010), pp. 37–68.

"The Ecumenical Consultation at Agapia Convent—Romania," *Romanian Orthodox Church News Quarterly Bulletin* 6, no. 4 (1976), pp. 25–29.

Ephrem (Archimandrite), review of *Le Ministère de la Femme dans l'Eglise* by Elisabeth Behr-Sigel, *Sourozh* 57 (1994), pp. 46–49.

Erickson, John H., "The Priesthood in Patristic Teaching," in *The Place of the Woman in the Orthodox Church and the Question of the Ordination of Women*, pp. 103–15 (ed. Gennadios Limouris; Katerini, Greece: Tertios Publications, 1992).

—Review of *Orthodox Women* by Constance J. Tarasar and Irina Kirillova (eds), *St. Vladimir's Theological Quarterly* 21, no. 3 (1977), p. 170.

Evdokimoff [*sic*], Tomoko, Letter to Michael Plekon, 1996.

Evdokimov, Michel, "Les Racines Russes de la Pensée Théologique d'Elisabeth Behr-Sigel," *Contacts* 59, no. 4 (2007), pp. 403–12.

Evdokimov, Paul, *Ages of the Spiritual Life* (trans. Sister Gertrude, S. P.; rev. trans. Michael Plekon and Alexis Vinogradov; Crestwood, NY: St. Vladimir's Seminary Press, 1998).

—"The Charisms of Woman," in *In the World, Of the Church: A Paul Evdokimov Reader*, pp. 231–42 (ed. Michael Plekon and Alexis Vinogradov; Crestwood, NY: St. Vladimir's Seminary Press, 2001).

—*La Femme et le Salut du Monde: Etude d'Anthropologie Chrétienne sur les Charismes de la Femme* (Paris-Tournai: Casterman, 1958). Published in English as *Woman and the Salvation of the World* (trans. Anthony P. Gythiel; Crestwood, NY: St. Vladimir's Seminary Press, 1994).

—*In the World, Of the Church: A Paul Evdokimov Reader* (ed. Michael Plekon and Alexis Vinogradov; Crestwood, NY: St. Vladimir's Seminary Press, 2001).

—*Le Mariage. Sacrement de l'Amour* (Lyon: Livre Français, 1944). Published in English as *The Sacrament of Love: The Nuptial Mystery in the Light of the Orthodox Tradition* (trans. Anthony P. Gythiel and Victoria Steadman; Crestwood, NY: St. Vladimir's Seminary Press, 1985).

—*La Nouveauté de l'Esprit: Etudes de Spiritualité* (Spiritualité Orientale, 20; Bégrolles: Abbaye de Bellefontaine, 1977).

—"Panagion and Panagia: The Holy Spirit and the Mother of God," in *In the World, Of the Church: A Paul Evdokimov Reader*, pp. 155–73 (ed. Michael Plekon and Alexis Vinogradov; Crestwood, NY: St. Vladimir's Seminary Press, 2001).

Fahey, Michael A., "Eastern Orthodoxy and the Ordination of Women," in *Women Priests: A Catholic Commentary on the Vatican Declaration*, pp. 107–13 (ed. Leonard Swidler and Arlene Swidler; New York: Paulist Press, 1977).

FitzGerald, Kyriaki Karidoyanes, "The Eve-Mary Typology and Women in the Orthodox Church: Reconsidering Rhodes," *Anglican Theological Review* 84, no. 3 (2002), pp. 627–45.

—"The Inter-Orthodox Theological Consultation on Women in the Church," *Ecumenical Trends* 18, no. 3 (1989), pp. 33–36.

—"The Ministry of Women in the Orthodox Church: Some Theological Presuppositions," *Journal of Ecumenical Studies* 20, no. 4 (1983), pp. 558–75.

—"An Orthodox Assessment of Modern Feminist Theology," in *The Place of the Woman in the Orthodox Church and the Question of the Ordination of Women*, pp. 287–318 (ed. Gennadios Limouris; Katerini, Greece: Tertios Publications, 1992).

—"Orthodox Women and Pastoral Praxis: Observations and Concerns for the Church in America," in *Orthodox Perspectives on Pastoral Praxis: Papers of the Intra-Orthodox Conference on Pastoral Praxis (24–25 September 1986) Celebrating the 50th Anniversary of Holy Cross Greek Orthodox School of Theology (1937–1987)*, pp. 101–26 (ed. Theodore Stylianopoulos; Brookline, MA: Holy Cross Orthodox Press, 1988).

—*Women Deacons in the Orthodox Church: Called to Holiness and Ministry* (Brookline, MA: Holy Cross Orthodox Press, 1998).

FitzGerald, Kyriaki Karidoyanes (ed.), *Orthodox Women Speak: Discerning the "Signs of the Times"* (Geneva: WCC Publications, 1999).

Florovsky, Georges, *Ways of Russian Theology: Part One* (ed. Richard S. Haugh; trans. Robert L. Nichols; The Collected Works of Georges Florovsky, 5; Vaduz, Liechtenstein: Büchervertriebsanstalt, 1987).

—*Ways of Russian Theology: Part Two* (ed. Richard S. Haugh; trans. Robert L. Nichols; The Collected Works of Georges Florovsky, 6; Vaduz, Liechtenstein: Büchervertriebsanstalt, 1987).

Gallaher, Brandon, "'Waiting for the Barbarians': Identity and Polemicism in the Neo-Patristic Synthesis of Georges Florovky," *Modern Theology* 27, no. 4 (2011), pp. 659–91.

Gavrilyuk, Paul L., "Harnack's Hellenized Christianity or Florovsky's 'Sacred Hellenism': Questioning Two Metanarratives of Early Christian Engagement with Late Antique Culture," *St. Vladimir's Theological Quarterly* 54, nos 3–4 (2010), pp. 323–44.

Giles, Kevin, *The Trinity and Subordinationism: The Doctrine of God and the Contemporary Gender Debate* (Downers Grove, IL: InterVarsity Press, 2002).

Gillet, Lev, *L'Offrande Liturgique* (Paris: n.p., 1988).

Ginn, Roman, "Paul Evdokimov on the Question of Women's Ordination," *The Priest* 41 (1985), pp. 40–45.

Graffion, Anne-Marie, "Elisabeth dans Sa Paroisse de la Crypte," *Contacts* 59, no. 4 (2007), pp. 474–75.

Graham, Ian, review of *The Ordination of Women in the Orthodox Church* by E. Behr-Sigel and K. Ware, *Sourozh* 83 (2001), pp. 49–55.

Hackel, Sergei, "The Agapia Consultation," *Sobornost Series* 7, no. 6 (1978), p. 431.

—*Pearl of Great Price: The Life of Mother Maria Skobtsova 1891–1945* (Crestwood, NY: St. Vladimir's Seminary Press, 1981).

—"Russian," in *The Study of Spirituality*, pp. 259–76 (ed. Cheslyn Jones, Geoffrey Wainwright, and Edward Yarnold; New York: Oxford University Press, 1986).

Hampson, Daphne, *Theology and Feminism* (Oxford: Basil Blackwell, 1990).

Hanna, Elaine Gounaris, "Crete Consultation Report," *MaryMartha* 1, no. 1 (1991), pp. 3–4.

Harrison, Verna E., "Eve, the Mother of God, and Other Women," *Ecumenical Review* 60, nos 1–2 (2008), pp. 71–81.

—"The Fatherhood of God in Orthodox Theology," *St. Vladimir's Theological Quarterly* 37, nos 2–3 (1993), pp. 185–212.

—"Male and Female in Cappadocian Theology," *Journal of Theological Studies* 41, no. 2 (1990), pp. 441–71.

—"The Maleness of Christ," *St. Vladimir's Theological Quarterly* 42 (1998), pp. 111–51.

—"Orthodox Arguments against the Ordination of Women as Priests," *Sobornost* 14, no. 1 (1992), pp. 6–24. A slightly shorter version of this essay appears in *Women and the Priesthood*, pp. 165–87 (ed. Thomas Hopko; Crestwood, NY: St. Vladimir's Seminary Press, rev. edn, 1999).

Harvey, Susan Ashbrook, "Feminine Imagery for the Divine: The Holy Spirit, the Odes of Solomon, and Early Syriac Tradition," *St. Vladimir's Theological Quarterly* 37, nos 2–3 (1993), pp. 111–39.

—Review of *The Ministry of Women in the Church* by E. Behr-Sigel, *St. Vladimir's Theological Quarterly* 37, no. 1 (1993), pp. 101–03.

Hinlicky, Sarah E., "Epilogue: Orthodoxy, Modernity, and Feminism Recovered," in Elisabeth Behr-Sigel, *Discerning the Signs of the Times*, pp. 137–48 (ed. Michael Plekon and Sarah E. Hinlicky; Crestwood, NY: St. Vladimir's Seminary Press, 2001).

—"Introduction," in Elisabeth Behr-Sigel, *Discerning the Signs of the Times*, pp. 1–3 (ed. Michael Plekon and Sarah E. Hinlicky; Crestwood, NY: St. Vladimir's Seminary Press, 2001).

Hopko, Thomas, "Apophatic Theology and the Naming of God in Eastern Orthodox Tradition," in *Speaking the Christian God: The Holy Trinity and the Challenge of Feminism*, pp. 144–61 (ed. Alvin F. Kimel, Jr; Grand Rapids, MI: Eerdmans, 1992).

—"The Debate Continues—1998," in *Women and the Priesthood*, pp. 249–57 (ed. Thomas Hopko; Crestwood, NY: St. Vladimir's Seminary Press, rev. edn, 1999).

—"Galatians 3:28: An Orthodox Interpretation," *St. Vladimir's Theological Quarterly* 35, nos 2–3 (1991), pp. 169–86.

—"God and Gender: Articulating the Orthodox View," *St. Vladimir's Theological Quarterly* 37, nos 2–3 (1993), pp. 141–83.

—"The Lima Statement and the Orthodox," *Journal of Ecumenical Studies* 21, no. 1 (1984), pp. 55–63.

—"On the Male Character of the Christian Priesthood," *St. Vladimir's Theological Quarterly* 19, no. 3 (1975), pp. 147–73. Reprinted in *Women and the Priesthood*, pp. 97–134 (ed. Thomas Hopko; Crestwood, NY: St. Vladimir's Seminary Press, 1st edn, 1983).

—"Preface to the English Edition," in Elisabeth Behr-Sigel, *The Ministry of Women in the Church*, pp. ix–xii (Redondo Beach, CA: Oakwood Publications, 1991).

—"Presbyter/Bishop: A Masculine Ministry," in *Women and the Priesthood*, pp. 139–64 (ed. Thomas Hopko; Crestwood, NY: St. Vladimir's Seminary Press, rev. edn, 1999).

—"A Response from Fr. Hopko," *St. Nina Quarterly* 3, no. 3 (1999), pp. 22–23.

—*The Spirit of God* (Wilton, CT: Morehouse-Barlow, 1976).

—"Women and the Priesthood: Reflections on the Debate," in *Women and the Priesthood*, pp. 169–90 (ed. Thomas Hopko; Crestwood, NY: St. Vladimir's Seminary Press, 1st edn, 1983).

Hopko, Thomas (ed.), *Women and the Priesthood* (Crestwood, NY: St. Vladimir's Seminary Press, 1st edn, 1983).

— (ed.), *Women and the Priesthood* (Crestwood, NY: St. Vladimir's Seminary Press, rev. edn, 1999).

Illies, Joachim, "Eva und das Heil der Welt: In der Sicht des russisch-orthodoxen Christen Paul Evdokimov," in *Die Sache mit dem Apfel: Eine moderne Wissenschaft vom Sündenfall*, pp. 116–26 (ed. Joachim Illies; Freiburg: Herderbücherei, 1972).

"In Memory of Elisabeth Behr-Sigel," *The St. Nina Quarterly Online Journal*, <www.stnina.org/online-journal/announcements/memory-elisabeth-behr-sigel> [accessed December 10, 2012].

"Inter Insigniores," in *From "Inter Insigniores" to "Ordinatio Sacerdotalis": Documents and Commentaries*, pp. 18–76 (Washington, DC: United States Catholic Conference, 1998).

Interview with Elisabeth Behr-Sigel, [transcript], b. 1907, *St. Nina Quarterly*, on May 30, 2003 at St. Vladimir's Orthodox Theological Seminary and June 3, 2003 at Holy Cross Greek Orthodox School of Theology (unpublished).

Jaquet, Demetra Velisarios, "Women in Orthodox Christian Traditions," in *Encyclopedia of Women and Religion in North America*, pp. 509–18 (ed. Rosemary Skinner Keller and Rosemary Radford Ruether; vol. 2; Bloomington and Indianapolis: Indiana University Press, 2006).

Jensen, Anne, "L'Eglise Orthodoxe: Est-Elle Patriarcaliste?" *Una Sancta* 40, no. 2 (1985), pp. 130–45.

Kalaitzidis, Pantelis, "Challenges of Renewal and Reformation Facing the Orthodox Church," *Ecumenical Review* 61, no. 2 (2009), pp. 136–64.

—"From the 'Return to the Fathers' to the Need for a Modern Orthodox Theology," *St. Vladimir's Theological Quarterly* 54, no. 1 (2010), pp. 5–36.

Kallis, Anastasios, "Presidency at the Eucharist in the Context of the Theology of Icons: Questions about the Ecclesial Representation of Christ by the Priesthood," *Anglican Theological Review* 84, no. 3 (2002), pp. 713–30.

Karkala-Zorba, Katerina, "The Ordination of Women from an Orthodox Perspective," in *Women and Ordination in the Christian Churches: International Perspectives*, pp. 54–63 (ed. Ian Jones, Kirsty Thorpe, and Janet Wootton; London: T&T Clark, 2008).

—"The Role of Women in the Orthodox Church Today," *MaryMartha* 5, no. 1 (1996), pp. 3–8.

Karras, Valerie, "Flesh of My Flesh—Greek Patristic Exegeses of the Creation of Eve," *St. Nina Quarterly* 2, no. 1 (1998), pp. 1, 9–10, 12, 19.

—"The Incarnational and Hypostatic Significance of the Maleness of Jesus Christ according to Theodore of Stoudios," in *Studia Patristica*, pp. 320–24 (ed. Elizabeth A. Livingstone; vol. XXXII; Louvain: Peeters, 1997).

—"The Mystery of the Trinity Revealed Cited Experienced: Language, Metaphor and Personhood," *St. Nina Quarterly* 2, no. 3 (1998), pp. 12–14.

—"Patristic Views on the Ontology of Gender," in *Personhood: Orthodox Christianity and the Connection between Body, Mind, and Soul*, pp. 113–19 (ed. John T. Chirban; Westport, CT: Bergin and Garvey, 1996).

—"Sermon: The Significance of the Maleness of Jesus Christ?" *St. Nina Quarterly* 1, no. 2 (1997), p. 12.

—"The Theotokos: Icon for Humanity," *St. Nina Quarterly* 1, no. 3 (1997), pp. 1, 7–8.

—"Women in the Eastern Church: Past, Present, and Future," *St. Nina Quarterly* 1, no. 1 (1997), pp. 1, 11–13.

Kasselouri-Hatzivassiliadi, Eleni and Sarah Hinlicky Wilson (eds), *"A Communion Lived in Faith and Love": Reflections on Elisabeth Behr-Sigel's Ecclesiology* (Doxa and Praxis; Geneva: WCC Publications, 2013).

Keenan, William J. F., "Rediscovering the Theological in Sociology: Foundation and Possibilities," *Theory, Culture and Society* 20, no. 1 (2003), pp. 19–42.

Khodre, George, "The Ordination of Women," in *Concerning the Ordination of Women*, pp. 61–64 (Geneva: WCC Publications, 1964).

Klofft, Christopher P., "Gender and the Process of Moral Development in the Thought of Paul Evdokimov," *Theological Studies* 66 (2005), pp. 69–95.

Kollontai, Pauline, "Contemporary Thinking on the Role and Ministry of Women in the Orthodox Church," *Journal of Contemporary Religion* 15, no. 2 (2000), pp. 165–79.

Lacelle, Elisabeth J., "Elisabeth Behr-Sigel," in *Penseurs et Apôtres du XXe Siècle*, pp. 375–86 (ed. Jean Genest; Montreal: Fides, 2001).

Ladouceur, Paul, "Aperçu de l'Oeuvre Littéraire d'Elisabeth Behr-Sigel," *Lumière du Thabor* 28 (2006), pp. 5–8.

—"Pensée et Oeuvre d'Elisabeth Behr-Sigel," *Contacts* 59, no. 4 (2007), pp. 430–54.

Lanne, Emmanuel, O. S. B, "Une Femme de Dialogue, Engagée dans le Siècle du Mouvement Oecuménique," *Contacts* 59, no. 4 (2007), pp. 455–58.

Lattier, Daniel J., "The Orthodox Rejection of Doctrinal Development," *Pro Ecclesia* 20, no. 4 (2011), pp. 389–410.

Lazareth, William H. and Bärbel von Wartenberg, "Preface," in *The Community of Women and Men in the Church: A Report of the World Council of Churches' Conference, Sheffield, England, 1981*, pp. ix–x (ed. Constance F. Parvey; Philadelphia: Fortress, 1983).

Lienhard, Marc (ed.), *La Faculté de Théologie Protestante de Strasbourg Hier et Aujourd'hui, 1538–1988* (Strasbourg: Oberlin, 1988).

"Liminaire," *Contacts* 59, no. 4 (2007), pp. 393–94.

Limouris, Gennadios (ed.), *The Place of the Woman in the Orthodox Church and the Question of the Ordination of Women: Interorthodox Symposium, Rhodos, Greece, 30 October–7 November 1988* (Katerini, Greece: Tertios Publications, 1992).

Liveris, Leonie B., *Ancient Taboo and Gender Prejudice: Challenges for Orthodox Women and the Church* (Burlington, VT: Ashgate, 2005).

—"Consultation Report: MaryMartha Editorial—Istanbul and Bossey," *MaryMartha* 5, no. 2 (1997), pp. 3–7.

—"Ecumenism at a Cost: Women, Ordination, and Sexuality: 'Disagree with the Umpire—Take the Ball, and Go Home,'" *Journal of Ecumenical Studies* 41 (2004), pp. 55–73.

—"Seminar Report: Feminine Images and Orthodox Spirituality Seminar, Ecumenical Institute, Bossey May 1992," *MaryMartha* 2, no. 2 (1992), pp. 12–13.

—"Seminars at Bossey 1994," *MaryMartha* 3, nos 3–4 (1994), pp. 42–46.

—"Women, Leadership, and the Orthodox Church in Australia: Always Second, Secondary, or Seconded," *Studies in World Christianity* 13, no. 1 (2007), pp. 13–32.

Lossky, Olga, "Une Chrétienne Engagée au Coeur de son Epoque," *Lumière du Thabor* 28 (2006), pp. 1–5.

—"Les Déjeuners du Samedi," *Contacts* 59, no. 4 (2007), pp. 498–502.

—"Elisabeth Behr-Sigel: Her Vision and Contribution," in *Many Women Were Also There . . .: The Participation of Orthodox Women in the Ecumenical Movement*, pp. 181–83 (ed. Eleni Kasselouri-Hatzivassiliadi, Fulata Mbano Moyo, and Aikaterini Pekridou; Geneva/Volos: WCC Publications/Volos Academy for Theological Studies, 2010).

—*Vers le Jour sans Déclin: Une Vie d'Elisabeth Behr-Sigel (1907–2005)* (Paris: Cerf, 2007). Published in English as *Toward the Endless Day: A Biography of Elisabeth Behr-Sigel (1907–2005)* (ed. Michael Plekon; trans. Jerry Ryan; South Bend, IN: University of Notre Dame Press, 2010).

Lossky, Véronique, "Compte Rendu de l'Atelier: Hommes et Femmes dans l'Eglise," *MaryMartha* 5, no. 2 (1997), pp. 31–33. Published in English as "Men and Women in the Church: Report of the Workshop, Vendee," trans. Colin Williams, *MaryMartha* 5, no. 2 (1997), pp. 33–35.

—"La Femme dans l'Eglise Orthodoxe," *Contacts* 44 (1992), pp. 221–32.

—"Le Ministère des Femmes d'un Point de Vue Orthodoxe: Une Relecture," *Contacts* 48 (1996), pp. 101–18. Reprinted in *MaryMartha* 5, no. 2 (1997), pp. 54–68. "Women's Ministry—From an Orthodox Point of View. A Re-reading," trans. Colin Williams, *MaryMartha* 5, no. 2 (1997), pp. 69–82.

—"La Place de la Femme dans l'Eglise Orthodoxe," *Contacts* 55 (2003), pp. 104–08.

Lossky, Vladimir, *A l'Image et à la Ressemblance de Dieu* (Paris: Aubier-Montaigne, 1967). Published in English as *In the Image and Likeness of God* (ed. John H. Erickson and Thomas E. Bird; Crestwood, NY: St. Vladimir's Seminary Press, 1974).

—"Catholic Consciousness: Anthropological Implications of the Dogma of the Church," in *In the Image and Likeness of God*, pp. 183–94 (ed. John H. Erickson and Thomas E. Bird; Crestwood, NY: St. Vladimir's Seminary Press, 1974).

—*Orthodox Theology: An Introduction* (trans. Ian and Ihita Kesarcodi-Watson; Crestwood, NY: St. Vladimir's Seminary Press, 1978).

—"The Theological Notion of the Human Person," in *In the Image and Likeness of God*, pp. 111–24 (ed. John H. Erickson and Thomas E. Bird; Crestwood, NY: St. Vladimir's Seminary Press, 1974).

—"The Theology of the Image," in *In the Image and Likeness of God*, pp. 125–39 (ed. John H. Erickson and Thomas E. Bird; Crestwood, NY: St. Vladimir's Seminary Press, 1974).

—"Tradition and Traditions," in *In the Image and Likeness of God*, pp. 141–68 (ed. John H. Erickson and Thomas E. Bird; Crestwood, NY: St. Vladimir's Seminary Press, 1974).

Manolache, Anca-Lucia, "Orthodoxy and Women: A Romanian Perspective," in *Women, Religion and Sexuality: Studies on the Impact of Religious Teachings on Women*, pp. 172–83 (ed. Jeanne Becher; Geneva: WCC Publications, 1990).

Marriage, Alwyn, *Life-Giving Spirit: Responding to the Feminine in God* (London: SPCK, 1989).

McDowell, Maria Gwyn, "The Hands of a Woman," in *"A Communion Lived in Faith and Love": Reflections on Elisabeth Behr-Sigel's Ecclesiology* (Doxa and Praxis; Geneva: WCC Publications, 2013).

—"The Joy of Embodied Virtue: Toward the Ordination of Women to the Eastern Orthodox Priesthood" (unpublished doctoral dissertation, Boston College, 2010).

—"Newness of the Spirit: The Ordination of Men and Women," *Word* 48, no. 5 (2004), pp. 9–11.

Meerson, Michael Aksionov, *The Trinity of Love in Modern Russian Theology: The Love Paradigm and the Retrieval of Western Medieval Love Mysticism in Modern Russian Trinitarian Thought from Solovyov to Bulgakov* (Quincy, IL: Franciscan Press, 1998).

Mercier, Jean, "Interviews d'Elisabeth Behr-Sigel et de Nicolas Lossky: Les Femmes-Prêtres Vues par des Orthodoxes," *MaryMartha* 3 (1994), pp. 24–25.

Meyendorff, John, *Byzantine Theology: Historical Trends and Doctrinal Themes* (New York: Fordham University Press, 1979).

—*A Study of Gregory Palamas* (trans. George Lawrence; London: The Faith Press, 1964).

Moberly, Elizabeth, review of *Women and the Priesthood*, ed. Thomas Hopko, *Sobornost* 6 (1984), pp. 86–89.

Monsaingeon, M.-J., "A Propos du Rôle de la Femme dans l'Eglise," *Contacts* 42 (1990), pp. 224–25.

Morelli, George, "Whose Church Do I Belong To: My Church or the Orthodox Church of Christ?" *OrthodoxyToday.org*, <www.orthodoxytoday.org/articles6/MorelliSecularism.php> [accessed December 10, 2012].

Morris, John, "Thoughts on Women's Ordination," *The Word* 48, no. 3 (2004), n.p.

Mounier, Emmanuel, *A Personalist Manifesto* (London: Longmans, Green, and Co., 1938).

Nichols, Aidan, O. P., *Theology in the Russian Diaspora: Church, Fathers, Eucharist in Nikolai Afanas'ev (1893–1966)* (Cambridge: Cambridge University Press, 1989).

Norris, Jr, Richard A., "The Ordination of Women and the 'Maleness' of Christ," *Anglican Theological Review* 6 (1976), pp. 69–80.

Oduyoye, Mercy, "Preface at Dresden to the Sheffield Recommendations," in *The Community of Men and Women in the Church*, pp. 81–83 (ed. Constance F. Parvey; Philadelphia: Fortress, 1983).

"Orthodox-Roman Catholic Consultation on Bishops and Presbyters," *Diakonia* 11, no. 3 (1976), pp. 293–95.

"Orthodox-Roman Catholic Reflections on Ministries," *Origins* 7, no. 44 (1978), pp. 702–04.

"Orthodox Women's Consultation, Orthodox Academy of Crete, January 1990. Church and Culture: Ministry, Human Sexuality, Participation and Decision Making," *MaryMartha* 1, nos 1–3 (1991–92), pp. 3–7.

Parmentier, Elisabeth, "Elisabeth Behr-Sigel's Theological Formation and Ministry in Strasbourg," in *"A Communion Lived in Faith and Love": Reflections on Elisabeth Behr-Sigel's Ecclesiology* (ed. Eleni Kasselouri-Hatzivassiliadi and Sarah Hinlicky Wilson; Doxa and Praxis; Geneva: WCC Publications, 2013).

Parvey, Constance F., "The Church—Women and Men in Community," in *The Community of Men and Women in the Church: A Report of the World Council of Churches' Conference, Sheffield, England, 1981*, pp. 2–18 (ed. Constance F. Parvey; Philadelphia: Fortress, 1983).

—"Held Together in Hope and Sustained by God's Promise: A Personal Reflection," in *The Community of Men and Women in the Church: A Report of the World Council of Churches' Conference, Sheffield, England, 1981*, pp. 156–83 (ed. Constance F. Parvey; Philadelphia: Fortress, 1983).

Parvey, Constance F. (ed.), *The Community of Men and Women in the Church: A Report of the World Council of Churches' Conference, Sheffield, England, 1981* (Philadelphia: Fortress, 1983).

—*The Ordination of Women in Ecumenical Perspective: Workbook for the Church's Future* (Geneva: WCC Publications, 1980).

Petrou, Ioannis, "The Question of Women in Church Tradition," *Anglican Theological Review* 84, no. 3 (2002), pp. 645–61.

Phan, Cho D., "Evdokimov and Monk Within," *Sobornost* 3, no. 1 (1981), pp. 53–61.

Phan, Peter C., *Culture and Eschatology: The Iconographical Vision of Paul Evdokimov* (New York: Peter Lang, 1985).

—"The Eschatological Dimension of Unity: Paul Evdokimov's Contribution to Ecumenism," *Salesianum* 42 (1980), pp. 475–99.

—"Gender Roles in the History of Salvation: Man and Woman in the Thought of Paul Evdokimov," *Heythrop Journal* 31 (1990), pp. 53–66.

—"Mariage, Monachisme et Eschatologie: Contribution de Paul Evdokimov à la Spiritualité Chrétienne," *Ephemerides Liturgicae* 93 (1979), pp. 352–80.

Pheidas, Vlassios, "The Question of the Priesthood of Women," in *The Place of the Woman in the Orthodox Church and the Question of the Ordination of Women*, pp. 157–96 (ed. Gennadios Limouris; Katerini, Greece: Tertios Publications, 1992).

Philips, Andrew, "Some Reasons Why the Orthodox Church Does Not Admit Women to the Priesthood," *Orthodox Life* 43, no. 2 (1993), pp. 43–47.

Pirri-Simonian, Terry, "Guest Editorial," *Ecumenical Review* 60, nos 1–2 (2008), pp. 1–6.

Plaskow, Judith, *Sex, Sin, and Grace: Women's Experience and the Theologies of Reinhold Niebuhr and Paul Tillich* (Washington, DC: University Press of America, 1980).

Plekon, Michael, "Becoming What We Pray: Three Images, Three Lives," *Ecumenical Review* 57, no. 4 (2003), pp. 395–405.

—"The God Whose Power is Weakness, Whose Love is Foolish: Divine Philanthropy in the Theology of Paul Evdokimov," *Sourozh* 60 (1995), pp. 15–26.

—"Interiorized Monasticism: A Reconsideration of Paul Evdokimov on the Spiritual Life," *American Benedictine Review* 48, no. 3 (1997), pp. 227–40.

—"An 'Offering of Prayer': The Witness of Paul Evdokimov (1901–1970)," *Sobornost* 17, no. 2 (1995), pp. 28–37.

—"Paul Evdokimov, A Theologian Within and Beyond the Church and the World," *Modern Theology* 12, no. 1 (1996), pp. 85–107.

—"Rendre Son Etre Perméable au Christ," trans. Françoise Lhoest, *Contacts* 59, no. 4 (2007), pp. 413–29. "To Become Permeable to Christ: Elisabeth Behr-Sigel's Theological Vision," *Ecumenical Review* 61, no. 2 (2009), pp. 165–76.

—"Sacrement Frère/Soeur chez Paul Evdokimov et Mère Marie Skobtsov," *Contacts* 56 (2004), pp. 5–28. "The 'Sacrament of the Brother/Sister': The Lives and Thought of Mother Maria Skobtsova and Paul Evdokimov," *St. Vladimir's Theological Quarterly* 49, no. 3 (2005), pp. 313–34.

—"Tradition's Freedom and Beauty: The Enduring Vision of Paul Evdokimov and Elisabeth Behr-Sigel," *Lutheran Forum* 37, no. 2 (2003), pp. 28–32.

—"Le Visage du Père dans la Mère de Dieu: Marie dans les Ecrits Théologiques de Paul Evdokimov," *Contacts* 47 (1995), pp. 250–69.

Plekon, Michael (ed.), *Tradition Alive: On the Church and the Christian Life in Our Time: Readings from the Eastern Church* (Lanham, MD: Sheed and Ward, 2003).

Poirot, Eliane, O. C. D. I., "Elisabeth Behr-Sigel et le Carmel Saint-Elie," *Contacts* 59, no. 4 (2007), pp. 459–66.

Raeff, Mark, "Enticements and Rifts: Georges Florovsky as Russian Intellectual Historian," in *Georges Florovsky: Russian Intellectual and Orthodox Churchman*, pp. 219–86 (ed. Andrew Blane; Crestwood, NY: St. Vladimir's Seminary Press, 1993).

Regule, Teva, "An Interview with Susan Ashbrook Harvey," *St. Nina Quarterly* 1, no. 4 (1997), pp. 5–8.

—"The St. Nina Quarterly: Bringing Together a Community of Women," *Ecumenical Review* 53, no. 1 (2000), pp. 101–04.

Rousseau, Olivier, "Le Professeur Paul Evdokimov (1901–1970)," *Irénikon* 43, no. 4 (1970), pp. 588–91.

Roussel, Jean-François, "Evidence et Indicibilité dans l'Apologétique de Paul Evdokimov," *Contacts* 47 (1995), pp. 287–307.

Ruether, Rosemary Radford, *Sexism and God-Talk: Toward a Feminist Theology* (Boston: Beacon Press, 1983).

Runciman, Steven, *The Great Church in Captivity: A Study of the Patriarchate of Constantinople from the Eve of the Turkish Conquest to the Greek War of Independence* (London: Cambridge University Press, 1968).

Saiving, Valerie, "The Human Situation: A Feminine View," in *Womanspirit Rising: A Feminist Reader in Religion*, pp. 25–42 (ed. Carol P. Christ and Judith Plaskow; San Francisco: Harper and Row, 1979).

Schaupp, Joan, *Woman: Image of the Holy Spirit* (Bethesda, MD: International Scholars Publications, 1996).

Schmemann, Alexander, "Concerning Women's Ordination: A Letter to an Episcopal Friend," *St. Vladimir's Theological Quarterly* 17, no. 3 (1973), pp. 239–43. Reprinted in *Sexuality-Theology-Priesthood: Reflections on the Ordination of Women to the Priesthood*, pp. 11–15 (ed. H. Karl Lutge; San Gabriel, CA: Concerned Fellow Episcopalians, 1973).

—"Roll of Honour," *St. Vladimir's Seminary Quarterly* (old series) 2, no. 1 (1952), pp. 5–11.

—"Russian Theology: 1920–1972, An Introductory Survey," *St. Vladimir's Theological Quarterly* 16, no. 4 (1972), pp. 172–94.

Shaw, Lewis, "John Meyendorff and the Heritage of the Russian Theological Tradition," in *New Perspectives on Historical Theology: Essays in Memory of John Meyendorff*, pp. 10–42 (ed. Bradley Nassif; Grand Rapids, MI: Eerdmans, 1996).

Stavrou, Michel, "La Question du Diaconat Féminin," *Contacts* 59, no. 4 (2007), pp. 483–90.

Streett, Matthew J., "Deacons, Apostles and the Place of Women in the Orthodox Church," *The Word* 48, no. 3 (2004), pp. 12–13.

Tarasar, Constance, "Orthodox Women's Consultation," *St. Vladimir's Theological Quarterly* 20, no. 4 (1976), pp. 242–44.

Tarasar, Constance J. and Irina Kirillova (eds), *Orthodox Women: Their Role and Participation in the Orthodox Church. Report on the Consultation of Orthodox Women, September 11–17, 1976, Agapia, Roumania* (Geneva: WCC Publications, 1977).

Theodorou, Evangelos, *Hè "cheirotonia," hè "cheirothesia" tôn diakonissôn* (Athens: n.p., 1954).

—"The Institution of Deaconesses in the Orthodox Church and the Possibility of Its Restoration," in *The Place of the Woman in the Orthodox Church and the Question of the Ordination of Women*, pp. 207–38 (ed. Gennadios Limouris; Katerini, Greece: Tertios Publications, 1992).

Thunberg, Lars, "Paul Evdokimov, Théologien Oecuménique," *Contacts* 47 (1995), pp. 270–86.

Timiadis, Emilianos, "The Concern for Women in the Orthodox Tradition," *Diakonia* 12, no. 1 (1977), pp. 8–23.

—"*Excerpts from* The Concern for Women in the Orthodox Tradition: New Challenges," in *Orthodox Women: Their Role and Participation in the Orthodox Church*, pp. 30–36 (ed. Constance J. Tarasar and Irina Kirillova; Geneva: WCC Publications, 1977).

"Toi, Suis-Moi," Mélanges Offerts en Hommage à Elisabeth Behr-Sigel (Iasi, Romania: Editura Trinitas, 2nd edn, 2003).

Topping, Eva Catafygiotu, "Heroines and Haloes," *Greek Orthodox Theological Review* 32 (1987), pp. 131–42.

—*Holy Mothers of Orthodoxy: Women and the Church* (Minneapolis: Light and Life, 1987).

—"Orthodox Women and Our Church," in *Project for Orthodox Renewal: Seven Studies of Key Issues Facing Orthodox Christians in America*, pp. 63–89 (ed. Stephen J. Sfekas and George E. Matsoukas; Chicago: Orthodox Christian Laity, 1993).

Ugolnik, Anthony, "Nymphios and Sophia: Gender as a Spiritual Dialectic in the Thought of the East-Slavs," *Logos: A Journal of Eastern Christian Studies* 35, nos 1–4 (1994), pp. 11–40.

Valliere, Paul, "The Liberal Tradition in Russian Orthodox Theology," in *The Legacy of St. Vladimir: Byzantium, Russia, America*, pp. 93–106 (ed. John Breck, John Meyendorff, and Eleana Silk; Crestwood, NY: St. Vladimir's Seminary Press, 1990).

—*Modern Russian Theology, Bukharev, Soloviev, Bulgakov: Orthodox Theology in a New Key* (Edinburgh: T&T Clark, 2000).

—"La 'Scuola parigina' di teologia: unità o molteplicità?" in *La Teologia Ortodossa e l'Occidente nel XX Secolo: Storia di un Incontro* (ed. Adriano Dell'Asta; Seriate: La Casa di Matriona, 2005). Reprinted in *La Nuova Europa 1* (2005). Published in Russian as "'Parizhskaia shkola' bogosloviia: edinstvo ili raznoobrazie?" in *Pravoslavnoe Bogoslovie i Zapad v XX Veke: Istoriia Vstrechi*, pp. 52–63 (ed. Aleksandr Kyrlezhev; Moscow: Khristianskaia Rossiia, 2006). Unpublished manuscript in English, "The 'Paris School' of Theology: Unity or Multiplicity?"

—"Sophiology as the Dialogue of Orthodoxy with Modern Civilization," in *Russian Religious Thought*, pp. 176–92 (ed. Judith Deutsch Kornblatt and Richard F. Gustafson; Madison, WI: University of Wisconsin Press, 1996).

Vasilevich, Natallia, "The Issue of Female Ordination/Priesthood in the Ecumenical and Inter-Orthodox Discussion," in *Many Women Were Also There . . .: The Participation of Orthodox Women in the Ecumenical Movement*, pp. 139–55 (ed. Eleni Kasselouri-Hatzivassiliadi, Fulata Mbano Moyo, and Aikaterini Pekridou; Geneva/Volos: WCC Publications/Volos Academy for Theological Studies, 2010).

von Arx, Urs and Anastasios Kallis, "Common Considerations: The Orthodox-Old Catholic Consultation on the Role of Women in the Church and the Ordination of Women as an Ecumenical Issue: Preliminary Remarks," *Anglican Theological Review* 84, no. 3 (2002), pp. 501–07.

Wahlburg, Rachel Conrad, *Jesus and the Freed Woman* (New York: Paulist Press, 1978).

Walker, Andrew, "Resexing the Trinity: The Spirit as Feminine," *King's Theological Review* 13 (1990), pp. 41–44.

Ware, Kallistos (Timothy), "God Hidden and Revealed: The Apophatic Way and the Essence-Energies Distinction," *Eastern Churches Review* 7, no. 2 (1975), pp. 125–36.

—"Man, Woman, and the Priesthood of Christ," in *Women and the Priesthood*, pp. 9–37 (ed. Thomas Hopko; Crestwood, NY: St. Vladimir's Seminary Press, 1983). Substantially altered for Thomas Hopko (ed.), *Women and the Priesthood*, pp. 5–53 (Crestwood, NY: St. Vladimir's Seminary Press, rev. edn, 1999). This latter version reprinted in Elisabeth Behr-Sigel and Kallistos Ware, *The Ordination of Women in the Orthodox Church*, pp. 49–96 (Geneva: WCC Publications, 2000).

— *Orthodox Theology in the Twenty-First Century* (Doxa and Praxis; Geneva: WCC Publications, 2012).

—"Orthodox Theology Today: Trends and Tasks," *International Journal for the Study of the Christian Church* 12, no. 2 (2012), pp. 105–21.

Wendebourg, Dorothea, "'Pseudomorphosis': A Theological Judgement as an Axiom for Research in the History of Church and Theology," *Greek Orthodox Theological Review* 42, nos 3–4 (1997), pp. 321–42.

Wesche, Kenneth Paul, "Man and Woman in the Orthodox Tradition: The Mystery of Gender," *St. Vladimir's Theological Quarterly* 37, nos 2–3 (1993), pp. 213–51.

Williams, George H., "The Neo-Patristic Synthesis of Georges Florovsky," in *Georges Florovsky: Russian Intellectual and Orthodox Churchman*, pp. 287–340 (ed. Andrew Blane; Crestwood, NY: St. Vladimir's Seminary Press, 1993).

Williams, Rowan, "Bread in the Wilderness: The Monastic Ideal in Thomas Merton and Paul Evdokimov," in *One Yet Two: Monastic Tradition East and West*, pp. 452–73 (ed. M. Basil Pennington; Kalamazoo: Cistercian Publications, 1976).

—"Christian Art and Cultural Pluralism: Reflections on 'L'Art de l'Icone,' by Paul Evdokimov," *Eastern Churches Review* 8, no. 1 (1976), pp. 38–44.

Women and Men in the Church: A Study of the Community of Women and Men in the Church (Syosset, NY: Department of Religious Education, Orthodox Church in America, 1980).

Yokarinis, Constantine, "A Patristic Basis for a Theological Anthropology of Women in Their Distinctive Humanity," *Anglican Theological Review* 84, no. 3 (2002), pp. 585–609.

Zenkovsky, V. V., *A History of Russian Philosophy* (trans. George L. Kline; London: Routledge and Kegan Paul, 1953).

Zernov, Militza, "Women's Ministry in the Church," *Eastern Churches Review* 7, no. 1 (1975), pp. 34–39.

Zizioulas, John, "By John Zizioulas (Greek Orthodox Church), Faith and Order Secretariat," *Study Encounter* 4, no. 4 (1968), pp. 191–93.

Index

Action de Chrétiens pour l'Abolition de la
    Torture (ACAT) 8, 112, 141
Adam 14, 18, 21n. 52, 24, 44, 61, 73, 75,
    116, 157, 164
Agapia 9, 29–34, 35, 40–2, 53–4, 71, 73,
    97, 101, 103, 105, 115, 119, 140, 143
Anglicanism 6, 153
anthropos 45, 61, 68, 95, 98, 147, 155
apophaticism 21, 38, 50, 88, 148, 156, 159,
    162n. 89
archetypes 17–19, 22, 24, 44, 47, 50, 51,
    58–60, 63, 65, 67, 69, 99, 161
Arianism 117, 156n. 64
Augustine 121–4

baptism 24, 32, 49, 82, 96, 99, 105–6, 114,
    118, 120n. 34, 156n. 64
Barth, Karl 123–4, 126–7
Basil of Caesarea 44, 64, 123, 156
Beauvoir, Simone de 15, 18, 137
Behr, André 3, 4, 6, 7, 86n. 31
Belonick, Deborah 64, 66, 69, 70, 158–9
Bible 40, 65, 100–1, 151
bishop, office of 23, 36, 144n. 13, 152
Bloom, Anthony 6, 70–1, 80–1, 89, 144
Bobrinskoy, Boris 7, 102–3, 125n. 67
Boegner, Marc 2, 127
bogochelovechestvo 136, 140
Bossey 72, 86, 96, 100, 114
Bouyer, Louis 50–1, 82
Bukharev, Alexander 6, 7, 12–16, 29, 30,
    48, 92, 113, 120–1, 134, 136–7, 139
Bulgakov, Sergius 3, 4, 6, 12–16, 22,
    37–8, 48, 59, 60, 64, 66–7, 93–4, 124–5,
    132–42, 149

Cappadocians 18, 22–3, 43, 65, 90,
    155n. 61
charisms 19, 20, 22–6, 28–9, 31, 34–5,
    38–40, 46, 50–1, 55–7, 59, 63–4, 68,
    70–1, 75–6, 82, 90, 93–4, 96–7, 99, 107,
    115–16, 141, 164

Chitescu, Nicolae 42, 69, 80, 101, 143,
    145n. 17, 153
Christ *see* Jesus Christ
Clément, Olivier 7, 40, 59, 87, 118, 137, 145
complementarity 13, 18, 27, 34, 70,
    156n. 66
conscience 2, 126–9
Corinthians, First Epistle to the 19, 26, 30,
    37, 54, 57, 62, 95
Crete 79, 88, 96, 110, 111

Damascus 72, 99, 111
deaconess 35, 55, 96, 105–7, 109,
    111–12, 143
deification 17, 44, 51, 96, 137–8, 163
diaconate 6, 10, 33, 35, 36n. 39, 41, 43, 47,
    55, 75, 105–12, 141, 143, 147n. 27
divino-humanism 116, 124, 140n. 148
docetism 67, 156

ecclesiology 3–5, 12, 57, 68, 78, 101,
    124, 128
ecumenism 2–3, 6–8, 28–9, 41–2, 46, 48,
    54, 66, 69, 71–3, 78, 81–2, 96–7, 103,
    112–14, 119, 120, 122, 124, 128, 130,
    134, 139
energies of God 22, 159
Ephesians, Epistle to the 16, 62, 91
Erickson, John 29n. 1, 73, 92, 118, 154
essentialism 158n. 74, 159, 163
eucharist 24, 37, 56, 82–3, 90, 94, 96, 100,
    105–6, 110, 120n. 34, 126, 152, 154–5
Evdokimov, Paul 3–5, 9, 11–28,
    29–36, 38–41, 46–7, 50–1, 54–5, 57–61,
    63–4, 66–7, 69–71, 74–6, 80, 87–8, 90–4,
    98–102, 106, 112, 114–16, 128, 136–7,
    140–2, 143, 148, 155–8, 161, 164
Eve 20, 21n. 52, 23, 61, 73, 75, 116–17,
    157, 164

Faith and Order Commission 3, 41–2, 46,
    54, 80, 86, 143

fatherhood *see* paternity
feminine ecumenism 46, 59, 78n. 108
femininity 13–15, 17, 19–26, 30, 32–4,
    36, 38–40, 44–5, 47, 50–1, 55–5, 58–63,
    65–8, 70–1, 76, 89, 91, 93, 96, 98–100,
    106–7, 114–17, 141, 154n. 54, 155,
    160n. 81, 164–5
feminism 9, 10, 15, 16, 19, 28, 31, 38, 41,
    45–6, 49, 50, 53–4, 56, 66, 69, 73, 78, 81,
    86–90, 98, 113–19, 145n. 17, 147n. 27,
    148n. 36, 150, 158–9
Florovsky, Georges 121, 130–3, 136, 149

Galatians, Epistle to the 31–2, 47, 54, 82,
    90, 99, 118, 150
gender 17, 29–30, 34, 40, 42–3, 46–7,
    49, 54, 57, 59–63, 68, 70, 76, 88, 90, 92,
    94, 100, 102, 134, 145, 147–8, 157–60,
    163–5
Genesis 21, 26, 44, 47, 59, 162
Gillet, Lev 3–5, 37, 81–2, 108, 118–19,
    126–7, 139
God the Father 17, 20n. 48, 21–2, 36,
    44, 46, 51, 61, 64, 91, 94, 96, 102, 138,
    154n. 55, 156, 159, 164–5
Gregory of Nazianzus 45, 103
Gregory of Nyssa 44, 58, 60, 93,
    148n. 31, 162

Harrison, Verna 88–90, 92, 94, 148, 159
Harvey, Susan Ashbrook 102, 118, 144
Holy Spirit 21–3, 28, 35, 37, 55, 57, 59–61,
    64, 66, 82, 84, 85–7, 89–90, 93, 95–6, 99,
    105, 121, 123, 143, 148, 153, 155, 157,
    159, 164–5
Hopko, Thomas 23, 47, 60, 63–6, 69–70,
    74–5, 80, 88, 93–4, 116, 135, 142, 146,
    154, 156, 158, 164
hypostasis 161, 164

icon 37, 50, 95, 153, 155, 156n. 64, 157
    see also liturgical symbolism;
    representation of Christ
image of God 21, 25, 36, 38, 43–4, 68, 76,
    93, 110, 162–3
impurity, ritual 25, 35–7, 41, 45, 56, 69, 75,
    80, 84–5, 95, 106, 145n. 17
Institute for Ecumenical Research 66, 113
Istanbul 72, 100, 111

Jesus Christ 2, 5, 15, 17, 20, 22–4, 26, 32,
    35–7, 40, 43, 45, 47, 50, 54–6, 59, 60–4,
    66–7, 70–1, 73, 75–7, 80–5, 87–90, 94–6,
    99, 100–2, 107, 109–11, 117, 122–4, 126,
    130, 138, 140, 147, 151–7, 161
Jews 1, 4, 8, 54, 82, 108, 126, 163
John Chrysostom 88, 123, 151–2, 155
John, Gospel of 54, 76, 100
John the Baptist 24–5, 47, 50
Judaism *see* Jews

Karras, Valerie 144, 148, 159
Khodre, George 42, 69, 86, 101, 143,
    145n. 17, 153
Khomiakov, Alexis 3, 6, 131
Klingenthal 42–3

Laodicea, Council of 63n. 42, 76
Levinas, Emmanuel 2, 61
liturgical symbolism 37, 77, 89, 90,
    92, 100 *see also* icon; representation
    of Christ
Liveris, Leonie 85–6, 88, 95, 118, 144
Lossky, Vladimir 3, 5, 6, 14n. 11, 21n. 52,
    44, 65, 71, 80, 124, 127–8, 132–3, 137,
    140–1, 149n. 37, 160–3
Luke, Gospel of 62, 125
Lutheranism 1, 4–5, 7, 66, 113–14, 119,
    121, 123–4, 126–8

maleness of Christ 90, 95, 153–7
manual theology *see* pseudomorphosis
marriage 12–16, 25, 41, 91, 96, 121,
    137, 154
Mary 16–17, 20–5, 36, 41, 47, 50–1, 61–3,
    66–8, 71, 73, 75–6, 84, 86–7, 89, 93,
    97–100, 106–7, 116, 124, 147, 157
masculinity 13, 21–6, 30, 32–5, 37–40,
    44–7, 50–1, 54, 56, 58, 60–3, 65–8,
    70, 73, 76, 89–91, 93, 96, 98–100,
    102, 107, 116–17, 128, 141, 155,
    160n. 81, 164–5
maternity 17–18, 20, 22–3, 36, 38, 41, 59,
    60, 62, 68, 70, 87, 93, 99, 155
Matthew, Gospel of 76, 125
Maximus the Confessor 18, 60, 64, 67, 99
Meyendorff, John 7, 133, 135
misogyny 28, 47, 74, 85–7, 89, 117–18,
    145, 158n. 74

modalism 65, 156
Monk of the Eastern Church
    see Lev Gillet
motherhood *see* maternity
Mounier, Emmanuel 5, 65

neopatristic school 48, 74, 110, 131–42,
    149, 161n. 84
Nestorianism 73, 156
new community 31, 40, 49, 57, 78, 109
Niederaltaich 42–3, 45–6

ordination 9–10, 29, 32, 34–5, 37, 42–8,
    50, 55–7, 60, 65, 68–76, 79–82, 84, 87–9,
    91–3, 96, 101–2, 105–7, 111–14, 119,
    139, 143–8, 150, 152–8
Origen 33, 124, 138
otherness 39, 57–63, 94, 161
ousia 161, 163–4

Paris 3–5, 7, 12, 15, 30, 97, 102, 107–8,
    111, 113–14, 119, 129
Paris school 133, 135n. 122
paternity 17, 20, 23, 51, 59, 102
patristic thought 12, 13, 44, 55–6, 58–60,
    64, 69–71, 84, 88, 92–3, 101, 116, 129,
    131–7, 139, 147–8, 151–2, 154, 157,
    159–60
Paul, St. 26, 33, 37, 47, 54, 56, 57, 62–3, 68,
    102, 123
personalism 5n. 14, 9, 65, 80, 98, 160–5
Peter, First Epistle of 12, 81
priesthood,
    Christ's 23, 37, 153
    clerical 23, 32, 37, 51, 70, 80, 91–2, 94,
        100, 117, 128, 151–7
    female 9, 11, 23, 31, 35, 38, 43, 53, 55–6,
        63–6, 69–78, 81–3, 87–95, 98–9, 101,
        105–7, 112, 118, 143, 145–6, 148, 150,
        152, 156–7, 160
    lay/royal 8, 12, 23, 32, 36–7, 80n. 2, 91,
        93, 97, 100, 128
Protestantism 1–5, 7–8, 10, 12, 20n. 48, 29,
    40, 67, 81, 86, 98, 113–14, 117–29, 134,
    139–40, 143, 149–50
pseudomorphosis 74n. 94, 122, 138,
    149, 155

Reformed church 4, 5, 112, 119, 124, 127

representation of Christ 51, 55–6, 64,
    76–7, 80–1, 95, 117, 152–4 *see also* icon;
    liturgical symbolism
Rhodes, Interorthodox Consultation at
    9, 10, 41, 53, 72–8, 79–80, 88–9, 92, 96,
    101, 111–12, 141–2, 145, 147n. 28, 153–4
Roman Catholicism 3, 5–6, 8, 21n. 52, 40,
    46, 50, 56, 67, 69, 77n. 103, 80, 82n. 10,
    86, 98, 106, 112, 120–3, 125–6, 128–9,
    134, 143, 146n. 19, 151–2
Russian school 131, 133–6, 140
Russian spirituality 3–5, 7–9, 29, 120–3, 139

St. Vladimir's Orthodox Theological
    Seminary 9, 88, 95, 102–3, 112, 129
saints 4, 36, 86, 88, 101, 107, 121, 127,
    144, 150
Saint-Serge Institute of Orthodox
    Theology 3, 8, 12, 101, 113
Schmemann, Alexander 131–3, 138,
    153, 155
schools of Orthodox theology 10, 13,
    114, 122, 129–42 *see also* neopatristic
    school; Paris school; Russian school;
    suprapatristic school
sexual differentiation 18, 20, 24–5, 33,
    35, 38, 44–5, 55, 58–62, 64–5, 69, 94–5,
    148, 159
Sheffield 9, 29, 42, 46–9, 53–4, 57, 81,
    100, 141
Skobtsova, Maria 5, 29, 107–10
sobornost 12, 128
Soloviev, Vladimir 13–17, 30, 59–60, 67,
    94, 130–1, 133–7, 139–41
Son of God *see* Jesus Christ
sophiology 6, 14, 17, 22, 26, 50, 59, 67,
    125, 133, 136–9, 149
soteriology 17, 20, 55, 61, 75, 95, 118, 123,
    150, 155–7, 164
Strasbourg 1–5, 42, 66, 119, 127
suprapatristic school 136–42

theological anthropology 8, 15, 17, 21–2,
    25, 42–7, 50, 54–5, 65, 70, 73–4, 88–90,
    92–5, 98, 101, 103, 106, 110, 117–18,
    128, 137, 140n. 148, 148, 150–1, 156n.
    64, 157, 160–5
Theotokos *see* Mary
Tikhon of Zadonsk 29, 121–3

Timiadis, Emilianos 32–4
Topping, Eva Catafygiotu 87–8, 144,
    150n. 43, 152
tradition 4, 13, 23, 31, 34–5, 37, 41, 45,
    48–50, 53, 56, 60, 62, 64, 69–74, 76–8,
    83, 89–90, 93–4, 100–1, 118, 121–41,
    145–51, 153, 155, 157, 159–60
Trinity 12, 15, 20–2, 34–5, 37–8, 40, 44,
    46–7, 57, 59–61, 64–6, 68–70, 78, 94,
    103, 133, 155, 159–65

Virgin Mary *see* Mary

Ware, Kallistos (Timothy) 6, 64, 96, 101,
    118, 144, 153–4, 158
women's movement *see* feminism
World Council of Churches (WCC) 9,
    29, 32, 42–3, 46, 48, 57, 72, 83, 85,
    120, 126

Zizioulas, John 145